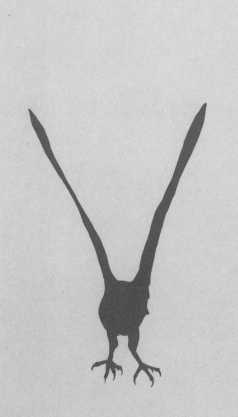

The
Birdlife
of
Britain

Mitchell Beazley Publishers Limited, London
in association with
The Royal Society for the Protection of Birds (RSPB

The Birdlife of Britain

A dramatic new way of identifying and
understanding the birds of Britain and Europe

We made this book because conventional field guides fail to understand the true needs of bird-watchers. Those earlier guides seem to concentrate on plumage, as if that were the exclusive clue to recognizing birds. But there is more to birds than feathers—and our book is, therefore, about birds in action, the way people really see them. That freedom of action is, after all, what makes aerial creatures so uniquely engrossing to watch.

For one thing, it brings them into our daily lives more than any other wild creatures. From an office window in any city centre there are Grey Wagtails to be seen on nearby roofs, or Kestrels circling church steeples. A Londoner may, with luck, see a Cuckoo over Oxford Street, and there are Tawny Owls in suburban trees. Grey Herons commute between parks. Feral Pigeons have been known to accompany commuters down the escalator to underground trains. It is not impossible for a Peregrine, the ultimate falcon, to appear over a railway terminus.

The Birdlife of Britain has been designed to give both beginner and expert the chance to develop and expand the pleasure of recognizing birds. While providing the uninitiated with the key to identification by behaviour, for the expert it illustrates an enormous range of plumage variations.

The same thinking has governed our choice of birds to be included in the book. Quite simply, they are the species which anyone is likely to see during a lifetime in Britain and Europe. Some are rare in the sense that their range is limited, but birds are excluded if in the ordinary course of events they are unlikely ever to be seen.

Moreover, the species are grouped together according to their resemblance to one another, rather than being forced into a taxonomic, or scientific, order. Again, this was done with the real needs of the observer in mind. A Hedge Sparrow and a House Sparrow look similar but belong to two different families. In a conventional field guide the two species are invariably separated by scores of pages. In this book they occur within three pages of each other. There is, however, a checklist of the common names of the birds against their scientific (latin) names, and this is based on Charles Vaurie's *The Birds of the Palaearctic Fauna*.

Phonetic renderings of bird sounds are notoriously meaningless to the uninitiated. Who can tell what "dweeje" sounds like in the wild? In order to eliminate this source of confusion, phonetic renderings are confined to the familiar (eg "cuc-coo") or to cases where they are an essential clue to a bird's identity.

The Birdlife of Britain has also broken new ground in accurate illustration. Every main illustration of every bird was painted either from a dead specimen or a skin—a stuffed bird. On average it required 38 separate measurements with scale dividers to construct the basic outline.

The specimens themselves came from a number of sources. One was the artist's own deep-frozen collection. Another was the national collection at the British Museum (Natural History) Sub-department of Ornithology at Tring, Hertfordshire. The museum's con-tribution to the book as a whole, including the personal assistance of Peter Colston and Derek Read, has been invaluable.

Planning the book would have been more difficult without the help of Dr J J M Flegg, until December 1975 Director of the British Trust for Ornithology. In addition, several members of the staff of the BTO generously helped the artist with additional specimens and with advice. They were Bob Spencer, Howard Ginn, Bob Hudson, Chris Mead and Tony Prater.

Peter Conder, until December 1975 Director of the Royal Society for the Protection of Birds, and Nick Hammond, Head of Publications at the RSPB, have been valued colleagues throughout their association with the book.

Most long-standing of all the artist's debts is to Cliff White, who nearly 30 years ago helped him to acquire the techniques of accurate observation and evaluation.

Both of us have arrears of gratitude to the publishers. Creating *The Birdlife of Britain* required skill and enthusiasm beyond our own, and we would like to thank studio, proof-readers, designers, production staff and particularly the editor and senior editor for having both in abundance.

Peter Hayman.

Philip Burton

Illustrated by Peter Hayman
Written by Philip Burton
Maps compiled by John Parslow

With ducks and geese, uncommon waders, Iberian, mountain and wetland birds painted by Robert Morton; special topics illustrated by John Davis and tonal drawings by Brian Delf

Consultant: Ian S. MacPhail

Editor	Andrew Duncan
Design assistant	Mary Ellis
Editorial assistant	Alice Bryson
Production	Barry Baker

THE BIRDLIFE OF BRITAIN was edited and designed by Mitchell Beazley Publishers Limited, 87—89 Shaftesbury Avenue, London W1V 7AD

© 1976 Mitchell Beazley Publishers Limited.
ISBN 0 85533 087 2
First published in U.K. October 1976.
First reprint December 1976.
Second Reprint July 1978.
Third Reprint January 1979.

Typeset in Great Britain by CE Dawkins, London
Colour reproduction by Fotomecanica Iberico, Madrid
Printed in England by Sir Joseph Causton & Sons Ltd., London and Eastleigh.

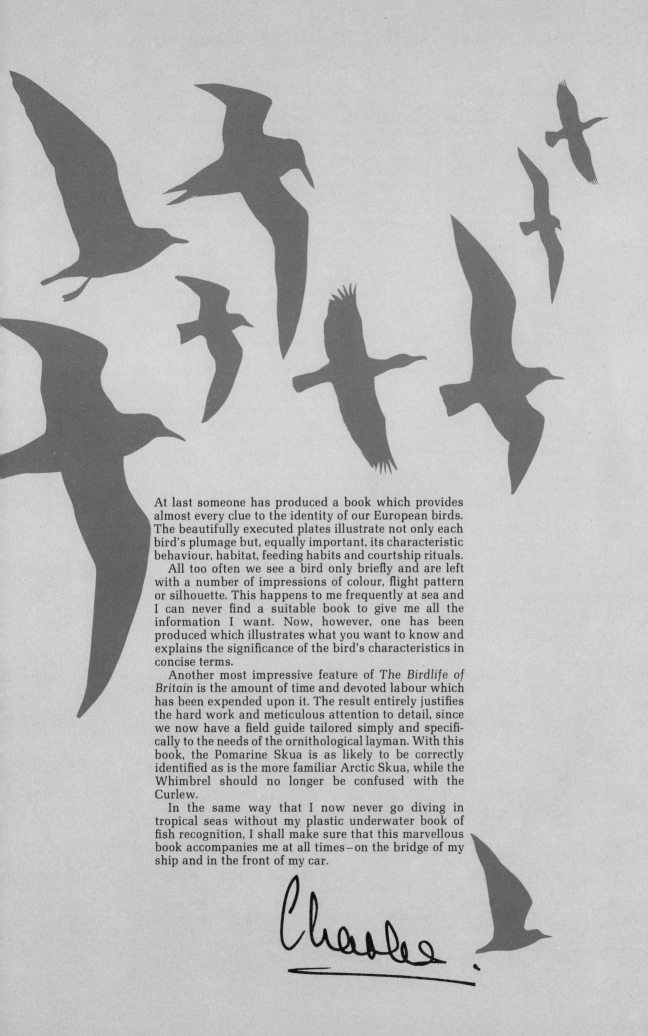

At last someone has produced a book which provides almost every clue to the identity of our European birds. The beautifully executed plates illustrate not only each bird's plumage but, equally important, its characteristic behaviour, habitat, feeding habits and courtship rituals.

All too often we see a bird only briefly and are left with a number of impressions of colour, flight pattern or silhouette. This happens to me frequently at sea and I can never find a suitable book to give me all the information I want. Now, however, one has been produced which illustrates what you want to know and explains the significance of the bird's characteristics in concise terms.

Another most impressive feature of *The Birdlife of Britain* is the amount of time and devoted labour which has been expended upon it. The result entirely justifies the hard work and meticulous attention to detail, since we now have a field guide tailored simply and specifically to the needs of the ornithological layman. With this book, the Pomarine Skua is as likely to be correctly identified as is the more familiar Arctic Skua, while the Whimbrel should no longer be confused with the Curlew.

In the same way that I now never go diving in tropical seas without my plastic underwater book of fish recognition, I shall make sure that this marvellous book accompanies me at all times—on the bridge of my ship and in the front of my car.

Charles .

An Introduction to Bird-watching
Dr Philip Burton

Reptiles with feathers

Birds have been described as "glorified reptiles with feathers" and certainly their reptilian ancestry, suggested even today by their scale-covered legs, is more obvious and far more recent than that of the mammals. Studies of the fossilized remains of the earliest known bird, the crow-sized *Archaeopteryx* which lived 130 million years ago, show that birds are the close relatives of the dinosaurs. This extinct group of

Fossil remains of *Archaeopteryx* indicate sophisticated primary feathers, but the poorly developed sternum suggests only weak flight

reptiles once dominated the land, but although many reached gigantic proportions there were many smaller species and all available evidence points to one of these as the direct ancestor of the birds. Though their life span on Earth lasted a thousand times as long as that of Man, the remaining dinosaurs have long since vanished and the closest surviving relatives of the birds are, curiously, the crocodiles and alligators. Nevertheless, birds are rightly grouped in a separate class of vertebrates, or animals with backbones, for their far-reaching adaptations have transformed them into the most vibrantly alive of all creatures—so successful that they have spread to every part of the Earth's surface and have colonized virtually every habitat save for the ocean deeps.

Pteranodon, giant even among the flying lizards, was the largest flying creature of all time: wing span, 27 feet

A unique adaptation

Birds were not, however, the first group of flying creatures to arise from reptilian stock. Long-extinct pterosaurs—the "flying lizards"—had remarkable powers of flight on membranous wings tautly stretched between the fore- and hind-limbs. But

with the development of feathers, their one truly unique feature, the birds were able to evolve versatile and efficient wings from the fore-limbs alone, leaving the hind-limbs free and so overcoming the most serious handicap of the pterosaurs, and, for that matter, the bats.

Feathers evolved before flight in birds, very probably as a heat-saving adaptation in ancestors which were already so active that they had become warm-blooded—that is, achieved a constant body temperature mechanism rendering them independent of the temperature of their surroundings. With this came an improvement and streamlining of the circulation in which the blood supply from the heart to the body was simplified from two huge arteries to a single main vessel called the aorta. Interestingly, this vessel passes to the right side in birds; in mammals it passes to the left of the body's centre-line. Feathers have provided the birds with far more than insulation and sophisticated flying ability: they show tremendous variation of shape and of colour and are the basis for the rich variety of plumages, and patterns of behaviour, which are among the most fascinating features of birdlife. The male Robin's

Common Buzzard contour feather

Kestrel tail feather

Marsh Harrier primary feather

bright red breast is his symbol of strength and authority when defending his territory against all-comers; the dappled plumage of the Nightjar enables it to remain almost invisible against its background; and the soft-edged feathers of the Barn Owl's wings are the key to its almost silent flight.

The fascination of birdlife

The ability to fly is, of course, of enormous value in evading danger from predators, and today flightless birds survive almost entirely on remote islands having no resident predators. For this reason, birds are generally able to pursue their activities in broad daylight, in full view of the observer, and here lies the key to their great popularity. Although mammals are equally varied and interesting in their behaviour, they are secretive and often nocturnal in habit and their study will most probably remain a specialist activity. By contrast, birds can be observed and enjoyed anywhere and this book has been designed to increase that enjoyment for beginner and expert alike.

The techniques of bird-watching
Simple identification of living birds is the starting point for all the many and varied activities that bird-watchers pursue. It may become an absorbing end in itself, or it may lead on to different, sometimes more specialized, areas of interest. Either way it is important at the outset to learn the basic techniques of bird observation. The way to make the best use of this field guide is explained in the following pages, but it should be realized that some species always cause difficulties—even to the most experienced observer.

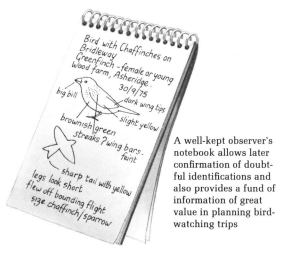

A well-kept observer's notebook allows later confirmation of doubtful identifications and also provides a fund of information of great value in planning bird-watching trips

The pitfalls are generally of two kinds; either the observer "sees" features that are not really there or fails to pick out features that are. The first often happens when only a fleeting glimpse is seen of the bird—and the errors are usually exaggerated when attempts are made to recollect details later. Seeing what is there is a matter of practice and self-discipline; assuming that you have a clear view, try to combine a part-by-part description— colour, pattern, size, shape of wing and so on—with a good overall impression of the bird. If in flight, note the style of flight, where the bird appeared from, where and how it landed, and what it did after landing. Birds are not identified purely by plumage pattern but by a combination of physical appearance, song or call, flight pattern and behaviour—all of which are clues to what the Americans call the "gizz" of the bird, the combinations of form and behaviour that make up the individual "personality" of the species.

Recording what you see
Right from the start it is advisable to adopt the habit of recording your observations; if on-the-spot identification is not possible, a simple outline sketch of major features, plus notes on where and under what conditions the bird was seen, will enable you to check the bird's identity at a more convenient time. Moreover, the bird-watcher's diary you build up over the years will provide a fascinating account of the changing aspects of bird activities throughout the seasons. Be very careful in estimating size, it is one of the most common areas of error; wherever possible, compare the bird with others of known size near by.

A developing interest
As your knowledge and interest grows you will aim to see more and more of the birds described in this book, and to do so will entail visiting a variety of habitats at different times of the year. If possible, make some of these visits with an experienced bird-watcher, or join a local bird-watching society—most of which organize visits to areas of interest, often led by guides whose detailed knowledge of the area is invaluable to the beginner.

Many observers become attracted to more serious studies of behaviour, populations or migrations and it is worth remembering that, although professional ornithologists have special facilities for certain types of study, there is ample scope for valuable work to be done by amateurs. Ringing programmes are organized in many of the European countries and, for those with the time to spare, and the enthusiasm, the effort is well rewarded.

Bird-ringing programmes, often implemented with amateur help, provide the key information in research studies

Ringing appeals to the hunting instinct in many bird-watchers and combines the excitement of a field sport with the opportunity to learn more about the lives and movements of birds. Counts of birds are often of great value in formulating long-term policies for their protection and conservation, and such research programmes always require the combined efforts of amateurs and professionals, often in many different countries.

Bird-watching in Town and Country

Garden sanctuaries

While holidays and country visits undoubtedly provide marvellous opportunities for observing birdlife, even the smallest urban garden may attract a host of avian visitors, given a little assistance, and city parks and formal gardens may often attract a surprising number of species.

The simplest way to attract birds into the garden is to provide them with food–the greater the variety of feeding material, the more species will be attracted. Hanging feeders are popular with tits, Greenfinches and Siskins, but spiral feeders should be avoided as they can trap birds by their legs. Flat-topped feeding tables are essential for Robins, Chaffinches and thrushes, while sparrows and Dunnocks usually feed most happily on the ground.

Suitable foods include sunflower and other seeds, nuts, flat-worms and mealworms, bacon rind and meat scraps. Bird tables should be cleaned and repositioned regularly to reduce the danger of bird diseases caused, and spread, by birds feeding under unhygienic conditions.

Birds may be encouraged to feed in gardens when berry-bearing bushes are planted and where seed-heads of flowering plants are left in place after the flowers have died

1 Hawthorn, 2 Holly, 3 Sunflower, 4 Berberis, 5 Cotoneaster, 6 Michaelmas Daisy, 7 Chickweed, 8 Dock, 9 Groundsel

Encouraging birds to breed

During the breeding season, a number of species may be encouraged to use nestboxes in the garden. These may be purchased or constructed easily in the home. The commonest type, ideal for members of the tit family, has a small circular entrance about 28mm in diameter; open-fronted nestboxes attract Robins and Pied Wagtails; larger boxes may be constructed for Treecreepers, while in larger gardens more specialized boxes may attract owls, doves, Jackdaws or woodpeckers. Details of the correct size, shape, entrance type and most favourable siting of nestboxes for different species is readily available from most national and local ornithological societies.

Hole-entrance and open-fronted nestboxes are easily made from odd pieces of wood; hinges may be leather or rubber

Bird-watching in woodland

Techniques of finding and watching birds in woodland vary according to the time of year. In the breeding season, the golden rule is to move about as little as possible–find a favourable spot and remain still; you will cause little disturbance and will see the birds acting quite naturally –displaying, building their nests, perhaps even feeding their young. Songs and calls will reveal the presence of many species, but give consideration to alarm calls. These are usually simple, sharp, penetrating calls–quite unmistakable even to the beginner–and if close may indicate that you are near a nest. In this case move away quietly; to remain may cause the parent bird to desert the nest, leaving the young to starve or fall prey to the predatory activities of a fox or a marauding Crow.

The changing seasons

As the breeding season ends, habits change. Parties of adults with young roam the woodland or neighbouring hedgerows, venturing far from their original nesting area. In late summer many birds will be moulting in preparation for migration and may become very difficult to locate. Pied Flycatchers, for example, seem almost to vanish at this time–but are probably feeding unobtrusively at the top of the woodland canopy.

As autumn progresses, the migrants leave and winter visitors may arrive. The techniques of finding birds may now become quite different. Birds will be patchily distributed, often in roving parties, and the observer may have to walk much farther to find what the wood has to offer. Look out for fallen fruit or nuts; fallen apples are attractive to Fieldfares and Redwings feeding in nearby fields; cherries to Hawfinches, whose powerful bills can tackle the hard stones of the fruit.

During winter, many birds such as finches and thrushes feed in flocks and roost together. These birds may be found in large numbers, roosting in thickets of evergreen laurel and rhododendron in woodland glades or along the margins of the wood.

Inland waters and marshland

Lakes, canals, rivers, reservoirs, sewage farms and gravel pits provide, in varying proportions, three main types of habitat—open water, waterside vegetation and exposed areas of shingle and mud. During the breeding season, waterside reed-beds, often with scattered willows, provide the main focus of activity, but this may be one of the most frustrating of all habitats for the bird-watcher: not only does it provide excellent cover for resident birdlife but it is also "out of bounds" to the observer. Boggy areas are dangerous to traverse, but, more important, it is impossible to do so without crushing vegetation, perhaps damaging nests or exposing the birds to the attentions of bird and mammal predators. The "sit and watch" technique is the only viable method in such areas and the hide is an invaluable piece of equipment.

The simplest hides consist of a light metal or wooden frame with a canvas covering

Residents and visitors

Though shy and skulking in habit, many reed-bed residents betray their presence with their loud songs and calls and the patient observer may be amply rewarded by some memorable sights—the nest-building mastery of the Reed Warbler, the camouflage of the Bittern, or the silent, deadly reed-skimming flight of the Marsh Harrier.

During migration periods, especially in autumn, open water and mud become areas of intense interest to bird-watchers. Waders of many species appear in large numbers as they pause in their journeys to feed and rest, while stretches of open water may be visited by gulls and terns passing through. In winter large flocks of ducks and geese will be the major point of interest and the fortunate observer may also see grebes.

Birds of the cliff and shore

Breeding waders and terns are found on flat coastlines, especially on banks of sand or shingle exposed at high tide. They are fascinating birds to watch, but their superbly camouflaged eggs, laid in a simple scrape, are vulnerable to careless feet and due notice must be taken of the alarm calls of adults. Similarly, cliff-nesting species such as Guillemots may panic if disturbed, knocking eggs from their precarious ledges or leaving them exposed to prowling gulls.

Many shore-nesting birds have superbly camouflaged eggs: those of the Little Tern, illustrated, being barely visible against the background of the nest scrape

The parade of seabirds

Outside the breeding season, visits to coast or estuary provide some of the most varied and popular bird-watching. During spring and autumn at favourable localities you may be able to observe the passage of seabirds throughout the day—shearwaters, ducks, Gannets and terns—the latter occasionally pursued by a skua. Many of these species fly close to the water surface making a high vantage point and either telescope or binoculars almost essential.

Some coastal headlands are also ports of call for migrant land-birds, and in areas of special interest observatories have been set up for the recording and study of migration. Pioneered at the turn of the century, there are now many such bases around the coasts of Europe, and for those who become interested in bird-ringing and its associated population and movement studies they are among the most interesting places to visit.

Waders and wildfowl

Muddy coasts and estuaries are not the easiest places in which to watch birds—but they are certainly the best, particularly if a hide is used. Extremely low tides should be avoided as the birds will be widely scattered; your visit should be timed to coincide with the high tide, when the birds are busily feeding on the mudbanks. You may also find wader roosts above the high tide line—sited on the same type of shingle banks as those used by breeding Ringed Plovers at earlier times of the year.

How to use the book

Even experts rarely identify birds on plumage alone. They piece together clues, such as overall colour, habitat, season and especially behaviour when feeding, flying, displaying or flocking. Thus, a blackish bird probing a lawn for food with its beak open can only be a Starling. This book illustrates as many as possible of those essential clues for identifying birds by behaviour.

Every image, including the smallest, is designed to capture the essential character of its subject. Even facial expression—notoriously elusive—is faithfully recorded so that a Marsh Tit can be told from the almost identical Willow Tit by the look in its eye. Simply memorizing feather markings is unnecessary. Instead, form a composite mental picture, using the whole illustration panel, of the bird in action.

Bear in mind that the symbols represent habitats which often overlap: salt-marsh may extend miles inland, bordered by fresh pasture.

KEY PARTS OF A BIRD

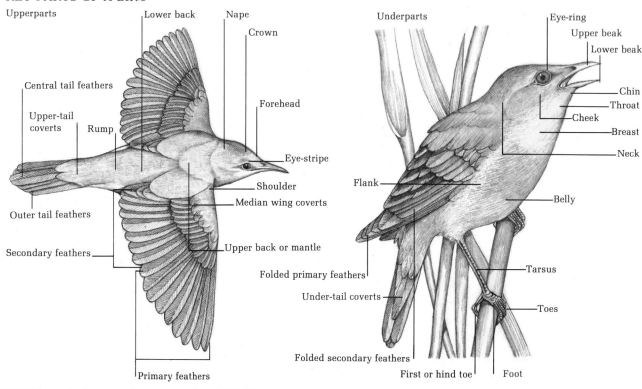

Upperparts — Lower back — Nape — Crown — Underparts — Eye-ring — Upper beak — Lower beak — Central tail feathers — Forehead — Chin — Throat — Cheek — Upper-tail coverts — Rump — Breast — Neck — Eye-stripe — Shoulder — Flank — Median wing coverts — Belly — Outer tail feathers — Upper back or mantle — Secondary feathers — Tarsus — Folded primary feathers — Toes — Under-tail coverts — First or hind toe — Foot — Folded secondary feathers — Primary feathers

 Any built-up area, from a city and its suburbs to a country town or village; urban parks and gardens; industrial sites and estates

 Very low vegetation, not usually exceeding three feet in height, or bare ground; moorland and the Mediterranean maquis

 A summer migrant to the British Isles. (Summer visitors migrate north from Africa to breed in the temperate European summer)

 Lakes and ponds; rivers, streams and canals; dykes and reclaimed or temporarily flooded land; reservoirs and sewage farms; bog and fen

 Low base vegetation, rarely exceeding three feet in height, but with low scattered trees (ie birch, hawthorn) usually not more than 30 feet high

 A winter migrant to the British Isles. (Winter visitors breed in the far north, migrating south for the comparatively mild central European winter)

 The seaside. Beaches, sandy or muddy; rocky coastline; estuaries; cliffs; salt flats and tidal creeks; dockyards and harbours; open sea

 Resident (ie non-migratory) and among the 60 commonest species encountered in the British Isles

 Denotes a non-migratory species, resident in Europe throughout the year. Some, however, may make seasonal movements within Europe

 All cultivated land, arable or pasture, including orchards and fruit groves in Mediterranean countries; small woods and copses situated on farmland; farmyards and farm buildings

 A summer visitor which happens to be one of the 60 commonest species in the British Isles

 A very rare or vagrant species

 Forest—whether coniferous, deciduous, or a mixture of both; plantations, extensive parkland and open forest

 A winter visitor which is among the 60 commonest species seen in the British Isles

 Some migrants, generally waders, pause in the British Isles while on passage during both summer and winter

Common name of species: traditional (scientific) classification is unnecessary for bird recognition. Instead, birds are grouped by their resemblance to one another. Species most easily confused are placed on facing pages for easy comparison. Flick through the book to find a species which looks something like the unidentified bird; not many pages away will be the bird itself. A checklist of scientific names appears on pages 256-7

At least one profile of every bird is painted to a marked scale. This standard illustration shows the bird in a characteristic pose. In most cases there is also a flight illustration to a smaller specified scale

A full explanation of the symbols appears on page 12. When two species occur on the same page, their habitat preferences and status are usually identical. Status, however, may differ, and the second status symbol added to the end of the row refers to the latter species in the page headline

Courtship, breeding and other displays comprise specific behaviour patterns, usually very conspicuous in the field, and their most obvious forms are widely illustrated

Every important variation in the appearance of the species is included, whether between male and female; adult, immature or juvenile; geographical race or stage of moult

When a bird is known for some special ability or physical adaptation, this is illustrated

Size is one of the essential clues to a bird's identity. Each standing silhouette has been drawn to the same scale as a House Sparrow for comparison. With experience, a flight silhouette can be used as a primary recognition point

Behaviour alone is so often the key to identifying a bird that the majority of illustrations on each plate is devoted to portraying the most characteristic habits of the species

Flocking habits, flock size and flock shape are clues, sometimes conclusive, to the identity of most species

Behaviour on the ground can reveal a bird's identity. Some species which have an unusual appearance when seen head-on are specially illustrated in this view. Useful identification features revealed only in flight are also shown

The main text describes the bird's natural history, breeding habits and survival prospects

---

Great Tit

Only the Great Tit, of the tit family, sings in spring from the treetops

Green back and pale nape patch are conspicuous features

(× ⅔)

The male's belly-stripe, bottom, is wider than the female's, top

Great Tits are distinguished from Blue Tits by their bold black and white head pattern, and from other European tits by the bright yellow breast. No other tit has white outer tail feathers

Males are seen posing aggressively on milk bottle tops when food is scarce

Acrobatic feeders. Great Tits attack nuts like Woodpeckers, and, right, can hold food in position in a crack in the bark with a foot

In winter, several species of tit will feed together in groups. Great Tits, the largest, stay near the ground, where they are easily identified by their white cheek patches

Great Tits readily take to nestboxes, in which they may use up to a cubic foot of nesting material. The bird's white cheek patches are conspicuous against the box's dark interior, and, turned side to side, are used in signalling

The Great Tit's distinctive "teechah... teechah" song is a welcome sign that spring has begun. It is common over most of Europe in woodland, agricultural and urban surroundings and has benefited from association with Man. Great Tits are the prime users of nestboxes, choosing them even where natural cavities are plentiful. They regularly visit gardens and show the strongest predilection for peanuts of all tits except the Marsh Tit. Bird tables are preferred to suspended food: Great Tits are less acrobatic than smaller tits. Such provisions are less useful at nesting time, for the young must be fed on insects. One woodland oak may provide as much food (especially weavils) as several gardens, where broods are generally smaller and less successful.

Clutch sizes average between nine and ten in woodland, and, in common with other tits, the eggs are buried in nest material when the female leaves the nest–a puzzling habit for a hole nester. Females are bold in defence of the nest, and males use the black belly stripe when trying to appear larger in territorial disputes. Great Tits have an extensive vocabulary: more than 80 different calls are recorded.

Over much of Europe, severe weather forces Great Tits to move west or southwest in winter, although in Britain this rarely occurs. This is a species which irrupts when numbers reach too high a level after a series of mild winters and good breeding.

J F M A M J J A S O N D

16

DISTRIBUTION MAP
■ Resident all year

☐ Summer quarters

■ Winter quarters

THE ORANGE BAND
☐ Months during which bird is not present

☐ Months during which bird is present but not breeding

■ Months during which bird is present and breeding

Note: the orange band shows the earliest usual date a bird may arrive and commence breeding in Europe; similarly it shows the latest usual date for the end of the breeding period and departure. The farther north, the later the event; the farther south, the earlier the event. In northern Sweden, for example, a Swallow arrives from Africa on June 1; in northern Spain, the same species arrives as early as March 15

Wren

(×³⁄₅)

The Wren's cheerful song is outstandingly loud for so small a bird

Left: the whirring flight over short distances close to the ground. Above: almost bee-like appearance in rear view. Right: characteristic confident pose, tail cocked, often accompanied by much bobbing

Wrens on the island of St Kilda, off the Outer Hebrides, are noticeably larger, greyer bodied and more heavily barred, but have the usual chestnut tail

Main food items are spiders, insects and other ground invertebrates. There are usually two broods of six, which tend to crowd the nest. The female bears the brunt of feeding the young

With feathers puffed out for warmth in cold weather, Wrens can look almost spherical

These birds are primarily terrestrial feeders, creeping through undergrowth or rocky crevices in search of food. This, and their habit of nesting in dark, cave-like places gave rise to their generic name *Troglodytes*: cave dweller. The low crouch is a typical Wren posture

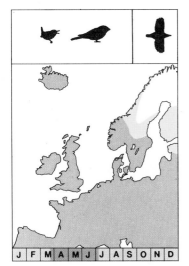

A tiny bird with a larger-than-life character, the Wren is the only Eurasian member of the large New World family, represented by ten species in the United States alone.

Known in America as the Winter Wren, our species must have crossed to the Old World in one of the milder periods of the Earth's past. It has become one of the most widespread species in Europe. Recent surveys have shown that in many British woodlands it is the most numerous bird. Able to adapt to both forested and open habitats, the Wren is found even on rocky oceanic islands such as St Kilda, where distinct races have evolved.

In spring, male Wrens will build several nests in their territory, only putting a feather lining in the one selected for laying. Some "cock's nests" are easy to find, but the chosen nursery is usually cleverly camouflaged to blend into a recess in a tree, ivy or bank. Nest boxes are sometimes used, but are more often chosen for roosting on cold winter's nights, when as many as 46 wrens have been counted, huddled in a feathery bundle, tails outwards.

The savage winter of 1962-3 was estimated to have killed 75 per cent of British Wrens, but with two or three broods a year and a clutch of five or six, normal population levels were regained after three years. The eggs have much the same colouring as tits', and Wrens have a long fledging period of 16 or 17 days.

J F M A M J J A S O N D

Firecrest-Goldcrest

Goldcrest

Firecrest

The bold black and white eyestripe and richer mantle colour distinguish the Firecrest from the drabber Goldcrest in the field. Note that the centre feathers of a displaying male Goldcrest's crown are just as fiery as the Firecrest's

(× ³⁄₅)

Although a less attractive songster, the Firecrest seems to dominate Goldcrests in territorial encounters

Nests built by both species are intricate hammocks of hair, moss and cobwebs suspended from a branch. Firecrests in particular are very shy when nesting, and should never be disturbed

Both species are as agile as tits, quite at home hanging upside down searching buds or foliage with needle-sharp beaks for insects, insect eggs or larvae

Goldcrests and Firecrests are similar in general colouring and habits to Willow Warblers and Chiffchaffs. Both can hover to catch flying insects or to pick aphids from under leaves

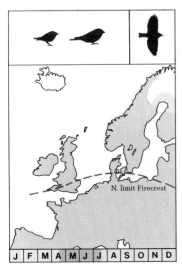

N. limit Firecrest

J F M A M J J A S O N D

These are the smallest European birds, about half the weight of a Blue Tit. Though sometimes amazingly tame (Goldcrests have been known to alight on a stationary observer), they can be infuriatingly difficult to locate as they flit restlessly about in dense foliage. They betray their presence with high-pitched calls, the Goldcrest's voice being thinner and less harsh than the Firecrest's: its song is a rapidly repeated jingle ending in a flourish which the Firecrest's entirely lacks. Once seen, the face pattern positively identifies either of the birds.

Both birds' nests are enchanting little hammocks of moss, hair and feathers, bound with spiders' webs and skilfully suspended under conifer boughs or amongst ivy. Seven to 11 eggs are laid, deep reddish cream in colour, and up to three broods may be reared each year. Such high productivity makes good sense for species which are extremely vulnerable to severe winters, when their insect food may be almost unobtainable. Goldcrests have the wider range but are more strictly confined to conifers – though cedars and yews in gardens and churchyards are as acceptable as forests and plantations. Firecrests inhabit cork oak woods in some of the southern parts of their range, and they have recently colonized places in southern England. In winter, Goldcrests regularly associate with tit flocks, which Firecrests rarely do. Both species are sedentary in southerly regions.

15

Great Tit

Only the Great Tit, of the tit family, sings in spring from the treetops

Green back and pale nape patch are conspicuous features

$(\times \frac{3}{5})$

The male's belly-stripe, bottom, is wider than the female's, top

Great Tits are distinguished from Blue Tits by their bold black and white head pattern, and from other European tits by the bright yellow breast. No other tit has white outer tail feathers

Males are seen posing aggressively on milk bottle tops when food is scarce

Acrobatic feeders, Great Tits attack nuts like Woodpeckers, and, right, can hold food in position in a crack in the bark with a foot

In winter, several species of tit will feed together in groups. Great Tits, the largest, stay near the ground, where they are easily identified by their white cheek patches

Great Tits readily take to nestboxes, in which they may use up to a cubic foot of nesting material. The bird's white cheek patches are conspicuous against the box's dark interior, and, turned side to side, are used in signalling

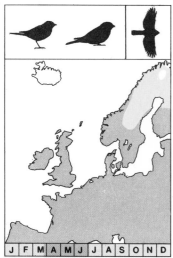

JFMAMJJASOND

The Great Tit's distinctive "teechah... teechah" song is a welcome sign that spring has begun. It is common over most of Europe in woodland, agricultural and urban surroundings and has benefited from association with Man. Great Tits are the prime users of nestboxes, choosing them even where natural cavities are plentiful. They regularly visit gardens and show the strongest predilection for peanuts of all tits except the Marsh Tit. Bird tables are preferred to suspended food: Great Tits are less acrobatic than smaller tits. Such provisions are less useful at nesting time, for the young must be fed on insects. One woodland oak may provide as much food (especially weavils) as several gardens, where broods are generally smaller and less successful.

Clutch sizes average between nine and ten in woodland, and, in common with other tits, the eggs are buried in nest material when the female leaves the nest – a puzzling habit for a hole nester. Females are bold in defence of the nest, and males use the black belly stripe when trying to appear larger in territorial disputes. Great Tits have an extensive vocabulary: more than 80 different calls are recorded.

Over much of Europe, severe weather forces Great Tits to move west or southwest in winter, although in Britain this rarely occurs. This is a species which irrupts when numbers reach too high a level after a series of mild winters and good breeding.

Blue Tit

The central belly-streak is characteristic, although the exact shape and length varies from bird to bird

Males spread their wings in a "butterfly" display flight, swooping down from their perch in a tree, then up towards the nest hole. The female collects material and builds the nest, but often the male will fly with her

Highly acrobatic perching and feeding postures, typical of the Blue Tit

In courtship the female solicits food by a wing-shivering display, to which the male responds with the typical offer of a green caterpillar. Extra food is vital for the female if she is to produce more than her own weight in eggs

(× 3/5)

A female Blue Tit with young brood. In suburban gardens, broods are small, but in woodland areas broods of ten to 12 are common

On the ground, Blue Tits have a characteristically alert feeding attitude. Alternatively the tail may be held cocked up over the back

Males in courtship display postures

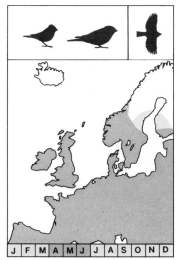

Brightly coloured and full of character, Blue Tits, next to Robins, must be the best-loved garden birds.

Like the Great Tit, the Blue Tit is a woodland species which has adapted to man-made environments. It is highly acrobatic, specializing in feeding at the extreme ends of branches. Natural food in spring and summer includes scale insects and larvae, and the timing of egg laying and clutch size are adjusted to produce young during the short-lived bounty of winter moth caterpillars. Blue Tits also take such items as oak buds and moss spore cases, and in gardens show varied tastes – they are the only tits that regularly eat bread. Many woodland Blue Tits are regular commuters to towns in times of food shortage or bad weather. Ringing shows that 1,000 or more individuals may pass through a garden in a year, even where it is unusual to see more than six at a time.

Blue Tits use the cobalt crown and wings during courtship, when the male flutters outspread wings in front of the female. The short crest is raised at all times of excitement. Clutch sizes in woodland average over 13 in some years. However, tits are in general single brooded, so the ten or so fledglings produced is comparable to a blackbird laying three clutches of four or five. Mortality is high: from a family party of 12 in early summer, just one adult and one young bird will, on average, live to breed the next year.

J F M A M J J A S O N D

The northern race of Willow Tit, found in Scandinavia, has very white cheeks and a greyer mantle

Willow Tit: a broader bulkier neck. The crown cap is more extensive than that of the Marsh Tit

(×³/₅)

The white cheek patches are obvious, even from above. Young birds, below, are almost impossible to identify

Bull-necked appearance of Willow Tit is still seen in back view. Note the slightly furry crown feathers

Marsh Tit: a smaller, rounder head. The crown feathers may sometimes look very glossy

(×³/₅)

Marsh Tits' outer tail feathers are shorter than the longest by up to 3 mm; Willow Tits' by 5 to 10 mm

Willow Tits have conspicuous pale edges to the secondary feathers on the wing, but these may be obscured in damp weather or in the breeding season

Marsh Tit, back view. Wing panels invisible, but neck clearly slimmer than the Willow Tit's, above

(×³/₅)

The Willow Tit (brown) is spherical in shape compared to the Marsh Tit (grey), whose build is much more typical of the tit family

Typical Marsh Tit profile—less puff-cheeked than the Willow Tit

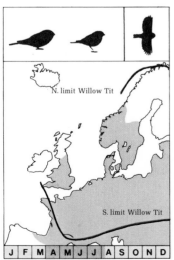

The Willow Tit was only separated as a new species in 1900, and for many bird-watchers, distinguishing it from the Marsh Tit remains a major problem. Through much of Europe their ranges overlap; in Britain the two races are most similar of all. In the diverse patch-work of its countryside, habitat preferences are ill-defined, but Marsh Tits tend to prefer drier, broad-leaved woodland, Willow Tits conifers and damper, deciduous woods.

Marsh Tits have a characteristic "pit-chew" call that the Willow Tit does not use. The then major distinguishing factor is nesting habits. Marsh Tits use natural holes; Willow Tits excavate a neat, flask-shaped hole up to one foot deep in soft, rotten wood, such as elder, and sometimes use nest boxes specially filled for them with soft, excavable material. Like all tits, both sexes excavate, but only the female builds the nest, which contains more grass, bark and wood chips than those of other tits. Both species' clutches average lower than other tits', and many Willow Tit nests are devoured by predators.

Outside the breeding season these birds are less gregarious than other tits; Marsh Tits show greater fondness for gardens, and in autumn often feed on seed heads of marsh thistle, honey-suckle berries or knapweed. Willow Tits spend more time feeding in low cover than other tits, and regularly take hemp nettle seeds in autumn. Both species are strongly sedentary.

N. limit Willow Tit

S. limit Willow Tit

J F M A M J J A S O N D

Coal Tit

Adult collecting beech fruit, a typical sight in autumn

The Coal Tit is distinguished by its glossy black crown, white cheeks and nape, and grey-buff belly plumage

The continental race is distinguished by its blue-grey plumage.

$(\times \frac{3}{5})$

The head is unusually large in proportion to the tiny body and short tail, and the black bib is more pronounced than on other tits

Typical feeding and perching postures. Note the fine, slender bill, well suited to probing for insects in narrow crevices

In winter, Coal Tits will feed in company with other tits, working over the trunk or branch-like treecreepers

The young bird, above, shows the drab colouring and much yellower face, nape and belly. The double wing-bar is a useful identification feature in flight

The Irish race, below, has yellow-buff cheeks and nape patch. In feeding posture the nape patch shows clearly

The nest is usually placed in a tree-hole or wall cavity, but the abandoned burrows of mice may also be pressed into use

J F M A M J J A S O N D

The Coal Tit is the smallest of our tits—less than half the weight of a Great Tit. Even in such an acrobatic family it stands out, flicking from branch to branch in a restless search for food. It is associated, though not exclusively, with conifers, and has become numerous in the many plantations which have been created in recent decades. Its spring song resembles a thinner, high-pitched version of the Great Tit's.

The relatively long, slender beak of the Coal Tit is more suitable than those of the Blue and Great Tit for extracting insects from cones or from behind flakes of bark. Coal Tits are assiduous food storers—a habit only useful to sedentary species and thus not often practised by Blue and Great Tits. Sites selected to store food are usually those which the bird would ordinarily search—clusters of pine needles, clumps of lichen on a branch, or crevices behind pine bark. Coal Tits commonly nest low down in rotten stumps. When these are eliminated from plantations, the burrows of rodents are used instead. A typical Coal Tit clutch contains seven to 12 eggs. As with other tits, the female builds the nest and incubates, though both parents feed the young, bringing spiders, aphids and miscellaneous small insects. Like other tits, the fledging period is rather longer than that of other birds of similar size—about 16 days. This reflects the greater safety conferred by hole nesting. Coal Tits are regular visitors to gardens.

19

Crested Tit

Like Greenfinches, Crested Tits circle treetops, trilling, in courtship display

The black and white crest (duller on immature birds) and the white face edged with a black "C" are unmistakable field characteristics. Its acrobatic behaviour is very similar to other tits, but the Crested Tit does not occur in large flocks

$(\times \frac{3}{5})$

Courtship feeding is started as early as possible to bring the female into optimum breeding condition

Nests can be located by following the Crested Tit's trilling song. Typical nest sites are holes in trunks of firs in old conifer forests

Crested Tits often feed on trunks in a similar manner to Treecreepers

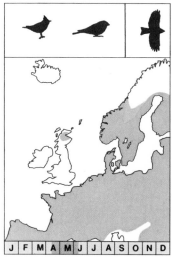

J F M A M J J A S O N D

Elegant in pattern yet sober in colour, this attractive tit is found in conifer forests through much of Europe, and several races have been distinguished. One of these is confined to Scotland, where its very localized population has been much diminished by the felling of old pine forest, though there are recent indications of recovery. Crested Tits tolerate some birch or alder mixed with the pine, and in southern Europe occur in deciduous woods with scattered evergreens and in cork oak forests. They feed in pine foliage at varying heights, and on the trunks and ground. The fine beak is ideal for extracting insects from clusters of pine needles, and the caching habit is well developed.

Like the Willow Tit, the Crested Tit excavates its own nest hole in a rotten stump: the scarcity of such stumps in plantations may explain their preference for natural pine woods. Hard wood is not removed, so the nest cavity is irregular, unlike the Willow Tit's. A few use nest boxes. Rather sparse nests are built, lined with deer hair, fur and similar materials. The clutch, averaging just over five, is small for a tit, and the eggs are more strongly marked than in other species. The incubation and fledging periods, of about 14 and 18 days respectively, resemble those of other tits.

The Crested Tit has a distinctive trilling call, but no regular song. It occasionally joins parties of other tits, and is highly sedentary.

Long-tailed Tit

Constantly changing their poses, Long-tailed Tits are lively, acrobatic feeders

(× ³/₅)

Upper- and under-parts of adult Long-tailed Tits are completely distinctive in their pink, white and black plumage

It is rare to see a party of Long-tailed Tits crossing between trees: they usually do so in ones or twos

The British race has a heavily patterned face

If the first nest fails – it is usually sited low in bushes – a second is often built high in the fork of a tree

During flight, which is rather erratic, the long tail is very conspicuous

The northern race shows a pure white head

A long tail is frequently seen poking out of the delicately constructed nest placed, typically, in a gorse bush

An adult feeding a young bird, which is distinguished by the brown plumage on its head

In winter, Long-tailed Tits roost communally for warmth and shelter

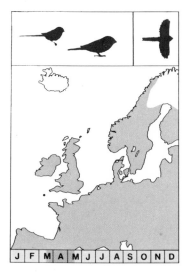

J F M A M J J A S O N D

The Long-tailed Tit's beautiful nest is usually seen in a low gorse or hawthorn, but some are found in trees up to 70 feet high. Possibly high sites were normal until Man's activities created hedgerows. Wherever found, the nest is a remarkable achievement: its feather lining alone may account for over 2,000 journeys. Lichens stud the exterior, but pollution has almost eliminated them around large cities, where paper or even polystyrene may be used instead. Eight to 12 eggs are laid early in April. With leaves barely out, hedgerow nests are conspicuous and may suffer predation. Extra adults sometimes seen feeding young may be birds whose own broods have failed. Though now considered only distantly related to typical tits, the Long-tailed is no less agile when feeding, and has a unique method of dealing with hard items – hanging from a twig by one foot while holding the morsel in the other and nibbling from it, human fashion. Diet consists of small insects, seeds and buds.

Long-tailed Tits are vulnerable to severe weather. Roosting on winter nights, parties of five to ten huddle together in a ball to conserve warmth – not a habit shared by other tits.

Lightest of all tits, the Long-tailed is nevertheless a regular traveller. Ringing recoveries are frequently over a 30-mile range, and one party of seven netted together moved 25 miles in four days. Continental birds cross the North Sea in some winters.

Dunnock

     R₆₀

The Dunnock, or Hedge Sparrow, is often seen flying across roads from hedge to hedge, and this habit has made it one of the most frequent casualties of the motor-car

A bird in worn plumage, below, has an almost grey head and very faint spots around the eye. The beak should be compared with that of the House Sparrow

Compared with the vigorous action of the House Sparrow, a Dunnock flies with an unhurried, undulating, almost delicate motion. Its grey head and streaked back are often visible in flight

(× ³/₁₀)

In new plumage, Dunnocks can be confused with House Sparrows: both have similar barring on the back. But Sparrows never have grey underparts, nor do they have streaked flanks. Also, a Dunnock has a distinctively delicate beak, rusty orange eyes and a grey head

Seen at close range the Dunnock's plumage is surprisingly attractive with its subtle patterning

(× ³/₅)

Birds sing and feed in hedges and bushes. Legs and feet are bright orange

These birds move about unobtrusively, creeping over the ground in a crouched posture, delicately picking at the surface. Although their usual pose is horizontal, Dunnocks, like Sparrows, can stand upright

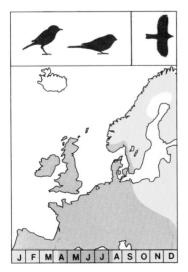

J F M A M J J A S O N D

American bird-watchers visiting Britain often surprise their hosts with eager requests to be shown a Dunnock. Their interest in this drab bird is due to its being the only common member of the accentor family – a small but distinctive group confined to Eurasia.

In the west of Europe and Britain, it is a common garden bird – rarely seen on the bird table, but often feeding beneath it, and quite approachable. Elsewhere, though equally numerous, Dunnocks are shy and secretive, best detected by the plaintive, rather penetrating call note. They have a wide habitat tolerance: some open ground is needed for feeding, but with cover of bushes or trees near by. The diet probably consists of small invertebrates in summer, replaced or augmented by seeds in winter.

In spring, males choose high perches from which to produce the warbled song which somewhat resembles the Wren's, only more subdued and without the terminal trill. Both sexes may be seen displaying on the ground, wings shivering and tails flicking as male chases female. Nests are built of grass, lined with hair and usually some bright green moss, contrasting pleasingly with the four to six bright blue eggs.

Despite the Dunnock's abundance, its migrations are poorly understood: in western Europe it is sedentary, but occasionally, when population levels are high, birds transfer to adjacent areas in wave movements.

Robin

Robins have an easy, slightly undulating flight

($\times \frac{3}{10}$)

The nest is often very well concealed

Robins sing from both open and well-concealed posts

An adult watching the ground beneath for insects. Robins have a characteristic way of turning and tilting their heads when looking for food

($\times \frac{3}{5}$)

Left, a bird about to pick up food, head tilted. Right, alert posture of bird moving about lawn

In rear view, the Robin's head is seen to be small and narrow

Robins acquire their red breasts gradually during the first summer. The back changes from spotted to plain brown at the same time

Below right, the threat display. Red breast puffed out, the bird sways from side to side. In extreme anger, the head may be thrown back

The juvenile has a spotted, scalloped breast

The young can be identified on behaviour alone: like their parents, they hop, hesitate, and then tilt the head to one side

The attacking attitude

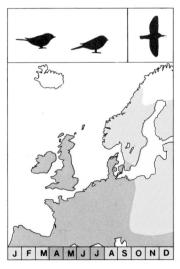

Britain's national bird, the Robin has lent its name to red-breasted birds throughout the world. Its popularity stems largely from tameness: birds regularly feed at gardeners' feet and are easily trained to enter houses or peck from the hand. Nevertheless, through much of the Robin's range it is a shy, woodland bird, better known for its "ticking" alarm call. Strongly aggressive, males attack ferociously even a bundle of red feathers. The fluffed-out red breast is used in threat by both sexes, as females too hold territories in winter, and also sing. In spring, territorial boundaries change, and the male's song becomes louder and more robust. With such aggressive temperaments and similar plumages, females entering a male's territory must adopt submissive behaviour to avoid violent rejection.

Nesting begins early, and three broods may be raised in a season. Notorious for choosing strange sites in houses and gardens, Robins may also be tempted into an open-fronted nest box. In natural habitats, the nest is cleverly concealed in a bank or tree crevice. Its thick foundation of dead leaves is as distinctive as the five or six creamy, rust-freckled eggs. Fledgling Robins have brown speckled plumage, which serves for camouflage from predators, and prevents arousing the anger of red-sensitive parents with new broods. The red breast develops during the first summer, equipping the bird for staking claim to winter territory.

J F M A M J J A S O N D

Tree Sparrow

A pair sitting still in a tree: very similar to the House Sparrow, except for the rufous-brown cap and slightly smaller size. They can also be distinguished by their call, once it is learned

In flight a Tree Sparrow closely resembles a male House Sparrow, sharing the same rufous-brown shoulder patch. Most reliable identification is by the white collar and the black spot on the white cheek

(× 3/10)

Unobtrusive while they feed, Tree Sparrows creep along the ground, picking around for food

Birds are frequently seen flicking their tails as they chirp from their favourite perches

Tree Sparrows nest in holes in trees, but also take to nestboxes

Male House Sparrow: grey crown, rufous-brown sides, large black bib

Unlike House Sparrows, adult Tree Sparrows of both sexes resemble each other

(× 3/5)

Front view shows a smaller black bib than on male House Sparrow

Female House Sparrow: pale beak and no colour on face

Large flocks of Tree Sparrows can gather in fields with House Sparrows and other species, when they are best distinguished from the former by their smaller size and neater appearance

Tree Sparrow: rufous-brown cap, white cheek, black spot

J F M A M J J A S O N D

In Europe, the Tree Sparrow is everywhere less numerous and more restricted in habitat than the House Sparrow, though in eastern Asia, where the House Sparrow is absent, it seems to occupy a similar niche, and in places reaches pest status. Generally, it is restricted to woodland edges, wooded gardens and the like, where it has trees near by for nesting, and access to cultivated fields or farmyards for feeding. The normal nest site is a hole in a tree, but buildings or haystacks are sometimes occupied, and Tree Sparrows are regular users of nestboxes, often ousting other tenants, such as Blue Tits. Their smaller size enables them to enter holes which a House Sparrow cannot negotiate.

The nest is an untidy one, similar to the House Sparrow's, but the eggs are distinctive – deep mottled brown, as opposed to the variable grey speckling of the House Sparrow's. Clutches vary from two to eight eggs, but most commonly contain five, and two or three broods are raised. Both sexes share in incubation, and this lasts 12 to 14 days. The fledging period is of similar length and both parents feed the young.

Tree Sparrows associate in flocks at all times, and these are at their largest and most obvious when feeding on grain in late summer – often in company with House Sparrows. The presence of Tree Sparrows among a flock of the larger species can be detected by their characteristically higher-pitched chirp.

House Sparrow

Chasing a pigeon

Flocks of sparrows occur in ripening cornfields

An adult male has a chestnut shoulder-patch and white wing-stripe

Frequent attempts to catch butterflies usually fail – but the Sparrow has greater success with moths

Parties of males display in groups, aggressively circling each other and chirping, then dispersing in all directions

$(\times\,{}^3/_{10})$

Adult female. The juvenile looks exactly the same

Adult plumage, below, is gained by the juvenile bird in August or September

Different postures produce visible changes in the pattern of the back feathers

The Common or House Sparrow usually builds its nest in a hole in a building, but nests found in hedgerows are recognized as the House Sparrow's by their domed shape and unkempt appearance

Always duller coloured than a male, the female has a buff back streaked with black

A country Sparrow is much brighter and cleaner in appearance than birds in most cities. This male is in autumn plumage – the black bib is less distinct than in winter

$(\times\,{}^3/_5)$

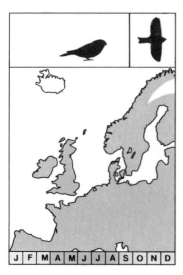

J F M A M J J A S O N D

Some people like the Common or House Sparrow for its cheeky opportunism, some hate it for eating grain and blocking gutters, but everybody knows it. Despite an apparent tameness, it is a wary, tough little bird which thrives not only in its native Eurasia but in other continents to which it has been introduced – notably North America.

The chirruping calls are varied, though instantly identifiable, but there is no distinct song. Males seeking mates build a nest and advertise by chirping incessantly near by. The birds visit their nesting colonies throughout much of the year – least often during the moult, which takes place in late summer or early autumn – but breeding is mainly confined to spring and early

summer. Nests are placed in cavities in buildings or in trees and ivy, and are exceedingly untidy structures of grass and straw lined with feathers, often domed. The clutch size varies from two to seven. First-year females tend to lay smaller clutches than older birds. Both sexes incubate, the male's share increasing throughout the incubation period. This is of variable length, but averages about 12 days – the issue is confused because incubation often starts before the clutch is complete. Hence the young may be of different ages. Fledging periods may be as short as 11 days, but 18 seems typical. Both sexes bring food, but at first this is mainly the job of the male, while the female broods the young.

Linnet—Twite

Male Linnet

Male Linnet

Juvenile Linnet

Female Linnet

Male Linnet

Bouncy, erratic flight characterizes the Linnet. Its wings are longer than the Twite's. The small size and the white in the wings and tail—easily visible in flight—identify Linnets whatever their age or sex

An adult male Linnet has a crimson crown and brownish-grey head. The breast is red and the beak is brown. The legs are short and the eyes comparatively small

$(\times \frac{3}{5})$

$(\times \frac{3}{10})$

Female Twite— a yellow beak

Male Twite— yellow beak, crimson rump

$(\times \frac{3}{10})$

Twites are darker, sepia-coloured versions of the Linnet and they have not nearly so much white in the wings

The female Linnet is duller than the male, with more streaking. Flight, shape, call and the white in the wings and tail will nevertheless reliably identify her

$(\times \frac{3}{5})$

The female Twite has a white lower belly and an orange-brown neck and upper breast

A young Linnet, duller than the female, and more heavily streaked

A Twite of either sex has virtually no white feathers in its tail

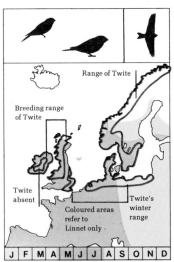

Range of Twite

Breeding range of Twite

Twite absent

Coloured areas refer to Linnet only

Twite's winter range

J F M A M J J A S O N D

Though one of Europe's most abundant finches, the Linnet has never become a garden bird, although often found near farms. Its diet consists of seeds from a variety of common plants, such as dock, charlock and goosefoot, and its English name probably derives from linen, the textile obtained from flax, a favourite food plant. Occasionally birds lose the sight of an eye through injury by the hooked seeds of plants such as burdock. Even during the breeding season, Linnets feed in restless, chattering flocks, and the cheerful twittering song is a characteristic sound of the gorse-studded heaths where they live.

The nest is a small, grassy cup, warmly lined with hair or feathers, placed low in a gorse, broom or bramble bush, several often being sited close together in small colonies. Four to six eggs form the clutch, incubated by the female, who is fed on the nest by the male. Feeding the young is by regurgitation. Though both sexes share in feeding the nestlings, the male may give his food to the female, who then passes it to the offspring. Linnets resemble most finches in consuming the young's droppings during the early days of fledging.

The Twite is a more northerly counterpart of the Linnet, resembling it in general habits, but choosing moorlands as a breeding habitat. The nest is normally sited in heather, and only one or two broods are reared compared to the Linnet's two or three.

Redpolls

Mealy Redpolls are the continental race, Lesser Redpolls the British and Alpine race

All Redpolls have the same circular, dipping song flight, accomplished with slow wing beats. They also sing from their perches and in ordinary flight

($\times$ $^{3}/_{5}$)

Male Lesser Redpoll

Male Lesser Redpoll

($\times$ $^{3}/_{10}$)

Above, a Mealy Redpoll is smaller and darker than an Arctic Redpoll, larger and paler than a Lesser Redpoll

($\times$ $^{3}/_{10}$)

($\times$ $^{3}/_{5}$)

Arctic Redpoll

($\times$ $^{3}/_{10}$)

A Lesser Redpoll in late summer. Its upper plumage wears to an almost uniform dark brown, underparts to a shiny white. The red cap retains its vivid scarlet all the year

Juvenile Redpolls—no red cap and no black bib. As acrobatic as tits, Redpolls are likely to be seen hanging head up or down from twigs or tall plants, or feeding on riverside alder in company with Siskin

An Arctic Redpoll (a separate species of Scandinavia and the high Arctic tundra) is the largest and whitest of the redpoll group

($\times$ $^{3}/_{5}$)

They are tiny, active birds, with pointed wings that look very long in proportion to the body. In spite of the profusion of races, the very clear twin features of scarlet cap and black bib reliably separate adults of the Redpoll group from all other species

Male Mealy Redpoll

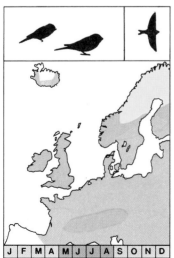

J F M A M J J A S O N D

Seen at a distance, Redpolls might easily be mistaken for Linnets were it not for their distinctive call—a staccato "ch-ch-ch-chaa", following the rhythm of the letter V in the morse code. In the breeding season, this is interspersed with trills made by the male as he flies around his territory.

In western Europe, Redpolls breed in Britain, the Alps and the Carpathians. Another species of Redpoll breeds in Scandinavia, and right round the sub-Arctic and low Arctic. Although primarily birds of birch and alder forest, Arctic breeders inhabit open tundra where the only cover is juniper or dwarf willow. In Britain, Redpolls have recently begun to colonize conifer plantations. Birch and alder seeds are im-

portant items of the diet, and a variety of grass and weed seeds is also eaten. During spring, buds and insects are consumed.

Nests are often fairly close together in loose colonies, and may be placed in almost any tree or bush, usually from three to 15 feet high, but sometimes much higher. Materials used are twigs and grass, with a lining of vegetable down. The usual clutch of five is incubated by the female alone for 11 days, and both parents feed the young with food carried in the throat. Fledging takes place after 12 days, and two broods are often reared. Arctic breeders are highly migratory and winter in many parts of Europe. European breeding birds are more sedentary.

27

Greenfinch

The erratic "butterfly" display flight takes place over the treetops

Predominantly green and yellow, this long-winged, strong-bodied species is unmistakable. Flight action—erratic and bounding—is typical of other finches. Young and females have darker colouring than this adult male, but always show the same yellow patches on wings and tail

(× 3/10)

Colour intensity of the male's plumage varies during the year according to season or stage of moult, but this specimen represents the basic pattern

(× 3/5)

Adult female

Juvenile

Frowning, aggressive behaviour characterizes Greenfinches—especially adults. At a bird table, they will spend more time fighting over peanuts than eating

On dull days, a female or young bird can look much like a female sparrow, and may be overlooked when feeding

Large flocks of Greenfinches gather to feed in fields with other species, such as Yellowhammers, Chaffinches and Sparrows

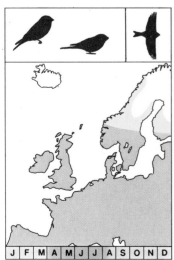

The bright plumage of the Greenfinch brings a frequent and pleasing touch of colour to suburban bird tables: over 1,000 different individuals have been ringed in some gardens during a single winter. Somehow, they can sense coming changes in the weather, and the arrival of large flocks of Greenfinches at the bird table is an excellent indicator of cold weather in the next few days. Sunflower seeds and peanuts attract them most, and by active feeding they will acquire an extra store of fat (perhaps 10 per cent of their body weight) to provide insulation and tide them over any food shortage.

Outside the suburbs, Greenfinches frequent woodland edges, arable land and waste ground. Dog's Mercury and elm seeds are common summer foods, with yew and hornbeam in autumn, rose and bramble in winter. On farmland and waste ground, chickweed, dandelion, persicaria, burdock and charlock are all taken. Greenfinches are rarely troublesome to farmers, despite a liking for cereals, hemp, flax and sunflowers.

The nest is rather untidy, lined with feathers, and often placed in a dense thorny bush, not as a rule very high. Nests are often grouped in small, loose colonies. Four to six eggs are laid, and two or three broods raised. The male defends his territory with a twittering song ending on a monotonous loud wheezing note, often uttered in a display flight.

J F M A M J J A S O N D

Goldfinch

(×³/₁₀)

Open wings of a Goldfinch in flight show their vivid and unique yellow pattern

Above: both sexes may take part in the moth-like display flight above trees. It usually precedes copulation

Goldfinches commonly perch on roadside wires

The white tail-spots show most clearly from below

Head of adult male: distinctive marking and a pale beak. More red than on female

Head of female. In winter both sexes develop the dark-tipped beak

(×³/₅)

The juvenile Goldfinch, also known as a grey-pate. It has the same yellow wing markings as the adult, which, though less extensive, are just as noticeable

Male singing from the top of an apple tree, a typical perch

Below left: a juvenile, recognizable by its streaked plumage. The species often feeds head down

The "pivot" display: wings drooping, tail slightly opened, feet anchored, the bird swings from side to side

Female at her small and precariously sited nest, which is covered in excreta from the young

Group working over thistle-heads: a typical Goldfinch feeding habit. The pattern of buff plumage on the breast may vary slightly from bird to bird

Goldfinches have a bouncing action in flight

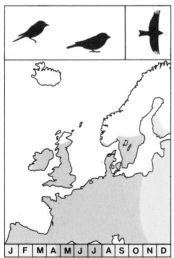

J F M A M J J A S O N D

The attractive plumage and cheerful twittering song of the Goldfinch have resulted in considerable persecution by Man. About 1860, at one site in Britain, an estimated 132,000 were caught each year. The species is now protected in this country, but in some places, especially Belgium, thousands are still being caught and caged.

Goldfinches are primarily birds of woodland edges and glades, and have adapted well to scrub and waste ground. The fine, sharply pointed bill is ideal for extracting seeds from groundsel or dandelion, and they also specialize in seed-heads of thistles, teazels and burdock. The short, stiff, red face feathers resist the prickles, but goldfinches occasionally get trapped on barbed hooks despite their agility on swaying stems. They are particularly adept at using the feet in feeding, and can be trained to pull in suspended food using the feet to hold successive loops of thread.

The nest is beautifully neat, made from grass, moss and lichens, with a startlingly white lining of wool or thistle overlain by a few contrasting black horsehairs. It is sited usually at the end of a flimsy branch, often in a garden or orchard. Clutches of five or six and two or three broods per year are usual. After a good summer, large flocks congregate on thistle patches.

Many Goldfinches winter in western Europe, but northern birds move to France, Iberia and North Africa.

Serin

There is a very con-spicuous yellow patch on the male's rump

The juvenile is buff overall, heavily streaked and has a pale yellow patch on the rump

Male Female

(×³⁄₁₀)

The Serin has long wings and a proportionally short tail. Absence of wing bars distinguishes it from the Siskin, as does the yellow rump

Males in characteristically active, fast-moving flight

The male has a yellow and green head. His yellow breast is as conspicuous as the yellow rump

(×³⁄₅)

A female's rump patch is marginally less obvious than the male's, her head pattern is indistinct and she is generally paler with more streaking on the plumage

Male

Female

Juvenile – like male and female, above, its head is rounded and eye and beak are small

Serins are tiny, often almost invisible on the ground

Viewed in flight from behind, Serins' yellow rumps seem to dance in the air

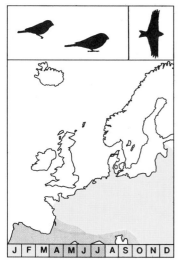

J F M A M J J A S O N D

A Serin's tinkling song is interspersed with trills very similar to the Canary's, reminding one of its close relation-ship to that familiar cagebird. Once an exclusively southern species, it has been spreading north and east for some 200 years, a trend which has accelerated during the past 20 years. Breeding first occurred in Britain and Finland in 1967, and the species has been regularly reported in the vicinity of Leningrad.

Serins prefer a mixed habitat, and thrive in the patchwork of wood, farm and town that covers much of modern Europe. In spring, important food items are elm buds, birch catkins and dan-delion seeds, while in summer they turn to a wide variety of grass and weed seeds, often visiting such places as allotments and railway yards or well-timbered gardens and town parks. Brassica and persicaria seeds are fa-voured in autumn, mugwort in winter.

These are the smallest of European finches, and might be confused with Siskins. However, they lack yellow tail patches, and instead have a very bright yellow rump and a yellow eye-ring and eyestripe. Serins have stubby beaks, Siskins have pointed ones, used for extracting seeds from cones.

The nest is hidden usually near the end of a branch, anywhere between three and 40 feet high. Normally four eggs are laid, and there are two broods in the northern part of its range, more in the south.

Siskin

Female

Male

(×³⁄₁₀)

Siskins have a fast, bounding flight. Their speed means that there is rarely a glimpse of the underparts, above and right. The usual view is of a silhouette

Siskins are very small birds with very long wings and short tails – all features which are noticeable in flight. They are the only European members of the finch family that combine greenish-yellow overall colour with bright yellow wing bars. The female, left, has no yellow patches on her tail

Black cap and bib distinguish the male from the female

The female has duller, streaked plumage, but shares the basic wing pattern of the male

(×³⁄₅)

A typical view of a Siskin feeding in alder. This is a young bird: it resembles the female, but is more heavily streaked, especially underneath

Immature

A female has no black on her head

Male in winter: crown and bib become grey

Birds quarrelling over peanuts

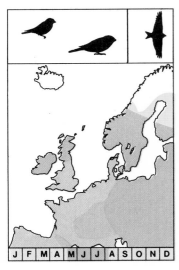

The fortunes of this tiny but attractive finch are, like the Crossbill's, linked with the crop of spruce seeds, though unlike the Crossbill it cannot force cones open, but must wait for their scales to part naturally. In good years, breeding begins in April, leaving time for a second brood. In poor years, this early brood is missed out, and for young hatched later, there are supplements such as pine cones (which ripen later than spruce), elm, docks and thistles. Its nest is small and neat, placed high in a conifer. Three to five eggs are laid, and incubated by the female. Males have a sibilant, twittering song, often uttered in a circling display flight. Out of the breeding season, the high-pitched, rather liquid contact note is a reliable guide to identification.

From July and August, birch seeds are an important food. These, too, fluctuate in quantity, affecting the Siskin's migrations. When birch crops in Scandinavia are good, Siskins migrate south later and in smaller numbers. Alder cones are an important food source in winter, and in many areas Siskins have taken to feeding on nuts and fat put out for them in gardens, finding the food especially attractive when placed in red or orange containers. Siskins are agile when feeding, and adept at using their feet to bring hanging food into reach. These habits make them popular as cagebirds, and large numbers are still caught in Belgium and around the Mediterranean.

Brambling

Bright yellow underwing markings show on the male in flight

Adult male, autumn or winter

Unlike a Chaffinch, the Brambling in flight shows no white feathers in the tail

($\times \frac{3}{10}$)

During winter, Bramblings form groups in trees

Bramblings in flight reveal basically the same markings as Chaffinches, except for the white streak up the back, which can be very narrow, and very inconspicuous

Adult male at nest

Adult female, autumn or winter

The female in winter: a grey-brown head with a distinct pale grey nape patch

An adult male in autumn: as winter progresses, the buff feathers on the back and head will wear away, leaving both jet black

($\times \frac{3}{5}$)

Bramblings puff themselves out while feeding, and in doing so display more than the usually visible amount of orange under-plumage. The white wing markings also stand out

This is a difficult species to identify. There is much finely marked detail on the plumage, which cryptically camouflages the bird against its typical background of woodland beech leaves. It rises very fast and erratically from feeding on the ground and the best approach is to look against the background of foliage for the flicking of the white wing-bars and the serpentine weaving of the white rectangular streak on the back

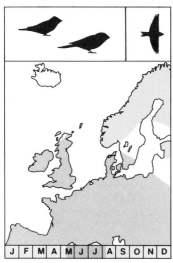

During the winter of 1951-2, an estimated 70 million Bramblings congregated in Switzerland in the neighbourhood of Hunibach, and the country as a whole may have held almost the whole population breeding west of the Urals. Concentrations of this size are unusual, but Bramblings are noted for the unpredictability of their migrations: birds wintering in Britain one year may be in Italy the next. This irregularity may be associated with the dependence of Brambling flocks on the seeds of a few trees (especially beech) that tend to be produced plentifully in alternate years in different localities. Thus, in many areas, bird-watchers will see large numbers of Bramblings roughly every other year. When beech mast is exhausted, Bramblings will flock with other finches on arable fields, feeding on weed seeds or grain.

The breeding range of the Brambling starts roughly where that of its close relative the Chaffinch stops. It is a common bird in Scandinavian birch woods in summer, second in abundance only to the Willow Warbler. Its melodious song, similar to the Redwing's, is heard only for a brief period. Like Chaffinches, Bramblings take a substantial quantity of animal food at all times, and this is specially important in northern breeding areas, where available insect food far outweighs suitable plant food. The nest resembles the Chaffinch's, but is bulkier, since the clutch it accommodates is larger—six or seven eggs.

J F M A M J J A S O N D

Chaffinch

Adult male

The conspicuous double wing-bar is not found on any other European finch

(× 3/10)

Adult female

Male

Female

There is little difficulty in telling Chaffinches apart from other small finches: markings, flight pattern and the jerky, cocksure ground movements are all quite distinct

Between bouts of flapping, the Chaffinch closes its wings completely, to produce the characteristic rising and falling flight

Below, displays used by the male Chaffinch

Between pair formation and nesting

During nest building

Territorial defence

A male in song. Chaffinches sing constantly during the breeding season

Adult female—markings almost identical to those of the adult male

(× 3/5)

A male bird in the crouching posture typical of Chaffinches

Feeding is typically done in a series of short, jerky hops. The white wing and tail markings are visible from behind, as is the nape patch. Despite their conspicuous patterning, these birds merge surprisingly well into the background

The female on her delicate lichen- and cobweb-covered nest

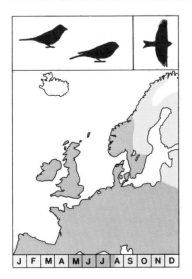

The Chaffinch's exuberant song is a familiar springtime sound throughout Europe, yet travelling bird-watchers can detect noticeable differences in local dialect even within a small country such as Britain. Its alarm call, however, is constant and closely resembles the Great Tit's call.

Though one of Europe's most numerous birds, the Chaffinch population has recently been decreasing. Numbers in Britain have dropped considerably since 1960, coinciding with the use of toxic seed dressings. As the bulk of the Chaffinch's food is weed seeds and cereal grains obtained from the ground, it is obviously vulnerable to such hazards. Other foods include beech mast, and the young are fed on insects.

Chaffinches breed in all types of woodland, scrub, hedgerows and gardens. The nest is a very neat cup, lined with feathers and flecked outside with lichens, often blending imperceptibly into a tree fork. Building is by the female alone, with the male in idle attendance. Five eggs are laid, with distinctive wine-coloured markings, and unlike other finches only a single brood is raised. Incubation is by the female and may be as brief as 11 days. Both parents feed the young.

Winter flocks feed in open fields, but roost in woods, preferably among evergreen bushes. The sexes migrate to different areas, and, in any one place, flocks are likely to consist entirely of either males or females.

Hawfinch

Inside the Hawfinch's beak: to give a firm hold on hard seeds, there is a plate of serrated ridges on the roof and on the lower jaw. Young birds have to eat soft seeds—the plates harden as the skull ossifies

A young bird has the same underwing pattern as an adult

Adult

(× ³/₁₀)

The Hawfinch is short-tailed and surprisingly long-winged. From above or below, its patterning is very conspicuous. In winter, the male bird's beak turns to pale yellow

Both head and beak are massive. This image is three-quarters life size

Adult male in summer, with a predominantly blue beak

(× ³/₅)

Crescent markings on the belly—not found on other finches—distinguish the young Hawfinch

A Hawfinch secondary feather has this unique shape, whose purpose is not known. The superb blue-green sheen is on both the secondary and primary feathers

This species has a habit of feeding unobtrusively on the ground, then rushing straight up into the trees without warning. Return to earth is slow and hesitant

Left, one of the male's courtship display postures. Its dignity tends to be marred by the hesitancy of his approach to the female, whose response is often aggressive. Below, the bill-touching ceremony

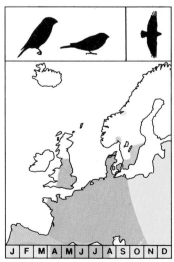

With its massive head and striking wing-bar, the Hawfinch should be easy to identify, but it is very shy and difficult to observe in its orchard or woodland habitat. The "tick" contact call—often used in flight—may help to locate it, as may the audible crunching of seeds produced by a feeding flock.

Its heavily reinforced skull bears powerful jaw muscles and the huge pyramidal beak has been calculated to exert pressures of over 150 pounds per square inch, adequate to crush hornbeam seeds, a favourite food, or to extract the nutritious kernels from the stones of damsons, sloes, olives and cherries. Stones are held vertically rather than horizontally between the jaws: this way they crack at lower pressure. In autumn or winter, flocks regularly feed under cherry trees on the stones of fallen fruit. In late winter, hips and haws are taken, and even oak buds. During early summer some caterpillars are eaten, and Hawfinches have been seen to catch large beetles on the wing.

During courtship, the male lays the foundations of the nest and sits on them, tempting females with feeding gestures. If she accepts regurgitated food with appropriate submission, all is well, and she completes the nest. The clutch contains four or five eggs, and two broods are usual. Hawfinches sometimes nest in gardens or orchards, but should not be approached, as they are extremely prone to desert.

Bullfinch

Bullfinches usually feed in pairs, methodically stripping the tree by working their way out to the end of each branch

The young bird is easy to identify – it has no black cap. The call is an irritatingly persistent double note, contrasting with the adult's single, soft whistle

Typical views of Bullfinch perching positions

Male bird, from below

Female in flight

$(\times \frac{3}{10})$

Below, diagram showing the unusual lateral location of the Bullfinch's feeding pouches (marked in black)

Male, female and young Bullfinches all have the distinctively square white rump and white under-tail coverts

$(\times \frac{3}{5})$

Above, preamble to the bill-caressing display. Below, the twig presentation to a female

An adult male in splendid pink, grey, black and white plumage. Head, wings and tail are a dark, glossy blue when seen at very close range. The northern race is larger and brighter than the southern- and central-European bird

Apart from the obvious difference in breast colour, the female Bullfinch has the same basic plumage pattern as the male

Bullfinches do feed on the ground

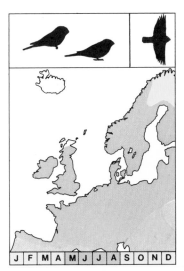

Loved for its elegant plumage, hated for its destructive attacks upon buds, the Bullfinch thrives none the less. In parts of Britain it is now commoner than the Chaffinch.

This bird's ravages on flowers and crops have caused its feeding habits to be closely studied. In gardens, lilac and forsythia may be stripped of flowers, while, on farms, currants, gooseberries and especially peas may be devastated. A single bird may strip up to 30 buds per minute. Curiously selective, Bullfinches favour Conference pear buds, but avoid Doyenné du Comice. Damage is worst near woods or hedges, where the birds can shelter when disturbed. Seeds of preferred trees (birch and ash) are produced in quantity every second year, and damage to buds tends to be worst in the lean years.

Bullfinches are quiet birds: the song is barely audible more than a few feet away, and the contact call is a soft, plaintive whistle. They are rarely seen in flocks of more than a dozen – and a single pair moving along a hedgerow is a more common sight.

The nest is frail but distinctive – a platform of twigs supporting a cup of fine roots, usually sited in a thorny bush. In it are laid five or six blue, maroon-freckled eggs, which the female incubates. Both sexes feed the young from a specialized throat pouch, which is developed only during the breeding season. Northern birds migrate, other birds move short distances.

J F M A M J J A S O N D

35

Crossbill

The adult female is a constant grey-green with yellowish underparts and rump

Crossbill plumage is extremely variable. Older male birds are usually red, but some birds are orange, or yellow or bronze, or a mixture of all three. Some may undergo colour reversion, from red to yellow

A juvenile is recognized by its streaked breast

(× ³/₁₀)

Long, narrow wings and a heavy head are apparent during the Crossbill's bounding flight

Signs of red appear on the back of a young male

These birds are acrobatic feeders

(× ³/₅)

Spruce cones before and after being attacked by a Crossbill

Seed extraction is done with the head laid sideways on the cone. It is not fully understood exactly how the crossed bill is used

Young bird — streaking on back

The nest is built high on the south side of a tree

Juvenile bird — beak is not yet crossed

Upper mandible is straight — the lower is crossed

Crossbills are seen drinking at puddles on forest tracks, and may descend to feed on fallen cones or seeds

While in the nest, a brood of Crossbills may consume some 85,000 seeds extracted from fir cones by the specialized bills of their parents. This remarkable skill enables Crossbills to exploit a major food source inaccessible to other birds (except the less efficient woodpeckers) until the cones open. Falling spruce, larch and fir cones are attacked by the common Crossbill; heavier-billed northern birds, which tackle pine cones, are usually regarded as a separate species, the Parrot Crossbill. Falling cones and explosive calls are a sure sign that a Crossbill party is at work above: the bird will twist a small cone right off its stem before extracting the seeds, and then discard it. Cone crops fluctuate from year to year, thereby causing irruptions (see opposite page).

Breeding starts in February, and nests are built in groups, high in conifers. Males utter a twittering song, sometimes in display flight. The female incubates the three or four eggs, fed by the male, leaving the nest briefly and infrequently. Both parents feed regurgitated seeds to the young, which develop unusually slowly. The fledging period is 25 days, and fledglings are dependent for a further month or so until the crossed bill tip has developed. Later in the year, Crossbills of all ages take aphids, using the tongue because the twisted bill cannot grasp them. In winter, they will eat salt thrown on icy roads—which can be a fatal mistake when poisonous substitutes are used.

Irruptions

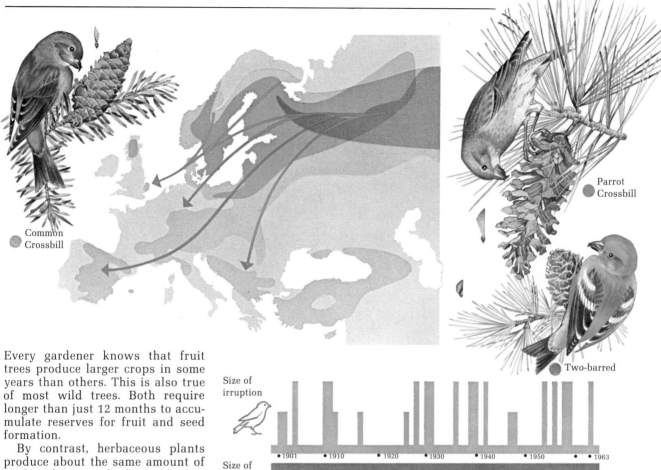

Common Crossbill

Parrot Crossbill

Two-barred

Size of irruption

• 1901 • 1910 • 1920 • 1930 • 1940 • 1950 • 1963

Size of cone crop

Every gardener knows that fruit trees produce larger crops in some years than others. This is also true of most wild trees. Both require longer than just 12 months to accumulate reserves for fruit and seed formation.

By contrast, herbaceous plants produce about the same amount of seed each year. The large number of birds which feed on herb seeds show small or insignificant fluctuations in their breeding populations: Linnets, for example, increase by at most 50 per cent from one year to the next.

A few species depend on trees for food. Their numbers show very marked fluctuations, which correspond to the size of the seed crops: Siskin and Redpoll populations, for example, increase by as much as four times between successive years. Such species differ from most birds by rarely migrating in a fixed direction. Instead, they cope with fluctuations in food supply by wandering until they find a new, more adequate feeding area. An influx of birds caused in this way is called an irruption.

Besides Siskins and Redpolls, other species showing well-marked irruptive movements include the Brambling, Pine Grosbeak, Waxwing and Redwing. Of all irruptive species, crossbills show the most specialized and sensational behaviour. Only in exceptionally lean years do they leave their breeding areas at all, and even then only one major movement is made in a single year.

Top: the Common Crossbill (which feeds mainly on spruce trees) has two other European counterparts, the Parrot Crossbill (which prefers pine) and the Two-barred (which prefers larch). All three irrupt mostly along the same routes into the same well-defined localities, with the exception of Common Crossbills from Scandinavia, which move to the United Kingdom. **Above:** the bar chart represents approximate sizes of Common Crossbill irruptions from Sweden between 1901 and 1963 and approximate levels of spruce cone crops in the same years. It shows that although many big movements coincide with poor crops, the two do not correspond exactly. Moreover, emigrations often start before the size of the new spruce crop has become apparent. Probably a high population level is necessary before emigration can occur, but once this level has been reached, the first inadequate crop will trigger an exodus. **Bottom:** after an irruption. Ringing experiments carried out in Switzerland suggest that some crossbills eventually return to their area of origin, but not until the second year after irruption. Unlike other birds away from their breeding ground, crossbills may raise young in the invaded areas

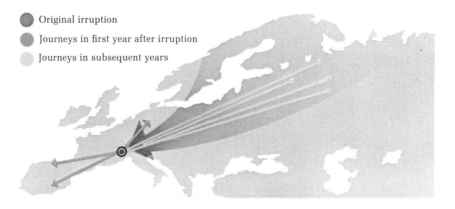

Original irruption

Journeys in first year after irruption

Journeys in subsequent years

Fan-tailed Warbler

Fan-tailed Warblers are most conspicuous in their high, jerky song flight over marsh and farmland. The dry "zeep ... zeep" is a good recognition point as the bird climbs into a blue Mediterranean sky

A side view shows the short, stocky build and alert posture. The plumage pattern is similar to that of the Sedge Warbler, but their physical characteristics differ

An adult perches above the delicate, purse-shaped nest, made mainly of cobwebs, hidden deep in grass. The back markings are conspicuous on this freshly plumaged bird, but duller, worn specimens are frequently encountered.

($\times \frac{3}{5}$)

Rear view of bird skulking into the undergrowth

No other Warbler has the stubby wings and rounded tail which gives this bird such a characteristic profile in flight

The feathers on the underside of the short, very rounded tail have characteristic white tips—not easy to identify in the field

($\times \frac{3}{10}$)

Although skulking birds, Fantail Warblers can be seen frequently in areas they favour

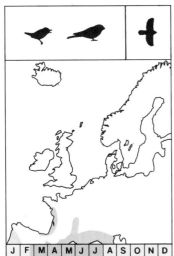

This tiny warbler, with drab, streaked plumage, is well suited for concealment against its surroundings of reeds or other vegetation. Nevertheless, it is often seen in its own habitat because of the male's conspicuous song flight: a surprisingly penetrating repetition of "zeep" calls. These are uttered as the bird bounces about on weakly fluttering wings, rising to 50 feet as if held on an invisible spring, undulating sharply with each "zeep". In many areas Fantailed Warblers have developed the habit of singing from roadside overhead cables.

The preferred habitat is reeds, salt scrub or other vegetation in marshy areas or by waterways, but Fan-tailed Warblers are also widespread in lowland scrub, on poor farming land, and often in apparently arid surroundings. In Europe it is a Mediterranean species, but it has an enormous range throughout the warmer parts of the Old World, and many close relatives occur in Africa. At present, populations are expanding northwards in Europe, breeding as far north as Brittany.

This bird builds a remarkable purse-shaped nest of cobwebs, reinforced with woven-in wisps of grass and lined with reed flowers and thistledown. It usually contains five bluish-white eggs, freckled with brown. Young in the nest are surprisingly noisy: both parents feed them and the male sometimes approaches while still singing—clues to an otherwise skilfully hidden nest.

Bearded Tit

Birds normally fly within inches of the reed tops, but departing on migration they rise direct from the reeds to two or three hundred feet. Returning, they drop out of the sky with just as little ceremony

Adult female

$(\times \sfrac{3}{10})$

Flight across the reed tops, tail wobbling uncertainly, is very fast, and ends inevitably with an abrupt dive back into cover

A young bird has much more black plumage than an adult: probably because it spends more time amongst the dark bases of the reeds

$(\times \sfrac{3}{5})$

Above, the male bird in a common perching position

A female at her nest, which is built right in the base of the reeds. The white spots in the bright red gapes of the nestlings evoke a feeding response in the adult

The Bearded Tit's combination of plumage and shape is unique in European birdlife. Particularly unmistakable is the male, with grey head and black moustaches. These actually hang loose as separate tufts, and their mobility explains why the bird's facial expression changes so constantly

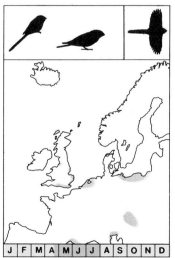

This elegant and charming bird has had a chequered history. Last century it was greatly persecuted by egg collectors, cage bird fanciers and others. Reprieved by protection, its populations recovered, though badly hit by occasional severe winters. Now it is expanding its range, and has colonized many new areas—notably in Holland (where reclamation has greatly enlarged its habitat), Germany and England.

Not a tit at all, this species is the only European representative of the huge babbler family of Asia and Africa. It is confined to beds of *Phragmites* reeds, where it takes insects in summer and *Phragmites* seeds in winter. On calm days, Bearded Tits may often be seen making short flights just above the reeds. Wind keeps them lower, but the "ping" call note betrays their presence. The nest is built near water level among reeds by both sexes, the male adding a lining, and five to seven eggs are laid. Both parents incubate and tend the young, which spend only nine to 12 days in the nest, often leaving while flightless. Up to four broods may be reared in a warm summer. Bearded Tit nestlings show a remarkable red, black and white pattern in the open gape, unlike any other European bird. Immature birds pair in their first autumn, and apparently maintain the pair bond for life. Once considered sedentary, it is now known to undertake extensive movements.

39

Grasshopper Warbler

When these birds produce their unique "reeling" song the head is turned from side to side and the beak is opened to reveal the yellow gape. The throat distends and vibrates with the effort—and so does the tail

Grasshopper Warblers often nest in young pine plantations

(× ³/₁₀)

Full views of the bird in flight are rare, but they reveal a rounded tail and oval wings

There are streaks on the under-tail coverts

Wing flicking and tail wagging form the male courtship display

A long-toed foot—efficient for walking on the ground

The extra-long central toe permits the bird to grasp two strands at once, enabling it to support its weight among the flimsiest stems. This facility assists the general adaptation of the feet for walking through or over vegetation

(× ³/₅)·

Rounded tail and streaked upperparts of uniformly plain colour—this is a nondescript bird

Sometimes Grasshopper Warblers look dumpy, at others remarkably slim

It is possible to mistake this bird for a mouse

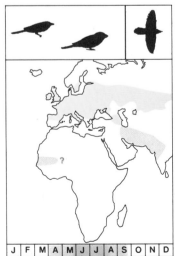

A bird that sings like an insect and behaves like a mouse, the Grasshopper Warbler is widely distributed but rarely seen. Any area of rough, rank grass or sedge is a likely habitat, but its presence often goes unsuspected. Song is the clue—a high-pitched trilling continued for two minutes or more at a time—but being ventriloquial it is difficult to locate.

Once the bird has been spotted singing—bill wide open and body vibrating—close approach is possible before it slips with astonishing speed through tangled undergrowth. Its skulking behaviour is aided by a foot with a relatively long central toe—ideal for walking or running and for grasping several stems at once, less good for grasping individual stems, as do Reed and Sedge Warblers. The female is all but invisible as she moves to and from the nest, which makes it difficult to find: searchers often walk one behind the other, since the bird slips off only after the first observer has passed. The nest is a simple cup of coarse grasses hidden deep inside a grass or sedge tussock. Five or six eggs are laid, prettily marked with dense, pinkish freckles. Two broods are usual.

Though more often seen on the ground than in flight, migrating Grasshopper Warblers are frequent casualties at lighthouses: hundreds have died in a night at some Irish Sea lights. Nevertheless, the species thrives and is extending its range.

Sedge Warbler

The contrast between the streaked back and plain rufous rump shows clearly in flight ($\times \frac{3}{10}$)

Wings are often held low, allowing a view of the rump ($\times \frac{3}{5}$)

A male chatters from a reed—one of the more exposed song posts chosen. The body is fatter, and posture more hunched than at other times

Two views of the conspicuous head pattern, left. Moustached Warblers (extreme southern Europe) have a near-black crown, and Aquatic Warblers (the far north of Europe) have a broad, cream central stripe. Both species are rare elsewhere in Europe

Sedge Warblers are skulking birds and build well-concealed nests, but they come into view more often than other reed-bed birds. Distinguished from other Warblers by their streaked upper parts

A displaying bird rises, then "parachutes" down, singing all the time

Left and below: the distinctive back pattern is formed by pale feather edges on the closed wings

Sedge Warblers may sing low in vegetation

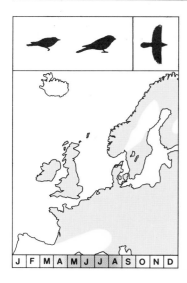

Commonest and most widely distributed of the European marshland warblers, Sedge Warblers frequent the dense vegetation along waterways and lakesides, as well as drier hedgerows and thickets. They are distinguished from most other reed-bed warblers by their streaked upperparts, dark crown and pale eyestripe.

Sedge Warblers spend much time low in vegetation, but can often be seen as they proclaim their noisy song, which is less repetitive than the Reed Warbler's. The deep, surprisingly bulky nest is well concealed, bound round stems in low vegetation, and holds four or five eggs. Two or three broods are usual.

Sedge Warblers winter in tropical Africa, and perform one of the most extraordinary of migration feats. Most migrants feed intensively before departure, storing energy as fat. Sedge Warblers take this to the extreme: they store fat in the body cavity, under the skin, even under the eyelids, some becoming almost spherical and having great difficulty in taking off. A few other species achieve pre-migratory weight increases of 30 per cent, but Sedge Warblers sometimes double their weight. Their store of energy is expended in a flight which traverses Mediterranean and Sahara in one hop. Recent drought conditions in western Africa seem to have affected the northward journey and Sedge Warbler populations have been considerably reduced.

Reed Warbler—Marsh Warbler

A Reed Warbler in song: fat compared to the perched bird, bottom centre

(×³⁄₅)

(×³⁄₁₀)

Reed Warblers build deep-cupped nests to protect the eggs in the violently swaying reeds

The warm-coloured, rufous-brown plumage of the Reed Warbler contrasts with the cold grey-brown of the Marsh Warbler, bottom right

A Reed Warbler in flight is indistinguishable from a Marsh Warbler

Typical view of Reed Warbler, below, "bouncing" at speed over the reeds

(×³⁄₅)

The juvenile Reed Warbler shows a marginally paler throat and more rufous plumage than an adult

Marsh Warblers have almost uniformly pale undersides

A juvenile Marsh Warbler: colour identical to the young Reed Warbler, but longer wing tips

Note the long wing tips of the Marsh Warbler

Adult Marsh Warblers have whiter eye rings than Reed Warblers

Marsh Warblers build a shallow nest in vegetation (not reeds). It is bound to surrounding stems with loose ends of the building material

Reed Warblers often adopt vertical (head downwards) and other acrobatic poses

Above, Reed Warbler's foot. Below, Marsh Warbler's

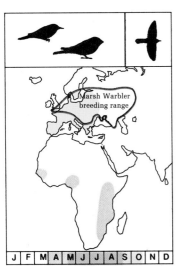

Marsh Warbler breeding range

J F M A M J J A S O N D

Reed Warblers' nests are renowned examples of bird architecture. Woven round a few reed stems, they are supported virtually by friction alone: there is no support beneath.

Reed Warblers arrive and breed late, most of their young being reared from June onwards. They almost invariably nest in beds of *Phragmites* reeds, from which the males deliver their harsh and repetitive song, reaching a crescendo during the two hours before dawn. The clutch of four is incubated by the female at night, and by both sexes during the day, when the female takes a 25 per cent larger share of this task than the male. Incubation starts with the second egg and lasts 11 to 12 days. The young are fed by both sexes, and at this stage parents often forage outside the reed beds, where saw-fly caterpillars on nearby willows are an important food source. They may leave the nest after as little as ten days, though it is a further week before they can fly. Frequently two broods are reared.

These birds do not show such spectacular pre-migration weight gains as Sedge Warblers, but make instead a re-fuelling stop in Iberia before crossing the Mediterranean and Sahara to tropical Africa. The main moult takes place in these winter quarters.

The confusingly similar Marsh Warbler differs from the Reed Warbler in habitat and behaviour. It lives in osier beds and marshy scrub, and males have a much more melodious song.

42

Savi's Warbler

Experience is required to tell Savi's Warbler from a Reed Warbler in flight, but it has a unique, sharp "spitz" call while on the wing and also when perching

$(\times \,^3/_{10})$

An adult in song revealing the pale breast and generally buff colouring of the underparts, which is quite distinct from the Reed Warbler's rufous-brown. The body shape and curved wings with stubby ends, which can be seen on the nesting bird, below, also set Savi's Warbler apart from the Reed Warbler

Cocking the tail

Underside view of tail shows the distinctive square-ended shape. It becomes rounder when the short, outer tail feathers are opened. The under-tail coverts are buff—unlike the Reed Warbler's

$(\times \,^3/_5)$

This bird's nest is mounted on a base of reeds or vegetation, quite unlike the Reed, Marsh or Sedge Warbler's

Savi's Warbler displays on the floor of the reed-bed by fluffing out its feathers, fanning the tail and slowly flapping its wings

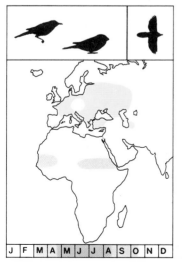

J F M A M J J A S O N D

Savi's Warbler is closely related to the Grasshopper Warbler, but, having unstreaked plumage, is more likely to be mistaken for the Reed Warbler. Its graduated tail and skulking, mouselike behaviour should distinguish it from the latter.

Savi's Warbler occupies wetter habitats than the Grasshopper Warbler, and is thus more vulnerable to drainage of marshland. It is much more patchily distributed, though having recently started to breed in England after a century's absence its status is improving. The typical habitat contains a mixture of willows, sedges and reeds, and some open shallow water is essential. Its diet consists entirely of waterside insects. The song resembles the Grasshopper Warbler's "reeling", but is usually delivered in shorter bursts, starting with a few ticking notes, and the individual notes in the trill are produced more slowly. The female is said to sing at times and a ticking alarm call is commonly used.

A rather bulky nest is built into the base of a sedge or rush tussock. Consisting of reeds and grasses woven around the plant stems, it is sometimes slightly domed. Four or five brownish eggs are laid and incubated by the female, who is believed to be almost entirely responsible for feeding the young. The incubation period is 12 days, the fledging period 14 days, and it is usual for the species to raise a second brood.

Cetti's Warbler

Cetti's Warbler is unusual among passerines in having ten tail feathers rather than 12, which can give the strongly rounded tail a ragged appearance. In song, far right, it is often heard, but rarely seen except early on spring mornings

Occasional upward flicks of the tail characterize the Cetti's behaviour in vegetation. The bird is generally more like the Garden Warbler or Blackcap than other marshland Warblers

Cetti's is the only uniformly rufous-brown Warbler, contrast being added only by the off-white eye-stripe. The underparts vary from off-white to pale buff

(× 3/5)

An extreme skulker at all times, Cetti's Warbler feeds low in scrub. It nests close to the ground (or occasionally over water) in the dark depths of plants such as brambles. The eggs, a dark, purplish brown, are adapted to concealment and so are the young, which are covered in dark grey or black down

(× 3/10)

Dark, rich brown plumage and a long, rounded tail make identification of this Warbler easy

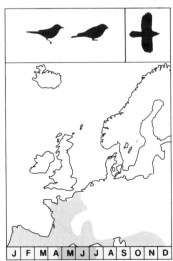

J F M A M J J A S O N D

This rather large warbler shares with the Dartford Warbler the distinction of being non-migratory in the true sense of the term. Thus, it also shares the Dartford Warbler's vulnerability to severely cold or long-lasting winters, which can cause massive population "crashes", most noticeably at the northern edges of its range. It is primarily a Mediterranean bird, common and widespread in southern and central Europe, and the present sequence of mild winters has encouraged a rapid expansion of the Cetti's Warbler's range northwestwards. Steadily increasing numbers now breed in southeastern England, but the next cold winter may well extinguish them all, making the bird once again a rare vagrant in Britain.

Cetti's Warbler spends much time low in vegetation, but can normally be seen (with a little patience) simply by standing still in a favoured area. Males advertise their presence with a startlingly explosive burst of song.

The habitat is bushes and scrub along marshland and irrigation ditches, or by lakesides, but occasional pairs breed surprisingly far from water. The birds are usually seen as they flick low between clumps of vegetation – especially when feeding young. Males may sing in open view on calm mornings in early spring, when the almost thrushlike shape can be clearly seen. The rather bulky nest, built in deep vegetation, usually holds a clutch of four striking brick-red eggs.

Great Reed Warbler

When seen singing amongst the reeds, Great Reed Warblers appear much bulkier than Reed Warblers, bottom right

($\times \frac{3}{10}$)

The flight of the Great Reed Warbler is slow and heavy, just above the reeds. Its long round-ended tail is often fanned in flight

($\times \frac{3}{5}$)

The bulky nest is woven about *Phragmites* reed stems, or less often in *Typha* bulrushes, willows and other trees. The bird high on the stem is a juvenile

Giant size, unstreaked plumage, long, rounded tail and massive beak typify the Great Reed Warbler. The extremely noisy "song" also provides useful identification in the field

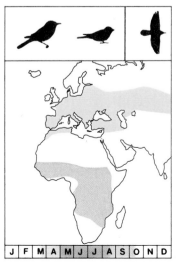

J F M A M J J A S O N D

An appropriately named bird which dwarfs the Common Reed Warbler. By far the largest of European Warblers, it is almost the size of the Song Thrush.

The Great Reed Warbler's plumage and general shape are similar to the Reed Warbler's, but the Great Reed Warbler may appear sandier when in worn plumage, and it has a longer, heavier bill. The flight is jerky, low over the reeds, and the long, rounded tail is partly fanned: it frequently crashes clumsily about as it moves through the reeds. The nest, woven round *Phragmites* stems, resembles the Reed Warbler's, but is bulkier, and four to six eggs are laid. Like the Reed Warbler, it is a frequent victim of the cuckoo.

Great Reed Warblers are widespread in continental Europe, especially in association with large reed beds, but never as numerous as their smaller relative. A rare bird in Britain, despite its abundance in nearby Holland, the Great Reed Warbler is expanding its range and may eventually breed here. It nests in sociable gatherings rather than colonies, with nests some distance apart.

Occasionally Great Reed Warblers will come into competition with, and drive off, Reed Warblers. Generally, areas with some open water are preferred, perhaps because water beetles, dragonflies and even small fish occasionally feature in their basically insect diet. In autumn they may fatten on sugar-rich berries before migrating.

Migration

There is something uniquely poignant about bird migration, particularly that of such small passerines as the many song birds which visit Europe each summer in order to breed. During June and July, most of these species are hatching their young—tiny scraps of life, blind, unfeathered and totally helpless. Within say eight weeks these same youngsters will set off one evening on a journey of many hundreds of miles towards a wintering place they have never seen. Perhaps even more incredible, those which survive may well be back near their birthplace the following summer.

Distances covered may be vast. Many European breeding birds, such as Swallows or Sanderlings, pass the winter in South Africa, a journey of about 5,500 miles. Arctic Terns travel a minimum of 8,000 miles from northern breeding grounds to their wintering places in Antarctic waters. Such trans-equatorial migrants enjoy permanent summer.

Of course, many birds are non-migratory, while others undertake only short movements, or more or less random dispersals from their point of origin. True migration involves regular movements between fairly well defined breeding and wintering areas, and its purpose is to ensure an adequate food supply at all times of year. Migration is confined to definite seasons, and should be distinguished from the weather movements which species such as the Lapwing or Redwing may undertake during hard weather.

Large birds generally migrate by day, but most small passerines travel at night—a safeguard against predators. Swallows and martins, which are day-time migrants, have protection in their flying skills. Very long journeys, like that of the Sedge Warbler (logged on the opposite page), last two days and nights.

Migration only starts during good weather, with clear skies and little wind. It may be thwarted by squalls, fog or heavy overcast: a fine spell following prolonged bad weather may produce a rush of migrants that have been accumulating at some departure point. Even when conditions are fine at the start, they may deteriorate during the journey, and when migrants are flying without landmarks over sea, cross-winds may blow them far to one side of their intended route. In such cases, they will either make a landfall off course or perish at sea.

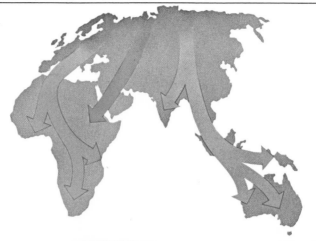

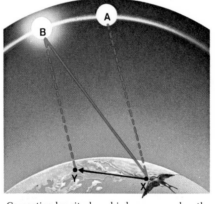

Correcting longitude: a bird can remember the sun's position, A, along its east-west track for a given time at home. It realizes that the observed sun, B, is not in that position. By flying eastwards from its present position, X, it "speeds up" the sun until on the home longitude, Y, the sun is at its accustomed position

Correcting latitude: a bird can remember the elevation, A, of the midday sun at home. It can also see that the observed sun, B, is not climbing as fast as it did at home. By flying south from its present position, X, the bird causes the sun to "rise" until on the latitude of home the sun is at its accustomed height

Migrations, as opposed to dispersals, are made in a very definite direction, which is known instinctively and not in any way learned or copied from older birds. This is clear by a comparison of the timing of migrations made by old and young birds: among many passerines, birds of the year set off first, while their elders moult into new plumage. Conversely, young Cuckoos migrate alone, well after the departure of their true parents, whom they never meet.

How birds determine their course, often over trackless stretches of sea, has been a source of much speculation. At present the most plausible theories are based on the role of the sun or stars.

The simplest form of navigation is that shown by a bird migrating in a fixed direction, as so many do. By day, the sun's position in the sky provides a compass orientation as long as the time of day is known, and there is good evidence that birds have accurate internal "clocks" for that purpose. This is shown by experiments with caged birds in a state of migratory restlessness, when they tend to flutter most in the direction they want to go; artificial suns and artificial alterations of day length produce the expected changes in direction. Similar results are obtained with night migrants caged under a starry sky, or even a planetarium. This need for visual clues explains why fog or heavy overcast can bring migration to a standstill.

Even more remarkable and intriguing is the capacity for homing, shown for example by the Manx Shearwaters transported from Wales to the USA which returned to their burrows in 12½ days. Orientation towards a definite goal from any direction requires the bird to know both its own position on the Earth's surface and that of the goal. Though other possible clues, such as magnetism or the Earth's rotation, have been considered, in these cases the sun is the most feasible.

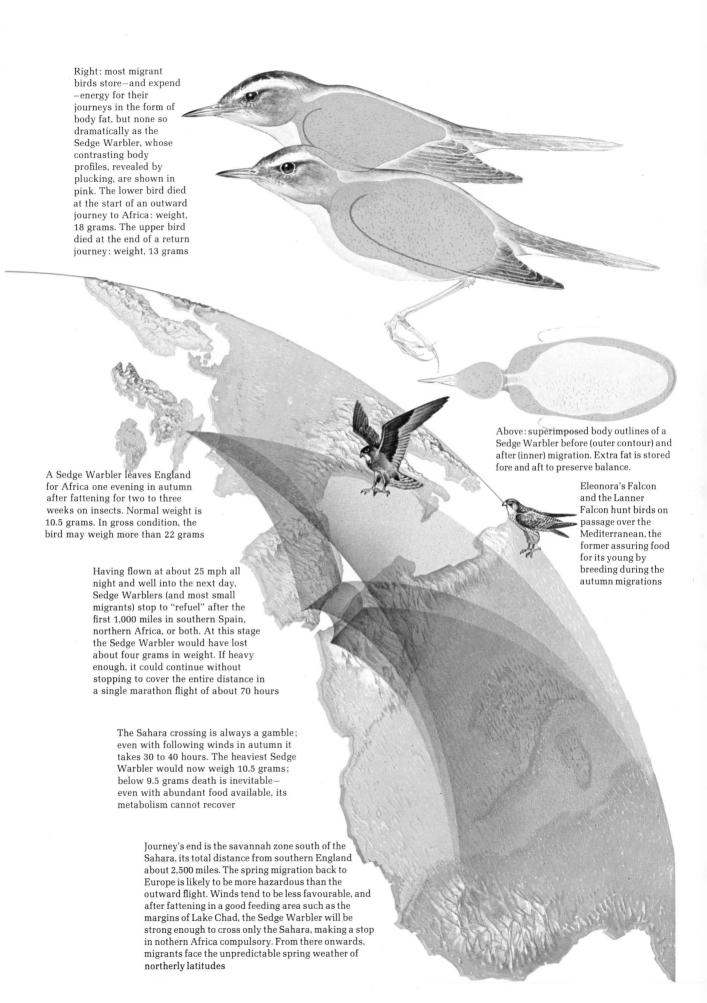

Right: most migrant birds store—and expend—energy for their journeys in the form of body fat, but none so dramatically as the Sedge Warbler, whose contrasting body profiles, revealed by plucking, are shown in pink. The lower bird died at the start of an outward journey to Africa: weight, 18 grams. The upper bird died at the end of a return journey: weight, 13 grams

Above: superimposed body outlines of a Sedge Warbler before (outer contour) and after (inner) migration. Extra fat is stored fore and aft to preserve balance.

A Sedge Warbler leaves England for Africa one evening in autumn after fattening for two to three weeks on insects. Normal weight is 10.5 grams. In gross condition, the bird may weigh more than 22 grams

Eleonora's Falcon and the Lanner Falcon hunt birds on passage over the Mediterranean, the former assuring food for its young by breeding during the autumn migrations

Having flown at about 25 mph all night and well into the next day, Sedge Warblers (and most small migrants) stop to "refuel" after the first 1,000 miles in southern Spain, northern Africa, or both. At this stage the Sedge Warbler would have lost about four grams in weight. If heavy enough, it could continue without stopping to cover the entire distance in a single marathon flight of about 70 hours

The Sahara crossing is always a gamble; even with following winds in autumn it takes 30 to 40 hours. The heaviest Sedge Warbler would now weigh 10.5 grams; below 9.5 grams death is inevitable—even with abundant food available, its metabolism cannot recover

Journey's end is the savannah zone south of the Sahara, its total distance from southern England about 2,500 miles. The spring migration back to Europe is likely to be more hazardous than the outward flight. Winds tend to be less favourable, and after fattening in a good feeding area such as the margins of Lake Chad, the Sedge Warbler will be strong enough to cross only the Sahara, making a stop in nothern Africa compulsory. From there onwards, migrants face the unpredictable spring weather of northerly latitudes

Ringing

Mist nets, made of very fine material, intercept birds in flight

Cannon nets are used to catch waders or wildfowl at roosts. They are carried over the birds by projectiles fired from small cannons

Permanent ringing stations are provided by Heligoland traps located on migration routes. Birds are driven down the net tunnel to a collecting box

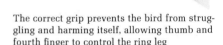

The correct grip prevents the bird from struggling and harming itself, allowing thumb and fourth finger to control the ring leg

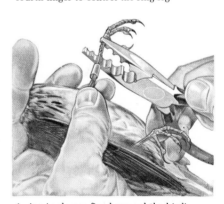

A ring is always fixed around the bird's tarsus above the foot, just loose enough to move freely.

Specially designed pliers are used to tighten the ring enough to ensure complete closure without risk of harm to the bird

Below, actual size rings ranging from those for Goldcrests and other tiny birds to those suitable for larger owls

All Robins look the same, even to an experienced observer, but by ringing, each becomes an individual subject for study.

The technique consists quite simply of placing around the bird's leg a ring bearing a unique number, and an address to which its discovery should be reported. As a refinement, colour rings are used for certain types of investigation, the colour codes being distinguishable through binoculars, thus eliminating the need for trapping birds in nets before checking their rings. Of course, the number of possible colour permutations is limited and the use of colour rings is normally confined to populations which are both local and resident.

Ideally, all birds should be ringed as nestings, so that age and birthplace are known exactly. Breeding seasons are short, however, and most birds are ringed while fully grown and able to fly freely.

Most of the facts about migration mentioned in this book have been revealed by ringing, and so has a great deal about life expectancy and mortality. It has been found, for example, that most small passerines live a maximum of eight to 11 years, and that their average life expec-

tancy at hatching is under two years. Larger species live longer, and the present record for longevity in the wild is held by a German-ringed Oystercatcher which lived into its 34th year. Ringing has shown that mortality is highest in the first year of a bird's life and subsequently levels off, although such factors as severe winters may lead to sharp increases. Ringing also provides a valuable check on the impact of these environmental changes on bird populations. Trapping birds for ringing provides opportunities to carry out additional studies, for instance on weight changes during migration, moult condition, presence of parasites and the changing colours of eyes, bill and beak.

Rings are made of light alloy, and their presence in no way hinders the life of a bird. This is essential on scientific, as well as humanitarian, grounds, for there must be no bias in results. The bird's interests always come first, and because of this, a high standard of skill is demanded of the ornithologists—mostly amateur—who carry out the work. Before a ringer is permitted to operate on his own, he must complete a period of thorough training and apprenticeship.

Barred Warbler

The Barred Warbler's extraordinarily large size – even compared with the Great Reed Warbler – its long wings and tail, the striking pattern on the underparts and overall grey colour make it an easy bird to identify. In certain lights the grey of the plumage can appear exceptionally pale

$(\times \frac{8}{10})$

Typical Barred Warbler postures including the cocked tail

An adult male, right. The female is practically identical. In no other species do the large size, long, square-ended tail and heavy bill combined with a pale eye all occur together

$(\times \frac{3}{5})$

The yellow of the eye can vary individually from bright to pale, but combined with the large beak and inimitable expression makes this species unmistakable. Barred underparts are unusual in a passerine

The juvenile bird is brown. It has a profile, and habits, identical to those of the adult bird

Birds pausing on migration may lurk in scrub along coasts. Often, all that is seen of the bird is a peeping head and a baleful, yellow eye

The juvenile Barred Warbler's colouring is very different from that of the adult. It has no barring. Some have the yellow eye – but it is very pale

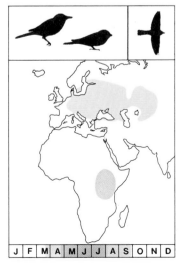

J F M A M J J A S O N D

Large size and heavy build distinguish the Barred Warbler. The heavily barred flanks of summer plumage are also distinctive, but birds in their first autumn show little barring, and but for their size might be confused with Garden Warblers. Narrow greyish wing bars and pale-tipped tail assist identification in all plumages, though the former may be lost by abrasion.

During the breeding season, Barred Warblers occupy a variety of scrubby habitats, including forest glades, woodland edges and tall hedgerows. There is also a marked inclination to choose sites near water. These preferences are shared by the Red-backed Shrike, and there is a distinct tendency for the two species to associate, despite poten-tial danger for the warbler. This association is even noted on migration, but its causes are difficult to surmise.

The male has a conspicuous song flight resembling the Common White-throat's, but Barred Warblers are generally skulking birds. The song is like the Blackcap's in tone, but briefer, and includes some scratchy phrases. Calls, given from deep cover, include a "chack" note like the Blackcap's and a "chur-ring" note recalling the Nightingale. The nest is often placed quite high in some dense bush, and a single brood is usual. Food includes soft-bodied arthro-pods and berries in autumn. Larger fruits, such as apples and pears, are also attacked on occasions. The African winter quarters are in acacia scrub.

Wood Warbler—Bonelli's Warbler

(×³⁄₅)

(×³⁄₁₀)

A Wood Warbler in display flight. The yellow under-plumage is distributed over its throat, breast and the leading edges of the wings

Bonelli's Warbler is best recognized in the field by its yellow shoulder patch, grey-green upperparts and yellowish tail. The yellow rump, not always visible, is also a distinguishing characteristic most often seen in flight

Typical posture of the Wood Warbler in song

Seen from beneath, Bonelli's Warbler has a silvery white throat and breast, separating it from the Wood Warbler

Juvenile Wood Warbler, left. A Wood Warbler is distinguished from Bonelli's Warbler by the larger eyestripe (which can vary in size), greenish back, yellow throat and white belly. Its wings are long and relatively narrow

(×³⁄₅)

Bonelli's Warbler builds a domed nest on the ground, often camouflaged with pine needles and other leaves. It is smaller than that of the Wood Warbler

Wood Warblers also build a well-concealed nest on the ground

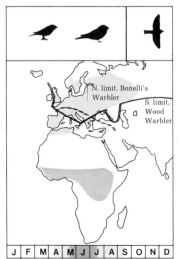

N. limit, Bonelli's Warbler

S. limit, Wood Warbler

J F M A M J J A S O N D

The Wood Warbler is the largest of the European leaf Warblers, and the most brightly coloured, with distinctive yellow-green upperparts, yellow breast and bright white belly. The song is a wonderful shivering trill, uttered with wings and tail vibrating, or sometimes in flight between perches. Song accompanies the butterfly-like display flight, when the male spirals down to a perch alongside his mate. There is a second quite different song – a repeated piping whistle – used about once every dozen trills.

In Europe, Wood Warblers are most often found in mature woods of oak and beech, preferably with sparse undergrowths. They spend most of their time high in the canopy, but build their nests on the ground. These are domed structures, with side entrances, often sunk in hollows. They lack the feather lining used by Willow Warblers and Chiffchaffs.

Bonelli's Warbler is a more southerly species, typical of Mediterranean hillside pinewoods and cork oak. Recent records indicate that it is increasing its range northwards. Its song is a trill somewhat like the Wood Warbler's, but lower pitched. The nest is similar, also lined only with grasses. The clutch, usually five, is smaller than the Wood Warbler's, but in both species a single brood is usual.

Both species winter migrate to Africa, but few details of the routes used are yet known.

Willow Warbler—Chiffchaff

Chiffchaff (× ³/₅)

Although both birds have similar shapes, the Chiffchaff's head is rounder. Its upperparts are nearer brown and the underparts closer to buff. Legs are usually very dark

Flight silhouettes hardly differ, but the Willow Warbler, left, shows longer wings than the Chiffchaff. Both species feed in the same manner, working actively high in the canopy, but also flycatching and hovering to pick insects from under leaves

Willow Warbler (× ³/₅)

A Willow Warbler's upperparts are more distinctly green and underparts more yellow. Legs are usually pale

The wings are often flicked as the alarm call is given

Both species are quite approachable while in song

A freshly fledged Chiffchaff, left, is all but indistinguishable from a freshly fledged Willow Warbler, but much yellower than an adult. The northern forms of Chiffchaff, centre, and Willow Warbler, below left, generally have browner upperparts and white underparts

Chiffchaffs build ragged nests, right, almost always placed above the ground, whereas Willow Warblers make weaker structures, left, placed in grass actually on the ground. Both nests resemble those of the Wren, comprising a domed roof and side entrance

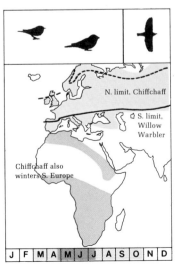

N. limit, Chiffchaff

S. limit, Willow Warbler

Chiffchaff also winters S. Europe

J F M A M J J A S O N D

First distinguished (along with the Wood Warbler) by the eighteenth-century naturalist Gilbert White, these two birds are still best identified by song. The Chiffchaff continually sings its name, while the Willow Warbler has a sparkling, descendant cascade of notes. Calls, too, are distinguishable, the Willow Warbler's much more di-syllabic. Silent birds are often perforce noted by the observer simply as "Willowchiffs".

The Chiffchaff's legs are usually black, the Willow Warbler's pale brown, but doubtful cases occur. In the hand, shape and length of primary feathers distinguish most individuals. Generally, Willow Warblers are longer-winged and slightly larger birds.

Differences in habitat are not clearly defined, but Willow Warblers generally occupy more open areas, and take to tall trees only where there is copious undergrowth. They penetrate far to the north in low birch scrub. Chiffchaffs prefer tall, mature woodland with less dense undergrowth. In western Europe generally, the Willow Warbler is considerably more abundant and in many woodland or scrub areas is the most numerous bird in summer.

Though both birds efficiently conceal their nests (a Willow Warbler's on the ground, the Chiffchaff's slightly above it), they betray them when feeding the young by giving repeated alarm calls—a warning which picnickers should heed, and then move on.

Icterine Warbler

A singing male often raises his crown feathers – as do both sexes when excited in display. Normally, Icterine Warblers are flat crowned and long beaked – reminiscent of Reed Warblers

Views of head from right-hand side and from above show the broad base of the beak, a feature shared with the Melodious Warbler

$(\times \frac{3}{10})$

In flight, the wings are detectably longer and more pointed than those of the Melodious Warbler. Note the differences in tail length between the two species

A fully grown juvenile is bright yellow underneath

In late summer, Icterine Warblers take berries, tugging them off with a highly distinctive backwards jerk of the head

Excellent points of recognition in the field are the long, protruding tips of the folded wings which extend to roughly half the length of the tail. So also is the pale, oblong patch on the wing

The bird on the right is a juvenile, much yellower than the adult on the left and without the pale wing-patch. Its tail is not yet fully grown

Migrating Icterine Warblers seen in autumn tend to have drabber, worn plumage, but the pale wing pattern is usually still distinct and the long wing-tips remain a reliable distinguishing feature

$(\times \frac{3}{5})$

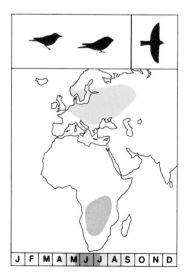

Pliny, the Roman encyclopaedist, mentions in his *Natural History* that a glimpse of the Icterine Warbler could cure a person suffering from jaundice. Presumably the superstition was connected with the bright yellow colour of the bird's underparts, and this curious idea is commemorated in the English and scientific names of the bird, which derive from the Greek *ikteros*, meaning jaundice.

Icterine Warblers are found in a variety of habitats, including parks, gardens and hedgerows, but generally keep to the tree canopy rather than the undergrowth beneath it. The typical nest site is six to eight feet up on a fork in the branches of a tree or bush. Both sexes build the nest, which is a neat cup of grass and roots lined with hair or feathers. Small scraps of paper or bark are often studded round the outside. Four or five eggs are the usual clutch, incubation and fledging periods each lasting 13 to 14 days. The duties of brooding eggs and feeding young are shared by both sexes; only a single brood is reared.

Harsh, grating noises interspersed with rich musical notes comprise the song, and, as with the Melodious Warbler, mimicry of other species is often included. The song is usually delivered from a regular perch, though sometimes in flight, and it is occasionally heard at night. The preferred habitats in winter quarters are cultivated land and palm groves.

Melodious Warbler

The long, broad beak is similar to the Icterine Warbler's, opposite page, but the head shape is normally flatter

In flight, the Melodious Warbler's wings are seen to be broader and rounder than the Icterine's, and the tail much shorter

$(\times\,^3/_{10})$

Bird in parachute display flight, similar to the Tree Pipit's

$(\times\,^3/_5)$

Melodious Warblers may emerge to sing on the sun-lit fringes of bushes, but spend most of the time deep in shrub cover

A juvenile is even yellower than an adult. The combination of green and bright yellow separates the Melodious and Icterine from all other Warblers. Leg colour ranges from lead blue to dark brown

Melodious Warblers are heavy headed, comparatively dumpy birds. The wing tips and tail are much shorter than the Icterine Warbler's and there is no pale wing patch

Some adults show very worn plumage, but can still be recognized by physical characteristics

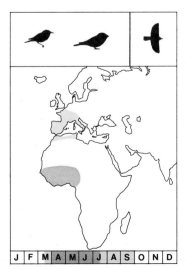

As the name suggests, this species has a genuinely tuneful song, lacking the harsh notes produced by the closely related Icterine Warbler. The song is sometimes continued for several minutes without pause, and often includes passages mimicking songs of other species. Other vocalizations include a sparrow-like chatter. The song is generally delivered from an exposed perch, revealing the striking orange gape, but also in flight, and there is a parachuting song flight recalling the Tree Pipit's.

The Melodious and Icterine Warblers show close similarity in colouring, and probably share a recent common ancestor. The last Ice Age is thought to have finally separated the two, leaving the Melodious in the south and the Icterine in the north. There is little overlap in range, or competition, between the two species, which are separated by habitat preferences. Although both are birds of deciduous woodland edges and glades, Melodious Warblers like dense scrubby cover beneath the trees, rather than their upper branches. This preference enables the Melodious Warbler to breed in lush gardens and parks, and also in overgrown citrus and fig orchards. The nest resembles the Icterine Warbler's, but is built low, in deep cover: brambles, oleander or hedgerows are common sites. Incubation is by the female alone, but both sexes share the burden of feeding the young. Incubation and fledging periods are each 12 to 13 days.

53

Blackcap

The adult male with its distinctive black cap. Nape and breast are grey, upperparts are a plain olive-brown and there is a pale patch on the belly

When this bird crosses high overhead between tall trees it appears very similar to a Garden Warbler, but it can be distinguished by its longer, slimmer tail

(×³⁄₅)

(×³⁄₁₀)

Raised crown feathers: one of the male displays

Males sing deep in foliage

The female has a brown cap. There is also a touch of brown on the otherwise grey breast. Her nest is a neat structure of fine twigs and rootlets

Adult male

Adult female – brown cap

Many Blackcaps have taken to visiting bird tables when wintering in Britain

Juvenile – rufous-brown cap

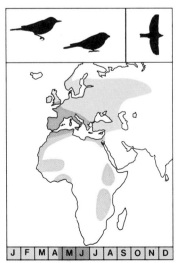

The melodious song of the Blackcap is commonly mistaken for the Nightingale's by the inexperienced, and for the Garden Warbler's by the more knowledgeable. However, it lacks the deep bubbling and long-drawn piping of the Nightingale's, and is briefer and richer than the closely related Garden Warbler's. A glimpse of the crown immediately distinguishes it from the latter.

Blackcaps favour more wooded habitats than Garden Warblers, often occupying areas with tall trees and sparse undergrowth. Where felling operations create a choice of environments, Blackcaps colonize territories with mature timber, Garden Warblers the scrubbier regions undergoing regeneration.

Nests, on average, are higher than Garden Warblers', but the two are similar, neatly woven structures of dry grasses. Five eggs are usual, and both sexes share incubation and feeding duties. Second broods occur mainly in the southern part of the range. Before autumn migration, adults moult completely, and juveniles moult body feathers, replacing dull brown caps with chestnut or black according to sex. Like many warblers, diet changes before migration from insects to fruit because its sugar content is easily converted into fuel reserves of fat. In southern countries, figs are favoured and several European languages name the bird "fig-eater". Autumn Blackcaps often show purple stains round the vent – the remains of elderberries or blackberries.

J F M A M J J A S O N D

Garden Warbler

Seen in flight, the Garden Warbler has a noticeably shorter tail than the Blackcap, and this feature distinguishes the two species when on the wing

(×³/₁₀)

Left, a Garden Warbler courtship ritual, in which the male chases the female around and into the undergrowth. Right, a more static display — the male opening his wings to the female

Adult

Juvenile

(×³/₅)

On first impression this seems the plainest of birds, but it has its distinctive features: the head is rounded; the bill unexpectedly short; there is a pale eyestripe and eye-ring and a subtle patch of grey on the neck. The face bears a distinct expression, for which the vacantly staring eye must be partly responsible

The female on her nest, which is placed low in a bush

The juvenile bird is very similar to an adult, having the grey neck patch — but there is a yellowish cast to its plumage

J F M A M J J A S O N D

Perhaps Europe's most nondescript bird, yet one of its most abundant summer migrants, the Garden Warbler is closely related to the Blackcap, but lacks its distinctive head colouring. It has most commonly been confused with the Willow Warbler and Chiffchaff or the Reed and Marsh Warblers. However, the former are smaller, with distinct eyestripes, and the latter have a quite different head shape. The Garden Warbler's song is entirely distinct from other birds', but easily confused with the Blackcap's. Usually the Garden Warbler sings in longer, less musical bursts.

The similarity between Blackcap and Garden Warbler extends to nest and eggs, which are difficult to distinguish reliably without seeing the bird — though Garden Warbler nests are usually less neat, and placed lower. The main difference is habitat, which is often much more open than the Blackcap's, extending into the birch scrub zone.

Garden Warblers share with Blackcaps and other *Sylvia* Warblers the habit of making "cock's nests", frailer in structure than the one actually used to hold the eggs. Both sexes share in rearing the young, which leave the nest after only some ten days, several days before they can fly.

Garden Warblers arrive later than Blackcaps and, like them, leave early. They moult in winter quarters throughout Africa, showing no tendency to overwinter in the north.

Whitethroat

Back view of the bird as it bounds away

An unmistakable display flight. The male bursts into the sky singing, then plunges back into cover

In flight, the Whitethroat is seen to have a slim build and long, thin tail

($\times$ 3/10)

The adult male: a grey head, white throat and pinkish wash on the breast

The crown feathers are often raised in song, anger or when the bird is inquisitive

Bird taking cover. This view reveals the white outer tail feathers

Rufous-brown feathers in the wing identify the female Whitethroat. The juvenile, below, is almost entirely rufous-brown

Adult male: eye colour varies

Adult female

Typical postures. Whitethroats often slip vertically out of sight

($\times$ 3/5)

Juvenile

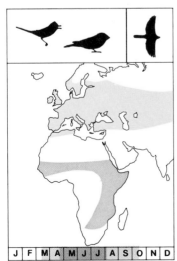

Until recently the Whitethroat was a familiar, numerous occupant of hedges and all forms of scrub (including woodland glades) throughout Europe south of central Scandinavia. The tumbling, parachuting display flight (often from heights of 100 feet) and chattering song made it additionally conspicuous.

In fact, until the autumn of 1969, the Whitethroat population had been steadily increasing. The following spring, only some 20 per cent of the expected number returned to western Europe. Researchers checked every possible cause, including weather on migration, use of anti-locust insecticides in wintering areas and the possibility of epidemic disease. They finally concluded that the extended drought in the Sahel region, south of the Sahara, had left the Whitethroats with insufficient food to "fuel up" for the return journey, so that many had perished attempting to cross the great desert. In most areas numbers are still much reduced.

The nest is built low in cover. Brambles or twigs in a patch of nettles are a favourite site, and first clutches (usually of five) are laid from mid-May on. The female incubates, but both sexes co-operate in feeding the young, betraying anxiety with harsh scolding calls from nearby cover when an observer approaches. Incubation and fledging periods are short (about 11 days), so there is frequently time for a second brood, which is generally smaller than the first.

Lesser Whitethroat

The juvenile Lesser Whitethroat has pure grey head plumage and dark ear coverts. Some birds appear very pale indeed in the field

($\times \frac{3}{5}$)

($\times \frac{3}{10}$)

In flight, the Lesser Whitethroat is seen to be a shorter-tailed, smaller bird that the common Whitethroat, but similar in shape

As with the common Whitethroat, there are some white under-tail feathers, just visible in side view

Lesser Whitethroats have a habit of feeding unobtrusively among leaves high in trees, when an observer sees only the pale underparts. They may also take insects on the wing

These are diminutive, stern-looking birds, which share many basic behaviour patterns with the common Whitethroat. Their under-plumage is colder-toned and plainer, the upper more uniform; the rufous-brown of the common Whitethroat is lacking

Adult male

Adult male

Adult female

Adult female

Juvenile

An observer can see daylight showing through the Lesser Whitethroat's finely built nest of twigs, roots and grasses

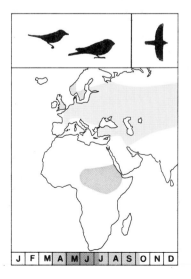

J F M A M J J A S O N D

Subtly handsome in grey and white plumage, the dark mask round the Lesser Whitethroat's eyes explains its old name of "mountebank": a quack who donned disguise to sell phoney medicines.

It differs sharply in habitat from the common Whitethroat, needing dense thickets with some tall trees, and unlike the common Whitethroat will occupy overgrown gardens and new forestry plantations. Scrubby woodland edges and deep hedgerows are also much favoured. Territories are large, with tree-top song posts sometimes several hundred yards apart. Males sing particularly actively in early morning sunshine, producing a far-carrying, monotonous rattle much

resembling the Cirl Bunting's song.

The frail nest is sometimes used for two broods. Since adults arrive late in spring, and moult before leaving in autumn, incubation and fledging periods are brief, and care of the young is short-lived. Despite this, the parent birds are usually active in defence of the nest. Like many Warblers, the diet changes prior to migration from primarily insects to primarily fruit.

Lesser Whitethroats have an unusual migration pattern. European birds move southeastwards via Italy, Greece and Cyprus rather than south through Iberia like the Common Whitethroat. Thus, on their way to winter in Ethiopia and the Sudan, they run the gauntlet of bird-catchers with lime traps and guns.

57

Dartford Warbler

Males are commonly seen perching on vegetation in brief song, or, as below, throat extended, exclaiming at some intruder. These birds have long, dark tails, which are often cocked. Underparts are good points of recognition, but vary individually and geographically

A typical view of the bird is to be had from behind as it bounces away over the scrub after being disturbed. On the wing, Dartford Warblers appear very dark — juveniles almost black. Flight is weak and erratic, with the tail weaving about in an uncertain manner

($\times$ $^3/_5$)

($\times$ $^3/_{10}$)

Males indulge in a song flight very similar to that of the Whitethroat

Birds perched in typical attitudes before diving into the scrub

A female feeding two chicks just out of the nest. Although not fully grown — note the short tails — they can already fly. The female is drabber than the male, but both sexes share the deep red eye-rings, orange legs, white flecks on the throat and pale-coloured belly

Patient observation rewards the observer. Dartford Warblers can come out of cover to feed or to scrutinize intruders. Most feeding is done very low among the vegetation

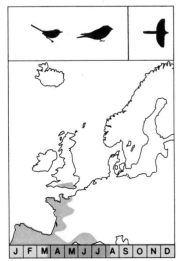

J F M A M J J A S O N D

The Dartford Warbler is one of the most characteristic birds of the thorny and impenetrable Mediterranean scrub called *maquis*. Farther north, its chosen habitat may be areas of gorse, lavender or broom, or even tall heather. Urban sprawl has long since banished it from the site of its discovery near Dartford.

Unlike most Warblers, it is to a large extent sedentary, and thus very vulnerable to severe winters. Heavy overnight snowfalls with large moist flakes, rather than persistent frosts, are the deadliest killers. Numbers fluctuate wildly, and the British population has at times been almost wiped out. Down to ten pairs in 1963, it was back to 560 pairs by 1975.

Dartford Warblers are skulking birds, especially on windy days. The bird-watcher's best approach is to wait and watch quietly, but in warm weather, males can be conspicuous, perching high or in dancing song flight. The song is a scratching, metallic warble, while contact and alarm calls are harsh — similar to the Whitethroat's.

The female builds the nest low and deep in cover, and the male assists with incubation. Two, sometimes three, broods are raised per year, and usually four eggs are laid. Small beetles, caterpillars and flies are brought to the young, and blackberries have been noted as an autumn food. How the birds manage in winter when adult insects are in short supply remains a puzzle: spiders and other arthropods may form the greater part of the diet.

Sardinian Warbler—Subalpine Warbler

Sardinian Warbler (male) flying up to tree

A male Subalpine looks very grey in flight, but otherwise resembles a small Lesser Whitethroat

$(\times \frac{3}{10})$

Male Sardinian Warbler: long tail and wing shape are distinct from other warblers

$(\times \frac{3}{10})$

A female Subalpine Warbler, right, has plumage colour of varying intensity

The female Sardinian Warbler, right, lacks the male's black cap, but her shape remains distinctive

A juvenile Subalpine Warbler's upperparts are predominantly buff

White under-tail coverts distinguish the juvenile Subalpine Warbler

The jerky flight and long, bobbing tail are easy to recognize

Males have red eyes

Above, a close view of the female Sardinian Warbler reveals the grey head and brown back. The brownish eye has a faint orange ring

$(\times \frac{3}{5})$

The brown-headed juvenile is rather dull, but comparatively easy to identify by shape

Red eye, black cap, white throat and grey plumage are all obvious in a close view of the male

A white moustache is the most striking feature of the rufous-brown and blue-grey male Subalpine Warbler

Juvenile Subalpine Warblers resemble small Whitethroats but lack the rufous-brown in the wings. Their under-tail coverts are white not buff

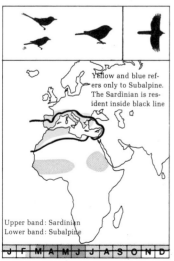

Yellow and blue refers only to Subalpine. The Sardinian is resident inside black line

Upper band: Sardinian
Lower band: Subalpine

J F M A M J J A S O N D

Related species with different lifestyles, the Subalpine Warbler migrates to tropical West Africa, the Sardinian Warbler is more or less sedentary, and suffers population crashes after bad winters.

Subalpine Warblers are birds of sunny hillsides up to 6,000 feet, preferably with ample cover of low, dense scrub, in which the birds lurk, often chattering noisily in alarm, but difficult to glimpse. Best views of them are usually to be had in spring, when the male is in song flight, or when both sexes are feeding young in a nest low in gorse, brambles or myrtle. Two broods are usual, and the drab young may be almost impossible to distinguish from young Whitethroats or, especially, the

Spectacled Warbler. Males superficially resemble the Dartford Warbler, but the shorter tail and white moustache immediately set them apart. The song is like the Whitethroat's but more musical.

Sardinian Warblers are alert, active birds, wary and elusive at times, yet they may be seen feeding unconcernedly a few feet from holidaymakers in hotel grounds, or skipping through almond or olive groves round houses and farmsteads. They are found on almost any open land. The scratchy song is uttered in flight or from high perches, and the rattling machine-gun-like alarm call is a characteristic sound of the Mediterranean. Clutches are generally larger than the Dartford Warbler's, and two broods are usual.

Stonechat

The back of this male will eventually wear to black and the buff on the tail coverts will wear off, leaving them white (× ³/₅)

Male summer plumage, left, is very striking, and the black head with white neck patches is unmistakable. Stonechats adopt upright postures with their plump bodies – always a good point of recognition – and often perch on wires

(× ³/₅)

Left, a male in worn plumage showing black back and white tail coverts

A female feeding two young. Females are drabber than males, but in winter brown feather edges tone down both sexes, making their differences less obvious

Male over bracken about to land on perch

(× ³/₁₀)

In flight, the white wing pattern and dark tail are visible. Stonechats are short-tailed, round-winged birds. Compare with Whinchat, facing page

Below, male head in winter. The buff feather-edges will gradually wear off until the head is completely black – exactly the same process as on the back

Stonechats feed on the ground much more often than Whinchats

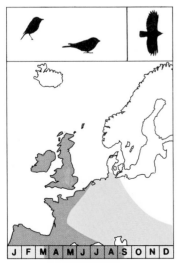

Stonechats, especially family parties, are noisy birds, and their commonest contact call resembles the click of two pebbles being knocked together – hence the name.

The male produces a tuneful jingle of song as he flutters in a bouncy flight up to 100 feet high. Like a Whinchat, the Stonechat inhabits rough, uncultivated open terrain, but favours drier areas with more bushes. A crucial factor may be its need for higher perches than the Whinchat. These include telegraph posts and wires, where they sit alert, wings and tail flicking, scanning the ground beneath for their insect food. Increasing reclamation of large areas of scrubby marginal land for agriculture has resulted in a recent decline of the European populations.

The breeding season is a long one, and an experienced female may produce up to four clutches of five or six eggs in a year, as opposed to a first-year bird, which usually manages only one or two broods. The nest is very deeply hidden, generally in the base of a gorse bush or grass tussock.

Stonechats have an extensive distribution, occurring across Eurasia to Japan, and south through Africa to the Cape. Numerous races have been described, varying in depth of rufous colouring below and extent of black above. Western and southern European birds are usually resident, but those breeding farther north must move south in winter.

Whinchat

An adult male has a striking head pattern, and both sexes share the bold white eyestripe

The back pattern, especially of the female, is unique – and reminiscent of dried grass

Adult male

(× ³⁄₅)

Juvenile

Except for the pale pattern either side of the tail, a juvenile Whinchat, below, is similar to a Stonechat

A female, about to alight, showing the white tail patches and white wing markings

The strong patterning on the wings and tail of the adult male are clearly visible in flight

(× ³⁄₁₀)

Female

White triangular patches on the tail either side of the rump distinguish the Whinchat absolutely from the Stonechat. In flight action and general behaviour both species are similar

Whinchats are migratory birds, and for this reason are longer-winged than the more sedentary Stonechats

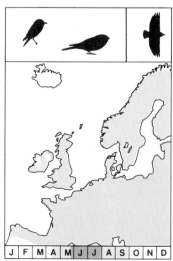

J F M A M J J A S O N D

Though similar in many ways to its near relative the Stonechat, this is a more strongly migratory species, which never winters in western Europe. Instead, it migrates to African grasslands as far south as Angola, but is most abundant in the wooded savannah zone extending from Senegal to Uganda. Rough grassland is also its choice of habitat in Europe, where heaths, commons, rough pasture or marshes may be utilized. It shows less preference for gorse than the Stonechat. With the increase in mechanized farming, hedges and rough areas generally are being eliminated, and Whinchat numbers have consequently decreased in many parts.

The Whinchat feeds on butterflies, moths and flies, gleaned mainly from grass stalks. Occasionally it catches airborne insects in the manner of a flycatcher. The nest is extremely well concealed in a grass tussock, under dead bracken or where grass grows through the base of a bush; it is sometimes reached by a distinct tunnel pathway, and is built mainly by the female from dry grass on a foundation of coarser grass and moss. It is lined with finer material, but no hair or feathers. The usual clutch contains five or six eggs, incubated by the female for 13 days. Fledging takes the same length of time, the young leaving before they are fully grown. Both sexes feed them and the family party stays together for some time after leaving the nest.

Bluethroat

The streaky plumaged juvenile would be difficult to identify were it not for the tail pattern

A stubby winged bird with a short, square tail. Bluethroats often look very dark in flight

(× ³/₁₀)

Above and below, left and right: next to its tail, the Bluethroat's eyestripe is its most reliable identifying feature. This remains constant through all the complex variations of plumage

Bluethroats are unobtrusive, skulking birds, best identified by their tails, which repeatedly flick as the birds land or hop about

It is possible, but not easy, to see the orange on the tail when it is closed

(× ³/₅)

Male Red-spotted Bluethroat

Male White-spotted Bluethroat. The white spot is small or absent

The orange and dark brown tail is unique

Typical fleeting view as the bird makes for cover

At the seaside Bluethroats commonly feed under Suaeda bushes

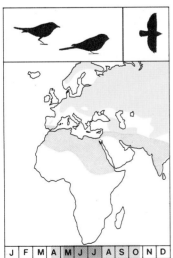

With gleaming sapphire gorget and superb song, the Bluethroat deserves wider acclaim. Its relative neglect by poets and ornithologists alike stems perhaps from its patchy distribution in western Europe. It frequents scrubby or open ground, with some marshy grassland, and this habitat has been much reduced by cultivation and development.

Western European breeders are of the white-spotted form. The Red-spotted Bluethroat breeding in Scandinavia is more numerous, and is one of the common birds of Lapland lakesides and birch scrub. The song is reminiscent of the Nightingale's, a close relative. Though less powerful, it is more varied, and includes frequent mimicry of other birds. It is delivered from a prominent perch or in a song flight. Females generally, and males outside the breeding season, are skulking birds, often only to be seen flitting from one bush into another.

The nest is like a Robin's, built in a depression in the ground, often under a bush. The five to seven eggs vary in colour from blue to olive. Incubation is by the hen, and feeding the young is done by both sexes. White-spotted Bluethroats occasionally rear two broods.

Red-spotted Bluethroats are common passage migrants through Europe, wintering in the Middle East and north-eastern Africa. Their breeding range extends right across Asia.

J F M A M J J A S O N D

Wheatear

Juvenile

Adult female

Adult male

(×³/₁₀)

Wheatears are shy but lively. They crouch almost flat on the ground or run at great speed, halting suddenly in a bolt upright stance. Flight is swift and rather jerky. The white-on-black tail pattern, resembling a blunt two-pronged fork, is highly conspicuous and quite unlike any found on other temperate European birds

Grey crown and back distinguish the male in spring plumage. In winter the grey gives way to buff, giving an appearance similar to the juvenile bird

Left, female freshly moulted

Juvenile, autumn plumage

(×³/₅)

Juvenile, rear view: a brown back

A Wheatear of the Greenland race, above right, is larger, longer winged and longer legged

A female Wheatear, spring plumage. Feather wear has dulled the bright colouring of the autumn bird

Though remaining faithful to the basic Wheatear pattern, plumage does vary considerably in brightness from bird to bird. The rump is always white

The birds inhabit open country, but nest in holes into which they bolt when alarmed

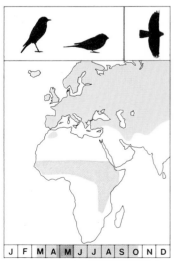

The Wheatear's name derives from Anglo-Saxon words meaning "white rump" – which is a conspicuous feature when the bird flies. This is a widely distributed species, inhabiting barren terrain throughout Eurasia, and also parts of the American Arctic. Mountains, tundra and shingle are all suitable habitats, but unlike several related species, the Common Wheatear is not a desert bird. Crevices among boulders provide nest sites, but oil drums and similar debris are used where available, and the birds sometimes make use of nestboxes. Typical sites have an entrance tunnel up to a yard long. The nest, built by both sexes, is of grass, roots and moss, with a lining of feathers and hair or wool from the rabbits or sheep with which it commonly shares its habitat. Five or six eggs are usual in western Europe, but Arctic breeders may lay up to nine. The female incubates, occasionally aided by the male, and both sexes feed the young. Incubation and fledging periods each last about two weeks, and the young are fully independent by the age of six days. Usually one brood, but sometimes two broods are reared.

Food comprises a variety of ground invertebrates. Berries are taken in autumn when the bird is fattening for migration, which may involve very long flights. Greenland breeders, for example, cover 2,000 miles to northern Spain in a single flight, using up a third of their starting weight.

Redstart

Adult male

A female, catching insects

$(\times \frac{3}{10})$

In summer the male bird has very grey upperparts, but by autumn the plumage fades to brown

The female has a pale eye-ring and rufous-brown underparts

Female and immature birds are similar, wing colour being the same warm shade of brown

$(\times \frac{3}{5})$

The male Redstart in full breeding plumage

Holes in trees or walls are the usual nest sites, but Common Redstarts frequently use nestboxes

Below, in front view the female's light brown underparts are undistinguished except for the pale throat markings. However, the dark orange tail showing below always indicates the bird's identity

On young males the face pattern is edged with white and there is an incomplete white V on the forehead

Young birds have crescent markings on their underparts and are much lighter overall than young Black Redstarts

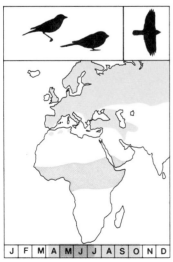

J F M A M J J A S O N D

This bird's name refers to the vivid russet tail, which contrasts beautifully with the male's elegantly coloured upperparts. He announces his presence in woodlands throughout Europe with a short jingling song. Both sexes have a two-syllabled anxiety note resembling that of the Chaffinch, Nightingale or Willow Warbler – an arrangement which may be of some mutual benefit to all these woodland birds. Redstarts prefer woods with a fairly open canopy and dense undergrowth interspersed with clearings. Deciduous woods are preferred, but pinewoods, parks and gardens may all be used. Males arrive in the breeding areas in April or May, slightly before the females. After pairing, the male chooses the nest site,

typically in a hole in a tree, but sometimes in a crevice among stones or under thick vegetation on the ground. The six pale blue eggs are incubated by the female for some 14 days and both sexes feed the young, tending them for two to three more weeks after the two weeks spent in the nest. A second brood may follow. Small insects, such as weevils, moths and flies, form the diet, and the young are fed on caterpillars.

On migration, Redstarts are frequent casualties at North Sea lightships. Numbers fluctuate locally, but a considerable longer-term decrease has occurred in southern England during the present century. In most areas, however, Redstarts remain common.

Black Redstart

Black Redstarts build nest holes in walls or in natural rock faces. The young have bright yellow gapes

A female in flight. Black Redstarts are larger, broader-winged birds than Common Redstarts and they have less red on their rumps

(×³/₅)

(×³/₁₀)

An adult male in summer plumage feeding a young bird. Compared with a young Common Redstart, the young Black Redstart looks sooty and lacks any rufous-brown

Left, the male from behind, orange tail conspicuous. Right, a Black Redstart often hovers to catch insects, rarely perching among branches

Females and juveniles, right and below, have overall dark plumage and appear nondescript until the orange tail is seen

Male in winter plumage. Black Redstarts can be seen taking food from the ground after flying down from a vantage point

Quiet feeders, Black Redstarts can be very unobtrusive

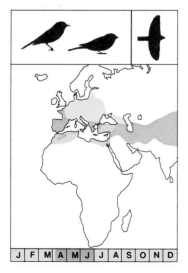

J F M A M J J A S O N D

A brief warble, followed by a noise resembling ball bearings rattled together, is a familiar sound in many European towns. This is the song of the Black Redstart. Once a species confined to mountainous areas, it has adapted to the industrial landscape, and is now one of the continent's most common urban birds. It shows special partiality for such places as docks, gas-works, railway sheds and power stations, and its spread in some areas was considerably helped by the devastation left by the Second World War – bombed sites have many features in common with the species' ancestral habitat. Farm buildings are also utilized.

The nest is usually placed on a ledge inside or outside a building; in natural habitats, a crevice among rocks is used. It is a bulky and rather untidy structure of grass and similar materials, lined with hair and feathers. Four or five white eggs are laid, and incubated by the hen. Both sexes feed the young during the rather long fledging period of 16 to 21 days. Polygamy has been recorded. There are two or three broods each year.

A variety of insect food is taken, including small beetles and flies. Midges from polluted water have been noted as a major food at one industrial site in Britain. Berries are eaten in autumn.

The migration pattern varies, and some populations are only partly migratory – Polish and German birds, for instance, have been recovered in Cyprus.

Pied Flycatcher

Large areas of almost pure black and white plumage make the Pied Flycatcher a smart bird, but the black can fade to brown by the end of the nesting season

(×⅗)

Male Pied Flycatcher in flight showing the conspicuous wing pattern

The Collared Flycatcher is extremely rare in the United Kingdom but distributed patchily on the continent, mainly in central Europe

In flight, the female and immature Pied Flycatcher are identical

(×³⁄₁₀)

A juvenile Pied Flycatcher looks very similar to the female except for some buff edging which shows in the wings. It has less white on the wings and tail. For this size of bird, the eye, with its pale ring, is rather large

The female Pied Flycatcher is plain brown overall, with some white on the wings and tail

Female Pied Flycatcher, rear view

Juvenile Pied Flycatchers are distinguished by crescent markings

A male Collared Flycatcher with the pronounced white collar. There are more white feathers in the wings than on Pied Flycatchers. The white wing patch varies from bird to bird

(×⅗)

A female Collared Flycatcher's tail, right; the female Pied Flycatcher's, left

Female Collared Flycatcher: pale collar and back patch are sometimes indiscernible

Male Pied Flycatcher: perching attitude

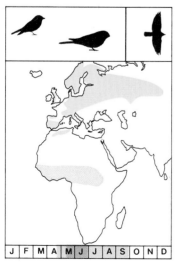

JFMAMJJASOND

Despite its name, the Pied Flycatcher feeds to a large extent on insects gleaned from foliage, and caterpillars are a major food source. It is primarily a bird of broad-leaved woodland, but can adapt to conifer plantations if provided with nestboxes. The natural nest site is a woodpecker hole in a tree, and inside this is built a nest made of bark, especially honeysuckle bark where available, and lined with fine grass. Six or seven, sometimes more, pale blue eggs are laid, early clutches averaging larger than late ones. The female incubates alone, fed frequently by the male. The eggs hatch in 12 days, and both parents feed the young during the 15-day fledging period. After they leave, in late June or early July, adults and young virtually disappear for a month or so prior to migration. During this time they moult into new plumage, and probably spend their time feeding quietly in the woodland canopy. The winter quarters are in tropical Africa, but before crossing the Sahara they spend time building up fuel reserves in Iberia: all Pied Flycatchers, even from the central USSR, converge here.

The Pied Flycatcher's European populations have undoubtedly been adversely affected by forest clearance, and it is very patchily distributed in Britain, France, Belgium and the Netherlands. Lack of nest sites is the principal problem, and provision of nestboxes can do much to encourage its spread.

Nightingale

Habitual tail cocking is a general feature of Nightingale behaviour

A Nightingale defends its nest against intruders with a noisy, deep-throated, scolding note, accompanied by aggressive flicking of the wings and tail, often coming to within a yard of the observer quite unperturbed

A plump, well-built bird, which might be confused with the Garden Warbler were it not for the rich rufous-brown of its upperparts. There is a comparatively large eye

A skulking bird, rarely seen in the open, the Nightingale usually flies at low level for short distances between cover

$(\times \frac{3}{10})$

An adult at a typical nest site, placed deep in vegetation. The young have a whitish flange around the edge of the entire gape – a feature which makes the presence of nestlings easier to detect in the gloom

$(\times \frac{3}{5})$

A male in display fans his wings and tail, and reveals the conspicuous yellow gape. The undertail colouring is rufous-brown, belly and throat are white, and the wing-pits are almost a pale orange

The juvenile Nightingale has under-plumage with the "scaly" look. Wing and tail colouring is very similar to that of the adult bird

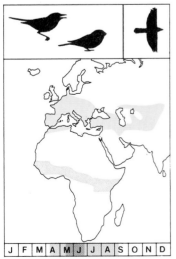

The Nightingale's song has been so praised in literature that comparing it unfavourably with other birds has almost become fashionable. Tastes may vary of course, but for richness, power and variety its song is hard to beat. Nightingales regularly sing at night, and are even heard in their winter quarters of African savannah scrub.

Nightingales arrive late in spring, and take up territories in thickets on the edges of woods—southern edges are often preferred. Shady, dense bushes and an undergrowth of nettles are characteristic habitats. The male has several song posts, some exposed, but most deep in a thicket, one of which may be near the nest. This is a bulky structure, much like a Robin's, with a similar foundation of dead leaves, sited in a depression amongst nettles, or just off the ground in a tangle of vegetation. The four or five eggs are deep olive-brown in colour, and are incubated by the female, who may feign injury when disturbed. The young are fed by both parents and leave the nest after only 11 or 12 days. A single brood is raised. Observers passing near by may hear the guttural, churring warning call, or a two-syllabled alarm resembling the Redstart's or Willow Warbler's.

In many parts of Europe, Nightingale populations have been decreasing. Changing forestry methods are largely to blame: growing coppice trees for poles, for instance, is dying out, thus eliminating a favoured habitat.

Spotted Flycatcher

A very unobtrusive bird with a quiet but insistent call

From sitting unobtrusively in a tree this bird will unpredictably sally forth

The Spotted Flycatcher is a sparrow-sized bird, with comparatively long wings and a medium-length tail. An effortless flyer, it can be brilliantly aerobatic while catching an insect

$(\times\,^{3}/_{10})$

The alert posture of a Spotted Flycatcher watching for insects. Wings and tail are frequently flicked before the dash after a victim

In certain lights a bird may look quite grey

Adults are streaked not spotted. There is a large black eye, flat bill and the wing feathers have some white edging. The short legs look weak. A very plain bird, but its shape and manner are unlike any other

The typical nest site is in a tree trunk, but Spotted Flycatchers are universal, and even bizarre, in their choice of sites

$(\times\,^{3}/_{5})$

Flight action in the chase after an insect

A Spotted Flycatcher often stands with its wings drooping, flicking them slightly from time to time

A juvenile bird really is spotted. This posture is typical

This species has a pointed beak with a broad base

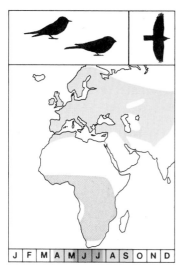

The skilled aerobatics of the Spotted Flycatcher as it sallies out to capture passing insects are an entertaining spectacle in gardens and parks over the whole continent of Europe. Originally a bird of woodland glades, it now exploits the man-made environment, though still preferring places with some tall trees. The feeding tactics of the Spotted Flycatcher can work only when flying insects are really abundant, and this state of affairs does not exist much before June. Summer migrants, which arrive in April and May, eat larval insects, or, like swallows and martins, fly unceasingly in pursuit of the few that are airborne. Because of its feeding habits, the Spotted Flycatcher is the last summer visitor to return, and its breeding season is very late: most birds do not lay until well into June. The natural nest site is a ledge on a tree against the main trunk, but buildings provide many excellent substitutes. Open-fronted nestboxes are popular, and disused blackbirds' nests on buildings are often occupied. The same site may be used in several successive years and the nest itself is a neat, compact structure of twigs, grass and moss, bound by cobwebs, and lined with finer vegetation and feathers.

Early clutches number four or five eggs; later ones contain fewer; and the second broods, which some pairs produce during July, may be only two or three strong. Both sexes incubate and feed the young.

Treecreeper

A slender beak for extracting insects

The Treecreeper's nest is built in a tree cavity, a hollow stump, or sometimes behind a loose piece of bark

A male approaching the nest – upper wing pattern and curved beak evident. Although the beak is shorter on young birds, they cannot be confused with other species

(×3/10)

A leisurely, undulating flight, but the observer is unlikely to catch a glimpse of the underwing feathers

The unusually stiff, pointed tail feathers sit firmly against the bark, providing support

Treecreepers roost in crevices in bark, and Wellingtonia trees are particularly favoured for this purpose because their bark is so easily excavated

(×3/5)

The extremely thick and fluffy feathers on the lower back and flanks can be puffed out round wings and body, disguising its profile and reducing heat loss. Tiny size, mousy colouring and mousy behaviour make the Treecreeper an easy bird to identify. It is a confiding bird – though rather than being tame it is probably indifferent to human beings

Working their way up a tree trunk, these birds look extraordinarily like mice. They procede in a series of spasmodic jerks – unhurried but never still

Standard Treecreeper feeding route

With its white underparts, a Treecreeper stands out best against a dark-coloured tree trunk

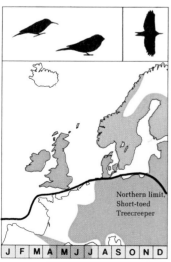

Northern limit, Short-toed Treecreeper

J F M A M J J A S O N D

Treecreepers seem almost to be part of the trunks and boughs on which they forage like animated pieces of bark. They inhabit almost any woodland or well-wooded parks and gardens, provided there is some old timber with loose bark for nest sites. Where their range overlaps with that of the very similar Short-toed Treecreeper, the common species seems to prefer conifers, while the Short-toed occurs in broad-leaved woods. Elsewhere, notably in Britain, the Treecreeper is more common in broad-leaved woods.

The nest is usually placed behind loose bark or ivy, sometimes in a crack in a shed adjacent to woodland. A bulky foundation of twigs is wedged into position, on which is built the cup of grass and bark strips lined with feathers and hair. This is constructed by both sexes, but incubation of the five or six eggs is mainly the female's task. Both sexes feed the young, and the fledging period is 14 or 15 days – the same as the incubation period. Second broods are unusual, but when they do occur they are often raised in the same nest.

Treecreepers are vulnerable to severe winters, but in their roosting behaviour at least show a valuable adaptation for surviving cold nights, choosing sheltered crevices behind bark or even excavating hollows in the soft, fibrous bark of Wellingtonia trees. This is a sedentary species, rarely travelling more than a few miles.

Wryneck

Rear view of Wryneck in flight

(× 3/10)

The extraordinary sky-pointing display, used in courtship and against threat or when the bird is held in the hand: simultaneously, the neck twists from side to side and the bird hisses

Undulating flight, reminiscent of a woodpecker's only faster. The pointed head and beak are noticeable on birds in flight

Full extent of the tongue

In the field the beak and feet appear flesh-coloured

(× 3/5)

The beak from above – its tip is very narrow and pointed

A Wryneck at its nest hole. This species can cling to vertical surfaces in the manner of a woodpecker. On horizontal branches it crouches almost flat

Unique amongst passerines, the Wryneck's highly cryptic plumage covered with intricate vermiculations somewhat resembles that of the Nightjar. The black mark (absent from juveniles) running from the nape down the back writhes about as the bird slowly twists its head from side to side

Progress over the ground is accomplished in clumsy hops, with tail slightly elevated

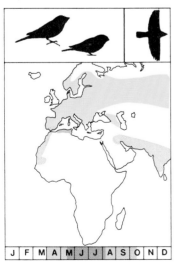

Camouflaged plumage gives the Wryneck a moth-like beauty when seen at close quarters, and its habits are of great interest. It is a matter for concern that its populations are decreasing throughout western Europe, and that it is almost extinct as a breeding bird in Britain. The causes of this decline are unknown, but may be climatic.

The Wryneck is classified as a member of the woodpecker family, but lacks many of their climbing and pecking adaptations. However, it does share with them the feature of an exceedingly long protrusible tongue. This is not barbed or spiny like a woodpecker tongue, but traps prey by means of a sticky coating ideal for gathering ants, which are a favourite food.

The bird derives its name from the extraordinary twisting postures of the neck during courtship and threat display. This latter is demonstrated in spectacular fashion when an incubating bird is disturbed: the neck writhes, the tongue flickers in and out, and fierce hissing noises complete a lifelike imitation of a snake.

Nests are located in natural holes in trees: unlike woodpeckers, Wrynecks cannot excavate holes. Old orchard trees are much favoured. The usual clutch contains seven to ten eggs and Wrynecks have the uncommon ability to lay more than one egg a day. The female incubates, aided occasionally by the male, and the eggs hatch in 12 to 13 days.

J F M A M J J A S O N D

70

Nuthatch

Nuthatches use cavities in tree trunks for their nests, and where the entrance hole is wide enough to admit another, larger species, the birds will reduce it to their own size by lining the inner circumference with mud

$(\times \frac{3}{10})$

Jerky, hesitant and flapping, this bird's flight seems like a Woodpecker's, especially if seen in silhouette, but the plain grey plumage of its upperparts will always set the Nuthatch apart

From beneath, the under-tail spots and rufous-brown coverts are easily visible. The Nuthatch flies very fast —not much more than a silhouette is seen of an airborne bird

This bird goes to extraordinary lengths adapting a nestbox to its taste: it narrows the entrance to its own size of girth and lines the interior with mud, rounding off the corners so the whole resembles the inside of a tree

Identifying Nuthatches is no problem: plain grey upperparts, a black stripe through the eye, orange-buff to whitish underparts. Seen close-to, they have a sinister, devilish look

The bird is entirely at home walking up tree trunks, negotiating the most impossible overhangs

Walking vertically down a tree trunk: as easy to the Nuthatch as climbing

$(\times \frac{3}{5})$

A Nuthatch sometimes feeds on the ground, where it hops about with jerky movements

The foot serves the same climbing function as a Woodpecker's, but its form is different

Nuthatches give out a loud, cheery contact whistle, which is a familiar sound in woods and parks—but few people connect it with the small bird high up on a bough. The song, a repeated whistle, has the same ringing quality and may be the prelude to a display flight in which the male floats downwards towards the female with wings and tail spread.

A Nuthatch's presence may be revealed by the loud tapping noises made as the bird hammers nuts. For this operation, the nut is jammed firmly into a crevice of a tree which will also be used as a store place. Nuthatches which acquire the bird-table habit may come and go at an astonishing rate, since many of the peanuts or sunflower seeds they take are simply hoarded. The mud smeared around the nest hole probably serves to reduce competition with other hole-nesting birds, but is also used inside the cavity to fill cracks and irregularities. Although Nuthatches quite often use nestboxes, they may be impossible to inspect, with the lid firmly plastered down from inside. The nest is a rather feeble collection of dead leaves and scraps of bark which conceal the eggs when the female is off the nest. There are six to nine eggs, which hatch after 14 to 15 days. The fledging period is 23 to 25 days—very long for so small a bird, though hole nesters generally have long fledging periods. Nuthatches rarely wander far from their area of origin.

Cirl Bunting

Adult male. The distinctive head pattern cannot be confused with that of any other bunting

(×³⁄₅)

Adult female

Flight is more dipping than the Yellowhammer's

A broader-winged, shorter-tailed bird than either the Yellowhammer or Ortolan Bunting

Immature

The female tends to be confused with the Yellowhammer or the Ortolan Bunting, but the species' plain olive rump will alone identify her

(×³⁄₁₀)

In flight the male is identified by his combination of rufous-brown back and olive rump

Male and female underparts are easily distinguished. The female's differ from those of the Ortolan Bunting by their heavier streaking, and from those of the Yellowhammer by their different pattern. The male's underparts are distinctive in their own right

A juvenile, like the adult, is distinguished from other similar species by its rump colour. Cirl Buntings have less piercing, aggressive expressions than either the Ortolan or the Yellowhammer.

Male

Female

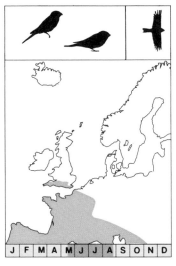

Male Cirl Buntings in breeding plumage are handsome birds, but the dull-plumaged females and juveniles are easily confused with other buntings. This is an unobtrusive species, easily overlooked. The best time to locate the birds is in spring, when the male is delivering his monotonous song from an exposed perch. This is simply a repetition of a single sharp note, and somewhat resembles the rattle of the Lesser Whitethroat.

Its most favoured habitat is more sheltered than many buntings prefer — parkland or woodland edges near cultivation. The nest is built by the female and is generally placed in the base of a bramble or other bush, or in a depression on the ground. The three

or four eggs are incubated by the female for 11 to 13 days, and she is fed on the nest by the male. After the young hatch, the male visits the brood with the female, normally giving his food to her for distribution. The fledging period is also 11 to 13 days. Two or three broods are commonly raised. Like several other buntings, Cirl Buntings disturbed at the nest may perform an "injury-feigning" display.

Family parties often remain together throughout the winter, feeding on stubble or in gardens, quite often visiting bird tables. The Cirl Bunting is largely resident, and having spread northwards during the nineteenth century, when it colonized Britain, now appears to be declining.

J F M A M J J A S O N D

72

Yellowhammer

The adult male Yellowhammer has a rufous-brown band across his breast, and his head is yellower than the female's, below right

In song, the Yellowhammer holds back its head and opens the bill wide. Bush tops or overhead wires are common perches

In flight, the yellow head is very conspicuous. Also, it may be the only clearly visible feature of the bird as it lands

(× 3/10)

(× 3/5)

A long-tailed, slim bird with fairly broad wings. The rump pattern contrasts with the Cirl Bunting's

White outer tail feathers – always noticeable

The Yellowhammer is distinguished from all other buntings by its vivid rufous-brown rump. The tail is constantly flicked

Female

Yellowhammers rest in trees before flying down to feed on a ploughed field. Flocks of these birds will mix with other species, such as Chaffinches, Greenfinches and Skylarks, as they feed on fields during winter and spring

Although it is less yellow than an adult, the young bird, below, has sufficiently distinct shape and behaviour to distinguish it as a Yellowhammer. When feeding, the species appears slim and long tailed

Yellowhammers have a monotonous song, often written as "little bit of bread and no cheese", which is one of the most familiar sounds of summer in most parts of Europe except the Mediterranean seaboard.

This is a bird with a wide habitat tolerance: almost any area will suffice that provides some open ground with rough vegetation and a few trees and bushes. Young conifer plantations in which there is still a dense ground cover of brambles support the highest density of Yellowhammers – up to 200 pairs per square mile in parts of Britain. The nest is built low down, often on the ground or in the bank of a ditch, or in a low bramble just off the ground. It is a rather bulky grass structure, lined with fine roots. Three or four eggs are the usual clutch, incubated by the female with occasional help from the male. Incubation and fledging periods each last 12 to 14 days. Both parents feed the young and, like many seed-eating birds, rear them on a diet of invertebrates, especially caterpillars and other insect larvae, but also occasional slugs and earthworms. Two or three broods may be reared, and it is scarcely possible to walk across a heathland in summer without hearing the anxiety call of a Yellowhammer with young near by.

Moult takes place in early autumn, and from then on, Yellowhammers associate in flocks feeding on stubble and roosting in vegetation or reeds.

J F M A M J J A S O N D

73

Ortolan Bunting

Duller head colouring distinguishes the female Ortolan from the male

Adult female

(× ³⁄₁₀)

Adult male

Confusing this species with the Yellowhammer can be avoided by observing the Ortolan's square-ended, as opposed to forked, tail, and longer, slimmer wings — but a juvenile Ortolan may have a slightly forked tail

Long tail and a slim build are revealed in flight

(× ³⁄₅)

An adult male. He and the female have a pink beak, not found on any other bunting. The Ortolan's facial expression is unique

Right, the usual extent of white on the edge of an Ortolan's tail. On some birds there may be more

A nondescript bird with a white eye-ring, the immature Ortolan has a yellowish tinge on its underparts and shares the adult's facial expression

An adult male has yellow, olivegreen and orange underparts

Ortolan Buntings are widely, though rather patchily, distributed throughout Europe, with the exception of northwest France and Britain. Their habitat requirements are simple—some bushes or other cover, and some open ground for feeding. These may be found on the treeless upper slopes of mountains in the Mediterranean countries, or on agricultural and scrub land farther north. Food consists of grain and other seeds, as well as insects, which form the main diet of the young. The insects taken include some fairly large species —beetles, crickets, and, in the winter quarters, locusts.

Males sing from bush tops or telegraph wires, the sound produced being a pleasant if somewhat monotonous series of six or seven notes, of which usually two are lower-pitched than the rest.

The nest is placed in a hollow in the ground, well concealed by overhanging vegetation or sometimes a rock. It is built by the female of dry grasses, roots and leaves, with a lining of finer vegetation and hair. Four to six eggs are laid, varying in colour, though always with some of the streaked markings characteristic of buntings. Incubation, mainly by the female, lasts 12 to 13 days, and she also takes the main share in feeding the young. These often leave the nest to fend for themselves before fledging, like various other ground nesters, sometimes as early as nine days after hatching.

Rock Bunting

On a young bird the inner secondary feathers, the upper tail coverts and the centre of the tail itself are a distinct rufous-brown

(× ³/₁₀)

In flight, the Rock Bunting is seen to have a long tail and fairly broad wings. There is a faint double wing bar and very conspicuous white outer tail feathers. A rufous-brown rump identifies the bird as an adult

Grey head, prominent eyestripe and black head patterning make this species instantly recognizable and unlike any other European bunting. The female bird is always slightly duller than the male, but both sexes vary in brightness depending on how recently the moult has taken place. The upper beak is dark, the lower is light in colour

(× ³/₅)

The juvenile bird is not easy to recognize, but at close quarters its basic shape, beak and tail pattern will distinguish it from other buntings

Apart from the almost sinister head pattern, a front view of the Rock Bunting reveals underparts of a warm orange-brown colour and very large white outer tail feathers

J F M A M J J A S O N D

Boulder-strewn mountain slopes are the characteristic breeding habitat of this species, but rocks are not essential: alpine meadows and even vineyards may be chosen. The male advertises his territory with a song that somewhat resembles the Yellowhammer's, but is much higher pitched, with the final note often repeated several times; its general effect somewhat recalls the Serin.

The nest, built by the female, is of the normal bunting pattern, largely made of grass, with perhaps a few bits of moss and bark, and lined with hair and fine plant material. Though normally sited in a hollow amongst rocks or on the ground, it is also frequently placed in a bush or small tree, sometimes six feet or more off the ground. The eggs, four to six in number, are remarkable for their markings—a rainbow network of fine lines, an extreme example of a characteristic shown by all bunting eggs. Incubation, by the female alone, is for 13 to 14 days, and the young are fed by both parents. The fledging period is uncertain. There is only one brood, and after the breeding season the birds move to lower terrain for the winter.

Northern breeders migrate south, some reaching the southern limit of the breeding range in North Africa. Here, Rock Buntings may be seen in quite large flocks with other buntings. The flight call is a rather liquid twitter, and a sharp note resembling the Cirl Bunting's is also used.

Reed Bunting

Male on song perch

In flight, the female shows distinctive red shoulders

$(\times \frac{3}{10})$

The adult male's breeding plumage is a black head, white neck and white stripe at the corner of the mouth

A double streak may develop on the back

The freshly moulted male has less definite but still pronounced streaking. His appearance changes when movement of posture or muscle affects the arrangement of feathers

$(\times \frac{3}{5})$

Top, the head of a freshly moulted male in autumn, the black plumage just showing through. By the following February the buff feather-edges wear away, leaving the full black of the breeding season, immediately above

Reed Buntings have conspicuous white outer tail feathers

Head and throat pattern distinguish the adult female from the male. Traces of the red shoulder markings are visible on the closed wings

The juvenile has a yellowish tinge overall, but especially on the belly. Reed Buntings constantly flick their tails, showing the white edges

Immature male, autumn plumage

J F M A M J J A S O N D

Many birds suffer from human activities—but a few show sufficient adaptability to profit from change and the Reed Bunting is one of these. Its typical habitat is wetland—marshy scrub with tussocks of rushes and sedge. Such habitats are gradually being eliminated throughout Europe, and many species which depend on them have declined drastically. The Reed Bunting has reacted by exploring drier habitats, and has successfully settled in such unpromising territory as barley fields. In the process, it has probably adversely affected other buntings, particularly the Yellowhammer.

Wherever it occurs during the breeding season, the Reed Bunting can quickly be located by its song—a simple and, to some, irritatingly monotonous repetition of three notes followed by a nasal whistle. This final note closely resembles the alarm call, which is readily delivered when an observer enters the territory.

Reed Bunting nests, made of grass, are placed low down in a sedge, rush or grass tussock. They usually contain five highly distinctive eggs, which are brown with heavy black spots and scrawls. When disturbed, the parent (male or female) often reacts by feigning injury. The eggs hatch after 13 to 14 days, and a further ten to 13 days completes the nest development of the fledglings, which are fed by both parents. Two broods are usual, but there are occasionally three.

Snow Bunting

Immature male, winter

Adult male, winter

Adult male

The long wings bear white markings unlike any found on other buntings

(× ³/₁₀)

Snow Bunting plumage is variable, but it generally takes the juvenile, above, about two years to develop the full white of the adult, far right

This juvenile shows the least amount of white that will be encountered on a Snow Bunting

Snow Buntings have unique facial expressions, and their beaks are very short

(× ³/₅)

An adult male's buff plumage wears away during the winter to produce this unmistakable breeding plumage

Male in winter plumage

Adult female— breeding plumage

Typical feeding ground—behind a beach

When feeding, these birds look long and slim and present a ground-hugging profile

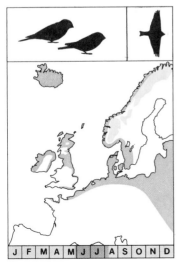

J F M A M J J A S O N D

A flock of Snow Buntings provides some of the most charming sights and sounds of winter on the coasts of western Europe. Feeding flocks frequently rise and fly around uttering melodious trilling calls, and resembling drifting snowflakes. The species is mainly Arctic—its only breeding outpost in western Europe is in the mountains of Scotland. It feeds mainly on seeds, gleaning them efficiently even from the surface of snow.

Males are first to return to the breeding areas, as early as March, even in Greenland. They immediately claim territories in the snowbound landscape, proclaiming them with a melodious song and defending them assiduously against neighbours. However, a new fall of snow brings a temporary cessation of hostilities, and the birds form flocks until conditions improve. Females arrive about a month later and are at first greeted with hostility by the males. When this provokes no reaction, the males' behaviour switches to courtship displays and chases.

The nest is bulky, built in a rock crevice, or occasionally, where available, in a building. It is constructed in three layers: moss outside, then grass and finally a lining of feathers. Four to seven eggs are laid and incubated by the female for 12 to 13 days. Both parents feed the young, which fledge in ten to 12 days. During the moult in early autumn, the birds are temporarily flightless.

Woodlark

Typical flight attitudes

(× ³/₁₀)

When it is flying, this bird can be distinguished from a Skylark by its slightly smaller size, much shorter tail and jerky flight movements. An additional point of recognition is the black-and-white patch half way along the leading edge of the wing

Path of song flight

An adult in fresh plumage – larks' feathers wear very easily, resulting in a paler overall appearance. The black-and-white patches on the mid-leading edges are visible on folded wings. It is a stubbily built bird

(× ³/₅)

Streaked breast and white eyestripe show well on Woodlarks of all ages, male or female

A young bird, which has left the nest, calls to a parent. At this early stage the wing feathers are very short. Young birds can run when they are only ten to 12 days old

The Woodlark's crest is fairly prominent. Rear view shows a tail strikingly shorter than the Skylark's, with white outer tips rather than white outer edges

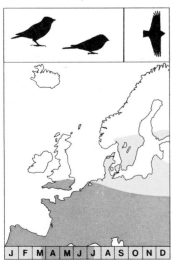

The Woodlark's song is less sustained than the Skylark's, but hauntingly beautiful. It is delivered from a circling song flight in short bursts, which include sad, liquid, descending phrases. Nowhere as abundant as the Skylark, this species prefers heaths and open areas with a mixture of short turf and longer vegetation and a few scattered trees – which may be used as perches and, occasionally, as song posts. Except in the northern part of their range, Woodlarks are extremely sedentary birds, spending most of the year in pairs or family parties in or near their territories.

Nesting commences as early as March – sometimes even during late snows. The nest is built in a depression on the ground, the outer layer being constructed mainly by the male from coarse grass, the female adding a lining of fine grass and hair. Three to four brown freckled eggs are laid, which the female incubates in spells of about 45 minutes, interrupted by feeding intervals of about eight minutes. Her immediate departure from, and return to, the nest is on foot, but she flies, accompanied by the male, to the feeding area, which may be over half a mile from the nest. Incubation lasts about 14 days, during which the male sings very little. The young are fed by both adults, and fledge in 11 to 13 days. However, they often leave the nest before this, and hide in hollows in the ground, between which pathways become established.

JFMAMJJASOND

78

Corn Bunting

This is the largest of the buntings, and in flight its bulk is quite striking. The wings are ample, the tail is medium length, the head and body heavy: all give the (quite correct) impression of a well-built bird

Beak shape provides an extra large opening for cracking seeds at the inner end of the gape, where the greatest pinching effect is obtained

(×³/₁₀)

Seen close to in flight near the ground, the Corn Bunting appears additionally substantial

The Corn Bunting's dark breast patch, resembling a necklace, is visible in the near distance. It is present on adults only, and varies between individuals

The male bird, in a typical posture, singing from a favourite perch

There are no special features in the plumage, but with short streaks overall it is quite distinctive in itself

(×³/₅)

Dangling the legs is a habit usually associated with the breeding season

A close view reveals the breast pattern. This is an immature bird – no breast patch

A Corn Bunting may be seen feeding quietly on the ground, when it appears slimmer than at other times and quite similar to a Skylark

Though one of the most drab plumaged of European birds, the Corn Bunting is an interesting species whose distribution and habits show puzzling features. It inhabits wide, cultivated fields, especially of cereals, preferring those without hedges. Hence, modern trends in agriculture are to its advantage. However, it is patchy and local in distribution, and during the course of this century has almost disappeared from Ireland, where it was once common.

Its breeding behaviour is also surprising. Unlike other buntings and seed-eating birds, the male takes little part in nesting. He may accompany the female while she builds, but incubation and feeding the young are her tasks alone. It was until recently thought that the male Corn Bunting was polygamous, but it now appears that this is by no means always so. The male has several song posts, often up to 150 yards from any nest, and his distinctive song resembles the jangling of a bunch of keys. During the breeding season his flight appears clumsy, with legs dangling – a habit which probably derives from the display flight he sometimes performs.

Every one and a half to two hours, the female leaves the nest to feed up to 400 yards away, where she is often then joined by the male. The nest is hidden on the ground, in a cornfield or on marginal land. The clutch contains three to five eggs, and up to three broods may be raised each year.

JFMAMJJASOND

79

Crested Lark

Wing action is mainly from the horizontal downwards

This species can quite often be seen perching on low trees or bushes

From beneath, the Crested Lark shows a pinkish-orange underwing, which contrasts with the plain brown of the Skylark's. The outer tail feathers are bright orange

($\times \frac{3}{10}$)

Portion of a juvenile's tail, showing the lesser extent of orange on the young bird

The rotund appearance of a bird with its feathers fluffed out in cold weather. By contrast, the hot climate makes Spanish Crested Larks appear slimmer than the norm

In flight, the Crested Lark shows a broad-winged, short-tailed profile. Its dumpy shape belies a remarkably buoyant flight

Larger than on any other European lark, the crest will frequently be seen raised. This species has a larger beak than the Skylark. There is a dark patch at the top side of the breast

($\times \frac{3}{5}$)

From behind, a clear view of the orange, as opposed to white, outer tail, which unfailingly distinguishes this species from the Skylark

Song perches are generally high

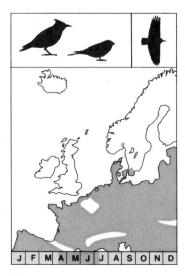

As pleasing as it is distinctive, the Crested Lark's call is a liquid whistle of four syllables which rises in the middle of the phrase. The bird's song, with its especially clear tone, rivals the Skylark's, but is usually briefer, delivered from the ground or a perch on a building. There is also a display flight, but unlike the Skylark, the Crested Lark rises and descends in silence, uttering its song in flight or from a perch only after it has climbed to about 200 feet.

Crested Larks frequent even more arid and sparsely vegetated terrain than Skylarks, and hence occur in such man-made habitats as roads, railway sidings and even bomb-sites. They nest in depressions in the ground, usually in the shelter of a shrub or grass tussock. Four eggs form the normal clutch, and the female incubates alone for 11 to 12 days. The young are fed by both parents on insects, although the normal diet of adult Crested Larks is grain and grass seeds. Like other larks, they leave the nest early, sometimes as soon as eight days, and a good week before they can fly. Two or three broods are raised.

Like many other larks, this species shows great variation in size and colour throughout its extensive range; colour differences are correlated with humidity and with the soil colour of its habitat. Fortunately, the four European races of this largely sedentary species are all very similar to each other.

Skylark

A Skylark can "hang" in the air as it sings, looking like a small bird of prey

The unmistakable Skylark song flight: a bird soars and hovers, then plunges towards the ground, straightening out into low-level flight, pouring out an unbroken, musical stream of song

Below, in winter, vast flocks gather over fields

In flight, a Skylark can be recognized by its short tail and ample wings with pale trailing edges

(×³/₁₀)

An adult bird. Skylarks often perch on posts, but never in trees

When alarmed, Skylarks stand bolt upright, often with raised crests. There is distinctive streaking on the breast and a black-and-white pattern easily visible under the tail

One phase of the song flight consists in circling low with whirring wings

An adult rising from the ground to begin the display flight

The young bird's plumage has a "scaly" appearance. This creeping posture may be adopted when the bird feeds

Adult Skylark. It has a very long rear claw

(×³/₅)

Skylarks have a triangular look from certain angles, produced by the sharp, straight slant of the wings on their downbeat. This is especially noticeable in the bird's low, flapping flight

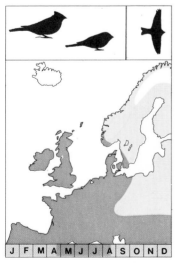

Although its remarkable song has earned the Skylark a place in literature, fame has not saved it from persecution. During the last century, Skylarks were netted in thousands daily in Britain, and they are still killed on a large scale for the table in Belgium, France and Mediterranean countries. The song is notable not only for quality and variety – including trills, warbles and mimetic passages – but also for duration. Individual song flights last several minutes and the song period covers more than half the year. As well as in flight, the song is sometimes delivered from a fence post or the ground.

Skylarks are birds of open fields and feed entirely on the ground, taking both plant items and small invertebrates.

Snow cover may force large-scale movements, and severe winters can markedly reduce populations. Scandinavian populations are strongly migratory, moving to France and Spain in winter. Southern populations are rather more sedentary.

The nest is a hollow on the ground. It is sheltered by vegetation – usually grass – but crops such as sugar beet are also employed. The female usually lays three or four eggs. Incubation, by the female alone, lasts only 11 days, and the young leave extremely early – from nine days onwards. They may return to the nest at night, but do not fledge for 20 days. During this dangerous time their scaly plumage provides excellent camouflage, and the adults are wary, only approaching the nest on foot.

81

Tree Pipit

(×³/₁₀)

Viewed from beneath, the Tree Pipit's breast markings are more prominent than the Meadow Pipit's—larger in size and fewer in number. It has white outer tail feathers

Tree Pipits have a "parachute" display flight, which finishes with the bird landing on a perch adjacent to that from which it started

(×³/₅)

This bird is much like a Meadow Pipit in flight—erratically surging and falling, a jerky, flitting spectacle. It also resembles a Meadow Pipit physically, except for its slightly longer tail, and longer, thinner wings: but these differences are so slight as to be hardly noticeable in the field

Close view reveals a more stockily built bird than the Meadow Pipit. The median wing coverts are very prominent indeed

The breast carries more yellow-buff than that of the Meadow Pipit, and the spots are more regularly spaced

Like Wagtails, Tree Pipits have the tail-wagging habit, but because their tails are shorter, the action is not so conspicuous

Legs are usually a bright flesh colour. A Meadow Pipit's legs are brown

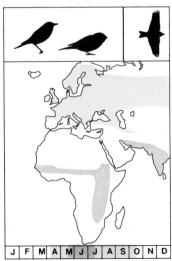

Less numerous and less widely distributed than the Meadow Pipit, the Tree Pipit has a more restricted choice of habitat—usually heaths with rough vegetation and scattered trees, clearings in woods, woodland edges and in high birch or oak trees in the depths of mixed deciduous woods. It has turned present-day forestry methods to advantage, for conifer plantations in their early stages provide an ideal habitat. Males arrive in late April, and quickly take up territories; females appear soon after. The female builds the nest, attended by the male. It is a simple grass cup, placed in a depression and usually well concealed under vegetation. During the four or five days before the clutch is complete and in-cubation can commence, both adults feed close to the nest and the male does little singing. Once incubation of the four to six eggs has started, he commences his song flights, often far away from the nest. After the eggs have hatched, 13 or 14 days later, his singing is again curtailed as he aids the female in feeding the young, which fledge after 12 or 13 days.

The adults moult wing and tail feathers before their autumn departure, which is mainly in September. The birds occur at all times, singly or in small parties, though roosts of larger numbers have been encountered. The food consists of live ground insects—beetles, grasshoppers, leatherjackets and spiders—and, occasionally, seeds.

J F M A M J J A S O N D

Meadow Pipit

Quiet, creeping behaviour while feeding

The white outer tail feathers are very conspicuous in low-level flight

The Meadow Pipit's appearance in flight is of a dumpily built, short-headed, short-tailed bird. The prominence of the two pale wing bars varies from individual to individual

(× 3/10)

Although they inhabit tree-less moorland, Meadow Pipits will readily perch in trees

Meadow Pipits may be seen rising individually, but then forming a flock. They progress in a weak, hesitant manner, rising and falling, as if in constant struggle to gain extra height. Wing beats usually sweep below the horizontal

Meadow Pipits do have pale eye-rings and the breast streaking is irregular but prominent

Bird with brown upperparts

Plumage varies little except for the basic colour of the upperparts, which can be principally buff, brown or greenish. Young birds especially have yellow-buff colouring

A long rear claw: not shared by the Tree Pipit

The pattern of breast markings varies from bird to bird

A Meadow Pipit wags its tail when walking about, but the tail, like a Tree Pipit's, is short and the movement is not so conspicuous as a wagtail's

(× 3/5)

Bird with greenish upperparts

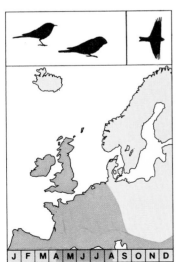

J F M A M J J A S O N D

On the bleakest, mistiest moorland, sometimes the only sign of birdlife for long periods of time is the sibilant call of the Meadow Pipit. Almost ubiquitous in such surroundings, the bird also thrives on downs, fresh marshes, sand dunes, and even on railway or motorway cuttings.

Breeding commences early, and the simple grass nest is sited in a depression in the ground under over-hanging vegetation, often in a cavity in the wall of a gulley. Analysis of British nest records shows that clutch size averages about four and a half at sea level, decreasing to four above 1,000 feet. Birds in northern parts of the range lay larger clutches. The female incubates for 13 days, and both parents feed the young during the fledging period of 12 days. Two broods are usual.

Only 54 per cent of Meadow Pipit eggs actually survive to hatch, and of those which do, only 30 per cent result in fledged young—figures probably typical of many small birds. Life expectancy at fledging is only ten months, but a bird surviving its first year can expect a further 15 months of life. In many areas, the Meadow Pipit is the most frequent victim of the cuckoo.

Meadow Pipits feed on ground invertebrates and in moorland areas crane flies and their larvae are an important part of the diet. In the southern part of its range, the species is only a partial migrant, wintering in Mediterranean areas and North Africa.

83

Rock Pipit—Water Pipit

Rock Pipit. This large pipit is particularly inconspicuous when walking on seaweed-covered rocks. Unlike any other pipit it has dusky, rather than pure white, outer tail feathers. It is also distinguished by its over-all smoke-coloured plumage, dark breast and pale eye-ring

($\times \frac{3}{5}$)

($\times \frac{3}{10}$)

Rock Pipit. In flight, its size, smoke-coloured plumage and dusky outer tail feathers are visible points of identification

Both Rock and Water Pipits have dark legs —either brown, lead grey or blackish— which separate them from all other European pipits

A Rock Pipit of the Scandinavian race. It can be distinguished in spring by its eye-stripe, pink flush on the chin and lighter breast streaking, but in winter is inseparable from its southerly counterparts

Above left, the outer tail feathers of a Water Pipit showing pure white tips. Above right, the Rock Pipit's are dirty, or dusky white

Male Water Pipit in spring plumage. The species has a strong eyestripe, pale, unmarked underparts with a pinkish wash and white outer tail feathers

($\times \frac{3}{5}$)

A Water Pipit in winter plumage

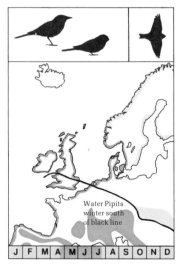

Water Pipits winter south of black line

J F M A M J J A S O N D

Rock and Water Pipits are actually members of the same species, of which the various races fall into two fairly distinct groups. Those called the Rock Pipits nest and forage along coastlines, while the Water Pipit group inhabits mountainous places.

The feeding habits of Rock Pipits have been closely studied in southwest England. They consume slightly more than their own weight of food each day, made up from enormous numbers of small periwinkles and the larvae of midges or flies gleaned from rotting seaweed. During the breeding season they forage mainly on grassy areas slightly inland. Members of the Water Pipit group feed on insects and spiders and some small snails. All members of the species build a simple grassy nest, the Rock Pipits in a rocky crevice, the Water Pipits in a grassy bank. The clutch of four or five eggs is incubated by the female for 14 days. The young remain in the nest for the rather long period of 16 days.

Communal roosting in rock crevices takes place around the end of the breeding season. In winter quarters, the birds are encountered occasionally, but regularly in ones or twos. In Britain, a few Rock Pipits may leave their permanent coastal quarters during the passage season to visit inland sewage farms, watercress beds and low-lying, wet localities. At the same time, visiting Water Pipits can be encountered in similar habitats.

Tawny Pipit

A graceful, bounding flight, which has more in common with the Yellow Wagtail's than the hesitant, jerky motion of the Meadow Pipit

Tawny Pipits are elegant birds – slim and long-legged. They have pale upperparts, but especially pale underparts, on which the streaking is sparse and sometimes entirely absent. The eyestripe is highly conspicuous, as is the row of spots formed by the wing coverts. There are off-white outer tail feathers

The typically alert posture. Stance has much in common with a Wagtail's. The long tail is especially evident in close view

Long tail and long wings give this Pipit a characteristic outline from a rear or side viewpoint

$(\times ^3/_{10})$

Markings shown up in flight vary little from the general pipit pattern, except that the back is unstreaked

The juvenile bird has similar markings to the adult but they are more definite

Foot and leg vary from a bright yellowish to a glowing flesh-pink colour. Unlike a wagtail, the Tawny Pipit has a short hind claw

Adult at typical nest site in a sand-dune

$(\times ^3/_5)$

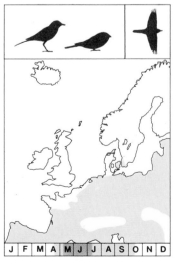

J F M A M J J A S O N D

The Tawny Pipit prefers more barren terrain than other European pipits, choosing extensive heaths, sand dunes, limestone hillsides and dry uplands. In some areas, such places have been planted with conifers, resulting in their abandonment by this species. It is, nevertheless, widely distributed throughout Europe and Asia, though only occurring in small numbers in Britain while on passage, and absent as a breeder from most of Denmark.

Tawny Pipits return to their breeding areas in late March and April. Males proclaim their territories with song flights, but the song is rather poor – a simple repetition of clear metallic notes. The nest is sited in a depression on the ground, concealed by a clump of grass,

bramble or heather. It is a rather substantial structure of grass, roots, even bits of seaweed, lined with fine grass and hair. Both sexes are believed to incubate, a process lasting 13 to 14 days, and both certainly feed the young during the 12-day fledging period. Four or five eggs are usual. Second broods may occur in southern parts of the range.

The main wintering areas of European and many Asian birds are dry and desolate plains in the southern Sudan. Here, they are usually seen singly or in pairs, but by the end of February they are associating in larger groups and indulging in courtship chases preparatory to their return to the breeding grounds.

Grey Wagtail

Pied Wagtail

Grey Wagtail

Yellow Wagtail

Viewed from beneath, the Grey Wagtail is distinguished by its yellow under-tail coverts and very long, thin tail

Juveniles and females lack the white wing bar

$(\times {}^{3}/_{10})$

Pied Wagtails – flying attitudes

All wagtails have the same sequence of flight movements. Wings flap rapidly, the bird gaining height; the wings close, and the bird curves downwards; then the process is repeated

The greenish yellow rump, present on birds of all ages, is conspicuous in flight

$(\times {}^{3}/_{5})$

A juvenile. Every Grey Wagtail has yellow plumage encircling the tail. Of all wagtails, it has the longest, slimmest tail

A male, winter plumage

A female, winter plumage

Grey Wagtails frequent town centres, equally at home on flat or sloping roofs

In summer the adult male develops a black bib

The female in winter. There is little problem in conclusively identifying the Grey Wagtail: grey upperparts contrast with the bright yellow under-plumage extending beneath and around the long, thin tail, which is constantly wagged

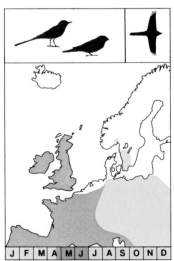

J F M A M J J A S O N D

This is the most graceful of the wagtails, its nimble actions and handsome plumage lending added enjoyment to a walk by a rushing stream. Because of a fondness for fast-flowing water, it tends to be found in hills and mountains, up to 8,000 feet in the Alps. However, it occurs in some lowland areas and occasionally well away from water when nesting in a man-made environment such as a bomb site or quarry. Such occurrences illustrate the birds' dependence on cavities for nest sites. Crevices in river banks, usually screened by vegetation, are the typical situation, but holes in brickwork on bridges or buildings are a favoured substitute. The nest is of grass and other vegetation, warmly lined with hair. It is built by the female, who also performs most of the incubation. The clutch of four to six eggs hatches in 13 to 14 days, and the young are fed by both parents, leaving the nest after 12 days. A second brood is often raised.

Grey Wagtails feed on a variety of insects found near water, including may-flies, gnats and beetles, as well as small molluscs and crustaceans. They regularly perch in trees, unlike other wagtails, and often make aerial sorties to capture passing insects. The call is high pitched and very brief; a long drawn note is used as an alarm, and a pleasant song incorporating a trill is to be heard in spring. European Grey Wagtails are residents or short-distance migrants.

Yellow Wagtail

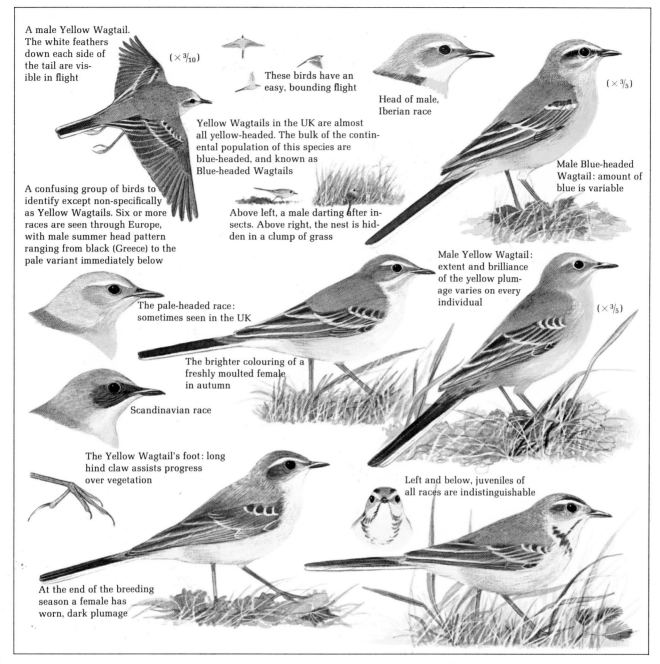

A male Yellow Wagtail. The white feathers down each side of the tail are visible in flight

(×³/₁₀)

These birds have an easy, bounding flight

Head of male, Iberian race

(×³/₅)

Yellow Wagtails in the UK are almost all yellow-headed. The bulk of the continental population of this species are blue-headed, and known as Blue-headed Wagtails

Male Blue-headed Wagtail: amount of blue is variable

A confusing group of birds to identify except non-specifically as Yellow Wagtails. Six or more races are seen through Europe, with male summer head pattern ranging from black (Greece) to the pale variant immediately below

Above left, a male darting after insects. Above right, the nest is hidden in a clump of grass

Male Yellow Wagtail: extent and brilliance of the yellow plumage varies on every individual

(×³/₅)

The pale-headed race: sometimes seen in the UK

The brighter colouring of a freshly moulted female in autumn

Scandinavian race

The Yellow Wagtail's foot: long hind claw assists progress over vegetation

Left and below, juveniles of all races are indistinguishable

At the end of the breeding season a female has worn, dark plumage

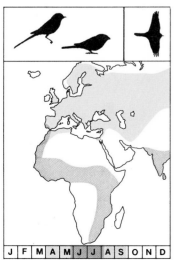

J F M A M J J A S O N D

Ornithologists are fascinated by the kaleidoscopic variety of male head patterns in the many geographical races of Yellow Wagtail, especially since birds identical to far-distant races may occur and breed amongst those of a quite different form. Thus, in Britain, the normal breeding birds are of a yellow-headed race, but here and there are small pockets of grey-headed birds identical to the form breeding in western Siberia. It is thought that such abnormalities occur through interbreeding with birds of other races. Whatever the colour of the male, all Yellow Wagtails have similar habits. They are typically birds of damp meadowland with a partiality for cattle pastures.

Males arrive about a fortnight ahead of the females and they nest in a depression in the ground, well hidden under vegetation and often lined with cattle- or horsehair. Five or six eggs are laid, densely freckled with yellowish-brown. They are incubated by the female and the young are fed by both parents.

These are exceedingly wary birds, the male calling the female off the nest when an observer approaches within 100 yards. Their behaviour at such times, and the "tsweep" alarm note, makes them seem more like (the related) pipits than wagtails. Two broods are usually raised before departure to the winter quarters. Yellow Wagtail populations in western Europe have recently shown signs of a decline.

87

Pied Wagtail

Male White
Wagtail, summer

Male Pied Wagtail

Female White
Wagtail, summer

Male Pied Wagtail, summer

Grey rump and grey
upperparts are
key points of recog-
nition on the White Wagtail

(×³⁄₁₀)

Pied Wagtails
are resident in the
United Kingdom. The White
Wagtail is the contin-
ental bird, occurring
in the UK only as a
scarce migrant

(×³⁄₅)

Adult Pied Wagtail,
front view: a large
area of white breast

When visible, the
White Wagtail's
flanks are pale grey,
the Pied Wagtail's
smoky grey

A first-year White
Wagtail. Its crown is
sometimes grey only

(×³⁄₁₀)

The male Pied
Wagtail shows a
greyer back in winter
plumage than in summer. In both
sexes the wing bars are prominent

A Pied Wag-
tail is commonly
seen walking on roofs or
walls in a deliberate,
stepping gait, head bob-
bing and tail wagging.
The latter is inter-
rupted with dashes
after insects

With a grey back, which sometimes
has a tinge of olive, the female
Pied Wagtail more or less resembles the White Wagtail. But
because she lacks the clean,
pale grey back and rump of that
species, her general appearance is much less bright

(×³⁄₅)

Young of both
birds are very
much alike

The elegant plumage and graceful actions of the Pied Wagtail are a familiar sight around human dwellings nearly everywhere in Europe. Almost any habitat will suit it if there are open areas where it can find insects and sheltered crevices to site the nest. Its natural choice is the vicinity of shallow streams, where shingle spits and adjoining grass provide feed and the banks offer nest sites, but it is equally at home feeding on lawns in a city park, with a nest in a nearby building. Insects are caught on the ground by sudden dashes and swerves. During June, roads through woodland attract many Pied Wagtails, which gather caterpillars that have fallen from overhanging trees to lie clearly exposed on the road. Despite this, these nimble birds rarely fall victim to passing cars. The nest is bulky and untidy, made of grass and coarse scraps, with a thick hair and feather lining. Nests around buildings are regularly sited on such strange places as farm machinery or ledges in sheds. The clutch of four to six grey spotted eggs is incubated by the female, the male helping for short spells with the first brood. When the young hatch, they may be fed mainly by the male while the female lays and incubates a second clutch.

Outside the breeding season, Pied Wagtails roost communally in thickets or buildings, sometimes in assemblies of several hundreds which are often found in glasshouses.

J F M A M J J A S O N D

Swallow

High-level flight is easy and languid

Juvenile | Adult female | Adult male

The adult male generally has longer tail streamers than the adult female. Congregating in excitable groups before migration is a habit common to all members of the swallow family

Three features conclusively identify Swallows: blue-black upperparts, reddish forehead and deeply forked tail

(×5/12)

Made from mud and straw, the Swallow's nest is usually placed on a beam or ledge in a shed or outbuilding. The parents can reach it through an astonishingly narrow opening, flying in at speed without hesitation

Adult

Individual forks from a juvenile tail, left, and an adult tail, right, showing their different lengths and the white spots

Juvenile

An adult gathers mud for nest-building, rolling it into an easily carried ball

The Swallow's low-level flight is one of the most familiar sights in early summer on open spaces, parks, playing fields and meadows

These are the only birds which fly at a constant height a few inches above the ground catching insects

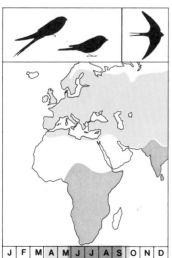

J F M A M J J A S O N D

The Swallow has been a welcome guest of human habitation from the earliest times. Unlike House Martins, Swallows generally nest inside buildings, showing a preference for farm sheds. They reach Europe between March and June, successive waves passing over earlier arrivals. Individual birds usually return to the same place, and may even reuse last year's nest, but the chances of both members of a pair surviving migration hazards are only one in five. Even when both return, reshuffling of pairs often occurs.

Four to six eggs are laid, and two or three broods are reared. Incubation and fledging periods are long, and nestlings may be found well into September. The Swallow captures aerial insects lower than House Martins or Swifts, often taking prey while skimming meadows or water. Although, unlike most passerines, it can feed on migration, it still suffers considerable mortality on its journeys, which from Europe involve a trans-Sahara crossing. Its routes and schedule are known in detail. British Swallows winter in southeastern and southern Africa, Dutch and German birds more centrally in the same region, and those from Russia to the north and west. Autumn migration lasts a leisurely two months, while spring return takes only one. Some Swallows have recently stayed to nest in South Africa, but with 15 native species of swallow to compete against, this is unlikely to become a general trend.

House Martin

Birds gather on wires, especially prior to migration

Typical nest-building sites under house eaves

Below right: adult feeds young bird in a mid-air meeting

Left: a common House Martin feeding habit – soaring or "towering" after insects

Birds often feed on woodland edges, above

Below: curious curved appearance of the wings while gliding

Above: open tail looks almost triangular

House Martins have a flicking action in flight. The underwing is dark, the body and throat pure white

The white rump is conspicuous, especially in flight low over the ground. Except at close range, the dark blue upperparts appear black. Closed, the tail is deeply forked

$(\times {}^{5}\!/_{12})$

The dumpy body shows in side-view

Birds stand carefully, bodies well above the wet ground, as they gather mud in small balls for nest building

White feet and claws – different to the Swift's

Adult's head showing the small beak

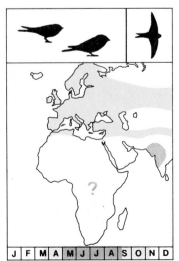

J F M A M J J A S O N D

The House Martin's nesting association with Man was well known to Shakespeare ("no jutty, frieze, buttress, nor coign of vantage, but this bird hath made his pendent bed . . ." – Macbeth, Act 1, Scene 6), but its ancestral home was mountains or coastal cliffs. There are House Martin colonies in towns and villages throughout Europe, varying from one or two nests to several hundred. Where pollution in cities has been brought under control, the aerial insect population has flourished and House Martins have moved in, nesting even on stark modern buildings. Colonies still occur on cliffs in remote mountainous regions, sometimes above the tree line at altitudes up to 14,000 feet.

House Martins can be tempted to nest under eaves in artificial nests, and once one pair is in occupation, others may come to nest near by. The major problem facing House Martins is the continuous take-over of their nests by House Sparrows. Clutches of four or five are normal. The parents share incubation duties, and other young from a previous brood may assist them in feeding nestlings. The fledging period is generally long – up to three weeks – and with two or three broods per year the last may leave as late as October.

House Martins arrive from Africa in April and May, congregating over reservoirs before dispersing to colonies. Return migration may be as late as November and late migrants sometimes fall victim to bad weather.

Sand Martin

This species is very gregarious at all times, and when away from the nesting colony will usually be found feeding in groups, especially over water. The Sand Martin's flight is a more fluttering, erratic motion than that of other martins

$(\times \frac{5}{12})$

Group vacating telegraph wires – a typical view of Sand Martins

The Sand Martin's most conspicuous features are its small size, mouse-brown upperparts, white body and brown throat band. The tail is only slightly forked

Sand Martins over water is one of the first signs of spring. Above, birds gather before descending to roost on reed beds

Below, attitudes adopted while roosting in reed beds

Adult at nest hole. The brown plumage has minor variations in shade

Below, colonies are always in natural or man-made earth or sand walls, the holes typically forming horizontal lines

Head of adult showing prominent throat band

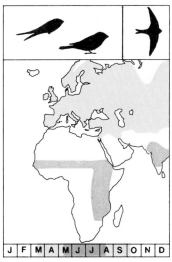

As more and more of the landscape disappears under a mantle of concrete, most birds find their habitats reduced. The Sand Martin is one of the few that do not: sand and gravel workings thrown up by the building industry provide it with an abundance of new breeding sites.

Natural sites for the Sand Martin's colonies of nesting tunnels are river banks or sand cliffs. The birds arrive early in spring, and cold spells may force small groups to huddle in tunnels for survival. Excavation, performed, incredibly, with the tiny feet, is an activity causing great excitement in the colony, and the resulting tunnels are two to four feet deep ending in a chamber lined with grass and feathers. Many birds make use of last year's holes, but if the sand face has collapsed in intervening months, they can establish new colonies at great speed.

Four or five white eggs are laid, and incubated mainly by the female. They hatch in a fortnight, and as with other hirundines there is a long fledging period of about three weeks. Newly fledged young remain around the colony for a few days, indulging in excited aerobatics and in chases (which adults may join), with a feather carried by one bird as an object of pursuit. While a second brood is raised, the first leaves for new feeding areas, often moving several hundred miles. By autumn, the birds have formed huge communal roosts in reeds or osiers.

J F M A M J J A S O N D

91

Swift

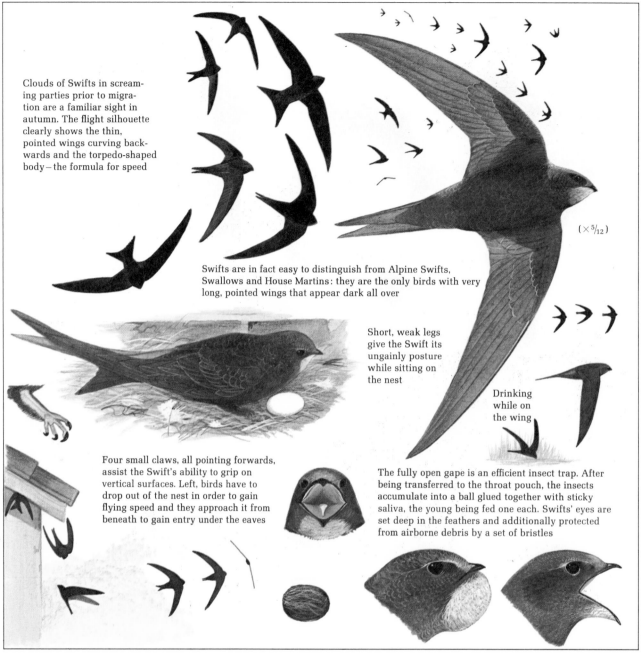

Clouds of Swifts in screaming parties prior to migration are a familiar sight in autumn. The flight silhouette clearly shows the thin, pointed wings curving backwards and the torpedo-shaped body – the formula for speed

Swifts are in fact easy to distinguish from Alpine Swifts, Swallows and House Martins: they are the only birds with very long, pointed wings that appear dark all over

Short, weak legs give the Swift its ungainly posture while sitting on the nest

Drinking while on the wing

(×⁵⁄₁₂)

Four small claws, all pointing forwards, assist the Swift's ability to grip on vertical surfaces. Left, birds have to drop out of the nest in order to gain flying speed and they approach it from beneath to gain entry under the eaves

The fully open gape is an efficient insect trap. After being transferred to the throat pouch, the insects accumulate into a ball glued together with sticky saliva, the young being fed one each. Swifts' eyes are set deep in the feathers and additionally protected from airborne debris by a set of bristles

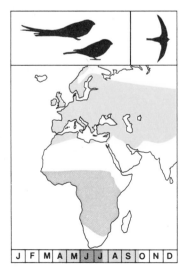

J F M A M J J A S O N D

Summer has come when parties of screaming Swifts flicker around the rooftops on knife-like wings. Their arrival at the nest sites ends a period of over nine months spent entirely on the wing, for these are the most aerial of birds, feeding, mating and even sleeping in flight. Their food is aerial insects, caught with the aid of an enormous gape. Their legs are tiny, with all four toes pointing forwards for clinging to vertical surfaces. The needle-sharp claws can be excruciating to an unwary human handler.

Nests are built in crevices in buildings, and the breeding cycle which takes place in these dark and secret places is remarkable. Nest material, which includes straws and feathers, is caught in flight and cemented with saliva. Two or three white eggs are laid, extraordinarily elongated in shape. In collecting the insect food, which is delivered to the young as a compressed ball, each parent flies some 500 miles a day. Cold, wet weather may force them to forage far from the nest for long periods. Consequently, the eggs are resistant to chilling, and the young can withstand several days of starvation. At such times, young Swifts become torpid at night, their temperatures falling from the normal 101°F to as low as 70°F. The young spend five to eight weeks in the nest – longer than other birds of this size: they depart for Africa immediately after fledging, for which voyage extra growth is required.

Alpine Swift

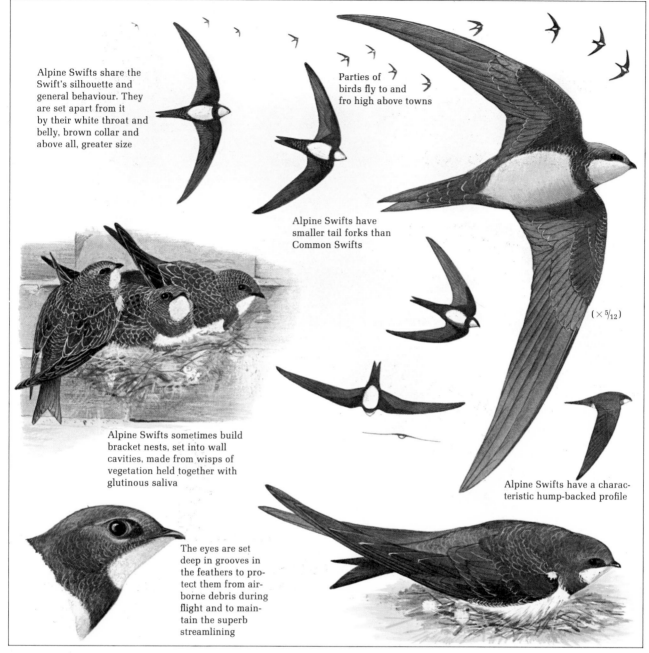

Alpine Swifts share the Swift's silhouette and general behaviour. They are set apart from it by their white throat and belly, brown collar and above all, greater size

Parties of birds fly to and fro high above towns

Alpine Swifts have smaller tail forks than Common Swifts

$(\times \frac{5}{12})$

Alpine Swifts sometimes build bracket nests, set into wall cavities, made from wisps of vegetation held together with glutinous saliva

Alpine Swifts have a characteristic hump-backed profile

The eyes are set deep in grooves in the feathers to protect them from airborne debris during flight and to maintain the superb streamlining

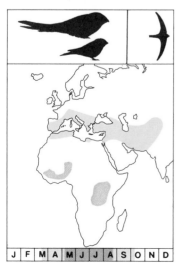

J F M A M J J A S O N D

Largest European representative of its family, the Alpine Swift's wings may span over 21 inches, with weight double that of the Common Swift.

Alpine Swifts show similar aerial specialization to their smaller relative, and probably fly even faster. Their food averages larger insects, including bees, and evidence suggests they select the stingless drones, though one bird examined had 11 stings in the gullet.

Breeding sites include mountains, caves and crevices in buildings. Some are age-old, as in medieval buildings and churches in Switzerland. Outside Europe, the species is by no means confined to mountain areas, nesting commonly in dilapidated buildings in Middle Eastern cities, where the loud trilling call mingles evocatively with the exotic hubbub around them. Displaying groups sweep silently round the nest sites, then burst into chorus. Like the Common Swift's, site entrances permit a free drop to reach flying speed, but inside, the birds are prepared to scramble or slide a long way to the nest. Nest material includes many outer cases of tree buds, mixed with saliva to form a cement. Two or three eggs are laid.

European Alpine Swifts winter in equatorial Africa alongside resident local races. During summer, weather movements sometimes occur: in 1917, a flock of 100, fleeing a depression, reached the southeastern coast of England.

Dipper

The continental race, known as the Black-bellied Dipper, has all dark underparts

Even in its very rapid flight up- and down-stream the Dipper's white breast makes it unmistakable. A fat, lively, bobbing bird

(× ³/₁₀)

When closed, the Dipper's white upper eyelid makes the bird look as if it is winking. This species uses its nictitating membrane, a transparent third eyelid, to protect the eye underwater

A young Dipper has grey upperparts and more white plumage below than an adult

Below the surface, the Dipper appears silver-grey, and the water pressure makes its outline sleek. Anchorage is a pebble on the river bed grasped in the strong claws

(× ³/₅)

Rufous-brown underparts distinguish the English race of Dipper. In this species, wear makes the feathers turn brown—a newly moulted bird has grey upperparts like the continental bird, top left

A Dipper will build its domed nest behind a waterfall, reaching it by flying through the torrent

Swimming with its wings open, right, the Dipper looks like a land bird that has alighted on the water by mistake. Below left, the bird walks rather than dives into the stream to forage for food

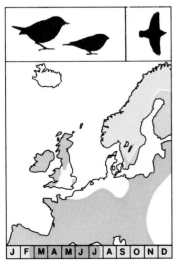

A strange and fascinating bird, the Dipper is hardly ever found away from swiftly flowing rivers. It is completely unmistakable, though the pied plumage can be surprisingly inconspicuous against a background of jumbled rocks and foaming water. The diet is a variety of water insects, including beetles, water boatmen and dragonfly and mayfly larvae, many of them obtained under water. To do this, the bird deliberately walks into the water, or sometimes dives, and then continues to walk over the bottom seeking food. This feat seems impossible, especially since the bird's buoyancy is increased by an insulating layer of air trapped in its unusually thick plumage. Nevertheless it happens, and is apparently achieved by continual wing movements to force the body down. The Dipper can also swim efficiently, despite its lack of webbed feet.

The territory of a pair of Dippers is a stretch of river about half a mile long, though this varies considerably. Both sexes proclaim their ownership with a loud song, which contains trills and grating noises. They usually build their nest in a crevice in a rocky bank, or very often in a bridge or weir, and sometimes behind a waterfall. It is domed, and made of moss with a lining of dead leaves. Four to six white eggs are laid, and incubated by the female for 16 days. The young remain in the nest from 19 to 25 days and two broods are normally raised.

This species has a wide range of stances, from upright to crouching. Its appearance on the ground is closer to that of a chat than a thrush

(× 3/5)

Adult female Rock Thrush

Newly moulted male Rock Thrush. August or September

Most reliable of the Rock Thrush's identifying features is the short red tail on either sex, visible from above or below. The eye is extraordinarily large. The wings are long, tapering sharply towards the tips. A wary bird, but less so when on migration

(× 3/10)

Adult male Rock Thrush spring plumage

Adult female Rock Thrush

Blue Rock Thrushes are seen on buildings

An adult female Rock Thrush has striped throat markings

Though essentially dull brown, the adult female Blue Rock Thrush's upperparts have a blue-grey wash

Adult male Blue Rock Thrush: entirely distinctive blue-grey plumage

(× 3/5)

In flight, the Blue Rock Thrush is identifiable on wing shape and on its long, square-ended tail alone

(× 3/10)

Juvenile Blue Rock Thrush

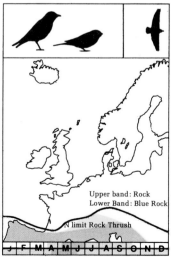

Upper band: Rock
Lower Band: Blue Rock

N limit Rock Thrush

J F M A M J J A S O N D

The Rock Thrush is a wary bird, and despite its vivid colouring is not always easy to see in its habitat of rocky mountainsides. Nimble and active while feeding, it seeks its food mainly on the ground. Insects form the bulk of the diet, many of them quite large, and even lizards and frogs are regularly taken. Melodious, warbling phrases make up the song, which is rather similar to that of the Blackbird. It is usually uttered from a prominent rock, but sometimes while flying. Courtship includes a spectacular display flight in which the bird glides down in circles from a great height. Nests are built in crevices among rocks and consist of grass, roots and moss. Building and incubation are carried out by the

female, the clutch of four to six eggs hatching after 14 to 15 days. Both sexes feed the young, which remain in the nest for 14 to 16 days. Rock Thrushes are fully migratory.

Blue Rock Thrushes are found in similar but even more barren areas than those favoured by the Rock Thrush: the rocks and cliffs around the ruins of Delphi are a typical example, and a perfect setting for such a beautiful bird. Generally similar to the Rock Thrush in most of its habits, it differs in being mainly resident, and in the appearance of its nest. Often very shallow, the nest of the Blue Rock Thrush is always more loosely constructed than the neat cup built by its close relative.

Song Thrush

The song perch is almost always elevated

Some are surprised to find that such a familiarly plain garden bird has an orange underwing, and take the Song Thrush for a Redwing

Alert and upright, head cocked to one side, the Song Thrush appears to be "listening" for a worm. In fact, the bird is scrutinizing the earth for signs of food

Flight is direct and only slightly undulating. Identifying the species in this view is difficult. Its wings beat a fraction faster than the Mistle Thrush's. Only the experienced can tell it from a Redwing, and then only by overall character

(× ³/₁₀)

Quite a different facial expression to that worn by the Mistle Thrush. Song Thrushes have gentle dispositions, backing away when, for instance, a Starling is aggressive

Song Thrushes are not as gregarious as they seem, usually going about in pairs. A party of ten on a football pitch is likely to be five pairs widely spaced. On the ground, Song Thrushes hop or run, but seldom walk

(× ³/₅)

Song Thrush eggs are sky-blue, as opposed to the Blackbird's overall reddish brown. The nest is traditionally lined with dung, but in suburban gardens mud is substituted

Snails are hammered open on stones

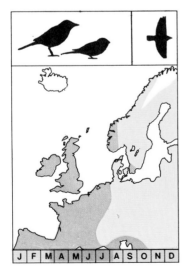

Mild weather in January will often trigger the first bursts of song from the common thrush, and because each phrase is repeated several times, it is probably the easiest to recognize of all garden bird songs.

Song Thrushes, along with Blackbirds, Robins and Starlings, are a familiar sight on lawns and flower beds throughout the year. Worms are their main food during the first half of the year, with caterpillars during May and June and fruit during autumn. Snails become important during cold winter weather or at any time when other food sources fail. They are smashed against a stone, which may be used repeatedly while the bird systematically clears snails from a nearby patch of ground: an almost legendary aspect of Song Thrush behaviour.

With four bright blue, black-spotted eggs against the unique mud lining, the Song Thrush nest is an attractive sight. Unfortunately, it is also easy to find, and the species suffers nearly as badly as the Blackbird from human predation. Bushes and trees are the usual nest site, ground situations and buildings being much less often used than by the Blackbird. Construction is effected by the female, who moulds the interior to a smooth cup with her breast. Ivy seeds are often used to ornament the rim. She alone incubates, but both sexes tend the young and two or three broods may be reared. The Song Thrush is a partial migrant.

Mistle Thrush

Singing from a bare tree-top in midwinter

A family party. Mistle Thrushes can look slightly pot-bellied

No other thrush has white on the tail feathers

A large, heavily built thrush, long winged, long tailed and distinctively undulating in flight. The juvenile is streaked black and white above, but identifiable as a Mistle Thrush on shape and behaviour

A white underwing, very striking in the field, and seen on no other thrush except the Fieldfare

The long wings and tail make a Mistle Thrush look lanky from behind. Rump and lower back are ochre

(× 3/10)

On this thrush the spreading of the primary feathers is particularly marked

Strikingly bold, the spots on the underparts are in a different pattern to those of the Song Thrush; upperparts are a colder shade of brown

(× 3/5)

Descending to a large, open space, the Mistle Thrush will make a long, undulating flight, opening and closing its wings, deliberately flattening out over the ground before landing. A highly distinctive habit— sometimes it seems the bird will never land

Whitish feather edges form a conspicuous pattern on the folded wings

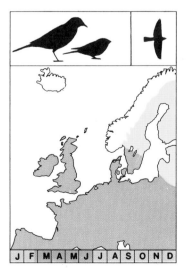

"Stormcock", the country name for this bird, is highly suitable: it sings loudly from high perches on blustery days in early spring. Mistle Thrush is no less apt a name, for it does indeed specialize in eating mistletoe berries in winter, and in the process renders invaluable aid to this parasitic plant in transporting its seeds to new host trees.

At other times, the Mistle Thrush may be seen seeking invertebrate prey in open areas such as playing fields, usually preferring these places to the small suburban gardens frequented by Song Thrushes. Possibly due in part to its feeding habits, the Mistle Thrush is nowhere as abundant as other thrushes, but holds unusually large territories.

Parkland, or suburban areas with tall trees, are typical breeding habitats, although orchards consisting of quite low trees are also favoured. Nests are generally placed higher than those of other thrushes, often on a horizontal limb close to the trunk. Site selection by the female may be seen in early spring as she squats in various likely spots before finally approving one. Three to five eggs are laid, incubated by the female for 13 to 14 days, and both parents feed the young for 14 to 16 days. Two broods are reared. It has been established that about 62 per cent of the young die before the end of their first year, but subsequently annual mortality drops to 48 per cent. These figures are likely to be much higher in a severe winter.

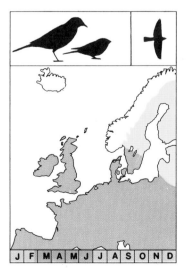

J F M A M J J A S O N D

97

Fieldfare

Flight action consists either in the wings flicking backwards, or, fully open, flapping normally

Above, the ragged look that epitomizes a Fieldfare flock

Fieldfares are part of the scenery in country lanes during autumn. They are frequently to be seen feeding on roadside hawthorns, often with Redwings

The pure white wing coverts are eyecatching. A Mistle Thrush is the only other thrush so marked

Long-winged and long-tailed, the Fieldfare has a build similar to but smaller than the Mistle Thrush

(× 3/10)

A juvenile – duller than an adult

(× 3/5)

When feeding on fields, the bird's habit of dropping its wings, exposing the grey rump, gives it a characteristic appearance, above and below

Grey head, rufous-brown back, grey rump and a dark tail distinguish the Fieldfare from all other species

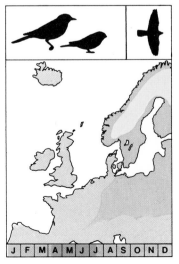

Harsh chuckling calls from passing Fieldfares are a characteristic sound of farmland in winter, but one which is being heard increasingly during summer, too, as the species extends its breeding range. Fieldfares first colonized central Europe in the early nineteenth century and a new phase of expansion has added them to the breeding list in Greenland (since 1943), Denmark (since 1960), Scotland (since 1967) and Iceland (since 1969). The spread may be due to climatic change, but must be aided by the fact that Fieldfares are no longer trapped for food – a practice conducted on a massive scale during the last century.

Typical Scandinavian breeding areas are in birch woodland, though various other habitats are now exploited, including parks and gardens in towns. Fieldfares nest colonially, with nests in adjacent trees – sometimes up to five in a single tree. Humans entering a colony face angry cries, dive-bombing and a liberal spattering of excrement. The nest is of twigs, grass and mud lined with finer grass. Four to six eggs are laid, which hatch after 13 to 14 days of incubation, mainly by the female. Both parents feed the young.

Slugs, insects and earthworms are staple foods throughout the year, supplemented by berries in winter, and flocks often visit orchards to feed on fallen apples. Fieldfares roost communally, preferring the ground to bushes or trees.

Redwing

During take-off the underwing pattern is conspicuous, and the eye-stripe visible

(× 3/10)

Redwing

Song Thrush

Only its smaller size and darker colour distinguish this species from the Song Thrush when seen from above. Redwings have a hurried, flicking action

Smallest of the thrushes, Redwings are quiet birds, but common on fields during winter, where they feed in company, especially with Fieldfares. Juveniles have plain brown upperparts, with no grey edging on the wing coverts and secondary feathers. The Icelandic race has much darker upperparts than other populations

The Song Thrush's underwing is orange not red, but this difference is not always clear

At dusk, birds seen diving into bushes such as hawthorn or rhododendron are likely to be Redwings returning to roost

At close range a Redwing is easy to identify. The combination of rich red flanks, eye-stripe and heavily streaked underparts is on no other species

(× 3/5)

Redwings feed gregariously on open fields

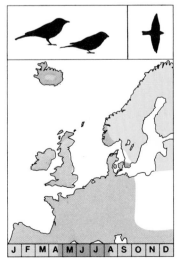

Snowfalls or hard frost may bring Redwings into suburban gardens. Their soft, lisping call can be heard at night over any part of England, including London; but for much of the winter they shun human habitation, feeding in open fields with Fieldfares, or sometimes Golden Plovers and Lapwings. Berries, such as holly and hawthorn, are eaten in large quantities, bringing the birds into hedgerows and thickets.

At night, Redwings roost communally in hawthorn scrub, laurel or rhododendron, flying in high in small parties and dropping down vertically to perch in the tops of the bushes. It is possible to trap large numbers of the birds for ringing at some roosts, which

has resulted in the discovery that Redwings are highly mobile throughout the winter, moving long distances to avoid hard weather, or to return to old haunts when conditions improve.

Like the Fieldfare, its breeding range is extending, and it now nests regularly in Scotland. Although nests tend to be grouped, unlike the Fieldfare it does not form clearly defined colonies. The nest is a typical thrush structure, made of grass and birch twigs, inside which is a mud cup lined with finer grass. Sites chosen are mostly low down, often on fine twigs near the base of birches. Five or six eggs are laid, and both sexes incubate them for 13 days. The young are fed by both parents and fledge after 12 to 14 days.

Blackbird

A Blackbird always flicks its tail on landing

(×³⁄₁₀)

Above, rising to a branch, the Blackbird progresses in a series of jerks, the wings not being lifted above the horizontal

Male in song

The all-brown female Blackbird has a profile and action in flight identical to that of the male

The male Blackbird is the only black garden bird with a yellow beak and yellow eye-ring

Blackbirds are noisy—incessantly so when a cat is present. They have a soft whistle, very difficult to locate, given when an aerial predator approaches. Below left, a Blackbird with partial albinism, common in this species. Below, a close view of the female reveals her pale breast and warm brown underparts

Before taking off, the bird takes one or two hesitant steps forward

(×³⁄₅)

A juvenile—ginger on head and breast

Below, left to right, typical behaviour on lawn or playing field: the noisy landing, tail cocked; the stoop to feed, tail flat; the forward hop, wings drooping

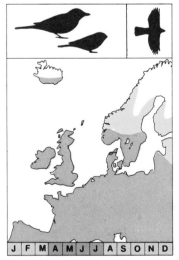

Often very easy to see and easily accessible, Blackbirds' nests are plundered by small boys more often than those of any other bird. Despite this hazard, the species remains one of the commonest in many parts of Europe, due to its versatility in exploiting new habitats created by Man. Originally a woodland bird, it now thrives on agricultural land and in urban areas, reaching maximum density in suburban gardens. Food eaten ranges from worms and other invertebrates to fruit and household scraps.

The nest is of grass, reinforced with mud and lined with finer grass. Bushes and small trees are typical sites, but nests on the ground or on buildings are common. Because so many Blackbirds'

nests are found, by ornithologists as well as vandals, a great deal of information has accumulated on their breeding biology. Nesting takes place from early March to late July or even August, but the greatest success rate is achieved by very early and by late nests. Early nests succeed because predators are less active at this time; late nests because summer foliage offers greater concealment. Three to five eggs are usually laid. Clutches are largest during May and are also higher on average in rural areas than in suburban ones. Incubation is by the female, but both sexes feed the young; three or more broods may be reared in a single season, during which the same nest is frequently reused.

Ring Ouzel

Ring Ouzels fly precipitately, wings flicking, tail cocking

Adult female, northern race

Adult male, northern race

($\times$ ⅙)

Ring Ouzels are most easily confused with Blackbirds when flying away from the observer at speed after being flushed

Partial albinism is so common among Blackbirds that occasional members of the species develop white markings about the throat with a passing resemblance to the Ring Ouzel's gorget. In such cases, the Ring Ouzel's pale wing-patches remain the sure distinguishing factor

Alpine Ring Ouzels are much paler than the northern race and have much more conspicuous wing-patches. Above is an adult male; right, an adult female

Adult male, northern race

An adult female Ring Ouzel has a much less distinct gorget than a male, but retains the distinct wing-patches and crescent feather edging

($\times$ ⅗)

A superficial resemblance to the Blackbird gives way at medium range to the Ring Ouzel's own outline: longer, narrower wings than a Blackbird, a long tail and white gorget

Juvenile, northern race

In moorland and mountain habitats the Blackbird is completely replaced by its near relative, the Ring Ouzel. This species particularly favours sheltered places in glens and gorges: unlike the Blackbird it is shy and shuns the neighbourhood of human habitation. Exceptions to this rule occur in autumn, when it may visit gardens to feast on cultivated berries, but even then such forays are usually confined to the early morning. At other times, various invertebrates constitute its diet. Clear single or double notes repeated three or four times after well-marked intervals comprise the Ring Ouzel's loud, piping song.

The nest resembles a Blackbird's in construction, but has a distinctive appearance due to the use of materials such as heather and moor grass. Vegetation overhanging the top of a cliff or peat bank is a common site, but low trees are occasionally used, and the alpine race sometimes nests quite high in conifers. Ring Ouzel nests are much more difficult to find than those of Blackbirds. One method which has been employed is the use of a border terrier: the birds have an unusually strong smell, which the dog detects with ease.

Two clutches of four eggs are usually laid, and incubation and fledging periods each last a fortnight. The duties of nest-building, brooding and feeding the young are shared between both sexes.

101

Golden Oriole

Adult female (See text)

Mature female

Juvenile

In flight, an adult female Golden Oriole is hard to distinguish from a juvenile, except by the juvenile's virtual lack of an outer wing-bar. Moreover, some fully mature females develop the full golden yellow of the adult male and these birds are only distinguished by their lack of black eye markings

The flight action is leisurely and rolling along a deeply undulating path. In courtship, the birds flit between tree-tops with remarkable ease. Confusion over identity arises only if the bird is seen in silhouette, when it somewhat resembles the Mistle Thrush

($\times \frac{3}{10}$)

View from beneath of the adult female, left, and the juvenile Golden Oriole, right. From this angle, the birds look similar

Adult male— black mark around eye and a brighter coloured beak than the female

From below, the adult male (or fully mature female) is unmistakable

($\times \frac{3}{5}$)

Despite the Golden Oriole's brilliant appearance, it can merge surprisingly well with the foliage

The adult female's yellow wing-patches are visible on folded wings

The juvenile is greener than the female and more heavily streaked

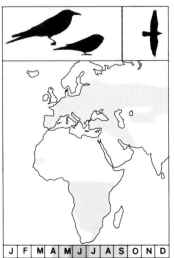

J F M A M J J A S O N D

It is the dappled background of sun and shade which allows the Golden Oriole to blend so surprisingly well with its normal habitat of the tree canopy. Younger females, with green underparts (rather than the golden yellow variant of the mature female), are the most difficult to locate of all. However, the birds are often revealed by their far-reaching and distinctive call, a liquid whistle of four syllables.

Golden Orioles occur in various woodland or parkland habitats, normally of broad-leaved trees. Foraging almost exclusively among the leaves, they capture a wide variety of insects, often rather large ones such as cockchafer beetles and even bumble-bees and hairy caterpillars. The prey is sometimes picked off leaves while the bird hovers. In late summer and autumn a great deal of fruit, especially figs, is consumed.

Suspended from a horizontal forked branch, the beautiful nest is built entirely by the female. Because it is frequently blown about, the nest cup is made very deep to reduce the danger of eggs or young tumbling out. Long strands of grass, leaf strips and bark are basic materials, with moss and lichens dotted about the exterior. Two to four eggs are laid, and incubation and fledging periods each last two weeks. Both sexes incubate and tend the young, feeding by regurgitation at first, and with whole prey later. As a rule, one brood is raised.

Starling

Starlings mob a predator by circling it in tight flock formation

($\times \frac{3}{10}$)

Above, a typical gathering. Left, singing with the wings partly open, flapping slightly, is commonplace behaviour

Sharp-winged, fat-bodied and fast, the Starling looks like an arrowhead in flight. In the distance, it appears jet black

Only Starlings form such dense black flocks over fields, rising, wheeling at speed and leap-frogging the next flock

Adult male in winter. Starlings have surprisingly intense markings and colour

The grey-brown juvenile is never far from an adult—in fact it often stands on the parent's heels

Flight is interspersed with glides during which the wings may be open or folded

Adult male, summer. Only Starlings peck with the beak held open

($\times \frac{3}{5}$)

Adult male, spring

Adult female, spring

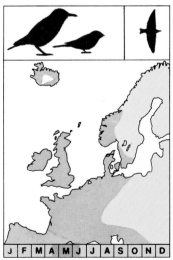

Starlings are noisy and dirty, but they are an impressive spectacle when they gather to roost, circling in dense flocks often many thousands strong. Two centuries ago they were much less abundant, depending on holes in trees for nesting, and for thickets or reedbeds for roosting. Now they make use of buildings for those purposes, and this has created a pest problem in many cities, not only in Europe but in the USA and various other parts of the world to which the species has been introduced.

These birds can find food almost anywhere, but their preferred feeding grounds are pasture or lawns. Worms and insect larvae are the prey in such situations, but Starlings differ strikingly in their feeding methods from the various thrushes which often search for similar prey alongside them. Whereas thrushes spread out widely and look around them for partly exposed prey, Starlings feed close together, moving in the same direction and excavating for invertebrates by repeatedly thrusting the bill into the ground and then opening it.

Rather surprisingly, in view of their abundance, most Starlings rear only one brood each year. Nest foundations are made by the male, and to his untidy mass of grass and straw the female adds a feather lining. Four to seven eggs are laid, hatching after 12 to 13 days. Fledging takes a comparatively long time—three weeks.

103

Waxwing

Waxwings can be acrobatic feeders

The bird's pointed wings and swift, buoyant flight in long undulations could be mistaken for a Starling's were it not for the trilling call, dumpy body and square-ended tail

$(\times \frac{3}{10})$

The pale underwing shows in flight

Obvious from this angle are the black throat, chestnut under-tail coverts and yellow band on tail

Astonishing alterations take place in the shape of a displaying Waxwing: here, the male (with extended rump) offers food to a female

$(\times \frac{3}{5})$

Females and first winter males have no yellow in the wing

Right, typical feeding postures. Changes in apparent size take place very quickly, the thinner usually signifying alarm

Waxwings are strange-looking birds, though none the less beautiful; with their crests, black masks and colourful wing markings they resemble no other common species. It is small wonder that their periodic visits in large winter flocks to areas where they were normally unknown aroused interest and sometimes even superstitious dread in times past. Like crossbills and Redwings, Waxwings show irruptive behaviour.

They are far-northern breeders, nesting in Scandinavia and the USSR. In most years, a sizeable population stays fairly close to home, while a smaller number migrate to central Europe. About every ten years, apparently as a result of population pressure, Wax-wings move *en masse* out of Scandinavia and the Russian taiga to winter in great numbers throughout Europe. In these years, they are seen regularly in southern Europe and Britain, where usually they are very scarce visitors.

Berries, particularly those of rowan, are the staple winter food – a resource for which they compete with Fieldfares and Redwings. In towns, cotoneaster and pyracantha are favoured. On the breeding grounds, food is mainly mosquitoes.

Waxwings nest in birch or coniferous forest. The chosen site is often a tree on the forest edge, or by a lake or stream. Conifer twigs, lichens and grass are the building materials, and the cup has a lining of hair and down.

On either species the pied colouring stands out, and both birds give the (misleading) impression of having weak, fluttering flight

$(\times {}^{3}/_{10})$

Lesser Grey Shrike. The Great Grey Shrike lacks the pronounced black forehead

$(\times {}^{3}/_{10})$

A Great Grey Shrike's first primary feather is much shorter than its second or third primary: the Lesser Grey Shrike's first primary is as long as its second or third. This is an entirely conclusive means of identification

A juvenile Lesser Grey Shrike has no black forehead

The Lesser Grey Shrike has narrower, more pointed wings than the Great Grey Shrike. It also has a stouter beak

Great Grey Shrike: the wing-patches vary in extent

Left, typical shrike postures when holding prey, resting or feeding. Below, a victim is usually impaled on a branch while additional food is sought

$(\times {}^{3}/_{5})$

$(\times {}^{3}/_{5})$

Whether the bird is perching or in flight, the Great Grey Shrike's tail is noticeably longer than the Lesser's

When the Lesser Grey Shrike folds its wings the primary feathers extend far beyond the secondaries, giving an appearance different from the stubby winged Great Grey Shrike

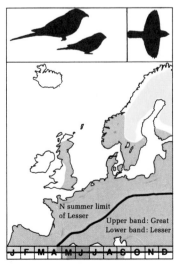

N summer limit of Lesser

Upper band: Great
Lower band: Lesser

J F M A M J J A S O N D

Shrikes are impressive birds which have evolved a way of life and physical structure resembling those of the smaller hawks. The Great Grey Shrike is the largest and most formidable species of the family occurring in Europe, its diet consisting of small birds and mammals (or, in the south, frogs and lizards), with a small proportion of large insects. The Lesser Grey Shrike eats beetles, mole crickets, grasshoppers and other insects. Shrikes are well known for their habit of setting up "larders" by impaling prey on thorns—or occasionally barbed wire: the Great Grey Shrike regularly treats its prey in this way, but the Lesser Grey appears to have abandoned this practice.

Northern populations of the Great Grey Shrike are migratory, often visiting the same territory regularly in successive years. They inhabit a wide range of country, including scrub, woodland edges and marshes; Lesser Grey Shrikes choose orchards, vineyards and wooded roadsides. Both species build large untidy nests in bushes or trees. Those of the Lesser Grey tend to be placed higher, and are often grouped in loose colonies. Clutches of five to six eggs are usual for both species, though in the north, where there is only time for one brood, Great Grey Shrikes may lay up to eight or nine eggs. Young Great Grey Shrikes fledge in about 20 days, but Lesser Grey fledglings leave the nest after two weeks, still barely able to fly.

105

Red-backed Shrike

Adult male

Left, the characteristic posture when looking for insects. Below left, the bird will maintain a face-on, crouching attitude to the observer. Bottom, swooping to the ground, where the bird will be seen feeding on insects

Adult female

Juvenile

The adult male. Red-backed are the only shrikes with no white in the wings

Slim and finely built, with an expressive tail, the Red-backed Shrike is generally a conspicuous, noisy bird, and the most beautiful European representative of its family. The adult male has a salmon-pink flush on his breast

(× 3/10)

An adult female has no black in the tail

(× 3/5)

An adult female. There is much variation in the extent of grey on female heads and rumps; also in the degree of rufous in immature and juvenile plumage

If in doubt as to whether the bird is a shrike, the beak should be examined first. Colour, shape and size will then distinguish this species from the Woodchat

With orange-brown plumage and crescent markings, the juvenile Red-backed Shrike is easier to recognize than a juvenile Woodchat

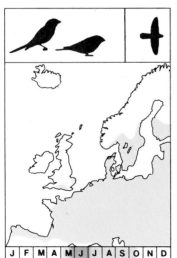

J F M A M J J A S O N D

Red-backed Shrike populations have declined seriously in the northwestern part of their range, and in Britain the species is rapidly becoming extinct as a breeder. There is no shortage of suitable habitats, and the beetles and bumble-bees which form much of its diet still seem common, despite alleged reductions in food supply due to climatic changes. A factor which must therefore be taken very seriously is the damage done by egg-collectors. Red-backed Shrike eggs vary extensively, and are therefore much prized.

In hunting and feeding methods the bird is typical of its family. Much of the prey is located from a look-out post, often at the top of one of the scattered bushes which are a prime requirement in its habitat. Occasionally the bird hovers to search a likely spot, or flies low past bushes to disturb possible prey. Victims include not only large insects, but nestlings or even adult small birds, lizards and rodents. These are often seized and carried with the feet, in the manner of a hawk, the beak being used for killing. The "larder" habit is well developed.

A thorny bush is usually chosen as the site for the large nest of moss, grass, wool and feathers, which is made mainly by the male. It is situated quite low, and the clutch varies from three to six eggs. Incubation is by the female alone, and lasts between 13 and 16 days. Both parents feed the young, which leave after about 14 days.

Woodchat

(×³/₁₀)

An adult male has a broader black band on the forehead than a female

Woodchats are commonly seen perching on overhead cables, when the large white V of the shoulder-patches and the glaring white underparts will identify the bird in rear, or in front view

Extensive, well-defined white patterning stands out on the adult male Woodchat seen in flight. A female is duller

The juvenile, right and below, seems to have plumage far removed from an adult's, and cryptic colouring makes it easily overlooked. The bird need not puzzle, however, if its basic shape is discerned, especially of head, beak and tail. The plumage is of the same pattern as an adult's, only faded

Although their basic pattern does not change, individual Woodchats vary considerably. Immature birds and sub-adults may have greyer backs and paler wings than adults. Some birds, like the male, top right, have pale edging on their inner secondaries

Adult female. At close range there is an appreciable difference between her head pattern and the adult male's, above

(×³/₅)

From behind, the white rump and wing-patches will catch the eye

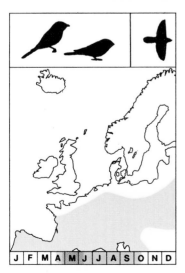

J F M A M J J A S O N D

Olive groves or forests of cork oak are the Mediterranean environment of this small and handsome shrike. In the north, various types of open woodland may be favoured, and, like the Lesser Grey Shrike, the Woodchat is often seen on telegraph wires along roadsides. Hunting methods and choice of food resemble those of the Red-backed Shrike, and the two occur in the same habitats in some places; "larders" are regularly used. Like all shrikes, the Woodchat utters harsh, chattering calls, but its song is superior to those of its relatives, including melodious phrases and imitations of other birds.

Woodchat shrikes generally nest a good deal higher than Red-backed, usually on an outer branch of a tree or tall shrub. Nest construction is rather neater: the deep cup of roots and leaves is lined with feathers, hair and wool. Five to six eggs are laid, showing variability similar to that which has had sad consequences for the Red-backed Shrike (page 106). Incubation is carried out by the female, fed on the nest by her mate, and lasts 16 days. The young are tended by male and female, and spend longer in the nest than those of the Red-backed Shrike – 19 or 20 days. Two broods are occasionally reared, though one is more usual.

North-bound migrants occasionally overshoot their Mediterranean breeding area, and small numbers of Woodchats are regularly seen in Britain during spring.

Roller

Lack of suitable holes in trees for nest-building affects Roller populations

Flight is easy and buoyant and, seen once, easily recognizable. Difficulty in identification arises only with birds flying away, when the blues are not very visible. Below, a Roller may be overlooked if not in flight: it sits quietly for long periods between dashing after insects

There can be no mistaking the brilliant blue underparts; with them the bird makes a breathtaking spectacle in its rolling, tumbling, display flight

($\times$ 1/5)

Below, a juvenile has a duller head and forewings than an adult. There is no black on the outer tips of the tail, which is rounded

From the side or rear, the chestnut-coloured back is a prominent feature. No other European bird has the size of a Jackdaw and such brilliant plumage

Proportionally, the head and beak are large. Legs are short

($\times$ 1/3)

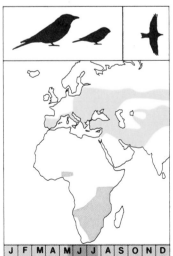

J F M A M J J A S O N D

One of Europe's most beautiful birds, the Roller is unfortunately decreasing in range, possibly as a result of changing climate. It breeds typically in open woodland or parkland areas, which provide it with tree holes for nesting and perches from which it can survey open ground for prey. For the most part this consists of large insects, but occasional lizards, small mammals and even small birds are added to the diet. In winter quarters, the grasslands of eastern Africa, European Rollers associate with the native Lilac-breasted Roller.

The English name of this bird derives from the male's springtime display flight, in which he flies to about 200 feet and then tumbles downwards, twisting and somersaulting as he does so. These are highly vocal birds, the usual call, a grating "kri .. kri .. kri", often being uttered on the wing.

Rollers are hole nesters, usually selecting an old woodpecker's hole, or other tree site, or occasionally a cavity among rocks or in a building. As a rule, they do not build any nest inside the chamber, although a sparse lining of debris and feathers may be added. Four to five white eggs are laid. Both male and female incubate for 18 to 19 days, starting before the clutch is complete. Young Rollers are fed by both adults, jostling and fighting viciously for the food items brought by their parents: they leave the nest after about four weeks.

Kingfisher

Males point aggressively at intruders on their territory, wings slightly drooping

An adult female about to feed her young. The large head and beak supported by strong neck muscles enable this bird to hold comparatively heavy fish

The plumage shows varying shades of blue, from deep blue to pale blue-green, according to the angle of the light

($\times \frac{3}{10}$)

A Kingfisher hovers, head pointing downwards, before plunging into water after fish. The bird's dark-coloured feet identify it as a juvenile

An adult male has an all-black beak. Length of beak varies individually

($\times \frac{3}{5}$)

Under the adult female's beak there is a pale orange patch

The impression given by the Kingfisher of having unreal proportions is caused partly by the extremely short tail. Its use is probably to facilitate movement inside the nesting tunnel

Left, attitude of bird as it flies up to the nesting hole. Right, flight profile from above, showing the long wings and pale blue streak on the back

An unusual foot, on which the three toes are partially joined

Almost spherical eggs (drawn on same scale as bird above) lie among fish remains and excreta

Left, a pale blue streak is often all one sees: the darker plumage blends with the background

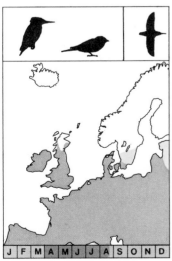

The Kingfisher's splendid plumage reminds us that it is a member of a predominantly tropical family. Although common enough on unpolluted waters, many people know it only from books, for it is shy and often surprisingly inconspicuous until it flies.

It catches fish by diving, either from a perch or after hovering. They are swallowed head first, and sticklebacks or bullheads are beaten unmercifully against the perch, for only when dead will spines or stiff fins flatten, making the fish safe to swallow. Courtship starts early in the year with high-flying aerial pursuits. Both birds excavate the nest tunnel, starting it off by flying at the river bank to drive in their bills. It may eventually extend three feet, and while one bird excavates, the other mounts guard outside. Seven white eggs are laid in early May on the bare soil of the nest chamber, and both parents share the three-week incubation period. The young spend three and a half weeks in the nest, fish remains gradually creating such filthy conditions that the adults have to bathe after each visit. Fledglings begin fishing practice soon after leaving, but their parents have to feed them until they are proficient. Many juvenile Kingfishers drown through diving too often and making their feathers waterlogged.

Young birds disperse in winter, some moving to the coast, while adults remain behind, male and female using different stretches of water until spring.

Bee-eater

Even when viewed from above, the Bee-eater's brilliant colouring merges unexpectedly with the landscape. The large V, formed by the yellow on the back, stands out well in the field

(× ³/₁₀)

Rear view of the recurved wing in the common sailing attitude

Flight is buoyant and easy, the bird soaring after insects then sailing down, ebullient, gay and restless

A Bee-eater is hardly to be confused with any other species, either by its colouring or by shape—the pointed wings and long central tail feathers are always conspicuous. But in a clear blue sky the bird can vanish completely in the glare of the sun, when only the rolling, liquid call reveals the Bee-eater's presence

Male or female, an adult looks the same. A juvenile is slightly duller and its central tail feather does not project

(× ³/₅)

Bee-eaters are seen sitting in groups between feeding forays

The Bee-eater's feet have three connected toes pointing forwards and a single rear toe

Nests are built in holes in river banks, but where banks are unavailable holes may be excavated in flat ground

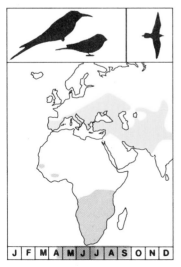

These birds are aptly named: their diet is largely honey-bees, supplemented with wasps and a variety of other flying insects. A single bee sting would be fatal for most small birds, but Bee-eaters overcome the problem partly by an unusual immunity to bee and wasp venom, but mainly by their skill in de-venoming the worker-bee by rubbing the sting out against a branch. The birds also have the ability to distinguish non-venomous drones. Extracting the sting always requires a return to the perch, and the considerable amount of feeding done in flight is presumably confined to non-venomous insects.

The European Bee-eater is a summer visitor, wintering in southern Africa and in India. Recently, European Bee-eaters have been reported nesting in South Africa during the period of the northern winter; they depart northwards with the rest, but it seems unlikely that they breed again in Europe during the northern summer.

Nest sites, usually colonial, are in tunnels made in banks or soft cliff faces. These tunnels, up to ten feet long, are excavated by both male and female mainly with the feet. Four to seven white eggs are laid, almost spherical in shape. During incubation, the nest chamber becomes carpeted with insect remains from the pellets which they disgorge as an alternative method of defecation. Both parents incubate and feed the young.

Birds of Iberia

Two great barriers, the Mediterranean and the Sahara, separate Europe from tropical Africa. Nevertheless, some birds of the hotter latitudes are endemic in southern Europe and nowhere is there a greater diversity of these than in Spain and Portugal.

Short-toed Eagle: large raptor with long, broad wings and an unmistakable white plumage. Spain, southern Europe, Asia east to Urals, NW Africa. Soars and hovers over lightly wooded country

Booted Eagle: pale phase, left, more common than dark, below. Spain, N Africa, C Asia, in hill forest

(×⅕)

Imperial Eagle: similar in size to the Golden Eagle but distinguished by white shoulders and pale nape. Spanish race now rare. Hunts over lowland forest, plains and marshland

(×¹⁄₁₁)

(×⅕)

Crag Martin: resembles Sand Martin but lacks throat band. Conspicuous white spots under tail. Spain, NW Africa; breeds on inland crags and coastal cliffs

(×⅓)

Red-rumped Swallow: distinctive russet rump and nape. Spain, NW Africa, eastern Mediterranean— on cliffs and buildings

Eleonora's Falcon: pale and dark forms. Superb aerial hunter. Breeds on Mediterranean islands

(×⅖)

Black Wheatear, above: cliffs and ravines in SW Europe; NW Africa

(×⅕)

Egyptian Vulture: distribution encircles Mediterranean. Scavenger in open rocky upland and lowland

(×½)

(×⅛)

Black-eared Wheatear: southern Europe, eastern Mediterranean, NW Africa. In dry open country with scattered trees and bushes

Mountain Birds

Some of these species, such as the Snow Finch, are confined to mountain tops. Others may occur in lowland areas which have features, such as cliffs, or cold climate, characteristic of mountains. Thus, the Chough is found on rocky coasts, and the Ptarmigan occurs at sea-level in the Arctic. Vultures, including the Lammergeier, are likely to be seen only in flight.

Griffon Vulture: long, broad wings and short tail. Usually seen soaring, when the wings are raised to form a V. Spain, the Alps, SE Europe

$(\times \tfrac{1}{22})$

$(\times \tfrac{1}{12})$

Black Vulture: Griffon-sized. Always soars with wings horizontal. Spain and SE Europe

Rough-legged Buzzard: has paler underparts than Common Buzzard. Breeds in Scandinavia and winters elsewhere in Europe

$(\times \tfrac{1}{14})$

Lammergeier: now gravely reduced in numbers. Spain, Alps, SE Europe

$(\times \tfrac{1}{11})$

Alpine Chough: yellow beak. Pyrenees, S France, the Alps

$(\times \tfrac{1}{5})$

$(\times \tfrac{1}{3})$

Snow Finch: resembles Snow Bunting, but has a dark (not white) head and different choice of habitat. Basically Alpine but also found in Pyrenees

$(\times \tfrac{1}{6})$

$(\times \tfrac{1}{11})$

$(\times \tfrac{1}{6})$

Chough: a long, red bill UK, Spain, the Alps

Ptarmigan, summer: male behind, and female. Scandinavia, Scotland, Alps

Ptarmigan, autumn and winter: autumn male behind, winter female and male in front

Rock Dove—Feral Pigeon

No other wild pigeon has two thick black stripes on the inner rear half of the wing, or a white rump

Landing

Rock Doves are fast fliers, skilled at gliding freely about cliff faces. To a cliff-top observer they frequently appear as tiny, flickering specks over the sea below. A pure white underwing is the mark of a truly wild Rock Dove, but may be seen on Feral Pigeons

Town, or Feral Pigeons, the domesticated descendants of the Rock Dove, occur in every conceivable plumage variation, from white, through chequered patterns, to black. Their beaks are shorter and stouter than those of Rock Doves. They may be seen feeding in fields with stray racing pigeons

For a pigeon, the Rock Dove has exceptionally pointed primary feathers—visible only on close examination

(× 1/5)

Feral Pigeons associate and breed with the Rock Dove in its natural habitat. True examples of the wild strain probably exist only in the remotest areas

(× 1/3)

Feral Pigeon in plumage phase most similar to that of the Rock Dove

Rock Dove

Feral Pigeons are widespread in cities, towns and villages throughout Britain and Europe. They may also be found in the vicinity of industrial complexes and in a great variety of habitats, including the sea-shore

A Rock Dove habitually perches on sea or inland cliffs, occasionally on buildings, but never in trees

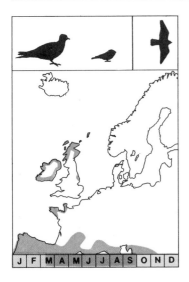

J F M A M J J A S O N D

Trafalgar Square or St Mark's in Venice would be different places without their crowds of Feral Pigeons. These birds are familiar in cities throughout the world, yet to find the Rock Dove—the wild species from which Feral Pigeons are descended—it is necessary to visit remote and wild sea cliffs, or crags, often in desert or arid areas.

Twin requisites for the Rock Dove's habitat are caves in which to nest and open ground on which to feed. Man's activities have greatly increased the supply of both: buildings are excellent substitutes for caves, and deforestation has enormously enlarged the extent of open ground. Domesticated and Feral Pigeons probably originated from wild Rock Doves which nested in buildings early in European history. Various weed seeds, especially those of vetches, are the bird's natural food, but in cultivated areas grain is a major item.

Rock Doves have exceptionally long wings and swift flight—features which, combined with an excellent homing ability, have led to the development of the domesticated racing pigeon. These characteristics probably owe their evolution in part to the Peregrine Falcon, which occurs in the same habitat as the Rock Dove and preys on it extensively.

Rock Doves nest socially on cave ledges, the male bringing twigs, heather or dry seaweed and the female assembling them. Breeding occurs throughout the year, during which three or four broods may be reared.

Wood Pigeon

Swift and capable fliers, as any sportsman knows, Wood Pigeons may be extremely wary birds, but in areas where they are not molested they are often surprisingly tame. When alarmed, these birds burst from cover with much noise

In display flight, the Wood Pigeon rises in an arc, performs wing clapping and glides down on bowed wings. The sound is caused by whiplash effect—not by the wings striking

Perching: note large body and small head

Young pigeons, or squabs, are most unusual-looking creatures with wide, fat bills specially adapted for taking the crop milk fed to them by the adult birds

Above, viewed from behind in display flight, white wing-flashes and pale rump are prominent features

(×⅕)

The small head, held high, is a characteristic seen clearly in silhouette

Prominent in almost every view, the brilliant white wing-flash separates the blue-grey inner wing from the almost black outer

The Wood Pigeon is an impressive bird and the largest member of its family; when standing it has a squat appearance, accentuated by the stout body and unusually small head

Below, the bird takes to the air with a clatter of wings

The striking tail pattern shows most clearly when viewed from below

(×⅓)

On take-off, the wings meet over the back. Tail is spread wide

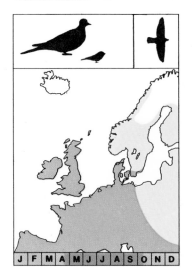

JFMAMJJASOND

Pigeons are unique among birds in producing a special fluid on which to feed their young. Because it is manufactured in the crop, and analogous to the milk produced by mammals, this fluid is known as crop milk, and it has an important influence on the birds' ecology. Many vegetarian birds are dependent on insect food when young, since this is the only diet providing sufficient protein for rapid growth. Consequently, their breeding seasons are fixed to the period of maximum insect abundance in early summer. Crop milk is a perfect substitute for an insect diet, and it emancipates pigeons from this strict seasonality. Consequently, their breeding seasons are spread over several months, though they may be affected by the availability of other food supplies.

Wood Pigeons show a peak of nesting activity and success in late August and September, when grain on recently harvested stubble gives the adult abundant food from which to make crop milk for the young. At one time, the lean winter months following this period inhibited breeding, but increased planting of clover for cattle fodder has expanded the breeding period by providing an abundant new source of winter food. In severe weather, Wood Pigeons may turn to other crops, such as brassicas or legumes, and their depredations at such times may be severe. This has earned them pest status in farming areas, where everyman's hand seems to be against them.

Stock Dove

Stock Doves have white on the outer web of the outer tail feathers

Stock Doves show black wing edging and pale central wing areas, a contrast to the Wood Pigeon

Gliding on slightly raised wings is an aspect of Stock Dove courtship behaviour

Left: even more eye-catching than the palest of pale grey rumps are the blue-grey wings with black borders. Right, the Stock Dove has its particular carriage in flight, probably more distinctive than its swift, dashing action

Among European pigeons, Stock Doves are the only tree hole nesters. They may also use rabbit burrows, cliffs or old buildings

(× 1/5)

(× 1/3)

This species is smaller, narrower winged and narrower tailed than the Wood Pigeon

Adult male in deep bowing display

Unlike an adult Wood Pigeon, the Stock Dove has no white on its neck or wings. It has a vinous breast with patches of iridescent green and two black bars on the inner wing

A juvenile has duller colouring than an adult

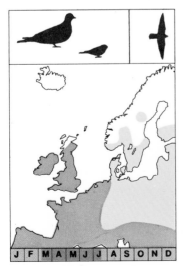

Parkland, with plenty of old timber, is the haunt of the Stock Dove. Such places provide the tree cavities which this hole-nesting pigeon needs for breeding purposes, though it will also resort to sea cliffs or deserted buildings. Unlike its relatives, however, the Stock Dove shows comparatively little tendency to exploit Man's environment. Although occurring regularly on farmland, and ready to add grain to its usual diet of weed seeds, in parks the bird ignores food which Wood and Feral Pigeons readily consume.

Because of their superficial similarity to Wood and Feral Pigeons, and their lack of distinctive field marks, Stock Doves often escape notice. Their presence can always be detected in the breeding season, however, by the cooing song, with its curious, gulping quality. Dead trees containing nest holes are situated close together in some places—a circumstance which often leads to fierce fighting between neighbouring pairs. The nest itself is often almost non-existent, though sometimes a typical pigeon's platform of sticks is built. Most pigeons depart occasionally from the typical clutch of two eggs, and the Stock Dove seems more prone than most to lay three. Two or three broods are usually reared and incubation lasts 16 to 18 days. The young fledge in about three and a half weeks, but may return to roost in the nest hole. Some northern populations of Stock Doves move south in winter.

J F M A M J J A S O N D

115

Turtle Dove

Turtle Doves have a flicking flight action, wings held well back. Before alighting, they reduce speed in a protracted series of distinctive braking movements. Migrating flocks fly at great speed

A male, far left, crooning to the female in a typical display

In display, the Turtle Dove rises with rapidly beating wings, then glides earthwards, often in a circle, wings and tail spread wide

(× ⅕)

Bare branches are much favoured for perching

No other dove has a similar neck pattern, which with the beautiful orange-and-buff-chequered upperparts and white-banded tail makes identification simple

The nest is a flimsy structure of fine sticks

(× ⅓)

White belly, pink breast and blue-grey underwing are exposed when the bird takes off

Chequered upperparts and white-banded tail are conspicuous on landing and take-off

The Turtle Dove's purring song seems to add the final soporific touch to a languid summer's day. Unlike other European pigeons and doves, this species is exclusively a summer visitor, its distribution closely linked with that of fumitory, the plant which is its principal food. Seeds of this and various other herbs make up its diet, and like the Collared Dove, the Turtle Dove will congregate around farm buildings to feed on grain—although the two species are rarely seen in the same farmyard together.

Although the Turtle Dove has the extended breeding season characteristic of pigeons, this has to be cut short in order to moult the flight feathers and build up fuel reserves for migration.

Consequently, although conditions are good for breeding during August, many late broods are deserted. Nests are built nearer the ground—sometimes only three feet high—than those of Wood Pigeons and Collared Doves. Hawthorn, brambles or similar dense cover are the location, and the nest itself is frail in the extreme—a simple platform of twigs and rootlets is typical, but one nest on record was made entirely of wire scraps. In common with all pigeons, the male brings material and the female builds the nest. Two eggs are laid, and both adults incubate. After two weeks they hatch, and the young are fed by both parents during the three-week fledging period.

Collared Dove

Markings vary individually

(×⅕)

Collared Doves look substantial in the air. Flight, superficially resembling the Turtle Dove's, consists of a series of deliberate, far-backward flicks of the broad wings. Considered with the long tail, it eliminates confusion with any other pigeon

Except for the black-and-white tail pattern a Collared Dove is nondescript when seen from below

Below, a juvenile is greyer overall than an adult and has no collar. The television aerial perch is typical of a species highly commensal with Man

In display, far left, the bird rises in the air much like the Turtle Dove and circles slowly with wings fully expanded and tail spread. The tail pattern is very conspicuous

Below, the landing approach is a remarkably hesitant series of checks and starts

Unemphasized colouring makes the upperparts none the less distinctive

(×⅓)

Below, the plumage pattern displayed on landing should be compared with that of the Turtle Dove

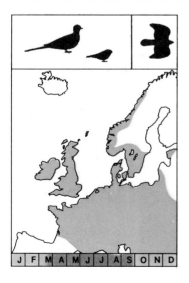

Since about 1930 this species has shown a dramatic expansion of its range, spreading from a foothold in the Balkans to cover most of central and northwestern Europe, including Britain and southern Scandinavia. What triggered it remains uncertain, but it is clear that the species' success is based on close association with Man. It is more timid and wary than Wood or Feral Pigeons, which is surprising in view of the fact that unlike them it is not a severe pest. Suburban gardens with a plentiful scattering of conifers are a favoured habitat, and the birds will also congregate in large numbers near farm buildings when grain is being processed, or on stubble in early autumn.

An additional factor in the Collared Dove's rapid spread must have been its astonishing reproduction rate coupled with low mortality. Pigeons generally have long breeding seasons, but Collared Dove nests can be found in use in any month of the year, even during winter in the north of its range. Four or five, perhaps more, broods may be raised each year, sometimes overlapping, so that a pair may be feeding one brood on crop milk while already incubating the next clutch. The nest is a frail stick platform, usually sited in a conifer. Yews or deciduous trees covered in ivy are also used, and in all such situations the nest can be surprisingly difficult to see, even when a bird is sitting. The dove may reveal its presence by repeatedly flying to the same spot.

J F M A M J J A S O N D

117

Green–Grey-headed Woodpeckers

(× ³/₅)

Adult male Green Woodpecker: the only other greenish woodpecker in Europe is the Grey-headed, which has less red on its crown and less black on its face

Below, an adult male Grey-headed Woodpecker. Compared with the Green Woodpecker this is a very shy bird, tending to remain out of sight behind a tree trunk

A juvenile Grey-headed Woodpecker

(× ³/₅)

Female Grey-headed Woodpecker

Both species have undulating flight paths

(× ¹/₇)

(× ¹/₇)

A Green Woodpecker is most likely to be seen feeding on grass, where it moves in clumsy hops, keeping an almost constant look out for danger by turning the head from side to side between bouts of pecking. Below: juvenile Green Woodpecker

Female Green Woodpecker

The Green Woodpecker's bright yellow rump is an unmistakable feature

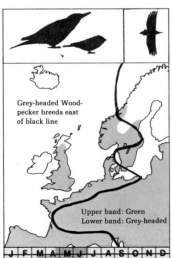

Grey-headed Woodpecker breeds east of black line

Upper band: Green
Lower band: Grey-headed

J F M A M J J A S O N D

Woodpeckers are known for their long tongues, a valuable adaptation by which the birds can feed on ants by probing the holes and passages of ant-hills or rotten wood. Green Woodpeckers have longer tongues, and a fondness for ants which brings them to feed on the ground more often than any other member of their family—they frequently visit lawns and playing fields. A mixture of old timber and open ground—typified by parkland—provides a favoured habitat, although almost any deciduous wood may prove suitable. Green Woodpeckers "drum" less than other woodpeckers, but have an extensive vocal repertoire.

Trees chosen for nesting are usually externally sound but rotten inside, and both sexes excavate the nest hole, which has a horizontal entrance tunnel and vertical shaft leading to the chamber itself. Five to seven eggs are laid on the wood chips which cover the floor. Both parents share the task of incubation, which lasts 18 to 19 days, and both feed the young. Many birds are evicted by Starlings.

The Grey-headed Woodpecker is closely related to the Green, and its habits are very similar. Although less widely distributed in Europe, its total range is much wider and it is at present spreading westwards. Habitats chosen include some mountainous terrain which the Green Woodpecker ignores, and the species also shows greater tolerance of coniferous woodland.

Black Woodpecker

Black Woodpecker flight looks not unlike that of the Jay. The bird's size is always striking: drawn to the same scale, far right, is a Lesser Spotted Woodpecker

Seen from below, a woodpecker is distinguishable from a Crow by its profile: head and tail project equal distances front and behind

The female has a small red patch on the back of her head, the male an all-red crown

The pale eye is startlingly prominent

($\times \frac{1}{3}$)

This species drums loud and often

($\times \frac{1}{6}$)

A Black Woodpecker climbs with its toes splayed out wide, more in the manner of a passerine than of a typical woodpecker

Below, when threatened, the bird performs a territory-marking display at the foot of its tree in a manner unique among woodpeckers

If a nest hole looks large for the tree, it is likely to be a Black Woodpecker's

There is no confusing this bird, the largest of the woodpeckers: it is as big as a Crow, and the simple contrast of scarlet and black makes it as easy to glimpse as to recognize. The bird is additionally distinctive in its manner of holding its head right back while poised to hammer

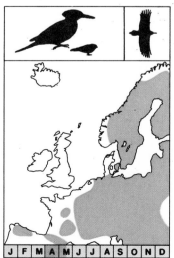

Stately plumage of scarlet and black, and large size, make the Black Woodpecker an imposing bird. Its habitat must include tall trees, of which conifers or beech are preferred. From the primary choice of mountain forest, the species has recently extended its range to include lowland areas in central Europe. Ants and other insects are the main food.

Black Woodpeckers, like the rest of their family, are strongly territorial, using "drumming" as a means of advertising territory during spring. This sound, audible for a considerable distance, is produced by a series of extremely rapid blows of the beak against a tree. It should not be confused with the normal feeding or nest-building noises of this and other woodpeckers, in which powerful blows are struck at intervals often several seconds apart. Occasionally, "drumming" is performed inside the nest cavity.

Perfectly healthy trees may be selected as nest sites. The task of excavation is undertaken by both sexes, and few holes are much lower than 20 feet from the ground. The cavity may be up to two feet deep. Four to six eggs are laid—incubation and feeding the young being carried out by both male and female. The eggs hatch after 12 to 14 days, and the young leave at 24 to 28 days. Jackdaws seeking nest holes often evict Black Woodpeckers, which is surprising in view of the latter's size and strength.

Great Spotted Woodpecker

Viewed from behind, the white shoulder-patches are an eyecatching feature

Flight is undulating—a series of rapid wing beats followed by momentary closure of the wings at the bottom of each dip

An adult male Great Spotted Woodpecker, left, has a conspicuous red patch on the nape. The female has not

$(\times\,^3/_5)$

$(\times\,^3/_{10})$

The Great Spotted Woodpecker is easily distinguished from the Lesser Spotted Woodpecker either by its white shoulder-patches or by the brilliant red of the under-tail coverts. This is a large, vigorous bird, with quite an aggressive manner and an explosive call which matches its personality. On a tree trunk it hops rather than climbs, working from side to side

An upwards swoop lands the woodpecker in its usual vertical stance on the branch of a tree

A young male shows only a small amount of red under his tail, but the red nape-patch is visible

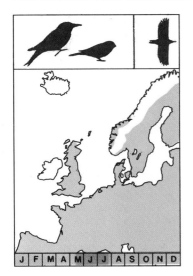

A feeding woodpecker sounds as if it is just tapping: in fact, the bird is hammering at the tree trunk with extreme force. A glimpse of the damage done always raises the question of how the bird's own physique can absorb the punishment of such blows. Study of head anatomy shows that the answer lies mainly in the design of the upper jaw, which normally would transmit the shock of the blows to the braincase. This shock is effectively cushioned by the action of the muscle which raises the upper jaw, and which is highly developed in woodpeckers. The Great Spotted Woodpecker is a highly effective hammerer: it not only exposes the tunnels of wood-boring insects, but also extracts seeds from pine and spruce cones during winter. The cones are wedged into crevices in tree trunks before hammering; oak-galls, containing the larvae of gall-wasps, may be treated in the same way. Bird-lovers who put up nestboxes in woodland may from time to time regret the Great Spotted Woodpecker's efficiency when it hews the boxes open to extract and eat eggs or young. Nevertheless, the bird is welcome at many bird-tables.

The Great Spotted Woodpecker's own nest is most often made in decaying tree trunks, either in deciduous or coniferous woodland. Four to seven eggs are laid, and both parents incubate them for 16 days. About three weeks are required for fledging to be completed.

Lesser Spotted Woodpecker

In spring, the male Lesser Spotted Woodpecker performs a "moth" display flight, floating from tree to tree, wings fully spread. He may also "parachute" from the top of a tree, displaying his upperwing markings to the female above

The Lesser Spotted Woodpecker's flight has the same undulating motion as the Great Spotted Woodpecker's

This species can be instantly distinguished from the Great Spotted Woodpecker because it lacks the latter's conspicuous white shoulder-patches

A tiny, sparrow-sized woodpecker, whose markings fully explain the species' former name of Barred Woodpecker. As well as its obvious plumage differences, the Lesser Spotted's head shape contrasts with that of the Great Spotted, and so do the proportions of its beak. Its character has an elf-like quality very different to the aggressive masculinity of the Great Spotted Woodpecker

(× ³/₁₀)

(× ³/₅)

Below, the female Lesser Spotted Woodpecker has a white crown

A juvenile lacks any trace of red. The face is dun coloured and the rest of its plumage resembles the adult's

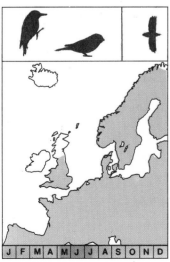

This tiny woodpecker finds its living mainly among the smaller dead twigs and branches of trees, rather than on the main trunks and boughs frequented by its larger relatives. Various types of woodland or parkland suit it, and it frequently occurs in old orchards. Insects make up most of the diet, particularly larvae of wood-boring beetles and wasps. Because it spends much of its time high among the smaller branches of trees, the bird is often overlooked, but the call may betray it—a shrill, repeated note rather like that of the Wryneck. Despite small size, the Lesser Spotted Woodpecker drums loudly and extremely rapidly—the frequency is 14 to 15 blows per second compared with the Great Spotted Woodpecker's

eight to ten. In common with several other woodpeckers, a display flight is performed by the male in spring. He may fly from tree to tree with slow flaps, or float down to the female's vicinity on trembling wings.

Nest holes are often in quite narrow branches, frequently on the underside of a sloping limb anywhere between near ground level and 80 feet. Soft decayed wood is usually selected, and with such a small entrance hole the nest can be confused with that of a Willow Tit. Four to six eggs are usually laid, and the two-week incubation is performed by male and female. Both also feed the young; they become extremely noisy once old enough to compete for food at the entrance hole.

J F M A M J J A S O N D

121

Hoopoe

Plumage is similar on the male, female and juvenile Hoopoe

On many Hoopoes the pink plumage is washed with grey. The black feathers always fade to dark brown by autumn

As exotic in its manner of flight as in appearance, the Hoopoe proceeds in a series of flicking jerks, the wings not often rising above the horizontal. This bouncing motion may be interrupted by abrupt changes of direction, of which the bird is a master

A dazzling effect is produced by the Hoopoe's flight action combined with the white barring on the back, and these may have developed for the purpose of confusing avian predators

The crest is raised when the bird lands, but also with great frequency at all other times, including flight

(× ³/₁₀)

(× ³/₅)

When feeding quietly in a field this species can be surprisingly inconspicuous. Often it will only reveal itself when spreading its wings to fly

On a perching Hoopoe the tail is conspicuously long—but in flight it appears short in comparison with the exceptional breadth of the wings

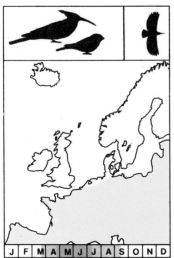

J F M A M J J A S O N D

Many birds have been loosely described as unmistakable, but, with its erectile crest, black-and-white-barred wings and long decurved bill, few can deserve the epithet more than the Hoopoe.

The decurved bill gives some clue to the bird's feeding habits. Although some of its prey (including such large creatures as mole crickets and even scorpions) is captured on the surface, the Hoopoe also obtains food by probing. Skull and jaw muscles show adaptations enabling the bill to be opened with considerable force against the resistance of the ground, and it is probably by excavation of this type that the insect larvae which predominate in its diet are found. The call, a far-carrying "oop . . oop . . oop", is uttered normally from the ground, with head lowered and neck distended.

Courtship displays often involve false feeding of the female by the male. Cavities in trees or among rocks are selected as sites for the nest, which usually has no lining. The birds make no attempt at nest sanitation: the combined effect of accumulated droppings and the Hoopoe's own distinctive smell creates a peculiarly unpleasant odour. Five to eight eggs are laid, quickly becoming stained by the mess. The female incubates, fed on the nest by her mate; hatching takes place after 16 to 19 days. At first only the male brings food while the female broods the young, but soon both birds are feeding their offspring.

Magpie

Magpies have beaks typical of the crow family to which they belong. The head is a matt velvet, rather than glossy black as with other crows

Gliding attitude

A young bird, below right, quits the nest with a short tail still growing

The long, bright green tail often appears almost black in the field

(×1/10)

Pied plumage, short, rounded wings and a long, wedge-shaped tail all make the magpie unmistakable. The underwing pattern is very different to that seen from above. Below, the black wing feathers show varied, iridescent sheens of blue

(×1/5)

The tail is sometimes partly opened in flight

Even in midwinter, when most other birds' nests have worn ragged, the Magpie's retains its conspicuous spherical shape. Formed of a cup made from thorny twigs, sheltered by a dome of similar material, the whole structure is larger than a football

Magpies eat any food, from insects and grain found on the ground to carrion, or even young birds taken in flight

Above right, Magpies are expert at locating other birds' nests, and frequently rob them

J F M A M J J A S O N D

An unmistakable and familiar bird with a flight as distinctive as its plumage – the long tail showing clearly, the short, rounded wings beating a few times between swooping glides. When socially or sexually excited, the Magpie's plumage is fluffed out, showing much white; a frightened bird shifts the emphasis to black by sleeking its feathers down. Always alert to danger, Magpies are happy to be viewed from a moving car, but vanish if it stops.

Magpies are notorious as predators of eggs and young birds. Pairs can often be seen working along hedgerows or woodland edge to the accompanying scolding of smaller birds. Otherwise predominantly ground feeders, and, like most crows, omnivorous, they show inquisitive interest in bright objects – hence the tales of "thieving Magpies".

The nest is built by both sexes and holds four to eight eggs, incubated only by the female, who is fed by her mate. It is impregnable to most predators, but Carrion Crows often attempt raids. In southern Europe, Magpies are parasitized by the Great Spotted Cuckoo.

Magpies walk energetically, tail slightly elevated, or hop for extra speed. In winter they can be seen foraging in small groups, though in places there are large communal roosts. In spring, they gather in social assemblies, where unpaired birds can find mates: it is here that individuals can be seen showing off the iridescent wing and tail feathers.

Nutcracker

(×¹⁄₁₀)

Seen from below, the Nutcracker has a unique, broad-winged, short-tailed outline. The white triangle of the undertail coverts is very conspicuous, as is the white terminal tail-band

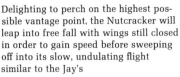 

Delighting to perch on the highest possible vantage point, the Nutcracker will leap into free fall with wings still closed in order to gain speed before sweeping off into its slow, undulating flight similar to the Jay's

A long "stabber" beak (it can and will be used to kill House Sparrows) contributes to the Nutcracker's general resemblance to a crow

(×¹⁄₅)

Front and back, the Nutcracker's plumage is heavily spotted. The white terminal band is visible on the upper- and on the undertail

Northerly distribution means that although the Nutcracker breeds in May, there are many years when it is obliged to incubate in a nest piled with snow

 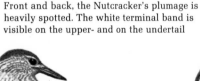

Under the beak there is a food pouch, used in autumn while collecting food for storage

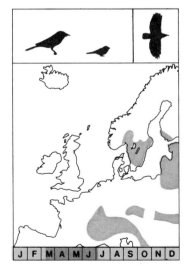

Pine seeds rather than nuts are the principal food of the Nutcracker, which provides an interesting parallel with that other pine cone specialist, the Crossbill. Both species nest early in the year, allowing the young plenty of time before the hardships of winter to gain experience in the highly skilled process of extracting pine seeds. Both have also evolved specialized means of coping with such a difficult food source, but their strategies are different. Crossbills are masters at opening even tightly closed cones with speed and efficiency; because of this, they have no difficulty feeding their young on the food available during their fledging period. Nutcrackers deal with the problem by storing food from the previous season

for use during the breeding cycle – a unique habit, because other food-storing birds consume their hoards during winter. To enable them to do this, Nutcrackers have large pouches in the floor of the mouth in which pine seeds can be kept as they are extracted, leaving the bill free to hammer and pry at the cone for more. A final similarity is that Nutcrackers, like Crossbills, show population fluctuations and periodic irruptions linked with the vagaries of the cone crop. Central European have thicker beaks than Scandinavian birds.

The Nutcracker's nest of twigs and earth is placed on a pine tree branch. Three eggs are laid, and incubated by the female for 18 days.

124

Jay

The extent of a Jay's wing beat is from just above the horizontal to well below it

One Jay flapping out of a wood after another is likely to be following it, even when the two are separated by a distance

A Jay's crest goes through bouts of constant motion, which vividly express the bird's mood and contribute to its wide variety of facial expressions. Under the lower mandible there is a food pouch

The familiar blue wing feathers are encountered in a number of human contexts, from headgear to anglers' artificial flies

Jays fly with jerky, flapping movements, sometimes at a considerable height

The most common view of a Jay is as it flies off. The most prominent feature of the bird's distinctive plumage is the white rump against a black tail, but the rows of thin white wing patches are also conspicuous

$(\times \frac{1}{5})$

There are slight local differences in plumage colour across Europe, some races having greyish backs, but the basic pattern is constant

The submissive posture – adopted by male or female

Attitude of bird taking off. Jays look clumsy, but they can twist through trees with great agility. The white rump shows clearly when the bird perches

On the ground, Jays tend to move with jerky, often sideways, hops. They will bury acorns, or other food, frequently by roadsides

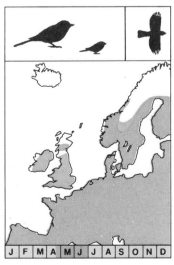

The oak trees which dominate so many European forests are in debt to the Jay, for it expends much effort during autumn in collecting and burying acorns for later consumption. Although the bird shows a remarkable memory for the places where it has buried them, inevitably a few are missed, and new oak trees start life in places they could otherwise never have reached. The burying process is carried out by excavating a hole in the ground with the bill, disgorging the acorn into it and covering it up. Apart from acorns, Jays take a great variety of animal and vegetable food, and their liking for the eggs of other birds sometimes makes them unpopular.

Heard at close quarters the familiar harsh screech of the Jay is almost deafening, but the bird also has a varied repertoire of other calls, and of postures, denoting subtle differences in emotional state. Excited gatherings of up to twenty birds may be seen in spring, with males displaying to females by turning the body sideways, raising crest and body feathers, and revealing the white and chestnut wing patches.

The nest, built of twigs with a lining of roots, is sited in a young tree or bush, not usually higher than 20 feet. The usual clutch is five eggs, which have a surprising similarity to those of the Blackbird in colour and size, although the Jay is not a nest parasite. Incubation is by the female alone.

Rook

Rook

Crow

Examination of a dead bird reveals differences between Rook and crow in the pattern of folded primary wing feathers. In flight, Rooks are set apart by the wedge-shaped tail. Below, flocks perform aerobatics near a rookery, an exhilarating sight on a blustery March or autumn day

Silhouette of the flapping flight—head held well forward and narrower wings than the crow ($\times \frac{1}{10}$)

Right, typical perching profiles

The Rook's usual flying attitudes, top. Compare with the squarer outline of the Carrion Crow, beneath

Calling in flight, accompanied by deliberate flaps of the wings

Bow-winged appearance of approaching bird

($\times \frac{1}{5}$)

The adult rook's whitish face and nearly straight-sided beak, centre, are unmistakable. Confusion can arise between the Carrion Crow, above, and an immature rook, below

Rear view of descent

Rooks have "shaggy trousers" where the legs join the body. Right, a displaying male. He bows to the female and calls vigorously

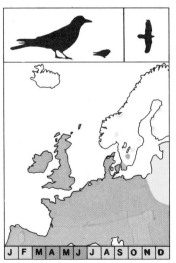

The noise that surrounds a rookery is as much a part of our villages and farmland as the sight of their bulky twig nests grouped in tall trees. Breeding starts in February or March, when the supply of large earthworms is at a maximum. Using binoculars, the display, the inevitable family squabbles and thieving of sticks from neighbours' nests can be easily observed. Most rookeries are from a handful to a hundred or so nests, but in Scotland several hundred, even two thousand nests may occur in a single rookery. During October, Rooks return to the rookeries in a brief resurgence of breeding activity, quickly extinguished by the dwindling number of daylight hours.

The Rook is widespread across cen-

tral and northern Europe, shunning places where trees are few or absent. Rook numbers in Britain increased between the wars, and a late 1940s survey showed a density of 35 birds per square mile. The latest survey, however, shows a sharp decrease in the population, the cause of which is still being investigated. Rooks are scarce in urban areas, unlike the Carrion Crow, which sometimes nests in the centre of major cities.

Always gregarious, Rooks often feed in mixed flocks with Jackdaws, and in winter the two species assemble in communal roosts. In Britain and France, winter numbers are swelled by migrants from central Europe. Rooks feed on grain and other vegetable matter.

Jackdaw

(× ⅒)

Flight profile shows rather pointed wings held slightly back

Soaring, the bird extends wing and tail feathers to their maximum spread

Flocks are often seen near ruins, cliff faces and large buildings, where they drop large quantities of nesting material

Jackdaws are superb flyers and play spectacular aerial games, especially around buildings or cliff faces

Adult

(× ⅕)

Head of adult with pale eye, glossy blue crown and grey nape, which is displayed at opponents as a submissive gesture

Pair at nest hole in tree – a typical situation

The head feathers are frequently erected

Small flocks are common

Normal flight is rather hurried, with wings beating mostly below the horizontal

Birds search along rooftops and gardens for food

A juvenile is blue-eyed and has a dark nape

Left, a bird with food in throat pouch. Jackdaws often nest in chimney flues

Jackdaws are smaller than Rooks

The Jackdaw is well entrenched in European folklore and literature. Not only does it frequently nest in buildings, but it makes an intelligent and interesting pet, and shares with some other crows a liking for bright objects — hence such tales as the Jackdaw of Reims. Like many species that nest in colonies, it has an elaborate system of communication by postures and calls, and these have been the subject of intensive study, which has revealed that a large proportion of the Jackdaw's social signals are learned, rather than inborn.

Natural nest sites are either cavities in groups of large old trees, or holes in cliffs. Buildings often provide suitable sites, and Jackdaws frequently create a nuisance by blocking chimneys. The nest is a heap of twigs lined with grass and other scraps, and huge amounts of such materials accumulate in traditional sites. Four to six eggs are laid, paler in colour than those of other crows — an adaptation to the dim light of the nest cavity.

Both sexes bring food, carried in the throat, though at first this task is performed mainly by the female. The fledging period is 30 to 35 days. Jackdaws have the same omnivorous diet as other crows, and are often seen foraging on rubbish tips. Outside the breeding season, they frequently flock with Rooks, their clucking calls standing out clearly from the harsh caws of their larger relatives.

127

Raven

($\times \frac{1}{10}$)

Soaring profile shows
slightly drooping wings

Out of breeding sea-
son, groups may
gather to soar, wheel
and perform aerobatics

Overhead, Ravens can be reliably identified by
their massive size, "fingered" wings, heavy head
and especially the wedge-shaped tail

Ravens have more pointed wings
than crows, and this is especially evident when they are soaring.
Relatively, their heads also
project farther forwards

Ravens are masters at using
the upcurrents around their
cliff nesting sites for
superb aerobatic displays

Profile of travelling flight,
in which the wingbeat
is strong and purposeful

The sedate walk,
a typical ground
posture. Note the
powerful feet

($\times \frac{1}{5}$)

A heavy head, massive beak and bristling
throat feathers, giving the bearded look, all
set the Raven apart at close quarters

Drooping wing attitude,
far right, often adopted
when the bird is hopping

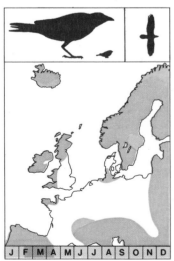

J F M A M J J A S O N D

Impressive and sinister in its usual setting of crags and mountains, intelligent
and amusing in captivity, the Raven
figures prominently in history and folklore. The deep guttural call enhances its
aura of menace and instantly confirms
visual identification. Carrion bulks
large in its diet, and Norse sagas record
Ravens in attendance at battles of the
Viking era: huge gatherings can still be
seen at whale strandings. Other food
includes small mammals, such as frogs,
eggs, insects and vegetable matter.

Nesting is early. Building may commence in mid-winter in England, and
the clutch of four to six is laid in
February. Deep blue-green with brown
freckles, the eggs closely resemble
those of the Rook and Carrion Crow.

The young are fed by both parents, at
first with insects, but soon with pieces
of meat. The food is often moistened,
and a captive breeding female is recorded cooling her young by wetting
her underparts before brooding. They
fledge at five to six weeks.

Amenability to captivity has permitted detailed studies of the Raven's
behaviour. Signals used in courtship
and threat involve ruffling the neck
feathers, stretching, bowing and holding wings out from the body, but actions
are less stereotyped than in many birds,
conveying a wider, more subtle range of
information. An extensive sound vocabulary is also used. Ravens are gregarious where common, and often form
large communal roosts.

Carrion Crow—Hooded Crow

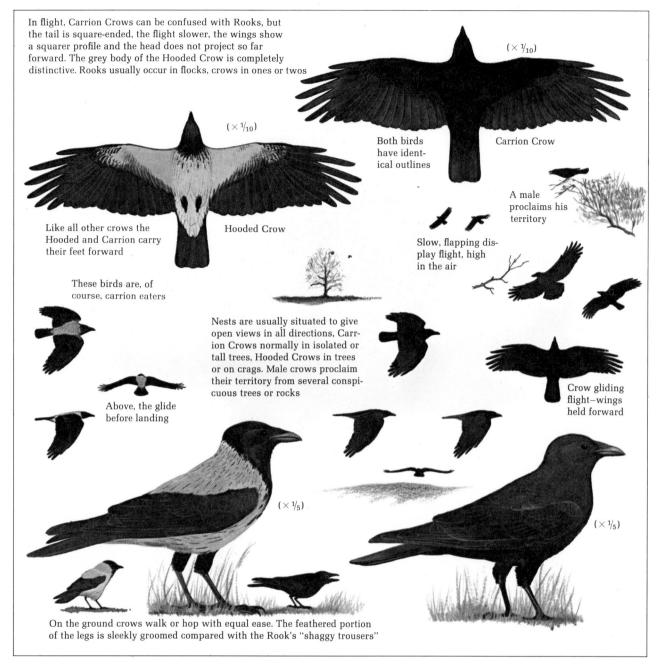

In flight, Carrion Crows can be confused with Rooks, but the tail is square-ended, the flight slower, the wings show a squarer profile and the head does not project so far forward. The grey body of the Hooded Crow is completely distinctive. Rooks usually occur in flocks, crows in ones or twos

(×¹⁄₁₀)

(×¹⁄₁₀)

Both birds have identical outlines

Carrion Crow

A male proclaims his territory

Like all other crows the Hooded and Carrion carry their feet forward

Hooded Crow

Slow, flapping display flight, high in the air

These birds are, of course, carrion eaters

Nests are usually situated to give open views in all directions, Carrion Crows normally in isolated or tall trees, Hooded Crows in trees or on crags. Male crows proclaim their territory from several conspicuous trees or rocks

Above, the glide before landing

Crow gliding flight—wings held forward

(×¹⁄₅)

(×¹⁄₅)

On the ground crows walk or hop with equal ease. The feathered portion of the legs is sleekly groomed compared with the Rook's "shaggy trousers"

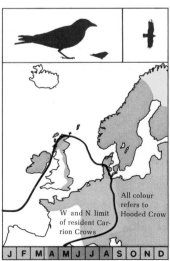

All colour refers to Hooded Crow

W and N limit of resident Carrion Crows

J F M A M J J A S O N D

Crows are usually solitary or operate in pairs—the birds often co-operating to steal food from other predators—even taking fish from Herons. One bird will hop quickly about in front of the Heron, distracting its attention, while the other attempts to sneak the fish from behind.

The diet resembles the Rook's, including earthworms, ground insects and grain, but in spring and summer especially, eggs, young birds and small mammals. Preying on game-birds has earned crows an evil reputation with gamekeepers. Shooting and poisoning have failed to control their numbers, and while other predators have declined, Britain's crow population has increased in recent years. Crows have

successfully invaded urban areas, perhaps aided by an ability to scavenge on rubbish tips and open spaces.

Less dependent on earthworms to feed their young than the Rook, crows breed about two weeks later. The solitary nest resembles the Rook's, but is often placed much lower, sometimes on the ground. Three or four eggs are laid.

Most crows are resident, but many Hooded Crows from the North move south in winter, occasionally reaching eastern England. The Hooded Crow occurs in Ireland, northern Scotland, Scandinavia and eastern Europe. The Carrion Crow is the bird of lowland Britain and southern and central Europe; hybrids occur in a narrow zone of overlap.

129

Corncrake chicks are jet black (×⅓)

Typical Corncrake profile, left; body held almost parallel to ground

(×⅙)

The Corncrake's fluttering flight appears very weak and the birds quite commonly strike overhead power cables when flying at night

The Corncrake is a skulking, elusive bird, and often very difficult to flush from cover; it has an astonishing ability to vanish in even the thinnest of cover

Male aggression, above and below; calling with wings open and drooped

Corncrake departs with fluttering flight, legs trailing untidily

Adult female

Adult male

(×⅓)

Quail invariably give the impression of very fast "buzzing" flight quite unlike the rapid beats and interspersed glides of most game-birds; the long, rather narrow wings resemble those of a wader. The birds commonly migrate at night

(×⅙)

Front and side views of the male Quail's head, below, show the very distinctive plumage pattern

Quail, above, are diminutive birds with dappled brown upper plumage very similar to the Partridge

During migration, Quail may be seen to rise suddenly from the most meagre cover or even from bare ground, where they walk about in a manner very like the Partridge. In breeding areas the birds are extremely difficult to flush unless dogs are used

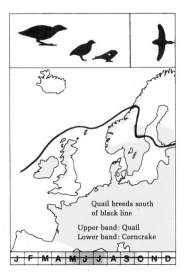

Quail breeds south of black line

Upper band: Quail
Lower band: Corncrake

J F M A M J J A S O N D

Astonishing dexterity at slipping through cover on foot frustrates most attempts to observe the Quail. Nevertheless, its call of "wet-my-lips" is still familiar in many parts of Europe, and immediately recognizable among the bird imitations in Beethoven's Pastoral Symphony.

In its winter quarters, this migratory game-bird occurs in sufficient numbers to rank as a major sporting target, while the Far Eastern race, domesticated in Japan, has achieved the doubtful distinction of use as a laboratory animal. The nest is exceptionally difficult to find, and probably many breeding occurrences go unrecorded; it is simply a scrape with a sparse lining amongst grass, cereal or vegetable crops, in which are laid seven to 12 eggs. Incubation by the female lasts 16 to 21 days and the young can fly by their nineteenth day.

The Corncrake—a rail—is not related to the Quail, but the two have much in common: they are skulking, meadow birds, known best by their calls, and gravely reduced in numbers by modern mowing methods. Breeding Corncrakes announce their presence by a rasping call, such as might be produced by dragging a stick across a comb. Their nests are made in sheltered hollows in clumps of grass or other plants, lined with grass stems. Eight to 12 eggs are laid, and the female incubates them for 14 to 21 days. Young Corncrakes are fully fledged at seven or eight weeks.

Red Grouse—Willow Grouse

Above, the grouse has a characteristic head-high, puff-breasted attitude viewed in flight

Red Grouse drawn to the same scale as the Common Partridge

(×1/6)

Seen from beneath, the Red Grouse's striking white underwing contrasts with the dark red belly plumage

The Red Grouse's dark tail is very evident on take-off

One of the most familiar birds of open moorland, the Red Grouse rises with a whirring sound, often calling loudly. Bursts of rapid wing beats are followed by long glides—the bird sometimes rolling from side to side. Parties may fly low at great speed, following the ground contours

The Norwegian coastal race of Willow Grouse has an unusual intermediate plumage colour

Willow Grouse in autumn plumage

Adult Willow Grouse in full summer plumage

Willow Grouse in winter plumage

Willow Grouse in summer: shape identical to Red Grouse but Willow has white wings in summer, partly white body in autumn, pure white in winter

(×1/4)

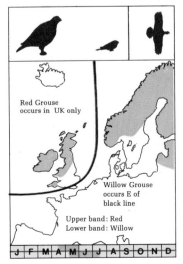

Red Grouse occurs in UK only

Willow Grouse occurs E of black line

Upper band: Red
Lower band: Willow

J F M A M J J A S O N D

Red Grouse and Willow Grouse belong to the same species, and are found in northern latitudes of the Old and New Worlds. Britain and Ireland are the home of the two races known as Red Grouse, which are distinguished by uniform red-brown coloration in summer and winter. All other races are known as Willow Grouse, and have white wings in summer and almost completely white plumage in winter.

Because grouse shooting in Britain is a highly organized sport, these birds have been intensively studied. Red Grouse feed mainly on young heather shoots, of which grouse-moor owners ensure a constant supply by regular burning. Willow Grouse live in a more natural environment, where they feed principally on birch and willow buds and to a small extent on heather.

Both Red and Willow Grouse are monogamous. Males stake territories in early autumn by means of display flights and much loud crowing. Pairs remain together until they have reared their young the following summer. Cocks which fail to gain territories, and most hens which fail to find a mate, wander into poorer habitats during the winter and die. Weakened by starvation, these birds often show a heavy infestation by internal parasites, which were once thought to cause the deaths. It is now understood that such birds are a doomed surplus, and that habitat condition is the main factor controlling the size of the population.

131

Black Grouse

In flight, the male Black Grouse is an impressive bird, its glossy black plumage set off by huge white wing-bars. The enormous lyre-shaped tail is quite unlike that of any other British bird

Usually seen in its open moorland habitat, the Black Grouse has the typical flight of a game-bird—rapid beats on stiffly held wings interspersed with long glides. The Black Grouse generally flies higher, and glides more, than the Red Grouse

Black Grouse commonly circle immediately after take-off and also before landing

Male

Female

(× 1/7)

Birds are often flushed from cover along woodland margins, particularly those at the edge of marsh or moorland. Plantation forest has extended the bird's range

The female is commonly known as a greyhen—a misnomer as her plumage is richly marked reddish-brown with two pale wing-bars. The male is also widely called the blackcock, and in some areas both male and female are called black game

Male

Female

Both male and female display their striking white underwing pattern when rising. The female should be compared with the similar Red Grouse

The male grouse has one of the most spectacular of courtship displays. Seen from behind, the tail is raised and spread—lyre tips almost touching the ground—while the under-tail coverts show as a great billowing white patch. The wings are drooped low and the red combs are expanded

Grouse often perch on trees, walls or fences

Rear view of the displaying male

Greyhen at lek

Wings drooped, combs expanded

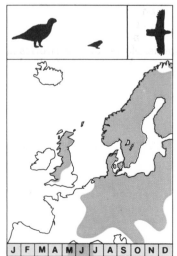

Black Grouse differ sharply from Red and Willow Grouse in their social arrangements. Like the Capercaillie and several North American grouse, they have abandoned the pairing system in favour of one in which males and females meet only for the purpose of mating, and the tasks of incubating eggs and rearing the young are carried out by the females alone.

Courtship and mating take place at a communal display ground called a lek, maintained over a long period. On it, up to 20 males defend small territories against their rivals by means of an impressive threat display accompanied by extraordinary noises—crowing, hissing and a bubbling call which can be heard two miles away. Performances like this are mainly confined to the early hours of the morning, and occur throughout much of the year. Central positions in the lek are held by older birds, and these dominant individuals achieve greatest success in mating with the dull-coloured hens who visit in small parties during spring. Although the hens make many visits to the lek, most will only mate once, and shortly after commence their domestic duties.

Black Grouse inhabit moorland areas, particularly near the edges of forests or cultivation. The nest is a simple scrape amongst rushes, heather or other thick vegetation. Six to ten eggs are laid, incubation lasts 24 to 29 days, and the young can fly well before they are fully grown.

Capercaillie

Female

Capercaillies are shatteringly noisy when leaving trees, but silent in flight. Below, males usually hold their heads well forward in flight, and the "beard" is evident

Either sex may feed in a pine tree, especially in winter, when the female, right, often roosts about ten feet from the ground

(× 1/7)

Above and below, the female. Her striking rufous tail, deep orange breast and white patches on the underwing are visible at long range, where her upperparts look grey

Left, an adult or juvenile female—both look similar. These are enormous, turkey-sized birds: close-to, even females are a striking size. Below, when anxious a Capercaillie raises its crown feathers and distends its throat. The birds tend to hold their heads high

Left, the male's incomparable song display. His body swells; the throat distends; at intervals he leaps some three feet in the air noisily flapping his wings. Below, two white spots are conspicuous in front view

(× 1/7)

(× 1/7)

At any season, Capercaillies are seen on the ground in thick woods or on open country. They flush when the intruder is about 30 feet away

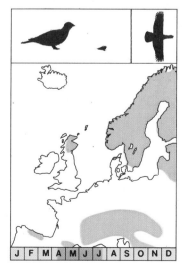

Capercaillies share with a few other large birds the ability to successfully intimidate human beings. Displaying males intent on defending their territory are occasionally aggressive enough to threaten intruders of any size, and have even been known to attack a moving vehicle, with fatal results for themselves. Spread tail and inflated throat feathers give the birds an impressive appearance, and their antics are accompanied by bizarre vocalizations—a succession of clopping noises like a horse, ending with a loud pop and a wheeze.

Exclusively birds of coniferous forests, Capercaillies are found in Scandinavia, central Europe and the Pyrenees. They were exterminated in Scotland by a combination of forest clearance and hunting during the eighteenth century, but birds from Sweden were reintroduced in 1837 and on several subsequent occasions in the nineteenth century. These now flourish, existing, as everywhere, on their unusual diet of pine shoots. This is an almost exclusive diet, and lends their flesh a resinous tang—which has not prevented them from being regularly hunted in many parts of their range.

Female Capercaillies are beautifully camouflaged to match the forest floor on which they nest. Although the nests are solitary, several may be situated in the vicinity of the male's display ground. Young Capercaillies can flutter short distances when about three weeks old, long before they are fully grown.

133

Pheasant

At distances where plumage is indistinct, a hen Pheasant is told from the cock by her shorter tail

The whirring ascent of a bird just flushed is followed, at sufficient height, by a glide. Normal flight is alternate flapping and gliding. One bird is recorded as having flown four miles (over water)—probably the maximum for sustained flight. The "kor .. kork" of the cock is an all-purpose call, uttered not only in alarm

Left, high-flying birds, a phenomenon of the organized shoot. Pheasants generally fly at low level

To clear trees, a Pheasant can rise almost perpendicularly

Common plumage variations, including the dark green

A hen Pheasant's tail is shorter than a cock's, but shorter still is that of a juvenile or moulting bird

($\times\frac{1}{6}$)

The cock is the only long-tailed game-bird. There are two main races of Pheasant in Europe, one with, one without the white collar

($\times\frac{1}{6}$)

Pheasants are not simply birds of wooded farmland; they occur on country as open as fens or on reed-beds and coastal saltings. They are partial to roosting over water. When flushed, Pheasants prefer to run for cover

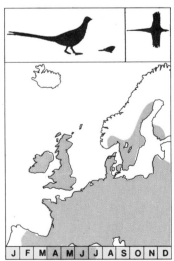

J F M A M J J A S O N D

Pheasants are unnerving—even to country people—when they explode under the feet with a whirr of wings and a loud crowing. Like most other game-birds, they are capable of rapid acceleration in the air, and can climb steeply to clear trees or bushes, but they lack the stamina for sustained flight. Muscles with this capacity for a high but short-lived rate of work happen to be good eating: and the sporting challenge provided by such a fast-moving target has of course made this family the shooter's ultimate bird.

Introductions of Pheasants to western Europe started early. Their origins are east of Europe, but with human aid they spread through the Continent and reached Britain during Roman times.

During the present century, Pheasants have been established in North America and New Zealand.

In spring, Pheasants like to eat young shoots of grass and cereals, but during the summer change to a diet of grain and other seeds, supplemented by some animal food. In winter, berries, acorns and beech mast are important items. Although many Pheasants are reared in captivity in order to boost natural stocks, they breed freely in suitable wild areas. Nests are scrapes with a scanty lining of vegetation and a few feathers, placed amongst undergrowth in a copse or wood edge. The young can fly weakly after two weeks, but thousands are killed by cars in the first two months of life.

Partridge—Red-legged Partridge

Reddish tail and buff, well-marked plumage distinguish the Partridge

Partridges are sociable by nature, often feeding in large groups. Tend to run, or walk, away rather than fly if intruders appear

Birds rise abruptly on take-off, often calling loudly, then fly low and fast over the ground. Flight is never prolonged—always consisting of short fast bursts and glides

(×1/6)

(×1/4)

Typical view of bird feeding in field

Above, the covey, or group, stays together even when flushed

Below, upright posture of alert birds; below right, more rounded when relaxed

Male Partridge has orange head, grey breast and horseshoe mark on belly; all pale or absent on hen

Red-legged Partridge in flight

(×1/6)

(×1/4)

Distinguished in flight by plain olive-brown upper-plumage—unlike the mottled light brown of the Common Partridge

Juvenile Red-legged Partridge is duller in plumage and lacks barring characteristic of the adult

Juvenile

Adult male Red-legged Partridge

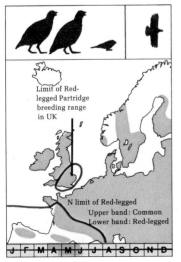

Limit of Red-legged Partridge breeding range in UK

N limit of Red-legged
Upper band: Common
Lower band: Red-legged

J F M A M J J A S O N D

Most Common Partridges inhabit farmland, but the species also occurs on heaths and commons. For nesting, they require hedgerows between fields which modern farming methods have tended to eliminate, with an adverse effect on their numbers. Even where conditions are ideal, Common Partridge populations fluctuate considerably and a cold, wet summer causes high mortality among young birds.

Red-legged Partridges show a wider habitat tolerance, but generally occur in more open areas than the Common Partridge and need more space. They have been introduced for sporting purposes into various regions, notably Britain, where they have thrived. Red-legs fly less readily than Common and,

rather than take to the air, family parties or "coveys" are more likely to disperse into cover when disturbed.

Both species site their nests on the ground, usually well concealed under a hedge or bramble-bush. Red-legged Partridges usually lay two clutches in separate nests, one of which will be incubated by the male, the other by the female. Sometimes they leave the first clutch apparently abandoned for some weeks before continuing incubation, and the habit can have strange consequences, such as Pheasants or Common Partridges adding their eggs to the unattended nest. Common Partridges raise only one brood a year. Both species produce clutches of up to 20 eggs; chicks fly feebly at three weeks.

135

Cuckoo

The rufous-brown juvenile superficially resembles a Kestrel

Of the two profiles above, the one on the right, long tail drooping, is by far the most often seen

Below, the adult (and first summer) female has a buff band on her breast

Long, thin, pointed wings with a long tail produce the unique silhouette

White spots stand out on the blue-grey adult's dark tail. Flight looks weak, with shallow wing beats; the head, small in proportion to the body, is held high (×⅕)

Below, a freshly hatched Cuckoo mounts the inner nest wall to eject a host bird's egg. Each one is balanced between the upturned, naked wings while the Cuckoo chick propels itself upwards with head and claws. At 35 days the Cuckoo dwarfs its foster-parent, here a Hedge Sparrow

Its head is inverted and the eyes are shut

Left, having laid her own egg in an occupied nest, the Cuckoo ensures deception by disposing of one host bird's egg

A nestling Cuckoo's head, three-quarters life-size; the white spot remains a feature of the nape until adult plumage develops

As much a part of the male Cuckoo's reputation as his call is his habit of raising the tail, drooping the wings and looking about while giving voice (×⅓)

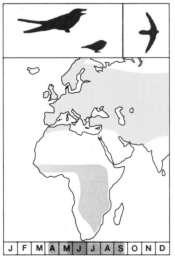

J F M A M J J A S O N D

Not everyone welcomes the Cuckoo's call as a symbol of spring: parasitic nesting habits arouse mixed feelings. A wide variety of small birds are exploited, but among the most frequent are Dunnocks, Meadow Pipits and Reed Warblers. A female Cuckoo usually keeps to the same host species, probably the one by whom she was herself reared, and her eggs often—but by no means always—show a strong resemblance to those of the host. Cuckoo eggs are larger than those laid by most of the host species, but are still remarkably small for this size of bird.

The female goes about selecting a nest soon after dawn, choosing one in which the clutch is incomplete and incubation has not yet begun. She keeps watch near by until ready to lay, which is usually in the early afternoon of the same day. Approaching the nest itself is accomplished by gliding down as unobtrusively as possible, preferably during the host bird's temporary absence, but Cuckoos are often attacked by angry parents. The whereabouts of parasitized nests can sometimes be detected by spotting a Cuckoo's feather amongst nearby vegetation.

Because a Cuckoo's egg has the surprisingly short incubation period of 12½ days, it usually hatches when the host nest contains only eggs or very small young. The nestling Cuckoo fledges after the fosterers have spent three weeks of frantic effort satisfying its voracious appetite.

136

Nightjar

When perching, the Nightjar sits lengthwise on the branch, almost hidden by its cryptic colouring

The unmistakable flight has a characteristic buoyant quality—bounding, wheeling and twisting after insects. Deliberate wing beats are interspersed with light, floating glides in which the wings are held in a deep V formation

(×¹⁄₃)

The male has white spots, usually three, sometimes two, on wings; two on tail

Male Nightjar

Head and gape of the male Nightjar

(×³⁄₄)

The Nightjar's beak is adapted to open both vertically and horizontally, giving the bird an enormous, almost circular, gape. The fringe of remarkably stiff bristles protects the eye from insect wings and legs and probably also effectively increases the size of the gape

An interesting feature of the Nightjar's foot is the deeply serrated underside of the middle claw. This adaptation enables the bird to clean dust and insect debris from the stiff fringe of bristles surrounding the gape

Nightjars always nest on the ground, even on the ballast of railway lines. The eyes are narrow slits by day (even on the young chick) and the bird is almost invisible against the ground

Female and juvenile birds lack white plumage markings

Night-flying insects are a rich potential food source almost entirely unexploited by birds. When darkness falls, it is the bats (with their highly refined system of echo location) which reap the benefit. Just one group of birds has evolved to bridge this gap, the nightjars—strange birds, with huge mouths and intricate camouflage resembling that of the moths on which they largely feed. Only one species of nightjar occurs in most parts of Europe, and it is a summer visitor to dry, open heaths, woodland clearings and young plantations.

From dusk, when the birds are most active, their presence may be revealed by the extraordinary song of the male—a prolonged, dry trill sounding like some piece of machinery and changing pitch periodically. He may also perform wing clapping during the breeding season, and both sexes have gliding aerial displays. No nest is made: the clutch of two eggs is laid on a bare patch of ground, among bracken or heather. The female is relieved at intervals by the male during the 18-day incubation and if disturbed reacts by feigning injury. Both parents feed the young, which fledge after two and a half weeks, but remain with their parents for a further four weeks. Two broods are often reared, the male taking sole charge of the young while his mate incubates the next clutch. Nightjars are decreasing in numbers, particularly in Britain.

137

Kestrel

A circling bird with sagging wings can only be a Kestrel

In certain flight attitudes the tail looks exceptionally long

A sub-adult's tail is grey but barred. Upperparts resemble a female's

(× ⅟₇)

Below, soaring, the wings are held slightly forwards. Only the Kestrel has such a prominent black tail-band

An adult female or immature Kestrel is simply identified by the conspicuous barring on upper and lower body surfaces

A very long tail is the Kestrel's principal point of identification. An adult male's, left, is plain grey with a broad, black band

Below, scrutinizing the ground from an overhead wire, a favourite perch

The characteristic manner of rising before the hover

City-nesting Kestrels are most likely to be seen near tall buildings

(× ⅓)

Above and left, various hovering attitudes. Among predators, only Kestrels hover (often over motorway margins) at heights between 30 and 300 feet, watching the ground for prey. The tail's angle of attack is continually adjusted to the wind speed. After the strike, prey is eaten at a perch

Adult male. Kestrels are changeable hunters—sometimes sluggish, at others capable of catching birds as vigorous as Starlings

At close quarters the barred and streaked female looks surprisingly different from the male. She retains the same profile and black tail-band

Gliding at height

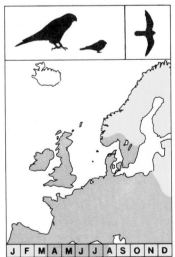

Pointed wings are the most obvious characteristic of falcons, which with hawks comprise the two main families of day birds of prey. The Kestrel is the commonest falcon in Europe; others included in this book are the Hobby, Peregrine and Merlin. Besides structural features, various habits and behaviour patterns distinguish the falcons from hawks: they make no nests of their own; they moult their flight feathers in a different sequence, and they let their droppings fall straight below the perch, rather than projecting them away from it.

In all these ways the Kestrel is a typical falcon, but its feeding and hunting habits are unusual. The diet is largely small rodents, varied with in-sects, frogs and a few small birds, and to search out most of its prey the bird employs an ideal method—hovering above open ground.

Nest sites are varied, including the abandoned nests of Crows or pigeons, or cavities in dead trees. Kestrels now breed in urban areas, where crevices in buildings furnish nesting places, and House Sparrows largely replace mice and voles as the staple food. Specially designed nestboxes attract them.

Four or five eggs are laid and both sexes incubate them for about four weeks. The young are fed by both sexes, and like all day birds of prey develop two successive coats of down before fledging, which takes place at 28 to 30 days.

Sparrowhawk

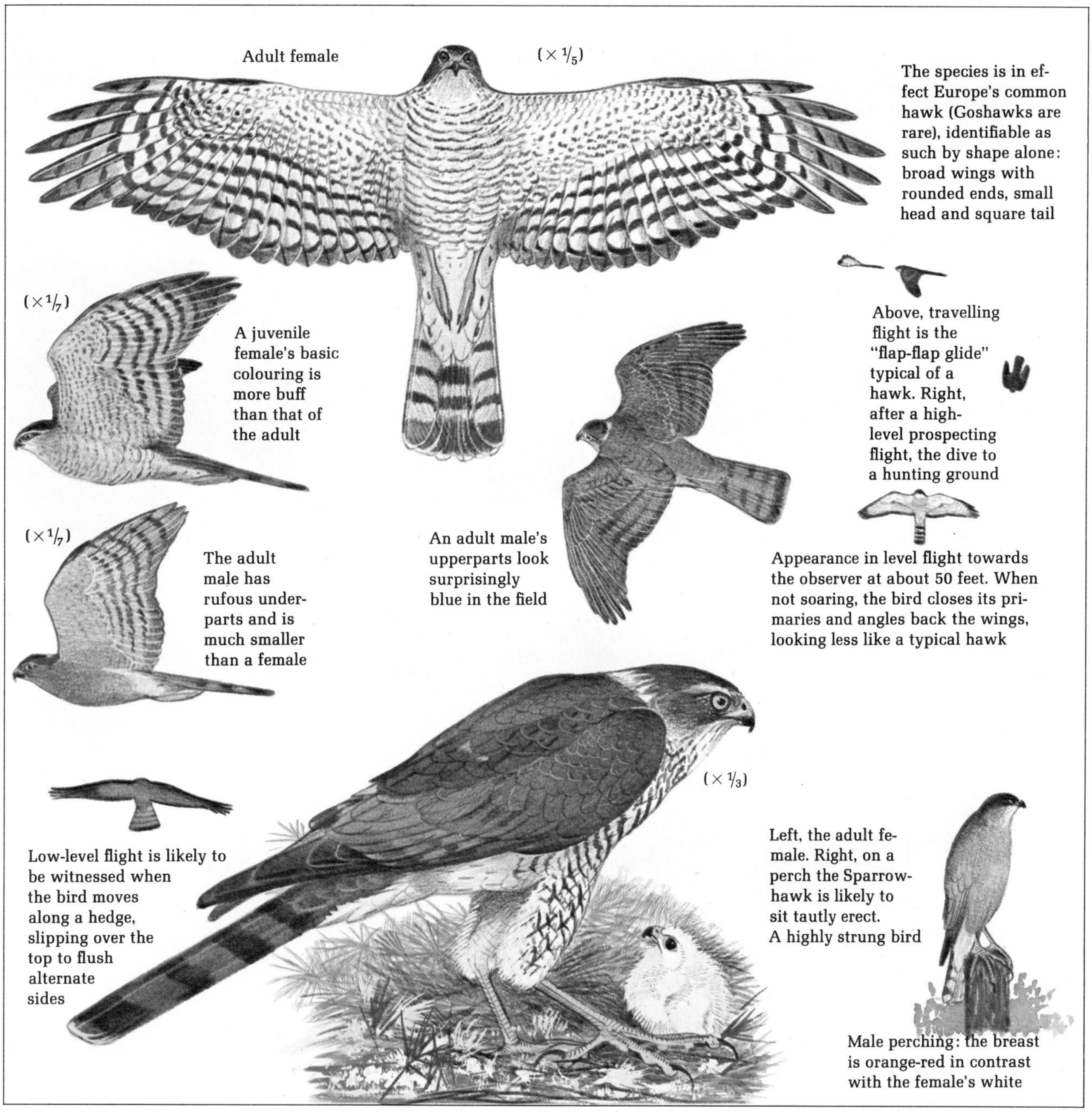

Adult female (× 1/5)

The species is in effect Europe's common hawk (Goshawks are rare), identifiable as such by shape alone: broad wings with rounded ends, small head and square tail

(×1/7) A juvenile female's basic colouring is more buff than that of the adult

Above, travelling flight is the "flap-flap glide" typical of a hawk. Right, after a high-level prospecting flight, the dive to a hunting ground

(×1/7) The adult male has rufous underparts and is much smaller than a female

An adult male's upperparts look surprisingly blue in the field

Appearance in level flight towards the observer at about 50 feet. When not soaring, the bird closes its primaries and angles back the wings, looking less like a typical hawk

(× 1/3)

Low-level flight is likely to be witnessed when the bird moves along a hedge, slipping over the top to flush alternate sides

Left, the adult female. Right, on a perch the Sparrowhawk is likely to sit tautly erect. A highly strung bird

Male perching: the breast is orange-red in contrast with the female's white

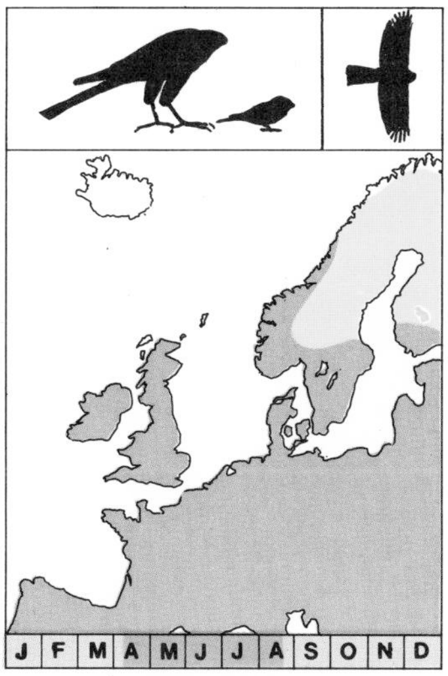

Swift yet manoeuvrable in flight, the Sparrowhawk is the supreme predator of small woodland birds. When hunting, it surprises them by flying fast and low along a hedge or woodland edge. Tenacious to the point of recklessness, Sparrowhawks sometimes pursue prey amongst buildings, and are not infrequently killed by flying into windows. A recent study in Holland shows that the smaller males concentrate on sparrows, finches and tits, while females capture more thrushes and Starlings. Prey is eaten at a regular plucking post, often at ground level, which may sometimes be an old nest or a specially constructed plucking platform.

Soaring display flights may reveal a breeding locality, but once nesting has commenced, Sparrowhawks efface themselves with great skill. The nest is a flat heap of birch or larch twigs sited on a branch near the trunk of a tree at a height of 30 feet or more. Small amounts of down are studded round the edges, more being added as incubation proceeds. Three to six eggs are laid, and the female incubates, leaving only briefly to eat food brought by the male.

Although usually high, the breeding rate has been reduced during recent decades. There have been occurrences of thin-shelled, fragile eggs and deaths of embryos during development, strongly linked with the use of organochlorine insecticides, which also caused a major mortality of adults in Britain between 1958 and 1960.

Hobby

When soaring, the Hobby holds its wings not forwards like a Kestrel but angled back. A juvenile is darker than an adult and has no red thighs

(×⅙)

Truly mercurial, Hobbies are overhead one moment, distant specks the next. At long range the outline may resemble a Swift's. Travelling flight is of the usual falcon pattern: a series of quick wing beats followed by glides

An insect is taken with the feet, then transferred to the bill

Breathtaking elegance in twisting after insects is matched by the Hobby's ability to take birds in the air without a moment's break in flight

In pursuit of House Martins

Elastic, even whippy, the Hobby's wing beat looks easier than a Kestrel's

Visible even half a mile away, the Hobby's black-and-white face pattern is certain identification: moustachial stripe and white cheek are much more pronounced than on the Kestrel

(×⅓)

The Hobby is a paragon among European birds of prey – superbly skilled in flight and handsome in appearance. Although its numbers have decreased, the decline has been less marked than among many raptors; in Britain there may even have been a slight recovery of numbers since the Second World War, probably due to stronger protection measures.

Hobbies breed later than many birds of prey, timing the emergence of their young to the period of maximum abundance of flying insects, for these are an important component in the diet of young Hobbies. Adults feed largely on small birds captured in flight, even such aerial experts as Swifts and Swallows. Insects taken include dragonflies, which are also no mean test of aerobatic technique. Heaths, downs or other open country with isolated clumps of trees are the typical habitat.

Displays take place early in the breeding season and include, appropriately enough, spectacular aerial performances, with one bird stooping at another or pairs exchanging food in flight. The clutch of three eggs is laid in the disused nest of another bird, often a Crow, less often a Magpie, Sparrowhawk or Wood Pigeon. Nests used earlier in the same season seem to be preferred to those from previous years, and there is a tendency to choose sites in conifers, though deciduous trees are often used. Young Hobbies fledge in about 30 days.

Goshawk

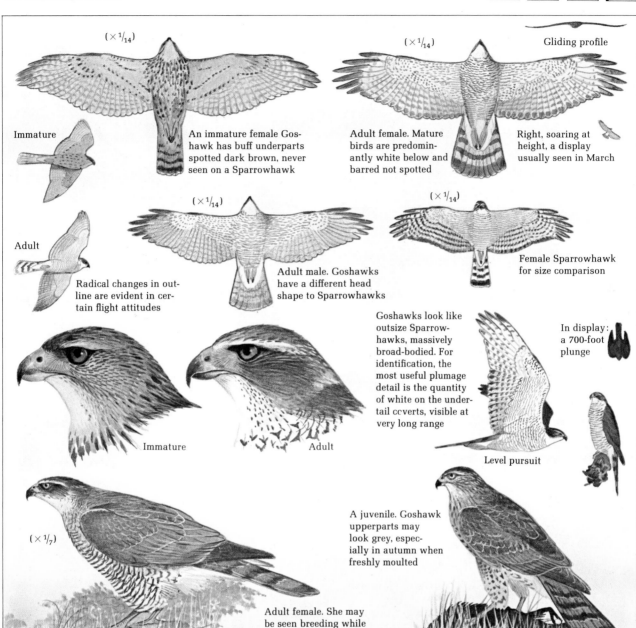

($\times \frac{1}{14}$)

Immature

An immature female Goshawk has buff underparts spotted dark brown, never seen on a Sparrowhawk

($\times \frac{1}{14}$)

Gliding profile

Adult female. Mature birds are predominantly white below and barred not spotted

Right, soaring at height, a display usually seen in March

Adult

Radical changes in outline are evident in certain flight attitudes

($\times \frac{1}{14}$)

Adult male. Goshawks have a different head shape to Sparrowhawks

($\times \frac{1}{14}$)

Female Sparrowhawk for size comparison

Goshawks look like outsize Sparrowhawks, massively broad-bodied. For identification, the most useful plumage detail is the quantity of white on the undertail coverts, visible at very long range

In display: a 700-foot plunge

Immature

Adult

Level pursuit

($\times \frac{1}{7}$)

A juvenile. Goshawk upperparts may look grey, especially in autumn when freshly moulted

Adult female. She may be seen breeding while still in immature plumage

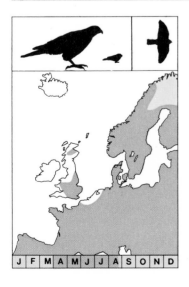

This superb raptor is in many respects a larger, more powerful version of the Sparrowhawk. Forests of all kinds are its habitat, and it stays more strictly within wooded terrain than its smaller relative. Hunting techniques include low-level flights similar to Sparrowhawks', and also short dashes made from some look-out post. Unfortunately, game-birds sometimes appear in the Goshawk's diet, and it has consequently been much persecuted by those concerned with game preservation.

In fact, its normal diet consists mainly of other birds, including many pigeons and Jays—species which themselves are considered pests. A recent study in Holland revealed differences in prey selection by males and females,

the former capturing more Jays, thrushes and Feral Pigeons, while females take more Wood Pigeons. Rabbits are also a common prey, taken mainly by females in winter, though male Goshawks capture many of the young rabbits available during the breeding season, when the female is busy incubating. Close relationship does not prevent the Goshawk occasionally killing a Sparrowhawk.

Goshawk nests are larger and more substantial than those of Sparrowhawks, and often include green conifer sprays in their structure. Old nests are often refurbished by the female; new nests are built mainly by the male. Both parents bring food, but direct feeding of the young is by the female only.

141

Peregrine

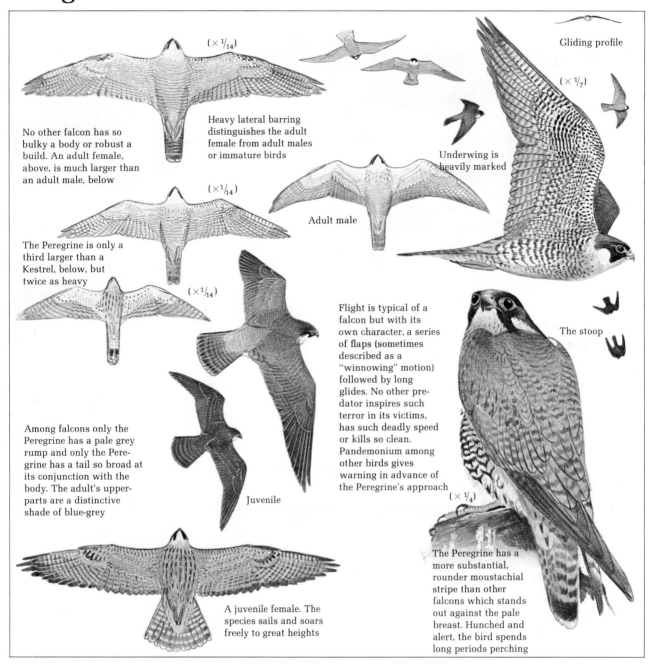

No other falcon has so bulky a body or robust a build. An adult female, above, is much larger than an adult male, below

(×1/14)

Heavy lateral barring distinguishes the adult female from adult males or immature birds

Gliding profile

(×1/7)

Underwing is heavily marked

(×1/14)

Adult male

The Peregrine is only a third larger than a Kestrel, below, but twice as heavy

(×1/14)

Flight is typical of a falcon but with its own character, a series of flaps (sometimes described as a "winnowing" motion) followed by long glides. No other predator inspires such terror in its victims, has such deadly speed or kills so clean. Pandemonium among other birds gives warning in advance of the Peregrine's approach

The stoop

Among falcons only the Peregrine has a pale grey rump and only the Peregrine has a tail so broad at its conjunction with the body. The adult's upperparts are a distinctive shade of blue-grey

Juvenile

(×1/4)

A juvenile female. The species sails and soars freely to great heights

The Peregrine has a more substantial, rounder moustachial stripe than other falcons which stands out against the pale breast. Hunched and alert, the bird spends long periods perching

These are the ultimate birds of prey, their renown deriving from a mastery of the stoop. This breathtakingly spectacular plunge to strike at flying victims has prompted some wild estimates of speed, ranging from 120 to 275 mph. A recent careful study using cinematography shows that the falcon levels out and slows up slightly just before striking, and final impact speed may be as little as 40 mph. Lethal damage is inflicted by the claw of the hind toe with the leg partially flexed. The victim is often allowed to fall to the ground. It is a method entirely different —and more elegant to watch—than that used by hawks, which strike from level flight with legs extended, killing with the front toes, and usually binding to the victim. A Peregrine may rise repeatedly above an elusive target—using a series of stoops until successful.

Rock and Feral Pigeons are favoured prey, and during the Second World War this obliged the British Air Ministry to order the destruction of Peregrines, fearing loss of carrier pigeons with vital messages. Though exterminated in southern Britain, they recovered only to face a far worse menace throughout their range—that of pesticides. Regular consumption of birds which have eaten contaminated seeds or insects allows some of those substances to accumulate in the Peregrine's tissue, causing sterility or death. Banning of certain chemicals has permitted a partial recovery, but the situation remains grave.

Merlin

An adult or immature female's upperparts appear uniform brown in the field. This is enough to distinguish her from the reddish-brown Kestrel

(× 1/7)

Adult male. The immature male has brown upperparts like those of the female

A Merlin exemplifies the predator's long reach

Although heavily patterned, the female's underwing is rarely of use as identification: swift flight leaves it indistinct

(× 1/7)

Least distinctive of the European birds of prey, this falcon is nevertheless completely individual: no other is so tiny, so fast or so habitually hunts near the ground

Chasing a Skylark

Extreme speed in every physical movement and obviously diminutive size are enough to distinguish Merlins in flight, even from falcons of similar appearance. Despite astonishing agility in following the victim's every twist or turn, a Merlin can be eluded by its prey

(× 1/5)

The bird may be seen darting over beaches or coastal marsh

An adult male Merlin is the smallest falcon with blue-grey upperparts. The species has much less distinct facial markings than any other bird of prey

A low-level perch is the most frequently used

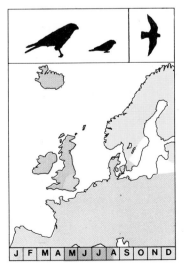

Smallest of the European falcons, the Merlin is none the less a fierce and dashing predator, living mainly on small birds, but occasionally taking species larger than itself, including Lapwings, Teal and Ptarmigan. Prey are captured in level flight, without the spectacular stoops of the Peregrine, but with remarkable speed and manoeuvrability. Common victims during summer are such birds as Meadow Pipits, Twites and Ring Ouzels, with which it shares its moorland habitat. During the winter Merlins occur on open country, especially around the coast.

Males arrive first at the breeding area, and before pairing make frequent short flights from perch to perch, calling. Nests are made on the ground amongst heather, or in old Crows' nests. Five or six eggs are laid at two-day intervals, and as incubation (about four weeks) begins before completion of the clutch, the young hatch at two-day intervals with the result that the eldest may be much larger than the youngest. This is usual among birds of prey, including owls, and is thought to be an adaptation to fluctuating food supplies: in lean years the youngest may die, but some of the brood will survive, whereas in an equally aged brood all would probably perish. Female Merlins perform most of the incubation, but both parents are extremely aggressive towards intruders. Food for the young is brought by the male and later by the female as well.

143

Marsh Harrier

(×1/14)

Immature, first summer

During the breeding season pairs of birds or single males in display soar as high as 700 feet

Juvenile male

Adult female

Adult male

Juvenile

Adult male

Left, the generally dark female has a pale crown, which, if the sun is low, may be observed shining as the bird hunts near the ground

(×1/10)

(×1/7)

Some males have duller plumage than this adult male, right

Marsh Harriers are the largest of the harriers. Their plumage differences with Montagu's or the Hen Harrier are self-evident. Harrier flight is characterized by its slowness, but the Marsh Harrier's is particularly so. It makes a few leisured flaps, then glides with the wings raised a little less steeply than others of the family

A predator hunting at very low level (perhaps 12 feet), frequently gliding with wings raised to form a V, can only be a harrier

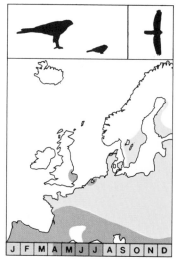

J F M A M J J A S O N D

There is a tendency to think of birds of prey as swift fliers, swooping on their victims at great speed. Some certainly are, but for certain types of hunting an ability to fly slowly is more valuable. Harriers are the masters of this technique, able to achieve air speeds of less than 20 mph. Flying into the wind, this may mean a ground speed of 10 mph or less, and brief hovers often intersperse their wheeling, buoyant progress. Minute inspection of the ground is possible at these slow speeds, and efficiency in detecting prey is further enhanced by keen hearing. The characteristic facial ruff of harriers conceals large ear openings, like those of owls.

Marsh Harriers typically frequent reed-beds or swamps of various kinds and will be seen flying rather faster and less buoyantly than Hen or Montagu's Harriers. Frogs comprise much of their diet, but small mammals, reptiles, insects and eggs and nestlings of marsh birds are also taken. A mass of reeds and willow twigs lined with grass forms the nest, usually sited in a reed-bed. Several nests may be close together. Incubation of the four or five eggs is performed by the female, and lasts about 36 days. Young are fed by the female, though the male brings food; they leave the nest before they can fly, at 35 to 40 days. Some males are polygamous.

Southern European Marsh Harriers are apparently more migratory than those which inhabit the north.

Hen Harrier–Montagu's Harrier

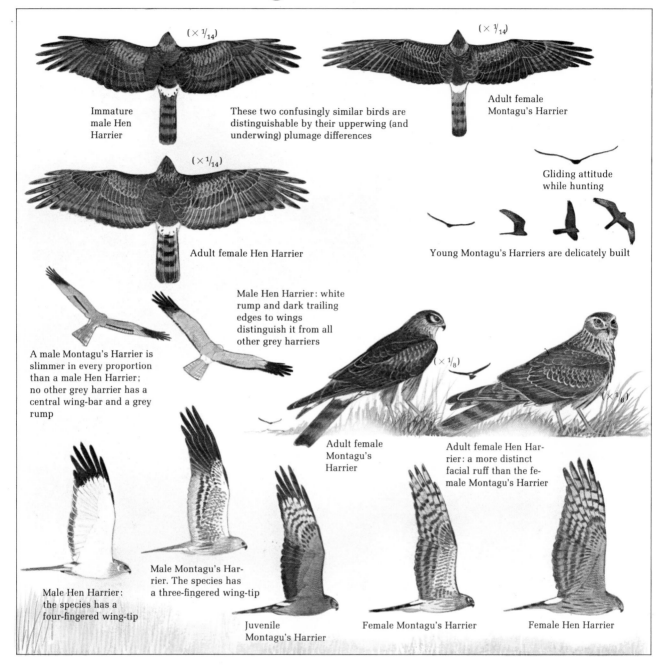

($\times \frac{1}{14}$)

Immature male Hen Harrier

These two confusingly similar birds are distinguishable by their upperwing (and underwing) plumage differences

($\times \frac{1}{14}$)

Adult female Montagu's Harrier

($\times \frac{1}{14}$)

Adult female Hen Harrier

Gliding attitude while hunting

Young Montagu's Harriers are delicately built

Male Hen Harrier: white rump and dark trailing edges to wings distinguish it from all other grey harriers

A male Montagu's Harrier is slimmer in every proportion than a male Hen Harrier; no other grey harrier has a central wing-bar and a grey rump

($\times \frac{1}{8}$)

($\times \frac{1}{8}$)

Adult female Montagu's Harrier

Adult female Hen Harrier: a more distinct facial ruff than the female Montagu's Harrier

Male Hen Harrier: the species has a four-fingered wing-tip

Male Montagu's Harrier. The species has a three-fingered wing-tip

Juvenile Montagu's Harrier

Female Montagu's Harrier

Female Hen Harrier

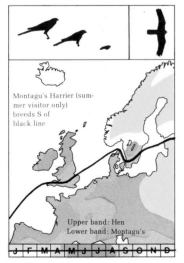

Montagu's Harrier (summer visitor only) breeds S of black line

Upper band: Hen
Lower band: Montagu's

J F M A M J J A S O N D

Hen and Montagu's Harriers are similar in both habits and appearance, but the former shows more tolerance of exposed and bleak surroundings. Its breeding range extends farther north, and northern Africa is the southern limit of migration for its western populations, many of which winter within Europe. Moorland is the Hen Harrier's breeding habitat, though marshes, heaths and even cornfields may be used. Montagu's Harrier has a more limited breeding distribution, but winters far south in Africa. Marshes, heaths, rough ground and young conifer plantations provide breeding places.

Both species may quarter the same favoured foraging area repeatedly on successive days. Their food includes various small mammals, reptiles and birds, usually taken by surprise on the ground, though Hen Harriers, which have been estimated to spend 40 per cent of the day airborne, sometimes pursue birds in flight, and have snatched wounded game-birds from under the noses of gundogs. Montagu's Harrier shows a particular fondness for adders. Both birds, but especially Montagu's Harrier, have the habit of roosting communally on the ground.

The whereabouts of breeding areas are revealed in spring by the climbing and diving display flights of the males—of which the Hen Harrier's is particularly spectacular. Both species make similar nests—pads of plant material of varying thickness placed on the ground.

Buzzard

(×¹⁄₁₄) Male

Above, the Common Buzzard soars with its wings held farther forward than a Honey Buzzard

Male

Adult male, sailing free. Among similar-sized predators, Common Buzzards have medium-length tails

Top, the soaring profile. Above, gliding profile

(×¹⁄₁₄) Female

Tails of immature bird, far left, and adult, left, show regular barring; Honey Buzzards have irregularly placed pairs of bars

Among buzzards, Common are the most habitual soarers. More than 20 may be seen wheeling in circles perhaps 500 yards across. Very variable in plumage, they remain distinct by a combination of broad, rounded wings and patchy marking

Male, gliding attitude

Gaining height to soar

Soaring

Rear view of turn

Common Buzzard

Honey Buzzard

Common Buzzards

Calling

(×¹⁄₇)

Like the eagle's, the upper leg is amply "trousered"; unlike an eagle's, the lower leg has no feathers

Upperparts revealed

Common Buzzards are seen searching on open ground for earthworms or beetles

Sitting for long periods in a tree watching for prey: behaviour common to all buzzards

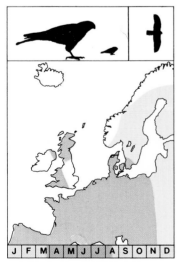

Compared with many European birds of prey, the Buzzard is a thriving species. Persecution by game preservationists has severely reduced many of its populations, but where this pressure has been relaxed, as in parts of Britain, they have recovered quickly. Rabbits are an important item of diet in many areas, and their decrease following myxomatosis led to greatly reduced breeding success in some Buzzard populations. Small mammals of other species, ground birds and reptiles make up the rest of the diet. Where prey is abundant, as on some Welsh islands, Buzzard territories may average as little as 120 acres per pair. The usual requirement is nearer 500 acres.

Buzzards prefer terrain consisting of a patchwork of wooded areas and open ground. The nest, made of sticks, heather, seaweed and often a few bones and sprigs of green foliage, is sited in a tree or on a cliff ledge between 15 and 60 feet up. Two or three eggs are laid, and incubation, by both sexes, lasts 33 to 35 days; fledging takes 40 to 45 days. On dispersal young Buzzards remain near their breeding ground. They probably first breed in their second summer, but before then three-quarters die, usually by shooting. The Buzzard's prospects improve after reaching maturity, and many are long-lived: one German bird reached nearly 24 years of age.

Scandinavian birds of all ages migrate to mainland Europe.

J F M A M J J A S O N D

Honey Buzzard

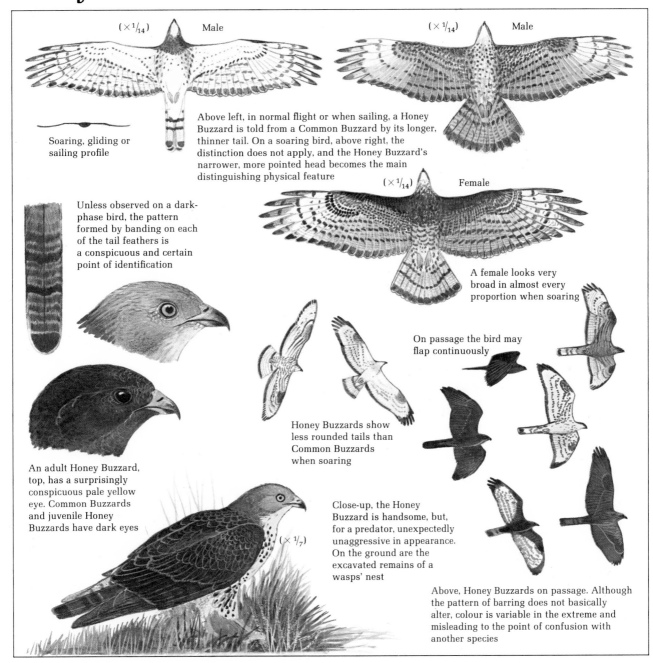

(×¹⁄₁₄) Male

(×¹⁄₁₄) Male

Above left, in normal flight or when sailing, a Honey Buzzard is told from a Common Buzzard by its longer, thinner tail. On a soaring bird, above right, the distinction does not apply, and the Honey Buzzard's narrower, more pointed head becomes the main distinguishing physical feature

(×¹⁄₁₄) Female

Soaring, gliding or sailing profile

Unless observed on a dark-phase bird, the pattern formed by banding on each of the tail feathers is a conspicuous and certain point of identification

A female looks very broad in almost every proportion when soaring

On passage the bird may flap continuously

Honey Buzzards show less rounded tails than Common Buzzards when soaring

An adult Honey Buzzard, top, has a surprisingly conspicuous pale yellow eye. Common Buzzards and juvenile Honey Buzzards have dark eyes

Close-up, the Honey Buzzard is handsome, but, for a predator, unexpectedly unaggressive in appearance. On the ground are the excavated remains of a wasps' nest

(×¹⁄₇)

Above, Honey Buzzards on passage. Although the pattern of barring does not basically alter, colour is variable in the extreme and misleading to the point of confusion with another species

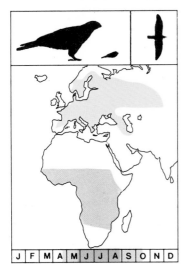

J F M A M J J A S O N D

Bees, wasps and their larvae seem strange food for a bird of prey, yet they are the Honey Buzzard's staple diet. Although this is varied with some small mammals and reptiles, adequate provision for a pair of Honey Buzzards requires a territory of some four square miles. Deciduous woodland, especially beech, is preferred, and some clearings are necessary for foraging. Adult wasps and bees have their stings bitten off before they are swallowed, but it is the grubs and pupae in nests of these insects which are the main objectives. Ground nests are dug out with the feet, while wasps' nests on buildings may be torn off in flight.

For their size, Honey Buzzards build rather small nests, but often on the foundation of a disused Crow or buzzard nest. Green sprays of beech are used liberally in its edges and lining. One to three eggs are laid, and are incubated for 30 to 35 days; fledging takes 40 to 44 days. The parents share duties equally, and either sex may brood or feed small young. At first, their food is brought largely in the form of wasps' nests and honeycombs carried in the parents' crops; these are regurgitated and larvae are picked out for the nestlings. Later, small vertebrates are also brought to the nest.

On migration, southward-bound birds, often in spectacular numbers, follow such well-defined routes as those over southern Sweden, the Bosporus and Gibraltar.

Osprey

The hover. If no fish is sighted the bird flies on

Above, the characteristic angling of the wings. So long are they that the bird may appear nothing but wings

Before diving, the bird hovers ponderously, often with the legs dangling

Head down, searching for fish. Slow, purposeful flight at about 30 feet marks a patrolling Osprey

$(\times \frac{1}{10})$

An Osprey either dives directly or, if the target is moving, with much checking and changing of course

Manner of holding wings while soaring, when the tail is fanned

White head and underparts are always conclusive identification

During glides the wings are sharply angled

The bird rises to about 50 feet before drying itself with a convulsive shake

$(\times \frac{1}{7})$

A fish is carried head first

Before plunging, the bird fully extends its feet. The dive may be aborted at a late stage

There are occasions when the bird is totally immersed, but not having waterproof plumage it flaps free almost instantaneously. Not every plunge produces a fish

A juvenile has buff edging on all the feathers of its upperparts, but, like an adult, looks predominantly white below

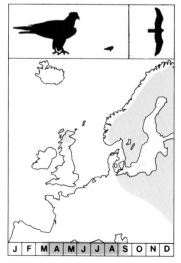

J F M A M J J A S O N D

Several birds of prey have turned to fish as a source of food, but by far the most successful and efficient of these is the Osprey. Its anatomy reveals that it diverged early from the main line of raptor evolution, and it is classified in a family of its own.

When fishing, it circles at between 50 to 100 feet, hovering briefly when it sights prey before plunging feet first. Fish of up to four pounds in weight are regularly captured, but accounts of Ospreys dragged under and drowned by larger fish should be viewed with scepticism.

Ospreys have a very wide distribution, including all continents except Antarctica. Sadly, their populations in Europe and North America have dwindled seriously, due to direct persecution and more recently to the effects of toxic chemicals released into waterways. Under strict protection their status has improved in some places, notably in Britain, but even these birds may be shot on migration.

Pines and spruces with dead branches high up the trunk are typical nest sites. Reused year after year, the nest of sticks, heather and grasses grows to a large size. Three eggs are normally laid and the 35-day incubation is undertaken largely by the female, though the male shares up to 30 per cent of the task during daylight. The female remains with her young while the male feeds the whole family a total of about three to five small fish a day.

Black Kite–Red Kite

Kite identified by angled wings and deeply forked tail

($\times^1/_{14}$)

Adult Black Kite, below, always looks dark brown; young birds especially have whitish wing-patches, easily confused with the adult Red Kite. Black Kite's tail less deeply forked than Red Kite

Adult Red Kite, above, has greyish head which becomes very pale in old birds. Immature birds are less red and have shallower tail fork. Neither species has a marked size difference between sexes

($\times^1/_{14}$)

Red Kite, above; wings virtually level when gliding. Wings always look slender when seen at a distance

Below, typical flight attitudes of Black Kite; ragged flapping flight interspersed with soaring

Viewed from in front in gliding flight, the kite's wings appear slightly angled. The Black Kite often hunts over lakes and rivers

Above, when viewed from beneath in soaring flight, the Red Kite's tail fork almost vanishes. Left, from above, pale wing-patches are prominent

When flying, the Black Kite, right, rises and falls, constantly changing direction—its tail twisting quite noticeably

Above, typical flight attitudes of Black Kite

Black Kite

Red Kite

Black Kite, left, always appears darker than Red Kite and has a much more upright posture when perching

The juvenile Black Kite, right, has paler wing-patches than the adult

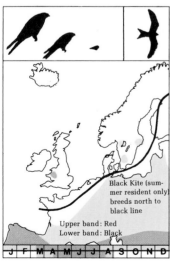

Black Kite (summer resident only) breeds north to black line

Upper band: Red
Lower band: Black

J F M A M J J A S O N D

Closely related but with different temperaments, this pair of species provides an illuminating case study of interaction between man and birds. Black Kites are bold and opportunist; although they have declined in parts of Europe, they are generally still common and have increased in some places. Red Kites are more beautiful, and also more timid: they have declined seriously during the past two centuries, becoming extinct as breeding birds in Denmark, Norway, Belgium and Austria, and reduced to a remnant in several other countries, including Britain.

Black Kites supplement a basic diet of small vertebrates and large insects with carrion and edible rubbish. Urban areas provide superb opportunities for exploiting the latter source, and Black Kites teem in many towns and cities in the warmer parts of the world. Their boldness is illustrated by numerous instances of birds snatching food from market stalls, even from people's hands, sometimes causing injury. Red Kites once took garbage in the streets of London, and still do in the Cape Verde Islands, but have never fully exploited refuse as a source of food. Deciduous woods bordering open country are now their main habitat.

Both species are tree nesters, building large structures of sticks and earth. That of the Red Kite is rather flat-topped and lined with grass or wool; the Black Kite's is deeper, and usually has rags in the lining.

149

Golden Eagle

No other eagle soars on raised wings. Sailing and gliding, the wings are flattened

An adult Golden Eagle has shorter wings and tail than a juvenile. Larger wings, ampler tail and a relatively small head distinguish the species from Common Buzzard

Wings clipped in at their junction with the body is characteristic of any eagle

Large size and obvious power set the Golden Eagle apart from comparable predators. It can cut through gale-force winds. Normal flight, a few measured flaps, takes the bird hundreds of yards, then it glides as far again; during a glide it may suddenly drop, then raise the wings without losing height. It is brilliantly aerobatic. Golden Eagles circle like buzzards, but cover more ground

The spectacular dive after prey

($\times\frac{1}{18}$)

($\times\frac{1}{7}$)

On the upper and lower surfaces of wings and tail an immature bird has striking white patches which diminish gradually during its first five years

Uninspiring dark appearance at long range belies the Golden Eagle's beautiful markings. The pointed, golden nape feathers are raised in anger

Skylines and crags are where to look for these birds: distance is required to encompass the scale of their movements. A pair may hunt about 20 feet above the ground, one usually behind the other and higher up the slope—behaviour shared by no other European eagle

Immature birds up to one and a half years old: wing-patches visible at great distance

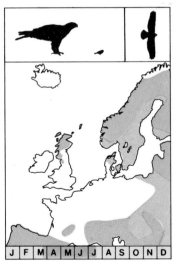

Traditional status as king among birds has not prevented the Golden Eagle from being mercilessly harried by gamekeepers, shepherds and egg collectors. More recently, its populations have been further imperilled by reduced fertility, and abnormal fragility of egg shells caused by organo-chlorine insecticides accumulated in the bodies of its prey. Perhaps its air of majesty may retain sufficient hold in people's minds to improve its prospects of survival.

Largest of the prey normally taken are hares or foxes, for anything bigger needs to be dismembered or partly consumed before being carried away. However, there is a recent record of an eagle killing a red deer calf, and eagles have been trained by Mongolian falconers to fly at wolves. Although lambs are occasionally taken, many are probably picked up dead, and the habit scarcely justifies the war waged on the bird by some sheep farmers.

Mountainous regions are the Golden Eagle's habitat, and its nest is usually placed on a cliff or in a tree. Made from sticks, heather and bracken lined with grass and rushes, the nest is used year after year, and successive additions of material can make it up to ten feet across and five feet deep. Two eggs are usually laid with a three- or four-day interval between. Incubation starts with the first, so that the eaglets differ in age. In 80 per cent of broods, the elder eventually kills the younger.

Tawny Owl

A bow-winged attitude is a characteristic of the Tawny Owl's swift and agile flight. Wing beats are interspersed with glides as the bird turns and twists through the trees

For long-distance flight, the owl has fairly rapid wing beats and the flight path is undulating. The bird is best seen in the very early morning, at daybreak

The perching bird has a plump, rounded look

An adult Tawny Owl at the nest with a month-old chick. The bird's head is very rounded, almost disproportionally large with huge, dark, liquid eyes. The tail is long but, owing to the breadth of the wings, appears to be of only moderate length

(×⅓)

In flight, right, the short, rounded wings and large head are unmistakable

The Tawny Owl has rich brown mottled plumage with fairly conspicuous white spots visible on the scapulars

(×⅙)

Left, the grey phase continental owl

Face and beak of the Tawny Owl, right, should be compared with those of the Barn Owl, which has an exceptionally long beak for an owl

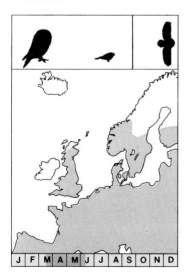

Over much of Europe this is the most common and familiar owl, its hooting call the archetype of all owl voices—though in fact rather unrepresentative.

The appeal of owls lies in their humanoid expressions, with large foreheads and eyes set at the front of a broad, flat face. Such features are actually adaptations for nocturnal hunting—the position of the eyes confers a wide field of binocular vision, important for accurate judgement of distance, while their size is a consequence of specializations for enhancing night vision. Sensitive hearing is also vital, and owls have relatively huge ears, their openings concealed just behind the facial disc of feathers surrounding the eyes.

Tawny Owls' ecology and life history have been very thoroughly investigated. They start nesting early in March, laying their clutch of two to five eggs on debris at the bottom of the nest hole. Incubation is by the female, starting with the first egg; 28 to 30 days are required for each egg to hatch, after which the male brings food—typically small rodents or shrews, occasionally small birds. Young fledge after five weeks, and the number successfully reared is strongly related to food supply. Young owls are dependent on their parents for some three months after leaving the nest, but then have to fend for themselves. Autumn and winter are times of high mortality, particularly for immature birds.

J F M A M J J A S O N D

151

Little Owl–Scops Owl

Scops Owl

Little Owl

Scops Owl, above, often perches on roofs: a vague form seen at dusk. In Mediterranean towns its persistent and monotonous call is often a nuisance ($\times \frac{1}{3}$)

The extreme slimness of its form, the very noticeable ear-tufts and the finely vermiculated plumage instantly identify Scops Owl, left, from the dumpy figure of the Little Owl. It is a tiny, stern-looking owl: flight is swift and wavering with no trace of the bounding motion characteristic of its relative

($\times \frac{1}{6}$)

($\times \frac{1}{6}$)

Right, Little Owl's under-side is heavily barred

Little Owl's flight, above, is an emphatic series of undulations

Above, the squat form of the Little Owl may often be seen perching on telegraph poles

The short spotted tail shows clearly on a departing bird

Agitated bobbing, a common sight

An adult Little Owl peers from its tree nest hole. Characteristically more open faced than Scops Owl

($\times \frac{1}{3}$)

Little Owl: typical short, rounded form. Bright-yellow eyes with black centres

Upper band: Little
Lower band: Scops

N Limit Scops

J F M A M J J A S O N D

Widely distributed in Europe, the Little Owl was introduced into Britain during the late nineteenth century and has successfully colonized most of England and Wales, although some decrease has recently occurred. One of the more diurnal owls, this species may often be seen on a telegraph wire or similar prominent perch, or flying overhead — when its undulating progress might for a moment confuse it with a woodpecker until the head shape is noticed. Little Owls have a mewing call, and during the breeding season members of a pair utter this alternately in a duet.

Hunting is carried out mainly at dawn or dusk. Insects, especially dor-beetles and cockchafers, are frequent prey, as are mice and slugs. Because of its capacities as a pest-destroyer, the Little Owl is popular with gardeners in some parts of Europe, but in many places small birds are its principal prey.

Little Owls normally nest in hollow trees, quite often near the ground; pollarded willows are a favourite. Eaves under the corners of old barns may also be used, and, wherever situated, the cavity usually has at least two exits. Three to five eggs are laid, and although incubation usually starts with the first egg, the female may not begin incubation until the clutch is complete. Hatching occurs after 24 to 25 days and the fledging period is three and a half weeks. Both sexes feed the young, and continue to do so for some time after they leave the nest.

Long-eared Owl

Owls have superb forward vision in normal flight

With wings upraised, the dark carpal patch is visible

In flight, above and right, the Long-eared Owl displays the differences in shape and proportion that distinguish it from the superficially similar Short-eared species. The Long-eared Owl has shorter wings but longer tail

$(\times \frac{1}{6})$

Like all owls, the Long-eared Owl is beautifully marked, with long, distinctive ears, orange eyes and delicately streaked breast. Facial expression varies greatly. This species usually nests in old Crows' nests or in abandoned squirrels' dreys

$(\times \frac{1}{3})$

A notable feature, right, of the Long-eared Owl's plumage is the very fine barring on the secondaries and inner primaries, giving the hind part of the wing a greyish appearance. Barring is more pronounced on the wings of the Short-eared Owl

Below, roosting birds often adopt a tight, upright, profile. When relaxed, the profile is more squat and rounded

In a display of aggression, below, an adult puffs out feathers and raises wings to appear larger

The young are typical of all owls—very rounded, covered in a thick, white down, and generally appealing. They are fed on voles, fieldmice and a variety of small birds

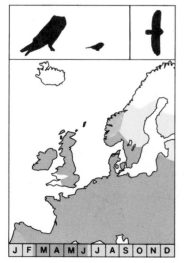

The wise old owl of countless children's tales is usually depicted as a Long-eared Owl. This character's origins are in Greek mythology, where, however, the archetype, which lacks ear tufts, seems more like a Little Owl.

Strictly nocturnal, except in the extreme north of its range, the Long-eared Owl is a difficult bird to glimpse, concealing itself very effectively while roosting—even though groups of up to 20 may sometimes do so together. Long-eared Owls generally prefer conifer habitats, but are by no means confined to them. Prey varies greatly with locality. In some places many birds are taken at roosts, and pairs of Long-eared Owls have been seen to hunt cooperatively, one flushing out victims while the other pounces. Small rodents are of prime importance in most areas, their cyclical population changes affecting the breeding success of the owls. In good years, more pairs nest, more eggs are laid and more young are produced. Disused nests of such birds as Crows and pigeons provide the usual site in which the clutch of three to eight eggs is laid, but sometimes eggs are placed on the ground under bushes or branches. Incubation, probably by both sexes, takes 27 to 28 days; both parents feed the young, which fledge in three and a half weeks.

Long-eared Owls tend to shun the vicinity of human habitation, and have not adapted to man-made environments as successfully as the Tawny Owl.

153

Barn Owl

Continental race, above; darker breast and extensively vermiculated plumage

Right, when flying at dusk, the Barn Owl is seen as a ghostly, elusive form—its flight slow, buoyant and wavering. The Barn Owl tends to patrol at greater height than the Short-eared Owl: it is commonly seen in daylight, especially when feeding young

British race

British race, right, has generally paler colour and a much whiter breast than the continental race. However, some of the continental owls are quite pale and are difficult to distinguish

The Barn Owl is easily identified by its large head, short, square tail, and medium-long wings. Colouring is a beautiful orange-buff above with grey vermiculation. The breast is either pure white or lightly marked with buff

(× ⅓)

(× ⅙)

The Barn Owl's long, spindly legs—rather "hairy" and also sometimes "knock-kneed"—give the bird a quaint appearance belying its hunting ability

Above: feathers removed to expose the large external orifice of the ear

In close-up, the head of the Barn Owl shows the long, thin beak, quite unlike that of the Tawny Owl. The position of the ear is also shown. Note that the beak points downwards when the head is held in the bird's normal perching position

It is ironical that the status of the Barn Owl in Europe should be causing concern to conservationists, for it is essentially one of the world's most successful birds, with a huge range including at least part of every continent except Antarctica. Its present decline in Europe results largely from the use of organo-chlorine insecticides—a factor which particularly affects this species of owl because it hunts over agricultural land.

Two colour phases of the species occur in Europe: the dark-breasted form is found in the north and east of its range, the white-breasted in the south and west, including Britain. Traditional farmland provides it with an ideal habitat, combining open ground for hunting with hedgerows and barns for roosting and breeding. Modern farming methods which involve the elimination of hedgerows and erection of less hospitable outhouses have been additional factors in its recent decline. Rodents are its main prey, although the diet appears to be more varied in southern Europe.

Large cavities in buildings or in dead trees provide nest sites. Like many owls, its breeding success is strongly correlated with the population fluctuations of rodents. Clutch sizes vary from three to 11, and the eggs are more pointed in shape than those of other owls. Incubation, by the female alone, lasts 32 to 34 days, and both sexes feed the young during their nine- to 12-week fledging period.

154

Short-eared Owl

Short-eared Owl in flight, left. Normal flight is low, but the bird may rise quickly to some height when flushed. In spring display, owls may fly high in full daylight. Displays also include sudden vertical drops and wing clapping

Short-eared Owls are wide-ranging birds of open country and often cover great distances. They are the longest winged of all the owls, but are characteristically short tailed; the head is very short and rounded

($\times \frac{1}{6}$)

Underwing, right, is pale with a noticeable carpal patch

Hunting technique, above: the owl typically hunts by patrolling an area with slow, wavering flight low over the ground. The bird rolls, checks, hovers and glides, then drops with raised wings—rising quickly if the "strike" is unsuccessful. Looks like a huge ghostly moth when seen on a gloomy winter evening

The eyes are yellow and unusually small

($\times \frac{1}{3}$)

The Short-eared Owl occasionally perches in a tree, more often on a post, but is most commonly flushed from ground cover. The body is carried in a more pronounced horizontal attitude than by most other owl species

The outstretched wing in flight clearly shows the dark carpal patch on the upper wing surface. The patch is encircled by a pale orange area, which appears buff at long range

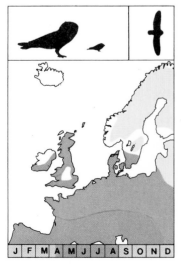

J F M A M J J A S O N D

Distributed around the pole in both the New and Old Worlds, the Short-eared Owl is clearly a flourishing species, yet its success is based on a strategy quite different from that of the more obviously common Tawny Owl. Short-eared Owls are nomadic, tending to congregate in areas where there is a temporary surplus in the population of mice or voles; Tawny Owls, on the other hand, make use of detailed knowledge of the wood or park in which they are resident. Much more diurnal than other owls, the Short-eared can regularly be seen quartering open ground, such as a field or salt-marsh, in broad daylight. Groups of the birds are quite often found hunting together in this way. Although rodents make up most of the diet, Short-eared Owls also take birds, even such swift fliers as Dunlin or snipe.

The nest is normally a scrape in dense vegetation on the ground, such as heather, rank grass or brambles. Four to seven eggs are usual, but up to 14 have been recorded in years when the rodent supply has been good. The female incubates, normally from the first egg, at first somewhat intermittently. Incubation lasts 24 to 28 days, and the young are fed by the female with food brought by the male. They may begin to make short forays from the nest from two weeks onwards, but do not fly until they are three and a half weeks old. Two broods may be raised in years when voles are abundant.

155

Ringed Plover

The bird is commonly seen as it takes off, wing and tail patterns showing clearly

Ringed Plovers have conspicuous white underparts, which flash as a flock turns in unison, alternately showing brown and white

The "butterfly" display flight, accompanied by continuous calling

(× ³/₁₀)

There are areas of white above the tail and a conspicuous wing bar

Head pattern varies slightly from individual to individual. The birds often fly low over the beach before landing

Left, display posture: rear end raised, tail fanned. Right, adult in broken wing display to lure away predators

Winter plumage is slightly less conspicuous than summer

Ringed Plovers have a hunched attitude and a slightly worried, fragile look

(× ½)

Juvenile resting on one leg. It has a delicate scaly pattern on the upperparts of the basically adult plumage

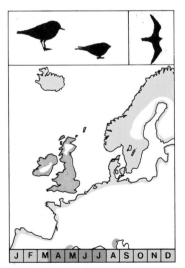

During summer, one of the characteristic sounds of shingly coastlines is the liquid call of the Ringed Plover. It is often uttered in alarm by adults with eggs or young near by, but this warning is rarely noticed by holidaymakers, whose disturbance of the birds leads to the failure of many clutches. The eggs are beautifully camouflaged in the simple scrape that serves as a nest. This protects them from marauding gulls, but increases the likelihood of them being crushed underfoot.

In some areas, Ringed Plovers nest inland, on heaths, or by gravelly streams. They usually ignore the industrial sites favoured by Little Ringed Plovers, but sometimes both occur together resulting in competition.

Ringed Plovers have been known to lay eggs in a Little Ringed Plover's nest and finally oust the smaller bird completely.

Egg-laying takes place any time between April and August. There are two broods, and extra clutches are laid to replace losses through disturbance or flooding by unusually high tides. Both sexes incubate for 24 or 25 days, and the young can fly after three and a half weeks. Outside the breeding season, Ringed Plovers may be seen feeding on sandy or muddy shores with other waders such as Dunlin or Knot, but are always distinguished by their typical plover feeding tactics of runs interspersed with short pauses. Prey is driven to the surface by a rapid paddling of the wet sand with one foot.

Little Ringed Plover

On a Ringed Plover, the black forehead pattern extends farther back, and half the beak is yellow

Adult

By comparison with the Ringed Plover, a Little Ringed Plover has less black on its forehead and a thinner, blacker beak. There is a pronounced white line running right round the crown and a pale yellow eye-ring

Adult

Unlike Kentish and Ringed Plovers, the adult Little Ringed Plover shows no obvious wing bar. In flight, its wings generally look all brown

(×³⁄₁₀)

In fact Little Ringed Plovers do have a minute wing bar which can sometimes be seen quite well on a freshly moulted bird – ultimately, it wears off

Juvenile Ringed Plover

Juvenile Little Ringed Plover

A juvenile Ringed Plover has a white eyestripe and a white forehead. The Little Ringed Plover has no eyestripe and its head is browner overall

A very typical view of the Little Ringed Plover, clearly revealing the frontal pattern, as the bird pauses before taking a few more steps forward

In flight the Little Ringed Plover is seen to have duskier underwing colouring than the Ringed Plover, and the wings are held farther back

A juvenile, below, has "scaly" plumage

(×¹⁄₂)

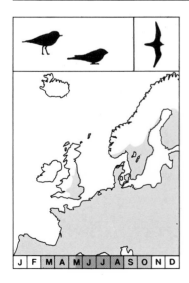

With the present steady reduction of wetland habitats, wader numbers are generally on the decline, but the story of the Little Ringed Plover in Europe provides a spectacular exception. Since the turn of the century its range has expanded dramatically northwestwards, and the spread is continuing.

This expansion has come about through the species' exploitation of man-made habitats, especially gravel pits and empty reservoirs. Natural choices are sand or gravel bars by inland lakes. Well-documented stages of its spread are those in Belgium and the Netherlands during the 1930s and in Britain since 1944. The British colonization started with two pairs; subsequent counts found 223 breeding

pairs in 1967 and 467 in 1973. In view of this expansion it is surprising to find that breeding success is low: many clutches of eggs are lost to predators such as Carrion Crows, or through flooding or disturbance. Dogged perseverance in producing repeat clutches helps compensate, and a few genuine second broods are produced. Both sexes incubate the four eggs in their simple scrape, expressing alarm when disturbed with a sharp whistle quite different from the Ringed Plover's liquid call. The young hatch after 24 to 25 days, and can fly at three weeks.

Food includes a wide range of small invertebrates, and "foot paddling" (see opposite page) is even more frequent than with the Ringed Plover.

157

Sanderling

During the winter months, Sanderlings have an overall silvery-grey appearance, right and far right, especially when seen in flight

$(\times \frac{3}{10})$

The dark-coloured tail with white rump patches either side is typical of all waders, but the Sanderling can be distinguished from the Dunlin by its striking wing bar

The juvenile's winter plumage, above, is a more distinctly mottled version of the adult's silver-grey, below

While moulting, the Sanderling has mottled plumage, above left. This contrasts with the scaled appearance of the black and rich orange summer garb, above right

Narrow lobes to toes

$(\times \frac{1}{2})$

On a resting bird the dark shoulder patch is largely obscured by breast feathers

Complete absence of hind toe

$(\times \frac{1}{2})$

The beak is short and straight like a Stint's. There is a distinctive dark shoulder patch

Winter adults, white against the beach, faces especially so

Feeding birds dash about like clockwork toys

Juvenile

Adult, autumn

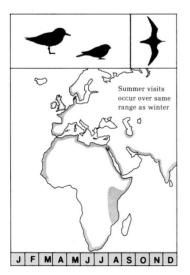

Summer visits occur over same range as winter

J F M A M J J A S O N D

A small silver-grey and white wader, the Sanderling is unmistakable as it speeds to and fro on twinkling black legs across the long sandy beaches to which it is restricted. In Europe it is primarily a bird of spring and autumn, smaller numbers staying to winter. In late spring, adults may be seen in mottled red-brown breeding plumage. A few first-year birds may stay the summer. Sanderlings feed on small crustaceans, seized as they follow the surf in and out.

The Arctic breeding season is short – as little as six weeks – and with some pairs the female lays two clutches in separate nests on arrival, incubating one herself and leaving the other to the male. Young are fed insects and larvae.

Sanderlings rank amongst the world's most travelled birds: Arctic breeders penetrate down South America to the Falkland Islands, through Africa to the Cape, and also to Australasia, always inhabiting sandy beaches.

They are confiding birds, often running away rather than flying, and rarely occur in flocks of more than a few dozen. European beaches serve as fattening areas for further journeys – studies have shown that their weight may double in a fortnight here. The journey from tundra to South Africa may thus be achieved in two giant flights. It is believed that only Greenland breeders make this long migration, while Siberian birds winter on European coasts.

Kentish Plover

The beak and eye are conspicuously large for a bird of this size

An adult male in flight shows the white wingbar – less conspicuous than the Ringed Plover's. This is a smaller, paler species

(× 3/10)

Below: oval appearance of the body of a bird facing an observer

Birds taking wing show their very white underparts

In flight, the Kentish Plover's tail shows more white and less dark colouring than the Ringed Plover's

Adult female Kentish Plovers do not have the dark collar of the "ringed plovers"

Plover-fashion, a male pauses before running. On hot, shimmery days, Kentish Plovers' plumage merges with the background

The colouring of an adult female is pale buff and white with dark legs and beak. This bird is shown in a more alert attitude than the male below, which displays the characteristic "hunched" posture of the plover

No other "ringed plover" has dark legs and this alone conclusively identifies the Kentish Plover

(× ½)

Female looking back at observer

There is no proper cause for the frequent confusion between this bird and the Ringed and Little Ringed Plovers. It is shorter in length; often pear-shaped; has longer legs and a larger head and beak

Adult males have a distinctive ginger crown. By autumn it can fade almost to the colour of the back

Juvenile plumage has a scaly appearance

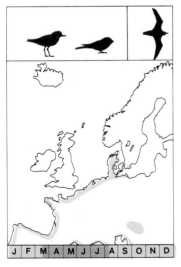

J F M A M J J A S O N D

This bird's English name is wildly inapt for a species distributed throughout four continents. Moreover, it ceased to breed in Britain in 1955.

The Kentish Plover is an active, nimble bird, which runs faster and more frequently than the Ringed Plover. It is also surprisingly confiding in the presence of human observers, unless there is a nest near by. When disturbed in the presence of the young, it reacts, like Ringed and Little Ringed Plovers, with a vigorous and realistic injury-feigning display. The nest is basically a scrape, as with the other two species of plover, but often has a sparse lining of shells, dead leaves or seaweed. Its situation varies considerably: like the Ringed Plover's, it may be built on open shingle, but dried mud, dead seaweed or grassy places are also occupied, though always close to the sea.

The display flight of the male, with slow, butterfly-like wing actions, also resembles that of the other two species. Three or four eggs are laid, and incubated by male and female in turn for about 24 days. Feeding places are sandy or muddy flats, where the birds feed well spaced out over the shore. "Foot paddling" is frequently used to stir up prey in shallow water.

Kentish Plovers are probably sedentary in many parts of their range, but more northerly breeders at least move south, wintering mainly on Mediterranean shores when they may be seen on passage in unlikely areas.

159

Dunlin

Commonest of all waders, the Dunlin in summer plumage can be identified by its black belly alone, which remains on most birds until September. Confusion, principally with the Little Stint, arises over full winter plumage, and over juveniles. For these the distinguishing factors are the Dunlin's down-curved beak, more portly appearance, more heavily streaked breast and spotted flanks retained until October

Adult, summer

Juvenile

Adult, winter

A juvenile in autumn plumage, below, can be confused with the Little Stint. The expert distinguishes the birds in flight on size alone

Adult, winter plumage

Dunlin of all ages and states of plumage retain the conspicuous wing-bar and tail markings

(× ³/₁₀)

Dunlin may prove exceptionally tame if approached slowly. They are frequently found inland on flooded terrain, sewage farms and reservoirs

Immature

An active feeder, the Dunlin alternates periods of rest with intense food-searching

Winter

Left, "stitching", the pattern left by a feeding Dunlin as it probes across the sand or mud

A massed flock of Dunlin, below, can be identified by its elongated shape. As the birds wheel, the whole mass flickers grey and white

Like other waders, the Dunlin is occasionally seen swimming

Adult, breeding season: a rufous back and black belly

Adult, winter plumage: a grey-brown back and slightly streaked breast

(× ½)

One-day-old chick

Juvenile: buff, as opposed to the grey plumage of the adult

Rising and falling like an animated plume of smoke, a flock of Dunlin performing aerobatics is an extraordinary spectacle. Such displays are usually seen at high tide, when Dunlin and other waders gather on shingle banks or fields to wait until the ebb tide exposes their feeding areas. Returning to the mud, they give an impression of bustling activity, feeding with scarcely an upward glance. Pecks at the mud surface and probes below it are interspersed with bouts of "stitching" – a rapid, mechanical series of shallow probes made as the bird moves forwards, leaving a track of dots. Its purpose is to discover prey by touch, and bouts of stitching often end in a deep probe to seize a tiny crustacean or worm. Surface pecks mainly capture a tiny snail (*Hydrobia*) which exists in enormous numbers on mudflats, providing food for many waders.

The Dunlin breeds on moorland, tundra or coastal marshes over much of northern Eurasia and America. Displays, pairing and establishment of territory are completed within two weeks of arrival on the breeding grounds, and the four eggs are laid in a scrape amongst low vegetation near water. They hatch after three weeks' incubation by both parents, and the young fledge after four weeks, feeding mainly on midge larvae, while adults concentrate on those of craneflies.

Dunlin of the Arctic sub-species winter in northerly regions.

Little Stint

Little Stints have the flight action and speed of flight common to small waders

Little Stint. Confusion with the Dunlin, below, is avoided by looking for the short, straight beak

A Juvenile. The Little Stint's white wing-bar, although not as conspicuous as the Dunlin's, is visible from a good distance

An adult in breeding season has a red back. The white lozenges on either side of the tail are standard on most species of wader

($\times \frac{3}{10}$)

Dunlin, southern race. A slightly down-curved beak

Two distinct Vs are formed by the back markings

Adult in winter

Dunlin, northern race. This specimen shows the longest beak to be encountered on the species

A deliberate walk and a picking action while feeding are characteristic of this species. It is also distinguished by its small size, short, black legs and a more elongated body than that of the Dunlin. Whatever the season, Little Stints have white underparts

Immature

Compared with the Dunlin this species has a cleaner appearance: its markings are more sharply defined

Adult, winter

Difficulty in distinguishing this species from the Dunlin is best overcome by discerning the neater, more delicate general look of the Little Stint at the same time as details of its plumage

($\times \frac{1}{2}$)

Adult, autumn

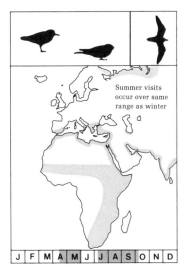

Summer visits occur over same range as winter

| J | F | M | A | M | J | J | A | S | O | N | D |

The Little Stint is one of the tiniest waders, conspicuously smaller than the Dunlin, from whose company it is rarely absent. Nevertheless, the two birds are related and their feeding methods are similar, with frequent rapid pecks interspersed with bouts of rapid, shallow test probes. Its rate of activity averages higher than the Dunlin's, reflecting its small size, and it concentrates more on molluscs or crustaceans found on the surface of mud or in shallow water. It also differs from the Dunlin in its choice of habitat on passage or in winter quarters, showing a greater preference for the edges of inland pools.

Spring and autumn migrations provide the main opportunity to see the Little Stint in western Europe. In its wintering places and on migration, it is occasionally found in flocks of several hundred, but on passage is usually seen in much smaller groups.

Its breeding areas are in the Arctic, well to the north of the scarcer Temminck Stint's. Grassy marshes or tundra are selected for nesting, and during the early part of the breeding season a prolonged trill is often uttered. This is presumably a song, though usually delivered from the ground; a hovering display flight has occasionally been observed. The typical wader clutch of four is incubated, mainly by the male, for about three weeks. The young fledge in approximately two to two and a half weeks.

Turnstone

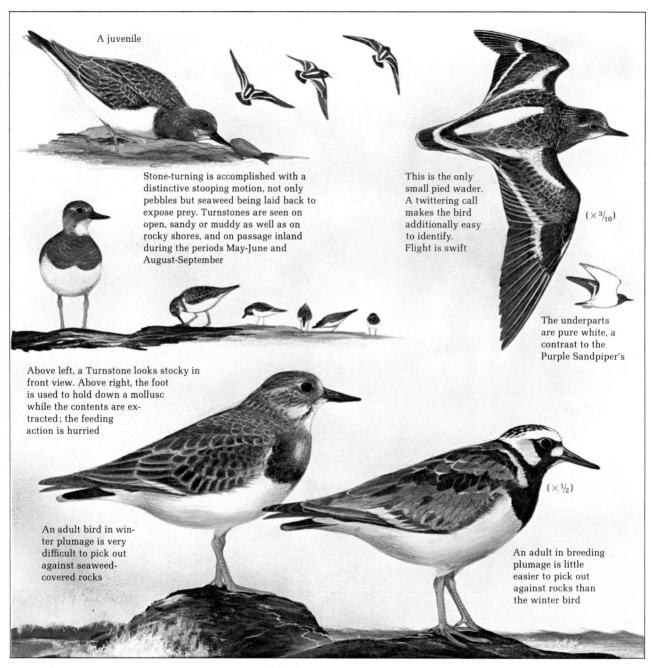

A juvenile

Stone-turning is accomplished with a distinctive stooping motion, not only pebbles but seaweed being laid back to expose prey. Turnstones are seen on open, sandy or muddy as well as on rocky shores, and on passage inland during the periods May-June and August-September

This is the only small pied wader. A twittering call makes the bird additionally easy to identify. Flight is swift

$(\times \frac{3}{10})$

The underparts are pure white, a contrast to the Purple Sandpiper's

Above left, a Turnstone looks stocky in front view. Above right, the foot is used to hold down a mollusc while the contents are extracted; the feeding action is hurried

$(\times \frac{1}{2})$

An adult bird in winter plumage is very difficult to pick out against seaweed-covered rocks

An adult in breeding plumage is little easier to pick out against rocks than the winter bird

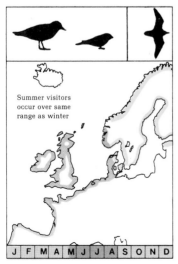

Summer visitors occur over same range as winter

J F M A M J J A S O N D

This bird's short, slightly upturned bill is adapted for prying under, or over-turning, all manner of seashore objects to find food. It also lays bare estuary mud by walking forwards, pushing back the fine covering of green seaweed into rolls with its beak. Sand-hoppers and similar crustaceans are the main prey found by this means, as well as small molluscs and worms. Turnstones also eat carrion washed up on beaches —ranging from dead birds to dead humans.

In Europe, the Turnstone breeds around the coasts of Scandinavia, chiefly on rocky islets. It is believed that year-old birds do not breed at all and even those of breeding age do not breed in every year. There is relatively little display at the nest sites, but males chase intruders away from their territory, returning with a butterfly flight, and tacking a trill on to the usual chattering call. Prior to laying, the male persists in making false nest scrapes. The female makes the final one, usually sheltered by a rock, and lays four eggs, often starting to incubate with the third, so that hatching (after 21 to 23 days) is spread over two days. Both sexes incubate, the female mainly by night, the male by day. After hatching, both parents tend the young, the male remaining with them for ten or more days after they can fly. Ringing experiments on Baltic breeders indicate that they migrate down the Atlantic seaboard to western Africa and beyond.

Purple Sandpiper

It is unusual to see the underwing pattern; the bird usually flies at low level

Despite its dumpy look, a Purple Sandpiper has the typical swift and easy flight of a wader. The all-dark upperparts with the pale but distinctive wing-bar (especially on the inner wing) provide conclusive identification. On either side of the dark tail are the white lozenges found on many waders

(×³⁄₁₀)

Purple Sandpipers are among the tamest of birds, but are very inconspicuous and easily overlooked. As well as their usual environment of rocky coastline they winter on mud or shingle beaches, and can also be seen on weed-covered breakwaters and slipways, especially at high tide

(× ½)

The sooty upperparts (faintly glossed with purple) merge easily with the bird's typical background of weed-strewn rocks. Leg colour varies from green through orange-yellow to brown. This adult is in winter plumage: a juvenile looks similar but has more patterning, and its feather edges are cream-coloured

In the breeding season adults develop buff edges to their back feathers and at first glance look entirely different from a bird in winter plumage

Seen at a distance, the flank markings appear to form longitudinal lines

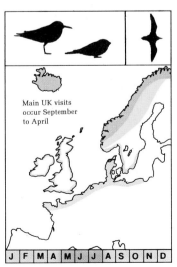

Main UK visits occur September to April

| J | F | M | A | M | J | J | A | S | O | N | D |

Tame in its behaviour, and charming to watch, the Purple Sandpiper should be one of the most familiar waders. In fact, it is much overlooked, probably because it is difficult to discern amongst the tumbled boulders of its rocky shore habitat, and spends much less time in flight than most waders.

Although closely related to the Dunlin, and similar – though plumper – in build, its habits are quite different. It rarely looks for food on sand or mud, and its bill is therefore scarcely used for probing or hunting by touch – most prey is found by sight. The great bulk of its diet in winter consists of small periwinkles and dog whelks. It feeds near the edge of the sea, moving up and down the shore with the tide. Its rate of feeding is highest in the middle region of the shore, where an average time of 17 seconds to pick up ten items was recorded in one field study.

It is largely silent in winter quarters, but on the Arctic breeding grounds a wheezy trilling song is used in display flight. Courtship also includes a wing-raising performance, sometimes seen in the wintering areas. The deep nest scrape is made amongst soft, lichen-covered ground, and the four eggs are incubated mainly by the male for 21 to 22 days. Birds disturbed while incubating employ the distraction tactic of leaving the nest with head lowered, looking remarkably like a vole or lemming, behaviour parallel to the injury-feigning displays of most waders.

Wood Sandpiper

The Wood Sandpiper usually nests on the ground, but also commandeers the disused nests of other species

This species has a pale underwing, unlike the Green Sandpiper's, which is black. Although a key point of difference between the species, it can be hard to discern on a dull day

($\times \frac{3}{10}$)

When flushed, the Wood Sandpiper rises quickly, flying off with a swift flicking action of the wings

Left, a typical view of this wader as it negotiates a particularly unstable patch of mud. In this posture the white open tail is eye-catching, as is the white shaft of the first primary feather

A Wood Sandpiper looks paler than a Green Sandpiper, but this test fails on dull days, when the Wood Sandpiper appears almost as dark as the Green. In flight, the Wood Sandpiper shows a greater length of trailing leg than the Green Sandpiper, and its wings are narrower

White first primary feather shafts are diagnostic of the Wood Sandpiper

Outside the nesting season, the Wood Sandpiper is rarely seen perching. This adult is in average breeding plumage—some birds have a more boldly chequered back with clear white markings. Most birds wear to a more uniform shade by late September. A more elegant, slimmer-built bird than the Green Sandpiper

($\times \frac{1}{2}$)

The pale-coloured head and white eye-stripe are characteristic Wood Sandpiper features, but not conclusive identification: adult Green Sandpipers have pale heads in spring, and in autumn they have a dark head with a white eye-ring

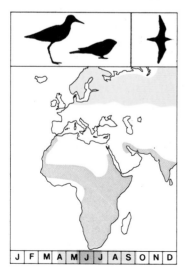

J F M A M J J A S O N D

Boggy clearings or lake shores among sub-Arctic birch or conifer woods are typical breeding grounds for the Wood Sandpiper, though farther north it nests on open tundra with only dwarf willow as cover. It is the most numerous wader in Finland, with an estimated 180,000 breeding pairs. A few pairs breed in Germany, Denmark and Scotland.

The breeding season starts with display flights, made by both sexes, consisting of alternating glides and flutters. There are two distinct songs, one of which sounds reminiscent of the clear, descending notes of the Woodlark, the other being indescribable. The nest is usually a simple hollow in the ground lined with grass. Four eggs are laid,

and incubated for 22 to 23 days by both sexes. The female takes the largest share of this task, but after the eggs hatch, she soon leaves the care of the young to her mate. Fledging takes about four weeks. Outside the breeding season, Wood Sandpipers are found mainly by pools on fresh marshes or sewage farms, rising with a characteristic call when disturbed. They feed both from water and by probing soft mud, obtaining small crustaceans, fly larvae, water beetles and the like.

In most of western Europe Wood Sandpipers are seen only on passage, usually in fairly small numbers, though gatherings of some thousands – mainly Scandinavian birds – occur in the Camargue, where the moult takes place.

Green Sandpiper

There is no white first primary feather shaft on the Green Sandpiper's wing, which is broader and darker in colour than the Wood Sandpiper's. Especially on dull days, a glimpse of the bird gives the initial impression that it is black and white

(× ³/₁₀)

In this typical wader posture, which the Green Sandpiper has in common with the Wood Sandpiper, it reveals a white tail with bold markings, which distinguish the species at all times

The adult in spring is very similar to a Wood Sandpiper, and identifiable only on general physical characteristics

A wary bird, which shoots twisting into the sky when flushed, uttering an explosive (even alarming) fluty call, quite distinct from the Wood Sandpiper's

The Green Sandpiper has a conspicuous white eye-ring, and its beak is longer, but not noticeably so, than the Wood Sandpiper's

Green Sandpipers are usually much less spotted than Wood Sandpipers, but this is not a conclusive means of identifying the species

(× ¹/₂)

An adult in winter plumage, which shows a darker breast and head than those of the Wood Sandpiper. The Green Sandpiper is a thicker-built bird with shorter legs

Typical alert resting posture of this nervous species. The tail is often bobbed

When the wings are lifted to assist balance, they are seen to be almost black underneath

Visits UK mainly from July to October

J F M A M J J A S O N D

Even more of a woodland bird than the Wood Sandpiper, the Green Sandpiper breeds almost entirely in either broad-leaved (birch and alder) or coniferous forest, but exceptions do occur, such as the pair which bred in Scotland in 1959, choosing wet moorland with only scattered pines.

During the early part of the breeding season the birds perform various ground displays with wings spread and tail fanned. Aerial display consists of alternating climbs, with rapidly beating wings, and steep downward glides. The song is a mixture of staccato, long-drawn and liquid notes. Usually, the nest site is the old nest of another bird, such as Fieldfare, Jay or Wood Pigeon, at heights of up to 45 feet or

more. The usual clutch of four eggs is incubated by both sexes for 20 to 23 days. On hatching, the young tumble to the ground, their light weight and thick down protecting them from harm. Fledging takes about four weeks, the male having sole charge of the brood after a few days. On passage and in winter quarters, the Green Sandpiper stays in situations providing plenty of cover, and is therefore likely to be unexpectedly flushed. While breeding, this species probes less than the Wood Sandpiper, mainly eating tiny aquatic animals.

Western populations of Green Sandpiper winter in Europe, from Britain south to Portugal, though birds from farther east migrate as far as Africa.

Uncommon Waders

Many birds come to Europe regularly but in very small numbers, either to breed or to pause while on passage. Others are intermittent and very rare migrants, including 16 North American species. The birds on this page are found regularly in suitable places.

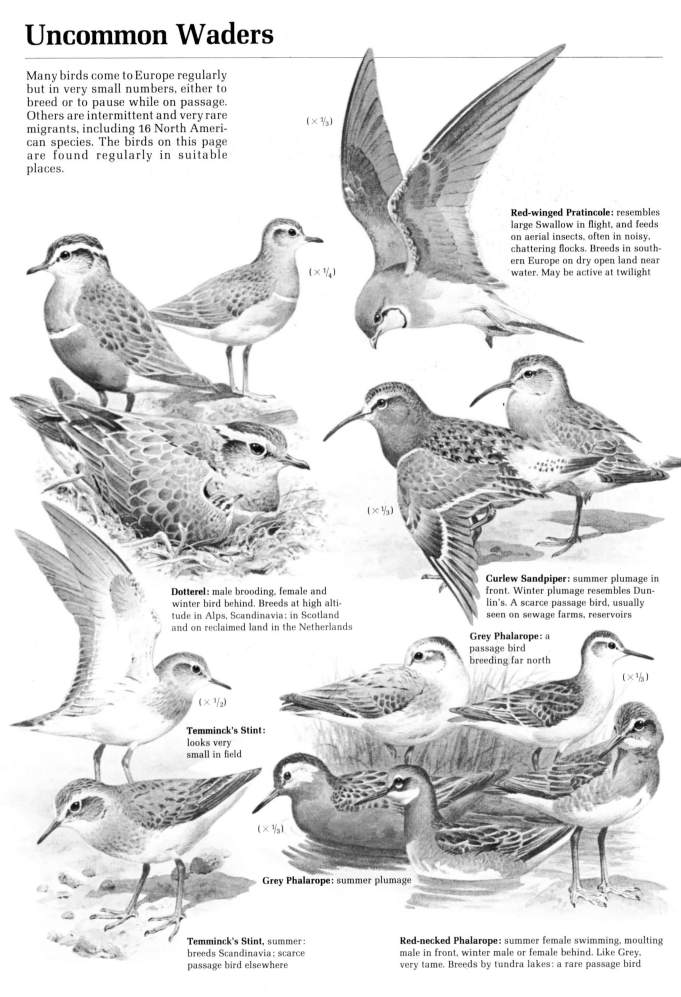

(×⅓)

(×¼)

Red-winged Pratincole: resembles large Swallow in flight, and feeds on aerial insects, often in noisy, chattering flocks. Breeds in southern Europe on dry open land near water. May be active at twilight

(×⅓)

Dotterel: male brooding, female and winter bird behind. Breeds at high altitude in Alps, Scandinavia; in Scotland and on reclaimed land in the Netherlands

Curlew Sandpiper: summer plumage in front. Winter plumage resembles Dunlin's. A scarce passage bird, usually seen on sewage farms, reservoirs

Grey Phalarope: a passage bird breeding far north

(×⅓)

(×½)

Temminck's Stint: looks very small in field

Grey Phalarope: summer plumage

(×⅓)

Temminck's Stint, summer: breeds Scandinavia; scarce passage bird elsewhere

Red-necked Phalarope: summer female swimming, moulting male in front, winter male or female behind. Like Grey, very tame. Breeds by tundra lakes: a rare passage bird

Common Sandpiper

Especially at dusk in autumn, a noisy party of Sandpipers may be seen flying about at some height—a preliminary to migration. At almost all other times the Common Sandpiper will be seen flying low over water

A striking and, for a wader, unusual underwing pattern, which is rarely seen in the field because the bird flies at low level. Useful in establishing the identity of a dead bird

Visible on an airborne Common Sandpiper are the white outer tail and white wing-bar. The flicking action of the wings, held stiffly and slightly forwards, is unique to (and typical of) the Common Sandpiper

$(\times \sqrt[3]{10})$

In summer an adult has dark streaking

$(\times \frac{1}{2})$

By the time it is two days old a Common Sandpiper chick forages for itself

Right, the extensions of the white breast plumage up the sides of the breast are a sure means of identification, visible in a front view

If disturbed when feeding at the water's edge, the Common Sandpiper will fly out over the water and swing round in a wide arc to return to the shore a few hundred yards farther on

This species incessantly bobs its tail

The young bird is more heavily barred than an adult, but this will only be seen at close range

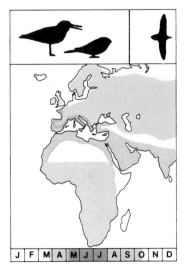

Swift-flowing rocky streams are the typical breeding habitat of the Common Sandpiper, though if sufficiently clear, still waters are suitable. Like the Dippers and wagtails with which it shares its living space, this trim little wader has the habit of making regular "teetering" movements—a feature of bird behaviour which has yet to be satisfactorily explained.

Common Sandpipers arrive at their breeding areas in April, and the pairing and courtship phase is marked by spectacular display flights in which the male circles higher and higher uttering a trilling song. He may dive at other males, and fierce fighting occurs on the ground. Both sexes make nest scrapes, the female choosing one to line with scraps of vegetation. The site chosen is usually in vegetation, but sometimes on quite exposed shingle banks. Both sexes incubate the four eggs, which hatch in 21 to 23 days. The young fledge in about four weeks, and there is only one brood. Injury-feigning is used to distract intruders from the young, and there are reports of adults carrying chicks between the legs to remove them from danger. Outside the breeding season, Common Sandpipers are seen in passage on a variety of waters and on the coast, where they prefer channels and creeks on saltings or fresh marshes to open shores. In all situations they feed by picking tiny animals from the surface of rocks, mud or shallow water.

Ruff

Ruff courtship ceremonial, below, takes place on an open display ground, or lek, on grassland or tundra. Periods of feverish, complex activity are interspersed with periods of sudden "freezing"

Adult female (Reeve)

(×1/6)

(×1/6) Adult male (Ruff)

Resident independent males, right, claim individual territories on the lek. Wing-flashing display heralds the arrival of "visitors" (white-plumaged, non-territorial males; marginal males trying to establish claims to territory, and females)

Male and female, above, in flight in winter plumage; immature birds are similar but have a slightly warmer tone to the plumage. Flight is strong with emphatic wing beats and the bird usually glides on landing. Faint wing-bar and the white patches at either side of the tail identify the Ruff

Male with ruff and ear tufts raised in display

Aggression display and actual fighting occurs between resident males and where a resident independent is challenged by a marginal male

Fighting ends when one of the protagonists shows submission by crouching and averting his head. A receptive female may meanwhile have entered the winning male's territory for copulation

(×1/4)

Medium-length, slightly curved bill and delicate head shape are identifying features. Seen in UK and western Europe on passage in spring and autumn; inland and coastal marshes and flooded fields

After the visitors have departed, the resident independent males adopt a unique upright stance, raising, relaxing and sleeking their ruffs

Leg colour is very variable and of little help in identification

Complex in breeding behaviour, beautiful in plumage, the Ruff is truly an amazing bird.

Display and mating take place only at communal display grounds, or leks. Several groups of birds throughout the world have evolved lek behaviour, and in Europe the Black Grouse provides another example. Among them the Ruff is unique because of its system of independent and satellite males linked with individual plumage variations.

Independent males establish leks, and acquire display territories on them by threatening or fighting other males. Satellite males may share territories with independent males, but do not take part in their defence. They show little aggression, otherwise indepen-

dent males would not tolerate them, and on large leks they achieve mating only infrequently. On small leks they are more successful, and their presence seems to have some value in attracting females to the site. Only males on territories have any chance of being selected for mating by the females that visit the lek; some, usually the young or very old ones, hold no territories, and can only linger around the margins of the lek. However, in time, the young ones will dispossess territory holders and establish themselves.

Nests are made in the general vicinity of the lek, but are often well hidden amongst rough grass or sedges. The female carries the entire burden of incubation and care of the young.

Knot

Adult, winter plumage. All Knot in winter plumage, and juveniles, have white underparts

Adult male, below, breeding plumage. The female is duller

Above, the appearance of winter birds in flight. Even at a distance, the wings look long

(×³/₁₀)

Above: an extreme example of the Knot's red breeding plumage; many birds are less intensely coloured

At close range, the Knot's very long wings are immediately striking. This adult in winter plumage has an overall grey appearance in the field, with a pale rump and a wing-bar which is not so marked as the Dunlin's

Knot form spectacular massed flocks with distinct shapes. A small one of about 1,000 birds, immediately below, is oval. A large one, bottom, containing 10,000 or more, narrows at the trailing end

At high tide Knot are seen resting. From medium range, they appear nondescript, but shape alone will identify them

The Knot is one of the largest of the European shore-feeding waders, with a noticeably stocky build, short, straight black bill and short pale legs. It will often be seen feeding in very large, dense flocks, the individual birds probing three or four times at one spot before moving

A juvenile. It can be distinguished by the dark penultimate rings on the back feathers

(× ½)

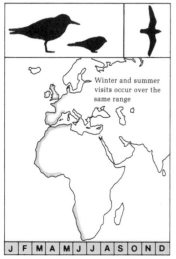

Winter and summer visits occur over the same range

J F M A M J J A S O N D

King Knut (Canute), who tried to turn back the waves, is said to have found these plump waders good eating, and their name is supposed to derive from his. Alternatively, as shore birds they may simply have been associated with the king whose reputation was made on a beach. Knot are larger than their near relative the Dunlin, in whose company they often feed. Their greater size is reflected in a slower feeding rate, illustrating an inverse relationship between size and activity which is general throughout the animal kingdom. Otherwise, their feeding behaviour is similar to the Dunlin's, though Knot concentrate more on surface prey such as small periwinkles and other molluscs. Knot are high Arctic breeders, nesting on open tundra sparsely covered by lichens. The four eggs are laid as soon as snow cover disperses, usually in the latter half of June. Both parents incubate, the eggs hatching in 21 days. The young are then led to more marshy ground, where insect larvae can be found.

Knot winter on the coasts of western Europe, as far south as West Africa; British coasts hold the largest number, 250,000 in mid-winter. Various schemes have been proposed for building tidal barrages or carrying out reclamation schemes in several of their main winter habitats, and to help forecast the effects of such developments on the Knot, its populations and migrations are the object of intensive research.

169

Golden Plover

 R

In winter the bird has a gold wash over dark upperparts, and a visible wing-bar

Breeding plumage of southern race

Winter plumage—all races, all sexes

Left, a male of the northern race; right, a male of the southern race. The farther south a Golden Plover lives, the less black there is on its breast

A solid-looking bird, with long, narrow, fast-beating wings. On this plover the rounded, almost bullet-shaped head is especially noticeable in flight

(× ⅕)

A Golden Plover looks identical to a Grey Plover from beneath, except for pure white, rather than black "armpits"

A recognizably gentle expression. Below, the wing-stretching habit, which often gives away the bird's location

(× ½)

Golden Plovers glide before landing, usually holding the wings up for a moment before folding them

Typical stance—one leg straight, one aslant

Golden Plovers look puff-breasted

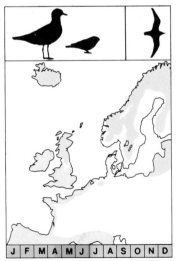

J F M A M J J A S O N D

Pasture and meadowland, often well inland, are the winter habitat of the Golden Plover, where its liquid calls are as much a sound of the country as the chuckling of Fieldfares. Moving from field to field, Golden Plovers fly in tightly bunched flocks, which spread out on landing to feed in the usual plover fashion—short runs alternating with brief pauses. When detected, prey is seized by sudden grabs, and the many earthworms captured usually break off near the head—a wasteful method compared with that of the Curlews often found on the same fields, whose long bills can extract worms much more completely. However, the run-and-snatch method is ideal for the capture of such surface prey as beetles, and the slugs and fly larvae often found under straw or grass roots are also eaten in large quantities. The shore (where small molluscs are the prey) is usually a subsidiary feeding place, except during hard frosts. However, in coastal areas it is used for roosting—though when there is bright moonlight, Golden Plovers stay feeding on the fields all night.

In early spring, birds still in winter quarters may be heard uttering their song—a beautiful trilling phrase, repeated in descending pitch—and many assume their striking summer plumage before leaving. The breeding habitat is moorland or tundra, where the nest is made in a depression amongst grass or lichen.

Grey Plover

Basic Grey Plover colouring is grey or brown, but there is slight variation according to season or the age of the bird

Highly conspicuous black armpit patches are present throughout the year on an adult or immature bird

A Grey Plover with the entirely black underparts of full summer plumage will sometimes be seen in Europe during May, June, July or August

Adult, full breeding plumage

While moulting, the upperparts are a mass of black and white spots

Both the white rump and barred tail are very conspicuous in the field. The long, thin wings carry a noticeable bar. This specimen is in winter plumage; juveniles are similar

($\times$ 3/10)

($\times$ 1/2)

An adult, winter plumage. The one-legged stance—a single toe protruding from the leg tucked up under the belly—is common among waders

Grey Plovers have a slow, ponderous walk. Their dejected expression and hunched posture seem to match their often bleak surroundings

The juvenile has a faint yellow wash

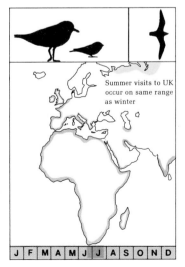

Summer visits to UK occur on same range as winter

| J | F | M | A | M | J | J | A | S | O | N | D |

Coastal mudflats are the habitat of the Grey Plover, a shore-feeding counterpart of the Golden Plover. The black "armpit" patch immediately distinguishes the Grey Plover in flight, as does the clear three-syllabled call—one of the most distinctive of all bird sounds. The Grey Plover is a more heavily built bird than the Golden Plover, and adopts a hunched posture—even on its infrequent feeding visits to fields, where a Golden Plover, with its upright stance, has a much better view over grass or stubble. On the shore, the longer, heavier bill of the Grey Plover enables it to take prey inaccessible to Golden Plovers, such as ragworms, which are excavated with sideways flicks of the bill. Crabs are a major food until they move into deeper water for the winter. Small molluscs are taken in quantity.

The Grey Plover is a high Arctic breeder and undertakes much more extensive migrations than the Golden Plover. European birds come from the populations breeding in Russia and Siberia. They migrate through the Baltic, and many continue via European coasts to winter on African shores as far away as Cape Province. Breeding habits resemble those of the Golden Plover: both have a similar song and "butterfly" display flight. The nest is a simple scrape amongst stones and lichen, where four eggs are laid at the end of June. The adults are extremely bold in defence of the young, which fledge in late August.

171

Greenshank

Very pale underwing

Greenshank on passage are seen either singly or in small parties

A Greenshank may be seen sweeping its bill from side to side in order to stir prey from the bottom of a pool

Unmarked wings are probably the cause of the Greenshank's reputation as a nondescript bird, but its pale head and white V extending right up the back are diagnostic of the species in flight, which is swift and erratic. The wings are usually angled back

$(\times \frac{3}{10})$

Greenshank give a predominant physical impression of leanness. Once learned, the deliberate and melodious call, uttered in three or four phrases, is unmistakable

$(\times \frac{1}{2})$

Below, posture adopted as the bird moves to new feeding ground

At close range, the green legs and the hint of green on the slightly upturned bill distinguish this species from all other waders. Greenshank take alarm at the slightest disturbance

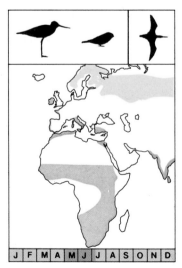

J F M A M J J A S O N D

Though it is undistinguished in plumage, the Greenshank's habits and life history are as interesting as any among the waders. It breeds in northern Europe and Asia on dry moorland or on boggy areas in tundra or forest clearings. From here it undertakes an extensive migration to winter on coasts anywhere from the Mediterranean to South Africa, or, for more easterly populations, southern Asia and Australasia. The bird is therefore seen mainly as a passage migrant in western Europe, feeding on mudflats, salt-marshes or fresh marsh pools. It is an active and nimble feeder, catching such prey as crustaceans and small fish in shallow water. It often makes rapid dashes to seize prey, and occasionally breaks into an astonishing, high-stepping dance, which is thought to stir prey into movement, thus revealing themselves. On the breeding grounds, water insects—especially beetles and water boatmen—are the main prey, but fish, newts and frogs may be snapped up.

The nest of the Greenshank is situated amid huge tracts of relatively featureless ground, and to find one is a major achievement in fieldcraft. This challenge, paradoxically, has made the Greenshank's breeding biology better known than many more common waders. Its rich song is uttered in a "switchback" flight, and a wide variety of displays is used in courtship. The eggs hatch in 24 to 25 days, and fledging takes about four weeks.

Redshank

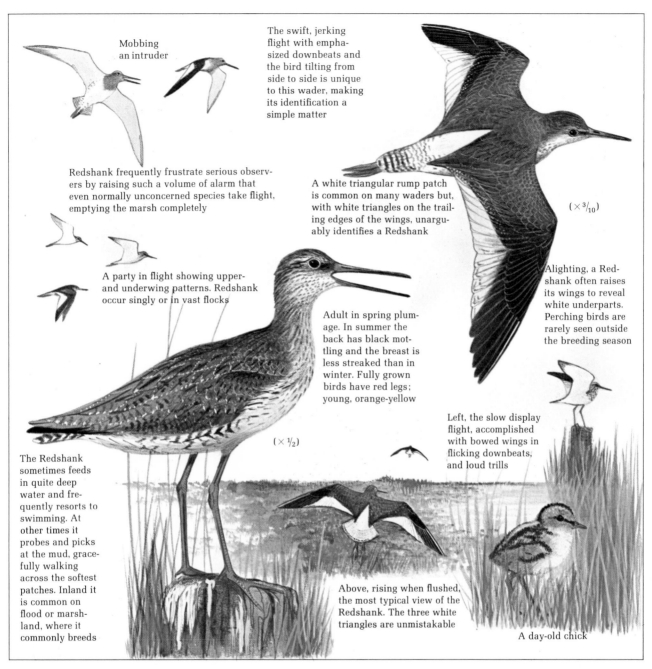

Mobbing an intruder

The swift, jerking flight with empha-sized downbeats and the bird tilting from side to side is unique to this wader, making its identification a simple matter

Redshank frequently frustrate serious observ-ers by raising such a volume of alarm that even normally unconcerned species take flight, emptying the marsh completely

A white triangular rump patch is common on many waders but, with white triangles on the trail-ing edges of the wings, unargu-ably identifies a Redshank

$(\times \frac{3}{10})$

A party in flight showing upper- and underwing patterns. Redshank occur singly or in vast flocks

Adult in spring plum-age. In summer the back has black mot-tling and the breast is less streaked than in winter. Fully grown birds have red legs; young, orange-yellow

Alighting, a Red-shank often raises its wings to reveal white underparts. Perching birds are rarely seen outside the breeding season

The Redshank sometimes feeds in quite deep water and fre-quently resorts to swimming. At other times it probes and picks at the mud, grace-fully walking across the softest patches. Inland it is common on flood or marsh-land, where it commonly breeds

$(\times \frac{1}{2})$

Left, the slow display flight, accomplished with bowed wings in flicking downbeats, and loud trills

Above, rising when flushed, the most typical view of the Redshank. The three white triangles are unmistakable

A day-old chick

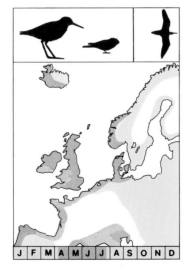

Rising with hysterical calls from a creek or pool at the approach of Man, the Redshank has aptly been called the sentinel of the marshes.

During autumn and spring its main feeding area is open mudflats, where it specializes in taking a tiny crustacean (*Corophium*) which lives in burrows in mud. Generally, these creatures lie near the surface, and are seized with brief pecks as the bird strides briskly over the mud: up to 100 pecks may be made per minute. Sight is the important sense for this type of hunting, but an alternative method, in which the bill is swept from side to side across the mud, seems to rely on touch, and is important at night. Studies show that a mud temperature below 37°F prevents the

Corophium from showing themselves, and when this occurs the Redshank switches to other prey, such as rag-worms and molluscs, or visits inland fields to take earthworms and leather-jackets. Redshank regularly feed inland in many areas, especially in the breed-ing season, when meadows near water are favoured.

Courtship includes a display flight performed with rapid, shallow wing beats, sometimes by several birds to-gether. The nest is a lined scrape, well hidden under a grass tussock or salt-marsh plants, usually with a definite side entrance. Both sexes incubate, sitting very tightly when approached. The four eggs hatch in 21 to 25 days, and the young fledge after four weeks.

Woodcock

Above, viewed from behind, the head shows eyes placed to give rear vision. This facility is enhanced by the slightly concave rear sides of the skull, apparent, left, on the head from above

Appearance of the male in the roding display flight, when his very slow wing action is something like an owl's

$(\times \frac{1}{5})$

Left, the conventional view of a Woodcock after being flushed, when it takes off with a considerable clattering. Larger than a snipe, with more rounded wings, it is additionally easy to recognize when flushed because it flies straighter, swerving to dodge through trees

If it has not just been flushed a Woodcock may be quite slow and hesitant in flight

Left, the very striking under-tail pattern is shown off during ground displays

Carrying a young bird between the thighs

With basically adult profile and plumage, for a newly hatched bird the young Woodcock is uncommonly recognizable as one of its species

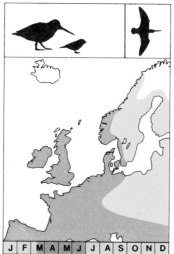

"For fools are known by looking wise, as men find Woodcock by their eyes." Such a feat of fieldcraft is beyond most people's ability, but it is undoubtedly true that Woodcock have very large eyes—an important feature in a largely nocturnal bird. Moreover, these eyes have a greater field of view behind the head than in front, providing early warning of danger while the bird is probing.

Prey is found mainly by means of the sensitive bill tip, and the capacity for raising the tip of the upper mandible, which many waders possess, is particularly highly developed in Woodcock and snipe, enabling them to grasp prey underground without the problem of opening the entire bill. The food itself is earthworms and insect larvae, found in moist places in woodland.

During the breeding season, male Woodcock perform a display flight known as roding. This takes place in the evening, and is a flight on a regular circuit, sometimes of several miles. The wing beats are characteristically slow, with intermittent pauses coinciding with a low croaking call. The nest is a scrape in the ground, often near the foot of a tree, with a clutch usually of four eggs. They are incubated by the female for 20 to 21 days, and the female tends the young, which fly after two and a half weeks. There is good evidence that females occasionally move their chicks by flying with them grasped between their thighs.

Snipe–Jack Snipe

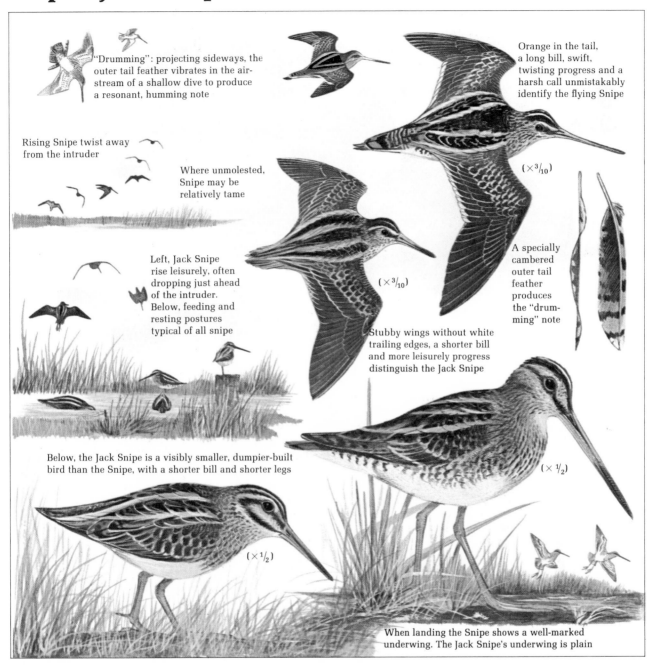

"Drumming": projecting sideways, the outer tail feather vibrates in the airstream of a shallow dive to produce a resonant, humming note

Orange in the tail, a long bill, swift, twisting progress and a harsh call unmistakably identify the flying Snipe

($\times\frac{3}{10}$)

Rising Snipe twist away from the intruder

Where unmolested, Snipe may be relatively tame

A specially cambered outer tail feather produces the "drumming" note

Left, Jack Snipe rise leisurely, often dropping just ahead of the intruder. Below, feeding and resting postures typical of all snipe

($\times\frac{3}{10}$)

Stubby wings without white trailing edges, a shorter bill and more leisurely progress distinguish the Jack Snipe

Below, the Jack Snipe is a visibly smaller, dumpier-built bird than the Snipe, with a shorter bill and shorter legs

($\times\frac{1}{2}$)

($\times\frac{1}{2}$)

When landing the Snipe shows a well-marked underwing. The Jack Snipe's underwing is plain

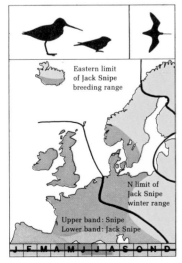

Eastern limit of Jack Snipe breeding range

N limit of Jack Snipe winter range

Upper band: Snipe
Lower band: Jack Snipe

J F M A M J J A S O N D

Zigzag flight must be an effective defence against the falcons or other winged predators which occasionally attack Snipe. Man, perversely enough, finds rising Snipe all the more attractive targets because they are so difficult to kill with a shotgun.

Their feeding methods make an interesting contrast with the Curlew's: they search in soft mud with straight probes, but indulge in none of the Curlew's vigorous contortions. Consequently, the bill needs less reinforcement, and there is room for a long tongue. By this means, many worms and insect larvae are drawn far up the bill even before it is removed from the ground. A small proportion of seeds is also taken. Snipe feed most actively at night, flighting to their feeding areas at dusk.

The "drumming" display flight is first heard in early spring over the wet woodlands or water meadows where the bird breeds. The nest is a simple scrape in a tussock with the usual wader clutch of four. The female incubates alone for 20 days, but both parents look after the chicks, which fledge in 18 or 19 days. Two broods are sometimes reared.

The Jack Snipe, a smaller bird, is a more northerly breeder than the Common Snipe, and though the two species associate together outside the breeding season, the Jack Snipe is never so numerous. Its feeding habits are generally similar.

Bar-tailed Godwit

Below, adults and immature birds are indistinguishable

A typical small flock pattern

Above and below, adults in full summer plumage. Birds moulting in or out of this condition in spring or autumn are much spotted with white

Length of bill is variable, but the female's is longer than the male's

A Bar-tailed Godwit is the only straight-billed brownish wader with a white V on its back. In flight the legs project only just beyond the tail

(× ⅕)

Bar-tailed Godwit flight is swift, powerful and direct. Before setting off in the desired direction on passage they can be seen methodically gaining height by flying to and fro. Above right, godwits indulge more than most waders in "whiffling" down to land—an erratic style of descent, during which birds can look temporarily insane

A large, long-billed wader with comparatively long legs. Before the spring moult, Bar-tailed Godwit plumage may in some cases be pure brown and white

(× ⅓)

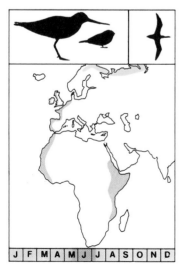

A feeding flock of Bar-tailed Godwits is an entertaining spectacle. Walking briskly across the mud, brief trial probes are made at frequent intervals, and when the sensitive bill tip detects prey, the bird continues walking without breaking step, but around its bill instead of straight on. This drives the bill deep into the mud to capture a worm or small bivalve mollusc. Occasionally, also, the birds will run in pursuit of visually located prey. Bar-tailed Godwits prefer to feed in firm, rather sandy mud, usually keeping well away from the tideline, unlike the longer-legged Black-tailed Godwits, which regularly wade in deep water. Though the birds feed in well-spread-out groups, they congregate in dense flocks at high-tide roosts. Single birds, or pairs, may also be encountered.

During winter, Bar-tailed Godwits have colouring similar to the Curlew and resemble them when in flight, but the godwit can be distinguished by its quicker wing beats even if the bill cannot be seen. These birds have a curious habit—shared, oddly enough, with the entirely unrelated grey geese—of suddenly losing height by plunging through the air in wild twisting dives. Their call is a wheezing squeak.

The Bar-tailed Godwit breeds in the Arctic, favouring marshy tundra with a scattering of dwarf willow or birch scrub. The nest is made on a dry hillock and the four eggs are incubated principally by the male.

Black-tailed Godwit

Adult Godwit in winter plumage; the juvenile is very similar but has a rufous tint on the neck and breast

The long trailing legs, long bill and broad white wing-bars are distinctive in flight. The black tail and white upper-tail coverts also show prominently, making the bird very easy to identify

Right, a male complains loudly at human, avian or animal intruders; gulls in particular are pursued mercilessly across the nest site

The white underwing and rather pied patterning show in flight

Passage birds occur singly or in parties inland at reservoirs and sewage farms. The species is more at home in inland areas than the Bar-tailed Godwit, but is often seen in large numbers in favoured coastal localities

The male has a remarkable "butterfly" display flight over his own territory and birds are easily observed during display periods

(× ⅕)

An adult bird in summer plumage has a very lean, long-legged appearance and stands much taller than the Bartailed Godwit. In summer, the neck and breast take on a chestnut colouring, but the under-tail coverts are invariably white—in contrast with those of the Bar-tailed species, which turn red

Wing and tail markings are clearly displayed as the bird glides in to land

Below left, the male shows off his tail pattern and raises the feathers on his back in a high-stepping display. Below, the female walks up to the nest scrape, made by the male, and crouches to make a close inspection

(× ⅓)

The adult in winter plumage is basically grey and white

Soft, treacherous mud, where men venture at their own risk, is the feeding ground of the handsome Black-tailed Godwit. It is a longer-legged bird than the Bar-tailed Godwit, and can therefore venture into deeper water. While feeding, Black-tailed Godwits move less hurriedly than Bar-tailed, and hunt more by touch, spending much of their time in long series of trial probes. Worms and molluscs are taken on the shore; insect larvae and such surface prey as grasshoppers, flies and beetles are taken inland. Seeds and berries are occasionally eaten on migration.

While on passage, the Black-tailed Godwit occurs inland more often than the Bar-tailed Godwit, and is a more southerly breeder, nesting in suitable areas of western Europe. It has recently returned to Britain as a regular breeder after more than a century.

The breeding habitat is fens or swampy grasslands inland. Laying commences in late April, and the nest, consisting of a thick pad of dead grass and sometimes down, is made in a hollow amongst rough grass. Normally there are four eggs in the clutch, and with the third or fourth, incubation commences. This lasts 24 days, and the male takes the main share of brooding. The young fledge after four to five weeks. Western European breeders migrate largely to central Africa; farther east, populations move to the Middle East and India. Many birds also winter in Britain, Ireland and France.

177

Curlew

(× 1/5)

Curlew flight can be slow and leisurely. Birds are seen singly, in small groups or in vast flocks. Migrating parties are seen half to one and a half miles offshore, at which range they may be confused with ducks

There is much barring on the under-wing, and a darkish neck and breast

All year, and even far inland, the loud call indicates a Curlew's presence long before the bird is visible. Size, long wings and a long decurved bill prevent confusion with all species except the Whimbrel. Both birds have a white V up the back, and a whitish tail; but Curlews have different head patterns and, in the case of females, much longer bills. The dark outer wings are evident on landing

Right, the longest of female Curlew bills is six inches in length—up to a third longer than the average male's bill, which ranges between four and five inches

(× 1/5)

Below, left to right, the Curlew's variable appearance: sleeping, alert and resting. Spangled plumage camouflages the bird efficiently on grass or moorland

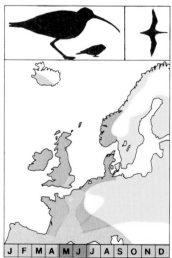

Stalking sedately across the mudflats of an estuary, a foraging Curlew presents an interesting contrast to the restless energy of the smaller waders. It hunts both by touch and sight, making frequent shallow probes by which the sensitive bill tip can detect subterranean animals, or locating them by such clues as surface holes and tracks. They are then extracted, often piecemeal, by deep and vigorous probes, the decurved bill shape aiding exploration underground. Ragworms and small bivalve molluscs are taken in this way on the shore, earthworms and leatherjackets on moorlands or pasture. Much surface prey is also taken.

The impression of sedateness is dispelled when a Curlew calls: its voice has a haunting quality, vividly evocative of the wild places it inhabits—moorlands or bogs when breeding, coastal flats in winter.

Most Curlews pair before arrival on the breeding grounds and are thought to return to the same territory in successive years. The territory is defended with boundary-marking flights and occasionally fighting. The nest hollow is selected from several made by the male amongst rough grass, and is then lined by both parents with grass stems. Four eggs are laid, and incubated for four weeks by both parents, who change places twice daily. The young fledge after six or seven weeks, but the bill does not reach full length for a further 12 weeks.

Whimbrel

Whimbrel on passage fly singly or in small flocks

A Whimbrel in flight looks smaller than a Curlew and its wings beat more rapidly. At close range the tail looks grey, but in the distance white

First indication of a Whimbrel's presence is usually its whistle. A single bird will often alter course to fly over an observer if he gives a life-like imitation of the call

The underwing is marginally whiter than the Curlew's

$(\times \frac{1}{5})$

From behind, Whimbrels have an outline typical of the group of waders, comprising curlews and godwits, to which they belong

This species is a smaller version of the Curlew, but easily differentiated at any season. Besides a visibly shorter beak than the Curlew, the Whimbrel has a dark crown with a central stripe, a conspicuous eye-stripe and a more dainty general appearance

The Whimbrel chick has a straight beak, and like other wader offspring is active soon after birth

$(\times \frac{1}{3})$

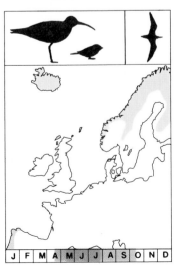

Tiny specks high in the sky, parties of migrating Whimbrel would often pass over unnoticed were it not for the call—a rapid series of whistles, descending in pitch, and usually seven in number. Heard in bleak surroundings, the call has an eerie quality, and in parts of Britain Whimbrel are called the "seven whistlers", with superstitious connotations. Seen at close range the bird is a smaller edition of the Curlew, but the bill is much shorter, though equally down-curved. Its feeding behaviour is similar, but the desultory trial probes of the Curlew are replaced by test jabs made close together in rapid sequence, somewhat resembling the technique of such small waders as Dunlin. Choice of habitat is rather wider than the Curlew's, with an apparently greater liking for rocky shores. Coral reefs are favoured in some of the wintering areas. Prey taken includes molluscs, worms and crabs.

The breeding habitat is usually treeless moorland or tundra. Display flights commence soon after arrival and consist of a long spiral climb followed by a gliding descent, sometimes varied with aerobatics. The accompanying song is a bubbling trill similar to that of the Curlew. Female often joins male in both the flight and the song. The nest is a depression, usually on a hummock giving a good view of the surrounding terrain. Both sexes incubate for 27 to 28 days, and the young are fledged in four weeks.

Black-winged Stilt

As unmistakable in flight as on the ground, the Stilt has quick, shallow wing-beats like a Tern. The legs are normally held close together and extend straight beyond the tail. Young birds are browner in autumn and greyer-backed in winter

Agitated Stilts will hover close overhead, legs dangling grotesquely, assailing the intruder with an unending scream of alarm calls. In the breeding season, females, left, have white crown and nape. On males, right, they are black

Stilts often hold their wings open to assist balance while rushing about

Juveniles, top, have brown crowns while second-year birds have grey napes, bottom. The male's crown and nape varies from an occasional pure white in winter, through the flecked dark grey of normal winter plumage, centre, to shiny black in summer

No other wader rivals the Stilt for length of leg. An incubating female's folded legs extend as far as the tip of the tail

($\times \frac{1}{3}$)

Newly hatched chicks have relatively short legs and beak

A rare visitor to northern Europe, the Black-winged Stilt is more widespread around the Mediterranean, where it is a characteristic bird of open marshland, lagoons and saltpans. It often occurs there in moderately large numbers, nesting in colonies on small islands or banks between saltpans. Individual pairs show considerable aggression, keeping up a fusillade of angry yelps.

Pink legs of quite extraordinary length and striking black and white plumage in all seasons make this one of the easiest birds to identify. Standing on mud, the legs may seem impractical as the Stilt half-crouches to take an insect or crustacean off the surface, or struggles to stay upright in a stiff breeze. The evolutionary benefits of feeding in deeper water than any other wader obviously offset this and Stilts are seen in their element pacing sedately in water nearly up to their bellies, where only the marsh terns are competitors for insects picked off the water surface with the delicate needle-sharp beak. Only rarely is the beak used for probing mud, though small fish are seized from the water.

The egg is typical in size and shape for a wader, but clearly the newly hatched chick, although able to run as soon as its down is dry, could not fit into a normal egg if legs and beak were of the same proportions as the adult. Thus, as it grows, beak and legs develop unusually quickly.

Avocet

In flight, Avocets are rounder-winged than most waders. Seen from below, they are largely white with black wing-tips. The narrow black chevrons on the back are diagnostic even when the upturned beak cannot be seen properly

Avocets sometimes swim, far left. A pair indulge in "mutual preening", centre, which often precedes copulation. Right, the male prepares to mount–the female indicating her receptiveness by crouching with spread wings

Very aggressive when protecting nest or territory, the Avocet's usual defence posture is to lower the head and run towards the intruder, sometimes with wings spread to heighten the effect. Below, a nesting female with belly feathers fluffed out to bring the brood patch into contact with the eggs

$(\times \frac{1}{3})$

Chicks have only a hint of the upturned beak, but they do show signs of the adult wing pattern and have the unusual webbed feet

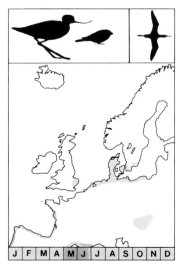

Avocets flying against a blue sky, melodious calls ringing over the marsh, are an enchanting spectacle. Surely the most beautiful wader, its name derives from the French *Avocat* (barrister), an allusion to the pied plumage. Related species in America and Australia have rufous colouring on head or neck.

The elegant upturned bill is a specialized feeding instrument. Small invertebrates are captured as the bird walks through water, sweeping the bill from side to side through the surface layers. It will also sweep the bottom mud, sometimes swimming and upending like a duck. Avocets nest colonially, choosing sites on open sand or mud near water. The small nesting territory is defended with a varied repertoire of displays and postures, but most commonly one in which the defender walks alongside the intruder, edging towards it. Pairs defending territories against neighbours display with legs flexed and heads lowered, often attracting other pairs. Pre-mating displays include bowing and bill-crossing. Nests vary from unlined scrapes to substantial platforms, the latter often a response to the threat of flooding. Four eggs are normally laid, in late April or early May in northern Europe. The chicks feed from birth, at first mainly by pecking, though sweeping begins while the bill is still quite short and nearly straight.

The Avocet colonies of eastern England date from 1947 (Avocets last bred here in 1842), and are now flourishing.

J F M A M J J A S O N D

181

Oystercatcher

Stabber bill

Young birds have a grey-tipped bill and white collar. Adults develop collar in winter

Hammer bill

In flight, the white undersides and the striking black and white wing and tail are conspicuous identifying features

A pair gives out the "kleep ... kleep" call together

An adult in "false sleeping" posture carefully observes the approach of an intruder

A convincing "broken wing" display is employed to lure an intruder away from the nest site

Roosting birds stand shoulder to shoulder on the beach, all generally facing the same way

Taking wing

After the shell has been forced open, the mollusc is neatly snipped free and washed in a nearby pool before being swallowed

$(\times \frac{1}{3})$

The young bird is well protected by the cryptic colouring of its down

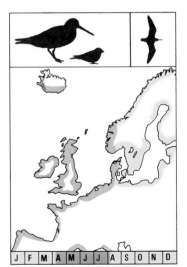

J F M A M J J A S O N D

Twinkling black and white wings and the wild, piping calls of a flock of Oystercatchers lend enchantment to many seashores.

The bird's vivid orange bill is adapted for opening bivalve molluscs such as mussels and cockles, and it may be used either to hammer them open or to stab the muscle which closes the shell. Birds learn from their parents to follow one method or the other, but "hammerers" suffer bill deterioration, which may place them at a disadvantage when probing for worms on shore or pasture—an important alternative feeding method. The nest is a simple scrape, often near a sheltering piece of vegetation. A territory around it is defended by a display with neck upstretched and bill pointed down, accompanied by loud piping.

Three or four eggs are laid, which hatch after 24 to 27 days of incubation by both parents. The young are among the few waders which are fed by their parents, since the main foods of the species cannot be obtained by chicks with their undeveloped bills. They learn feeding techniques gradually from their parents, staying with them even after they can fly at about five weeks.

Oystercatchers first breed at the age of five (males) and four (females), and many birds apparently live into their twenties. Most Oystercatchers move south in winter, though long-distance movements are mainly limited to northern populations.

Lapwing

Broad, rounded wing of male

Narrower wing of female

Slow wing beats and a ragged flock pattern distinguish the Lapwing in flight. An erratic tumbling display flight is particularly noticeable in the breeding season

Intruding crows are driven from the nesting site

Birds hunch up when facing into wind, below. Below right: typical stance adopted on landing

(× ⅓)

Adults are easily identified by the long crest and black and white underside markings. On young birds, left, the crest is shorter and the feathers have pale edgings

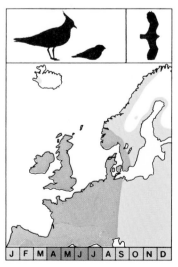

JFMAMJJASOND

Mewing calls and the exuberant, tumbling display flight of the male Lapwing seem to capture perfectly the feeling of exhilaration that comes with the start of spring. This advertisement flight soon attracts a mate, to whom the male displays in an exaggerated version of the movements by which a nest scrape is made. The couple prospect likely sites together, and the female signifies her approval of one of them by returning the display. Mating follows, and the first egg is often laid in March. Both sexes incubate, though the female takes much the larger share.

The eggs hatch in 24 to 31 days, exact time taken appearing to vary with altitude. Soon after hatching, the young are led away from the dry, exposed nest site—a ploughed field is typical—to a damper area with grass to provide them with cover. They fledge in four and a half to five weeks.

Outside the breeding season, Lapwings feed on pasture and ploughed fields, using the typical plover tactic of repeatedly running a short distance, then pausing, sometimes to pounce on a victim—often an earthworm, leatherjacket or moth larva. Vigorous excavating movements are used to extract prey from the roots of grass tussocks. Foraging becomes difficult when fields are frozen, and in hard weather, movements of Lapwings may be on a large scale. Sometimes Lapwings heading south-west overshoot drastically and end up in North America.

183

Spoonbill

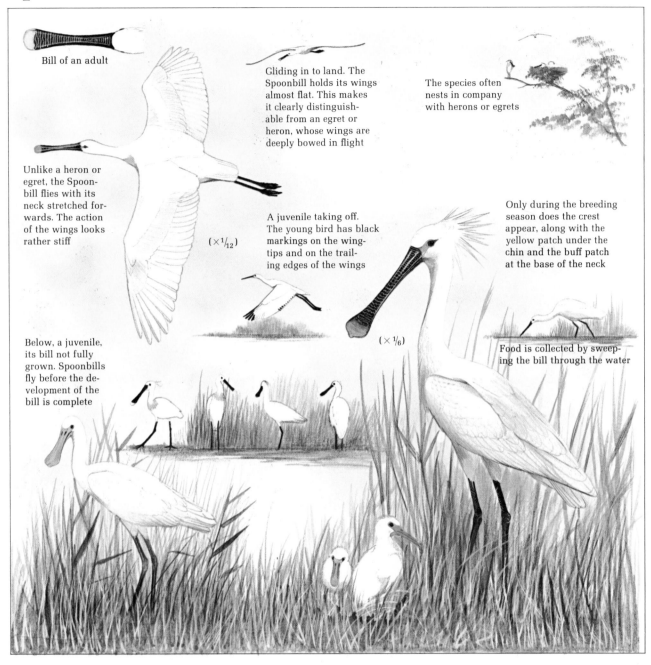

Bill of an adult

Gliding in to land. The Spoonbill holds its wings almost flat. This makes it clearly distinguishable from an egret or heron, whose wings are deeply bowed in flight

The species often nests in company with herons or egrets

Unlike a heron or egret, the Spoonbill flies with its neck stretched forwards. The action of the wings looks rather stiff

A juvenile taking off. The young bird has black markings on the wingtips and on the trailing edges of the wings

Only during the breeding season does the crest appear, along with the yellow patch under the chin and the buff patch at the base of the neck

$(\times \frac{1}{12})$

$(\times \frac{1}{6})$

Below, a juvenile, its bill not fully grown. Spoonbills fly before the development of the bill is complete

Food is collected by sweeping the bill through the water

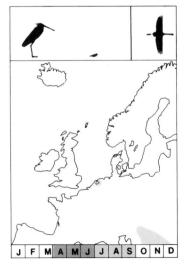

Spoonbills look beautiful and ridiculous, and, extraordinary though it may appear, the huge bill is an efficient feeding instrument: as it is swept from side to side in shallow water, numerous tiny crustaceans, fish, worms and molluscs are snapped up. Abundant nerve endings in the bill render it sensitive to the slightest touch or vibration, and probably most prey is detected by this means rather than by sight.

Breeding places must be near shallow lagoons suitable for feeding, and with continuing reclamation of wetlands these are becoming increasingly restricted. Nevertheless, the Spoonbill is showing a slight tendency to expand its range, perhaps as a result of protection, and there are hopes that it may eventually nest in the south of France or even eastern England, where it bred regularly until the mid-seventeenth century. Europe's most accessible breeding colonies are on the Naadermeer, outside Amsterdam.

The usual nest site is a reed-bed, but bushes are often used, and in some places nests are built quite high in trees. Little more than a platform of reeds and twigs, the nest usually holds a clutch of four eggs, laid at intervals of several days. Incubation and care of the young are shared by the parents, and the eggs hatch after three weeks to reveal chicks with short, almost normal bills and a sparse covering of white down. They may leave after as little as four weeks.

White Stork

In flight, Storks always carry their beaks angled downwards. The neck can be seen to sag a little about halfway along its length. Wing beats are slow and easy

Storks exploit thermals to soar to great heights when travelling locally or migrating. They delight in spiralling round after each other in enormous "stacks", rising as high as the warm upcurrent will take them before gliding off in a straight line to the base of the next thermal

Legs dangling, a Stork performs spectacularly steep descents

Left, bill clapping—a pair of adult Storks greet each other with this ceremony far into the breeding season

The threat display, used to warn off intruders

An adult will cover the eggs or chicks in the nest with a wing when an intruding Stork appears

Tree Sparrows may nest in the base of the Stork's nest

A stately gait, and a benevolent expression. Adults and young are much alike, except that the beak and legs of a younger bird are a paler red

(×¹⁄₁₂)

Like other large birds, the Stork glides with its first primary feathers up and the others drooping

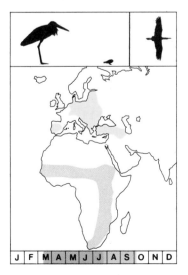

White Storks are surely the most conspicuous European birds, and since they also nest regularly on houses it is hardly surprising that their arrival is regarded as a significant event in the year. This strong association with rebirth no doubt underlies the Stork's role as a bringer of babies.

Despite the affection in which it is held, the bird's numbers in Europe are dwindling. It is strongly protected in most countries, and in some towns special nesting platforms are constructed. Direct persecution can therefore be ruled out. One cause of the decline may be the proliferation of modern buildings, but probably more serious is the use of insecticides in its African wintering areas. The chemicals are ab-sorbed by consumption of its favoured foods, locusts and grasshoppers.

Around their breeding areas White Storks forage principally in damp, grassy places, feeding on frogs, small mammals and large insects. Their huge stick nests are used year after year. Males are the first to arrive, and advertise for mates from the nest with a bill-clattering display. Six to eight eggs are laid, and incubated for 29 to 30 days. The parents share the duties of incubating and caring for the young.

Dependence on thermals (which occur only over land) to assist progress on long journeys means that storks choose the shortest possible sea crossings—Gibraltar in the west, and the Bosporus in the east.

Grey Heron

Display used by bird to the returning mate

Underwing pattern contrasts with that of the Purple Heron

There is no problem identifying a Grey Heron in flight. Its passage through the air is slow and ponderous; the legs trail and the long neck is drawn in, producing the conspicuous bulge

Viewed in flight from behind, the Heron's very broad, deeply bowed wings and drooping neck are especially noticeable

(×1/12)

Below, herons frequently adopt the one-legged stance. The bird on the left is an unusually dark-backed juvenile—fairly rare

(×1/6)

Long black head plumes and white plumes on the back denote the adult in breeding season

Immature bird fishing: distinguished from the adult by its head markings

For a short period during the breeding season the colour of the beak changes dramatically

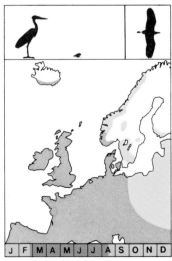

J F M A M J J A S O N D

Standing gaunt and motionless in the shallows, a Heron can be mistaken for a dead branch or a post. Even when walking, its movements are so slow and stealthy that it easily escapes notice. Eventually a fish will pay the price of negligence as the Heron's kinked neck is straightened with startling speed and the sharp beak seizes its victim. Frogs, small mammals and young water birds are taken, but fish are the primary food and, because of this, the Heron is sometimes shot as a pest.

Despite some persecution, and loss of habitat due to drainage, the Heron still maintains sizeable populations in most European countries. Because most Heron nests are conspicuous structures in tree colonies, fairly accurate counts can be made. Recent figures show populations of over 5,000 pairs in Britain, the Netherlands and Germany (including East Germany); figures for most other European countries are less than 1,000. Hard winters cause marked decreases, but normal numbers may be regained in two or three years.

Most heronries consist of less than 200 occupied nests, though a Dutch colony, now extinct, once numbered 1,025 nests. The first egg is normally laid in March, and the normal clutch contains three to five. Both parents incubate and hatching takes place after 25 days. The young are fed by both parents.

Purple Heron

White plumes on the back mark an adult in the breeding season

Action in flight is no different from the Common Heron's—deep, slow beats of the bowed wings—but the Purple Heron's grey and rufous underwing contrasts with the plain grey of the Common Heron's. Migrating herons arrive and depart at a great height

Drawn in for flight, the Purple Heron's neck makes an even larger bulge than that of the Common Heron. The trailing legs look enormous in flight—an effect produced by the very long toes

($\times 1/12$)

A lanky, highly coloured heron with scaled-down, large-bird features making it look bigger in the field than its actual size, which is appreciably smaller than the Common Heron's. Below is a second-year bird. Five years may be required to achieve adult plumage

A very long, and sometimes extraordinarily thin neck with conspicuous patterning. Deep red and black underparts are visible at close range

($\times 1/6$)

A juvenile has brown coverts

From above, brownish rather than grey wing coverts and back make a juvenile Purple Heron especially easy to tell from the Common Heron

Juvenile from behind

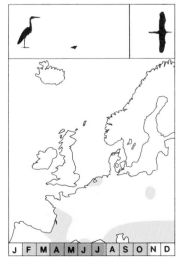

J F M A M J J A S O N D

Thinner and more angular than its larger relative the Grey Heron, a Purple Heron can be reliably identified by shape, even in poor light when its colours are indiscernible.

It also differs from the Grey Heron in choice of habitat, normally nesting in dense reed-beds. However, in the breeding season, Purple Herons do feed around the small ponds and dykes also favoured by Grey Herons. Unfortunately, large reed-beds are becoming fewer as human activities encroach on wetlands, and the Purple Heron consequently has a patchy and diminishing distribution in Europe. The Purple Heron is less often seen in groups than the Grey Heron, and is more often silent, though it has a similar harsh

call. It often remains active after dark.

Dead reeds are the main material for the nest, which is usually situated near water level, though occasionally higher in bushes. Although Purple Herons, like other herons, are colonial breeders, they build their nests in quite widely scattered groups. Four or five eggs are laid, and the nesting season is generally later than the Grey Heron's. Both sexes incubate, usually from the first egg, and hatching takes place in 24 to 28 days. The young fledge after six weeks and are independent after two months; a single brood is reared.

The main Purple Heron migration route passes over Tunisia, Sicily and Corsica, where in spring the birds are commonplace.

187

Birds of Fenland, Coast and Marsh

Of all bird habitats, the wetlands are the most seriously threatened. Over the centuries, Europe's marshes and fens have been progressively reclaimed for use in farming or for building, and the process still continues in many areas despite attempts at national and local control.

Only recently has the balance been slightly redressed in favour of bird-life by the creation of artificial waters such as reservoirs and gravel pits, but few of these provide the rich habitats found naturally. Some of the most valuable wetlands have been designated as nature reserves, but are still vulnerable to pollution and disturbance.

Wetlands harbour several bird groups, most having extremely skulking habits. Among them are warblers, crakes and rails, which enliven the reed-beds with a cacophony of chattering and squealing. Besides waterfowl, however, the various types of heron which predominate these two pages are the most characteristic wetland species.

Cattle Egret: more stocky than Little Egret, paler than Squacco. Feeds in fields with livestock (on which it perches). SW Spain, N Africa

$(\times \frac{1}{5})$

Little Egret: slender build, pure white plumage, contrasting yellow feet and black legs. Once persecuted for the long plumes of breeding plumage. SW Spain, N Africa

$(\times \frac{1}{6})$

$(\times \frac{1}{15})$

Crane: distinguished from Heron in flight by outstretched neck. Breeds in Scandinavia, N and E Europe; migrates through Europe in majestic formations, calling loudly

$(\times \frac{1}{5})$

Winter plumage in foreground

Red-necked Grebe: resembles Great Crested but smaller and lacking pale eye-stripe in winter. Breeds in C and E Europe; winters on estuaries and coastal waters

Squacco: smallest white European heron, appears buff at rest. Crest of long plumes in breeding season. S Europe and NW Africa

$(\times \frac{1}{15})$

Flamingo: huge white bird with startlingly pink legs and large bill specially adapted for filter feeding. Breeds in S France, SW Spain in localized areas; winter range slightly extended, coastal, also winters NW Africa

Night Heron: adult identified by black cap, white underside, grey wings; young are dark with buff spotting. Hunched posture at rest. Mainly nocturnal in habit. Summer in Holland, S Europe, NW Africa

$(\times \frac{1}{4})$

$(\times \frac{1}{8})$

Little Bittern: tiny heron easily identified by pale wing-patch. Skulking habits, climbing about in reed-beds. Like Bittern, freezes when alarmed. Summer throughout mainland Europe south of Baltic

$(\times \frac{1}{9})$

Bittern: large, brown skulking heron, spends much of its time in reed-beds. Plumage provides superb camouflage when bird freezes in upright posture. Present and breeding throughout Europe and NW Africa; summer only in S Sweden, E Europe

189

Red-throated Diver

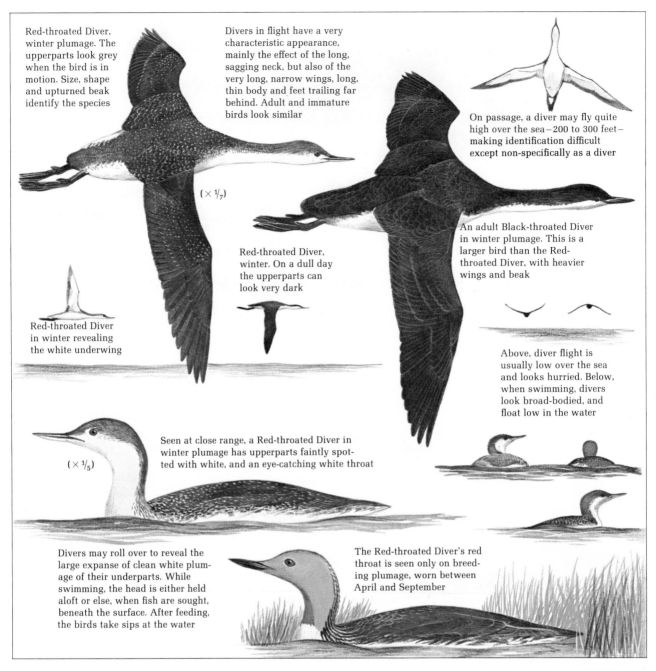

Red-throated Diver, winter plumage. The upperparts look grey when the bird is in motion. Size, shape and upturned beak identify the species

Divers in flight have a very characteristic appearance, mainly the effect of the long, sagging neck, but also of the very long, narrow wings, long, thin body and feet trailing far behind. Adult and immature birds look similar

On passage, a diver may fly quite high over the sea—200 to 300 feet—making identification difficult except non-specifically as a diver

Red-throated Diver in winter revealing the white underwing

Red-throated Diver, winter. On a dull day the upperparts can look very dark

An adult Black-throated Diver in winter plumage. This is a larger bird than the Red-throated Diver, with heavier wings and beak

(× 1/7)

(× 1/5)

Seen at close range, a Red-throated Diver in winter plumage has upperparts faintly spotted with white, and an eye-catching white throat

Above, diver flight is usually low over the sea and looks hurried. Below, when swimming, divers look broad-bodied, and float low in the water

Divers may roll over to reveal the large expanse of clean white plumage of their underparts. While swimming, the head is either held aloft or else, when fish are sought, beneath the surface. After feeding, the birds take sips at the water

The Red-throated Diver's red throat is seen only on breeding plumage, worn between April and September

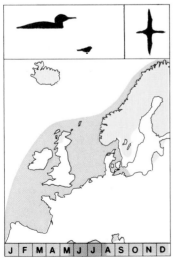

Although not closely related, divers and grebes share many physical specializations for swimming above and under water. Particularly striking in both groups is the position of the legs, which are set far back along the body. This provides efficient propulsion in the water but renders the bird hopelessly clumsy on land.

Commonest and most widely distributed of the divers is the Red-throated, which is also the smallest in size. During the breeding season it frequents lakes amongst tundra or moorland, and although some quite small stretches of water are chosen for nesting they are always close to the sea or a large lake, where the birds can fish.

Divers are noisy on their breeding grounds and in Scotland, the mewing and growling calls of this species are said to foretell rain. Displays may be seen throughout the summer: they involve dives, chases and posturing on the water by up to five birds at a time. A courtship flight, rising to tremendous heights and accompanied by cackling, is seen only before brooding commences.

Varying from a simple scrape by the shore to a substantial heap of vegetation in shallow water, the nest usually holds two eggs. Like those of all divers they are unusually elongated. Nest building, brooding and care of the young are tasks shared by both sexes. Incubation starts with the first egg and lasts 24 to 29 days.

Great Northern–Black-throated Divers

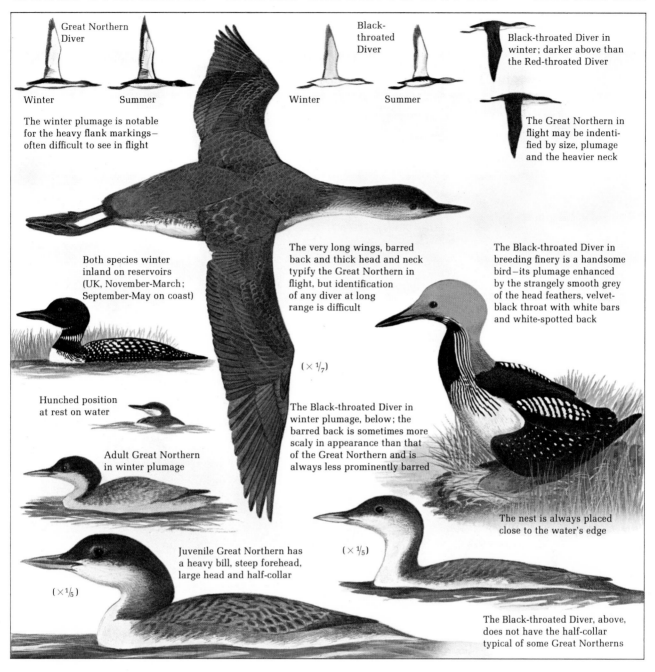

Great Northern Diver

Winter   Summer

The winter plumage is notable for the heavy flank markings—often difficult to see in flight

Black-throated Diver

Winter   Summer

Black-throated Diver in winter; darker above than the Red-throated Diver

The Great Northern in flight may be identified by size, plumage and the heavier neck

The very long wings, barred back and thick head and neck typify the Great Northern in flight, but identification of any diver at long range is difficult

Both species winter inland on reservoirs (UK, November-March; September-May on coast)

The Black-throated Diver in breeding finery is a handsome bird—its plumage enhanced by the strangely smooth grey of the head feathers, velvet-black throat with white bars and white-spotted back

$(\times \frac{1}{7})$

Hunched position at rest on water

The Black-throated Diver in winter plumage, below; the barred back is sometimes more scaly in appearance than that of the Great Northern and is always less prominently barred

Adult Great Northern in winter plumage

The nest is always placed close to the water's edge

$(\times \frac{1}{5})$

Juvenile Great Northern has a heavy bill, steep forehead, large head and half-collar

$(\times \frac{1}{5})$

The Black-throated Diver, above, does not have the half-collar typical of some Great Northerns

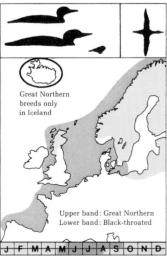

Great Northern breeds only in Iceland

Upper band: Great Northern
Lower band: Black-throated

J F M A M J J A S O N D

Scotland and Scandinavia harbour a regular breeding population of Black-throated Divers, but the Great Northern Diver had until recently been seen only in winter or on passage on European coasts or inland waters. In 1970, a pair of Great Northerns with two young were seen on a Scottish loch, and the following year at the same place a Black-throated Diver was seen with a hybrid Great Northern/Black-throated Diver and a well-grown chick. Though there have been no further breeding records, these occurrences raise the hope that the Great Northern Diver may eventually establish itself as a breeding species in Britain. Such an event would be most welcome, for divers have had to face severe pressure from mankind. Great Northern Divers are hunted for their plumage during summer, while the Black-throated's nests are sometimes destroyed by fishermen fearing the bird's impact on trout stocks. Moreover, all divers face a grave threat from oil pollution during their winter sojourn on the open seas.

The breeding behaviour of both species is generally similar to that of the Red-throated Diver, although incubation and fledging periods are a little longer, and neither of them is prepared to nest by such small sheets of water as the Red-throated Diver. Both are highly vocal during the summer, and the long-drawn, trembling wail of the Great Northern Diver is one of the most stirring of all bird sounds.

Black-necked–Slavonian Grebes

R

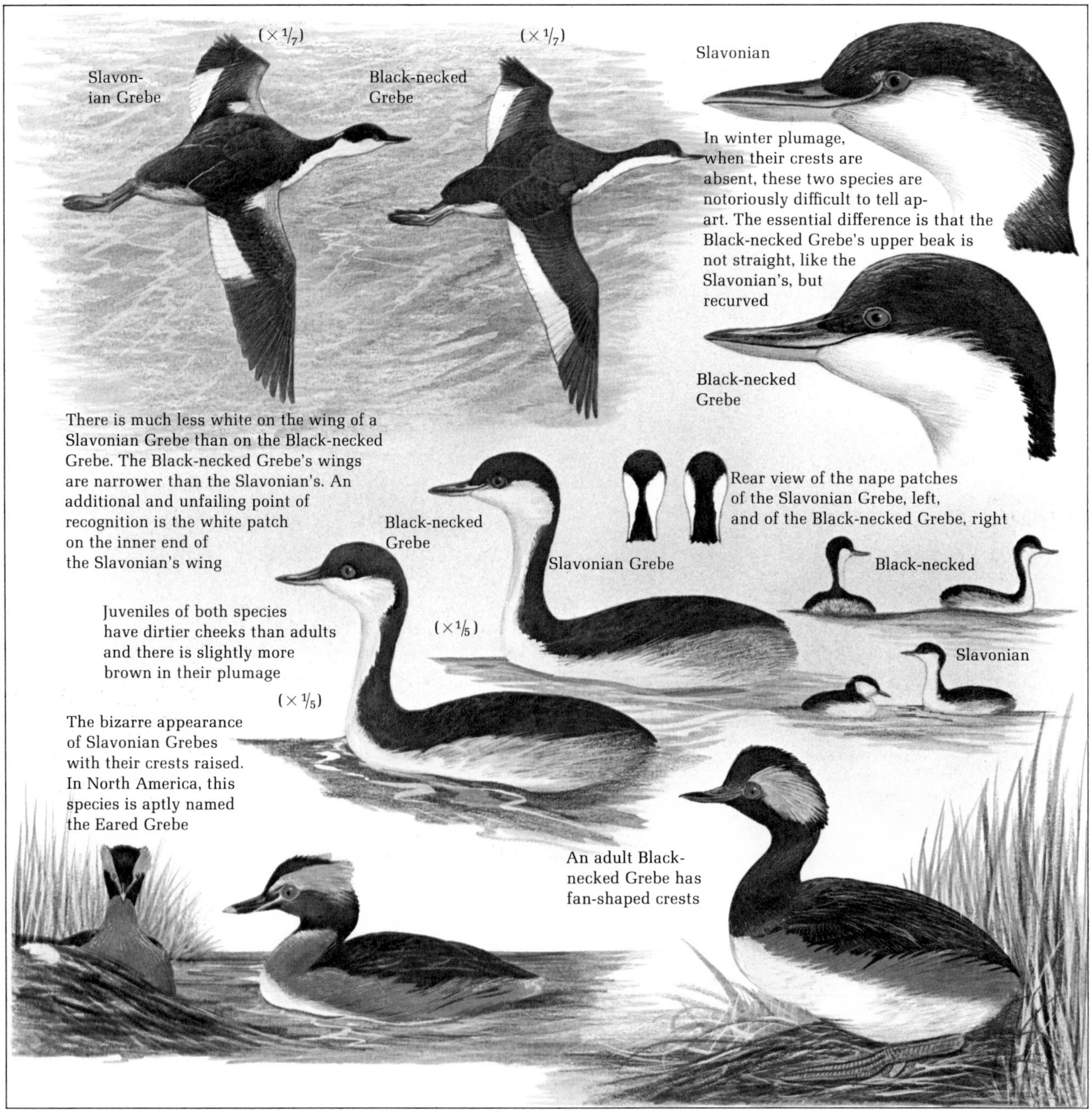
(× 1/7)
Slavonian Grebe
(× 1/7)
Black-necked Grebe
Slavonian
In winter plumage, when their crests are absent, these two species are notoriously difficult to tell apart. The essential difference is that the Black-necked Grebe's upper beak is not straight, like the Slavonian's, but recurved
Black-necked Grebe
There is much less white on the wing of a Slavonian Grebe than on the Black-necked Grebe. The Black-necked Grebe's wings are narrower than the Slavonian's. An additional and unfailing point of recognition is the white patch on the inner end of the Slavonian's wing
Black-necked Grebe
Slavonian Grebe
Rear view of the nape patches of the Slavonian Grebe, left, and of the Black-necked Grebe, right
Black-necked
Juveniles of both species have dirtier cheeks than adults and there is slightly more brown in their plumage
(× 1/5)
(× 1/5)
Slavonian
The bizarre appearance of Slavonian Grebes with their crests raised. In North America, this species is aptly named the Eared Grebe
An adult Black-necked Grebe has fan-shaped crests

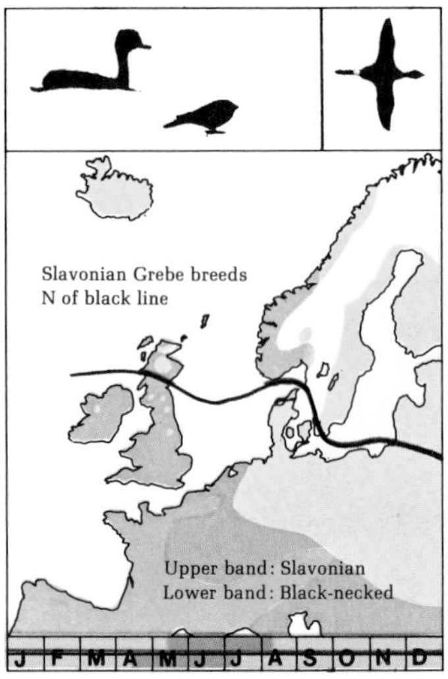
Slavonian Grebe breeds N of black line
Upper band: Slavonian
Lower band: Black-necked
J F M A M J J A S O N D

Both of these beautiful small grebes are widely distributed through the New and Old Worlds, their ranges overlapping extensively, although in Europe the Slavonian Grebe is generally a more northerly breeder. In summer, the Slavonian inhabits lakes or ponds with substantial areas of open water in addition to a well-vegetated fringe, while the Black-necked Grebe occurs on more densely overgrown swamps and meres. During the winter, the Slavonian frequents estuaries, but the Black-necked is usually seen on inland water, particularly reservoirs. Fish appear to be a more important item in the diet of the Black-necked Grebe, and in its winter quarters at least, it is the most assiduous and energetic diver of all European members of its notoriously submarine family.

In their breeding biology, these species show rather more differentiation of male and female roles than the Great Crested and Little Grebes, and territorial defence appears to be primarily the male's task.

Courtship displays involve raising and expanding the ear tufts by both sexes and the female responds to the male's advances by stretching the neck forward along the water or the nest. The nests are floating heaps of soggy vegetation. Both species tend to breed colonially, sometimes congregating among colonies of gulls and terns, whose fierce reactions to intruders offer some protection.

Great Crested Grebe

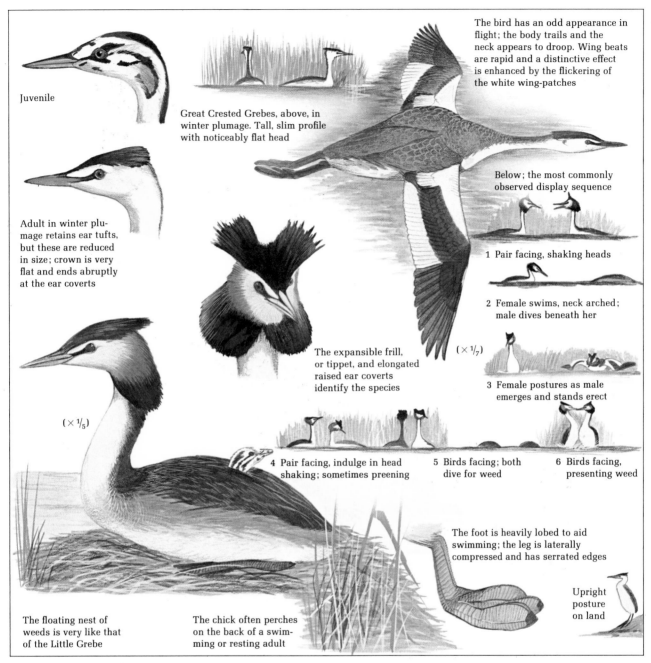

Juvenile

Great Crested Grebes, above, in winter plumage. Tall, slim profile with noticeably flat head

The bird has an odd appearance in flight; the body trails and the neck appears to droop. Wing beats are rapid and a distinctive effect is enhanced by the flickering of the white wing-patches

Adult in winter plumage retains ear tufts, but these are reduced in size; crown is very flat and ends abruptly at the ear coverts

Below; the most commonly observed display sequence

1 Pair facing, shaking heads

2 Female swims, neck arched; male dives beneath her

The expansible frill, or tippet, and elongated raised ear coverts identify the species

$(\times 1/7)$

3 Female postures as male emerges and stands erect

$(\times 1/5)$

4 Pair facing, indulge in head shaking; sometimes preening

5 Birds facing; both dive for weed

6 Birds facing, presenting weed

The foot is heavily lobed to aid swimming; the leg is laterally compressed and has serrated edges

Upright posture on land

The floating nest of weeds is very like that of the Little Grebe

The chick often perches on the back of a swimming or resting adult

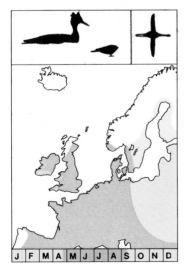

At a time when wildlife seems to be under pressure from every side, some reassurance can be gained by considering the change in attitudes which has taken place over the past 100 years in most countries of Europe. Today, the Great Crested Grebe is well known for its beautiful and intricate courtship ceremonies, but during the nineteenth century it was regarded simply as a source of millinery decoration. Intensive hunting gravely reduced its numbers, but it was saved in time by legal protection and changing fashions. Nowadays, as industrial activities create new lakes in abandoned gravel pits, it is actually increasing.

Courtship is principally confined to the early stages of the breeding cycle, before laying commences. Since first clutches may be laid at the end of February, this phase of behaviour may sometimes be observed as early as mid-winter. The displays are notable not only for their variety but also for their self-exhausting nature—that is, each may be complete in itself, rather than leading on to another more intense display. Another feature of interest is that both sexes take a nearly equal part in display, although the "trumpeting" performance in which one bird seeks the attention of another by vocal means is mainly used by females. Both sexes incubate the three to six eggs on a floating nest of rotting vegetation anchored to reeds near the water's edge. Two or three broods are raised.

193

Water Rail

Head of adult. The long beak is unlike any found on other rails or on crakes (× ³⁄₄)

Greyish wings and olive and black streaking on the coverts are visible on the Water Rail in flight. The legs are always dangled while the bird is in flight (× ¹⁄₆)

The most usual view of a Water Rail, below, as it takes to the air after being flushed. Alternatively, it may run for cover. Flight, although appearing weak, is strong. Water Rails are frequently brought down by accident during shoots

There is quite pronounced white marking on the underwing and belly, but such details are rarely seen because the bird is almost always observed at low level after being flushed

Long-necked appearance of bird standing upright

Feeding posture

(× ¹⁄₃)

A juvenile Water Rail has a yellowish beak and whiter, more heavily streaked underparts than an adult

Creeping into cover, left, a Water Rail reveals an extremely narrow body. This lateral compression enables the bird to pass between narrow gaps in the herbage

Conspicuous cream-coloured under-tail coverts are revealed as the bird cocks its tail

Identifying this species is never a problem because no other wader of comparative size or shape has such a long red beak. Additional, and easily seen, points of recognition are the grey underparts and barred flanks. It is a bird of contrasting moods, feeding unconcerned in the open or casually crossing roads, sometimes genuinely tame, at others making for cover with remarkable speed if alarmed

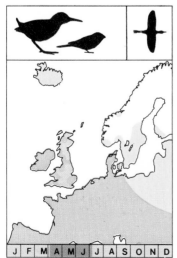

J F M A M J J A S O N D

Water Rails are seen nearly as often dead as alive: although shy and secretive in their habitat of waterside vegetation, on migration they have a remarkable flair for flying into lighthouses, cables and other man-made obstacles. Flight itself looks weak, with legs dangling. At other times, they prefer to run from danger. Nevertheless, they make substantial movements, southwards from the British Isles through Europe, or from Scandinavia and the Low Countries to the United Kingdom and Ireland.

The breeding season commences early in April, but the presence of nesting Water Rails in a reed- or osier-bed would often be unsuspected but for their strange calls. Most often uttered at dusk or dawn, these sounds are a weird mixture of grunts and squeals, which have been likened to the cries of a dying pig. Dead reeds are the main material for the nest, which is very well hidden in reeds or sedge. The clutch of six to 11 eggs is incubated by both sexes for 19 to 20 days. Young Water Rails leave the nest soon after hatching and are tended by both parents, the female brooding and the male feeding them. Fledging occurs after seven to eight weeks. Parent Water Rails have been seen to remove their young and even eggs from danger by carrying them in their bills. Foods eaten include seeds and berries of waterside plants, insects, molluscs, fish and even small birds.

Little Grebe

Far left, an adult has a pale yellow patch on the inner end of its beak. Left, a fully grown bird still in juvenile plumage

(× 1/7)

Rufous-brown plumage is apparent on a Little Grebe viewed from the rear, but is not as obvious from the side. Its fluffy tail is similarly inconspicuous when viewed from the side

This species has the appearance in flight of a typical grebe, but it is the only bird of the family to show no white on the upperwing

Below, an adult in winter is much duller and browner than in summer

Head of bird in winter plumage, three-quarters life-size

Left, a young grebe can swim within hours of hatching. Below left, a Little Grebe viewed from above looks almost circular, evidence of the exceptional width of its body

Below, adults with a day-old chick on the floating nest. This is anchored by the plant or branch around which it is built. Decomposing vegetation, from which the nest is made, generates heat, which assists incubation

(× 1/5)

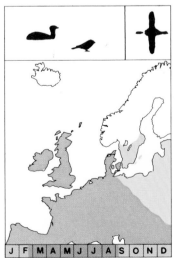

Though more widely distributed, the Little Grebe, or Dabchick, is less often seen than the Great Crested Grebe, for it spends little time on broad sheets of open water and dives readily when alarmed. Its favourite habitats are ponds, sluggish rivers and canals, with plenty of vegetation growing in their shallow margins. Often, the only indication of its presence is the curious tittering call, resembling high-pitched, hysterical laughter. This cry has a sexual function, and is often uttered as a duet by members of a pair, facing each other with necks upstretched. As the rest of their displays are less elaborate than those of other grebes, and the head lacks tufts or frills, it appears that sound largely replaces

sight in the Little Grebe's courting activities.

The nest is a floating mass of rotten vegetation, similar to that of the Great Crested Grebe but smaller. Both sexes incubate, and, when changing places, the approaching bird brings a strand of fresh green material to add to the nest. Little Grebes are highly territorial, and male and female defend their stretch of water vigorously, intruders being repelled by a series of short rushes with wings half raised. The clutch of four to six eggs hatches after about 20 days. Brooding adults slip quietly off the nest at the least sign of danger, after quickly covering the eggs with nest material. Many young fall victim to predators such as pike or herons.

195

Coot

The Coot flies with fast, shallow wing beats, achieving fair speed and momentum when under way

From this angle the dangling legs are particularly conspicuous

Groups are seen resting or grazing where there is grassland at the water's edge

A Coot must laboriously patter over the water for some yards in order to reach take-off speed

$(\times \frac{1}{5})$

Below, the white frontal shield and beak are an obvious feature at any range. Coots dive constantly, jumping clear before entering the water

Fighting or aggressive bluffing games are commonplace

While grazing, the Coot will be seen turning its head on one side in order to crop vertical stalks of grass

A comical, fat bird with generally grey plumage (which looks jet black at a distance), white frontal shield and improbable feet—as easy to identify as to spot

$(\times \frac{3}{10})$

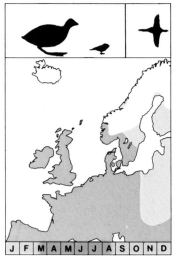

Coots spend much of their lives afloat, swimming early with the aid of their lobed feet. They dive frequently for food, mainly vegetable, although small fish, worms, molluscs and even ducklings also figure in their diet. Coots inhabiting park lakes may often be seen grazing on lawns near the edge of the water, though they are reluctant to venture as far ashore as the Moorhen. Highly territorial, Coots display strong aggression towards intruders, sometimes even attacking ducks and grebes as well as other Coots. Loud metallic calls and much splashing accompany these encounters.

The nest is of reeds and grasses with a thicker foundation than that of the Moorhen and usually placed among reeds well away from the shore. It is built mainly by the female, while the male collects building materials. Both sexes incubate, but the male continues to bring material even after laying has commenced, so that sometimes one or more eggs are accidentally buried in the nest lining. Four to eight eggs are laid, and incubation lasts 21 to 24 days. The young remain in the nest for three or four days, returning there for a few further nights to be brooded. During this time the male feeds them and the female broods. They are independent at about eight weeks, and two broods are usual. Birds from northern and central Europe move southwest in winter, sometimes as far as Iberia and northern Africa.

Moorhen

At night or at dusk the Moorhen flies over towns or country at about 50 feet, uttering a soft "cock . . cock"

While swimming, the Moorhen scarcely interrupts its bobbing of the head and flicking of the tail except to dab at some morsel on the surface

Left, the bird in flight, its legs dangling in the normal position. Below, the appearance of a Moorhen as it is often seen flying with quick, shallow wing beats before landing on water and swimming to cover

In flight (and on the ground), a Moorhen has the typical profile of its family, the rails. Being half as big again as any bird in the group, there is no difficulty in identifying it on size alone

(× ⅕)

A juvenile Moorhen is brown

Left, typical Moorhen feeding postures. In summer, when on inland waters, the birds may feed at the water's edge, hundreds of yards from cover

Repeated flicks of the tail are given as the bird walks away

The red frontal shield and yellow-tipped bill make this species unlike any other in Europe. Its bronze upperparts, grey underparts, white flash and green legs are all easily visible features

(× ³⁄₁₀)

The chick — black legs and a minute frontal shield

Very long toes equip the species for both walking and swimming

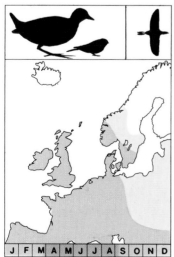

Found in nearly every part of the world except the polar regions, the Moorhen is a highly successful bird, although many of its fellow members of the rail family are endangered or even extinct. A key factor in its survival is an ability to adapt to environments altered by Man. Practically any patch of water surrounded by vegetation suits it, including ponds amid cultivated fields, or in parks and gardens.

Although a shy bird in parts of its range, it is comparatively tame in many parts of Europe, sometimes foraging openly on lawns. Nevertheless, the Moorhen moves quickly when alarmed, running for the nearest thick cover, into which it vanishes as though by magic. Moorhens also dive skilfully,

evading danger by surfacing under an overhanging river bank, screened behind hanging grass or nettles. Floating vegetation also provides cover under which a bird may remain submerged for some time, obtaining air by stealthily protruding the bill above water.

The nest is made of dead reeds or flags, usually built just above water level on a mudbank or tussock in a pond or stream. Alternatively, the birds may nest in bushes, often utilizing the abandoned nests of other birds. Males are strongly territorial, repelling intruders by display or by actual fighting. The clutch of five to 11 eggs is incubated by both parents and hatches in 18 to 22 days. The young are able to fly after six to seven weeks.

J F M A M J J A S O N D

197

Teal

Below, the drake Teal. No other duck has a Sienna red and green head pattern set off with a cream-coloured line in a hairpin bend around the eye

$(\times \frac{1}{6})$

At take-off the wing stroke is highly exaggerated

Full male plumage. This is complete from October to July; eclipse is from the end of July to the end of August

With Garganey, Teal are the smallest of the ducks. They are distinguished from the former by their green and black speculum. The female Teal, above right, reveals two narrow wing-bars in flight

Above, the female rising

Springing into the air: only Teal can achieve near-vertical take-off. They are capable of enormous acceleration

Teal tend to fly low and fast, swooping and wheeling like waders. Two or more flocks of small ducks seen turning in unison are likely to be Teal

Swivelling of the heads is a sure sign that the birds are about to take off

Male in eclipse (see main text)

Exquisitely vermiculated plumage on the back and flanks is visible on the drake at close quarters

The cream and black under-tail coverts are conspicuous at long or short range

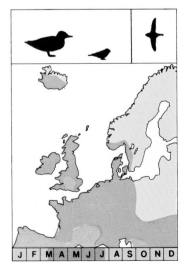

J F M A M J J A S O N D

Ducks can be divided on the basis of feeding behaviour into two groups: surface-feeding species and diving species. Surface-feeding, or dabbling ducks, include the Teal, together with the species on the following five pages, and the Shoveler. These birds rarely dive for food, but obtain most of it in shallow water, often by up-ending, or even on land. Dabbling ducks have their legs set well forward on the body, and like the Teal most have a bright patch of colour on the wing called the speculum.

Teal frequent both inland and coastal habitats. On salt-marshes and brackish places important foods are the seeds of marsh samphire and tassel pond weed, and tiny snails gleaned from the mud surface. Inland, the seeds of spike-rush and creeping buttercup, together with aquatic midge larvae, are common items of diet.

Like many water-fowl, Teal carry out complicated displays during courtship. These take place on the water, with a group of drakes swimming around a duck, and involve flicking water towards the female followed by posturing to show off the green speculum and distinctive head markings. Peat moorland, with plenty of rushes and small pools, is the characteristic breeding habitat.

For about a month after breeding, the male undergoes a radical change of plumage, the eclipse. His resulting appearance is virtually the same as female or juvenile.

Garganey

Unmistakable enough at close quarters, the drake Garganey's white eye-stripe can become obscured when seen at long range

Double wing-bars against pale grey wings identify the drake Garganey in flight and are always the first feature to catch the eye. Full drake plumage is seen from February to August

Above, the female Garganey, usually to be seen with the drake, has a paler eye-stripe than the female Teal

Garganey "pump" their heads before take-off

Drake Garganey have a calling display, above left, uttered with the neck fully extended, and sometimes in flight during spring. Above right, the drake's preening display – wings raised

The female in flight. Garganey are longer winged and shorter bodied than Teal – a difference discernible only to the experienced

Having moulted his primaries, the drake in eclipse is flightless and during this vulnerable period the unostentatious plumage probably has some value as protective camouflage

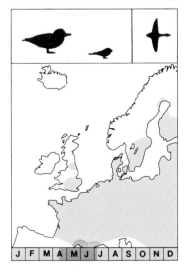

Garganey are trim, elegant little ducks, about the same size as Teal but only distantly related to them. Among European birds, the Shoveler is their closest relative. Besides the blue forewing, the two species share many features of behaviour: for instance, their intention to take flight is signalled by vertical head pumping, rather than lateral head shaking as in other dabbling ducks. Garganey have a mainly southerly distribution in winter, and throughout most of Europe are consequently seen only during the breeding season.

Shallow fresh waters of various kinds are chosen for breeding, and Garganey are usually seen only in pairs or small groups, although large flocks occur at winter quarters. During their displays, male Garganey utter an extraordinary crackling sound, produced with the aid of an enlarged vocal apparatus. It is usually uttered with the head laid back and bill pointed upwards – a posture also used by the female, who utters a quieter quacking note. Nests are usually in coarse grass near a pool or water meadow, lined, like those of most water-fowl, with thick down, which the female plucks from her breast. The ducklings fledge in five to six weeks.

Garganey feed in a similar way to other dabbling ducks, but spend less time up-ending. Animal foods seem to be important, though the Garganey's diet has been less closely studied than that of many ducks.

199

Pintail

Obvious at close range, the drake's long tail feathers prevent confusion with any other duck. In the distance, he has conspicuous identifying features in the neck-stripe, white breast and extensive blocks of cream and black on the rear quarters

A drake's full plumage is seen between October and late June

The sleekly built Pintail flies fastest of the ducks, its wings making a hissing sound

(×⅙)

To maintain the up-ended position while feeding, a Pintail paddles with the feet, and adjusts its balance by tilting the tail. Below, displaying males may cock their tails or swim with the neck held erect

At long range, drake Pintail look grey, white and brown

Above, the drake dips his beak at the start of the water-flicking display, above right

Above left, the drake is in eclipse from mid-July to early September. Right, the female

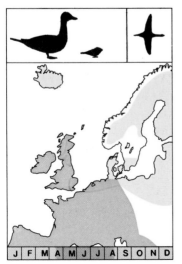

Slim and graceful in build, with long, rather narrow bills, Pintail are easily recognized in any plumage. Their breeding range is mainly northerly, and over much of Europe they nest sporadically and in small numbers. Winter populations are augmented by migrants, largely from Russia, and moderate numbers can be seen on most estuaries—though really large concentrations are mainly at inland sites. Pintail up-end a great deal while feeding, and obtain seeds, roots and leaves from various pond weeds and from eel-grass. Grain, rice and even acorns are eaten in parts of the bird's range. Animal food includes insects, molluscs, fish and tadpoles. Pintail are largely nocturnal feeders.

Courtship displays are elaborate, and the drake's posturing shows off the white head-stripe, long tail and speculum to good effect. Breeding grounds range from marshland to moorland, but in general nests are sited in rather more exposed positions than those of many ducks, often in quite short grass. Pintail tend to nest socially, sometimes forming small colonies on islands in lakes. The drake Pintail remains fairly close to the nest while the duck incubates the seven to nine eggs—a task lasting 23 to 24 days. He also stays in attendance while she tends the ducklings, and the female's behaviour is strongly protective. She will drive intruders off if possible, or utilize injury-feigning to lure them away from the nest.

Wigeon

At close quarters, Wigeon stand out from other ducks by their head and bill shape

The drake's white wing-flashes extending to the fore-wing are unique among ducks. On a folded wing they show as a horizontal bar tapering at each end. The silver-grey of the back is in reality fine black lines on white feathers

$(\times \frac{1}{6})$

Below, Wigeon will graze near the water's edge with other species, here Brent Geese. Left, the Wigeon also grazes on inland fields, marshes or partly flooded agricultural land

In a flock, Wigeon may form irregular lines. Usually at the sight of a human or a gun they will brake in mid-air with an audible fluttering

A first-winter drake's forewing is very like the female's

Following eclipse, the drake develops full plumage. It is complete between November and June

Wigeon are thoroughly gregarious, gathering to rest in large flocks on the sea or on a suitable patch of inland water

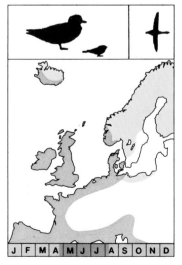

With short, stubby bills and high fore-heads, Wigeon have head profiles quite unlike other surface-feeding ducks. This difference is connected with their feeding habits. Primarily grazers, they spend little time dabbling: hence, they do not need the long, wide bills which their relatives possess for straining food particles out of water. Mudflats and salt-marshes are their main winter habitat, and eel-grass, green seaweeds or salting grass are their foods—a diet similar to that of the Brent Goose. It is common to see the two species feeding close together and Wigeon probably benefit by gleaning scraps left by the Brent. Wigeon also visit inland sites to feed on grass, showing preference for the vicinity of large lakes or reservoirs.

Drake Wigeon call with a far-carrying whistle, which once heard is never forgotten a nostalgic sound especially to wildfowlers, for whom this species is a traditional quarry. Even females are easily recognized by their quacks, which have an unusual growling quality. Pairing takes place before return to the breeding grounds, and there is relatively little courtship display in this species, which is more strictly monogamous than most dabbling ducks. Nests are sited near shallow lakes, often quite small ones, amid tundra or moorland. Nine is the commonest clutch size in northern parts of the Wigeon's range, seven to eight farther south. The young fledge in six and a half weeks.

Gadwall

The drake is in eclipse from early June until October. Behind him is a female

$(\times\frac{1}{7})$

White wing-patches are the most striking feature on a flying Gadwall. Its sobre colouring reduces to simple grey and brown in the distance

As a consequence of walking on land, a dabbling duck has a smaller rear toe than a diving duck, whose foot is larger overall

Below, the duck and, right, the drake, which at close range is characterized by finely vermiculated grey plumage, and at longer range by his black rear quarters

In common with all surface-feeding duck, Gadwall land on the water with necks stretched forwards, taking the impact with their feet

While up-ending, Gadwall can be distinguished from Mallard by their orange-yellow, rather than orange-red, legs

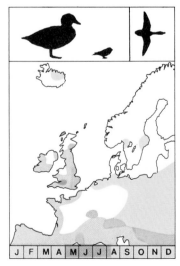

Drake Gadwall look dull by comparison with the males of other surface-feeding ducks, yet their finely barred plumage is attractive at close range. Although Gadwall are very similar to Mallard in size and shape, the two are not believed to be closely related. Behavioural studies suggest the species is related to the Wigeon—both, for example, share a distinctive bill-lifting ceremony, used between members of a pair after a clash with rivals.

Gadwall breed in both Eurasia and North America, but are rather sparsely distributed and breed sporadically over much of their range. Nevertheless, the species seems to be on the increase: it has been deliberately introduced to North America, and in Britain a stock of hybrid Gadwall and Mallard has become established in one locality. In the Old World, greatest breeding density is reached between the Caucasus and the Caspian, and in Europe Gadwall are generally more abundant in eastern countries.

These are exclusively fresh-water ducks, rarely seen on estuaries. Water plants of various kinds are the diet, but animal food is also important, especially during the egg-laying period. When feeding on plants, Gadwall show a preference for the succulent parts, and are much less inclined than most ducks to eat seeds.

Nests are usually well hidden in vegetation, but are sometimes built in exposed places among gulls' and terns'.

J F M A M J J A S O N D

Mallard

Domesticated varieties

Rouen

Crested

Aylesbury

Khaki Campbell

Indian Runner

Drake Mallard in flight; the dark centre region of the lower back is bordered by paler areas. The double wing-bar is clearly visible at considerable distance

($\times \frac{1}{6}$)

A small proportion of Mallard regularly nest in cavities in trees, commonly pollarded willows, in the vicinity of water

Drake Mallard in eclipse (late July-September) is distinguished from the duck by his broad yellow bill

Female

Swimming with neck drawn in

Bill-dipping

Mallard displays, left: several drakes gather round a single duck, competing for attention. Displays include bill-dipping, swimming with neck drawn well back, or (foreground) rocking two or three times with breast immersed and tail raised

Rocking display

Below, only the Mallard has curled, black tail coverts

Female with ducklings: her otherwise soft plumage is brightened by the purple speculum edged with black and white

Drake in winter, (October-June); legs and feet are a bright orange-red

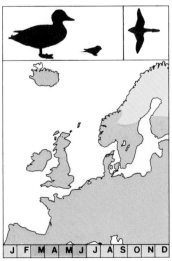

Common throughout Europe and in many other parts of the world, the Mallard shows the great adaptability characteristic of a successful species. Its ready acceptance of almost any kind of waterside habitat, including many in man-made environments, was no doubt a key factor leading to its domestication. Versatility is also a feature of the Mallard's feeding habits. Much information on its diet has been obtained by analysing the stomach contents of birds shot by wildfowlers, and these show a great range of foods, varying from year to year as well as between different habitats. Seeds predominate, mostly from small plants, including sedges, pond weeds, shore-growing spinach and many other water plants, but in some places acorns are eaten in great quantities in years following a good oak crop.

Mallard behaviour has been investigated in great detail, and in its general pattern resembles that of other dabbling ducks. The main courtship displays are those leading to pairing rather than mating, and as with other ducks involve mock preening, drinking, water flicking, and head-up, tail-up postures. Mallard nests vary greatly in situation, and are often far from water. Nests on pollarded willows or holes in trees are common, and freak sites among buildings are regularly recorded. Nine to 12 eggs form the usual clutch, and incubation lasts 28 days: the young fledge in seven weeks.

Red-crested Pochard

Below, the drake in full plumage is among the gaudiest of European wildfowl

Revealing the most extensive wing-bar of any duck, chestnut-coloured head and black neck, the drake is unmistakable in flight

$(\times \frac{1}{7})$

Although Red-crested Pochard are diving ducks, in shallow water they will feed by reaching down or up-ending like surface feeders

Female on nest

Female

The drake is distinguished by his red beak, even in eclipse

Eggs are covered over when a female leaves her nest

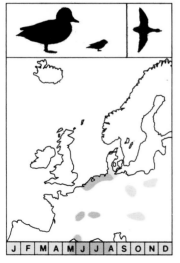

J F M A M J J A S O N D

Diving ducks, of which the Red-crested Pochard is an example, differ from surface feeders in a number of ways. Their legs are set farther back on the body, making them clumsy on land, and they have to hold their bodies more erect than dabbling ducks. Stockier in build, they have a different appearance in flight, with thick necks and narrower, differently shaped wings. When taking flight, most diving ducks patter across the surface for some way before becoming airborne and then fly with very rapid wing beats. Diving ducks are generally rather silent, and on the whole sober in plumage. The male Red-crested Pochard is an exception with his bright russet head and red bill.

Deep lakes, either fresh or brackish and preferably with a fringe of reeds, are the typical habitat of this species. Its nests are well hidden in vegetation near the water, and the usual clutch consists of six to 12 eggs. The female incubates for 26 to 28 days from completion of the clutch and cares for the young alone. Six or seven weeks are required for fledging.

During the last four decades or so, the Red-crested Pochard has extended its range northwards, and now breeds regularly in Holland. Unfortunately its spread is difficult to trace with certainty, because the species is widely kept in captivity, and escaped specimens cause much confusion. It is believed that northern European breeders winter in the Camargue.

Pochard–Ferruginous Duck

Pochard group showing plumage variations: female in winter, left; drake in winter, at right, and female in eclipse in foreground

Winter drake Pochard are identified by the chestnut head and the black areas separated by silver-white back

Ferruginous drake, lower left, has white wing-bar like Tufted Duck but is identified by the white eye

$(\times \frac{1}{6})$

Ferruginous drake in display adopts a kink-necked attitude; the white triangular area shows prominently

$(\times \frac{1}{6})$

Above, Pochard in display postures

Ferruginous duck, winter

Ferruginous drake, winter

Ferruginous Duck patter along the water when taking off. The white underwing is clearly visible

Ferruginous drakes have pure-white under-tail coverts

Pochard commonly use the jump-diving technique when feeding, preferring water between three and eight feet in depth

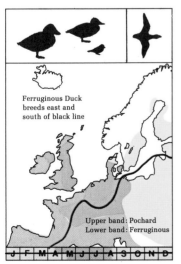

Ferruginous Duck breeds east and south of black line

Upper band: Pochard
Lower band: Ferruginous

J F M A M J J A S O N D

Pochard often associate with Tufted Duck, but in most places are usually less numerous and more shy in behaviour, preferring to keep well away from the water's edge. Their breeding requirements are rather more exacting, a dense fringe of reeds and rushes being a basic necessity before any lake is used for nesting. Primarily a freshwater feeder, the Pochard obtains most of its food by diving, but some feed by dabbling in the shallows. Stonewort provides them with much of their food, but various seeds are taken, as well as a small amount of animal matter.

During courtship, groups of drake Pochard may be seen swimming round a duck. Their principal display consists of laying the head down along the water with the neck feathers raised, giving a strange, thick-necked appearance. To accompany this performance, a curious note is uttered, which has been described as resembling an asthmatic man taking a deep breath at his doctor's request. The nest is usually made in rushes; though substantial and well concealed, it often has only a very sparse lining of down.

Ferruginous Duck have a limited breeding distribution in Europe, largely confined to the southeast, but are more widespread in winter, when they are seen as far west as Britain. Occurring more frequently on salt water than the Pochard, their diet appears to include more animal matter, such as molluscs and small fish.

Tufted Duck—Scaup

Female in eclipse

Male and female Tufted Duck in eclipse plumage (July-September). Female belly plumage varies from all brown, left, to nearly white

Adult male in eclipse

Scaup, below, use feet and wings (including the alula or "bastard" wing) when diving for food

Adult male Tufted Duck in winter plumage

Adult male Scaup in flight, showing the characteristic pale grey back. The bird is larger than the Tufted Duck but has a similar wing pattern

($\times \frac{1}{6}$)

At a distance, adult Tufted Duck appear all black and white, but the bright yellow eye is a distinct feature

($\times \frac{1}{6}$)

Above, on landing, ducks use their large feet as rudders

Below, the female Scaup has a white blaze round the bill

Female Tufted Duck often nest together on an island in a lake

In addition to the grey back, Scaup have longer, broader bills than Tufted Duck. Neither sex has a crest on the head

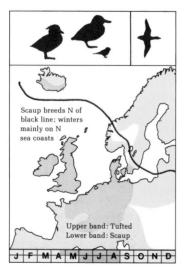

Scaup breeds N of black line; winters mainly on N sea coasts

Upper band: Tufted
Lower band: Scaup

J F M A M J J A S O N D

Tufted Duck have habitat requirements very similar to those of the Pochard, though they are even more strictly tied to fresh water. However, it is a basic rule of ecology that two species with identical requirements cannot live together, so it is not surprising to find that the diets of these two ducks differ considerably. Tufted Duck take much more animal matter during their diving forays to the muddy floors of lakes or reservoirs, the usual items being insect larvae, molluscs and crustaceans, with relatively small amounts of water plants and their seeds.

Nesting habits are also different from the Pochard's. Tufted Duck usually site their nests in drier positions sheltered by a grass tussock, but often make up for their greater exposure by nesting on islands—an effective deterrent to some predators, especially foxes. As islands are often small, Tufted Duck tend to be social nesters. Always well lined with down, the nests hold seven to 12 eggs, which hatch after 23 to 27 days' incubation; the young fledge in about six weeks.

Scaup are mainly winter visitors to the UK and are seen from October to March. Outside the breeding season, they are salt-water ducks, congregating often in very large flocks on bays and estuaries where there are extensive mussel beds. Northern lakes, amongst moorland, fells and forest are the breeding habitat, and like Tufted Duck they may group their nests on islands.

Goldeneye

The uniquely high forehead, the beak shape and the circular white face-patch identify the drake at close range or in the distance

Below, the female: same head and beak profile as the drake

In flight the drake flickers black and white, an effect enhanced by rapid wing beats. Goldeneye are among the swiftest wildfowl

(× 1/6)

In common with all diving duck, Goldeneye patter the surface during take-off

Above, the jump-dive, which begins an underwater foray. Goldeneye are among the strongest divers, staying submerged long enough to hinder relocation

Below left, an immature bird. Below right, the drake

During courtship drakes display by throwing back the head, stretching forwards along the surface and kicking water in the air behind with their feet

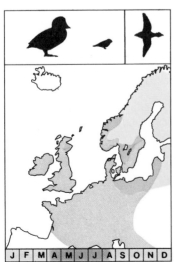

Flying, or swimming, Goldeneye are easy to identify. Passing overhead, their wings make a loud whistling noise which at once distinguishes them from other ducks. On the water they show a characteristic head shape, with high foreheads and short bills. Goldeneye dive deeply, and seek much of their animal food by turning over stones at the bottom of lakes or estuaries. For this purpose, a short, robust bill is a more suitable implement than a long one. The high forehead allows a large air space to be accommodated in the roof of the skull. This is an unusual feature in diving ducks, most of which have denser skull construction than surface feeders for the purpose of reducing buoyancy. Possibly the air sinuses in a Goldeneye's skull provide an air reservoir to permit more prolonged dives.

Forested areas, with plentiful lakes and waterways, are the habitat chosen for breeding. Trees are a necessity because the normal nest site is a cavity in old timber. Inside it, a mixture of wood chips and down provides the bed for six to 15 eggs, which are incubated for 26 to 30 days. On hatching, the young remain in the nest for about 24 hours to dry out, and are then called by their mother to the ground below. They tumble out, preserved from injury by their small size and thick down, and are able to fly after eight to eight and a half weeks. A few pairs probably breed in Scotland.

207

Long-tailed Duck

Drake Long-tailed Duck are self-evident. Females confuse, but they are identifiable by the brown face-patches and head and beak shape. The species looks less squat than other diving ducks

Left, the drake and, below, the duck in winter plumage (October-February)

Long-tailed Duck roll from side to side in flight, alternately exposing pale belly and dark upperparts. The wings are slightly curved back, and their up-stroke does not rise much above the horizontal

(× 1/7)

Below, a juvenile

Female in winter

Above, a drake in summer plumage; right, in winter

Distant hounds, or the skirling of bagpipes: both similes have been applied to the calling of Long-tailed Duck, but neither quite captures the haunting quality of the sound. It is frequently heard in spring, for courtship starts before the ducks have left their wintering areas for the high Arctic breeding grounds. Parties of drakes gather round a duck to display by raising first tails, then bodies, calling with increasing intensity until the whole group takes off in a headlong chase.

Shallow seas rather than estuaries are the favoured winter habitat—Long-tailed Duck like to forage in clear water. Suitable conditions are found in many parts of the Baltic, where the species congregates in huge flocks sometimes many thousands strong.

The actual breeding environment is among tundra pools. Pairs tend to be scattered, although they regularly nest in association with Arctic Terns. The birds arrive just before the thaw has ended, and wait offshore until conditions improve. In such barren surroundings there is little cover for the nest, which is a simple hollow lined with grass and down. The five to nine eggs are, like those of any duck, incubated by the female alone, but the male does stay near the nest at first. Hatching occurs after 23 to 25 days; no precise fledging period is recorded, but the young are independent after five weeks. Crabs, periwinkles and various bivalves are the major food items.

Smew

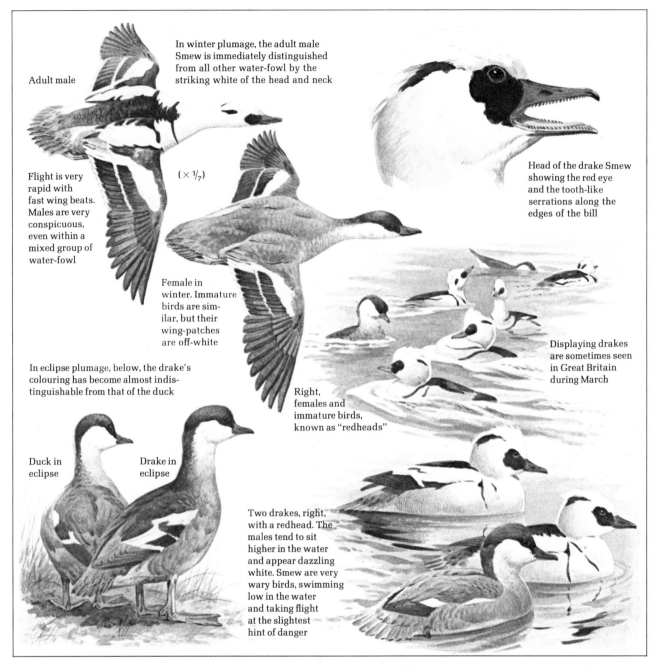

Adult male

In winter plumage, the adult male Smew is immediately distinguished from all other water-fowl by the striking white of the head and neck

(× ¹/₇)

Flight is very rapid with fast wing beats. Males are very conspicuous, even within a mixed group of water-fowl

Head of the drake Smew showing the red eye and the tooth-like serrations along the edges of the bill

Female in winter. Immature birds are similar, but their wing-patches are off-white

In eclipse plumage, below, the drake's colouring has become almost indistinguishable from that of the duck

Right, females and immature birds, known as "redheads"

Displaying drakes are sometimes seen in Great Britain during March

Duck in eclipse

Drake in eclipse

Two drakes, right, with a redhead. The males tend to sit higher in the water and appear dazzling white. Smew are very wary birds, swimming low in the water and taking flight at the slightest hint of danger

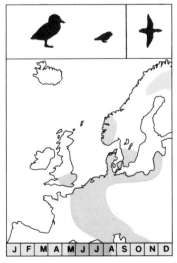

Utterly charming in its almost entirely white plumage, the drake Smew could almost be mistaken for one of the floating fragments of ice which litter its winter habitat. Females and young drakes are more conventionally attired, though still quite distinct from other ducks—but in poor light it is possible to confuse them with Black-necked or Slavonian Grebes.

Smew, together with Goosanders and Mergansers, belong to the sawbill group of ducks: the margins of their beaks are studded with tooth-like projections which help to grip fish. Compared with the other sawbills, Smew are smaller and shorter billed, and their diet includes quite large quantities of prey other than fish. Fish are nevertheless the main source of food in winter, when the Smew's day is occupied with spells of intensive fishing lasting 25 to 30 minutes, separated by five-minute pauses to rest and preen. Paired Smew dive together, and sometimes large flocks fish in unison—a habit also observed in other members of the sawbill family.

Winter habitats include various shallow waters, such as harbours and reservoirs; the summer environment is a lake or river surrounded by woodland. Holes in trees, or sometimes nest-boxes, provide nest sites, and a clutch of six to ten eggs is laid. Throughout the 30-day incubation period the male remains near by, but when the young hatch he leaves to moult.

209

Goosander

An adult male Goosander looks whitest of all the water-fowl, with the exception of the much smaller drake Smew

Set off against so much white plumage the green head, long red bill and black back stand out at considerable range—up to half a mile. A Goosander looks long

(×⅙)

Above, drakes gather in parties while the females incubate. Left, Goosander are expert divers, staying submerged for surprisingly long periods

A female or immature Goosander, right, is known as a red-head and shows a clear-cut border between brown neck and white breast. Red-head Red-breasted Mergansers do not

Female at nest hole in a tree, which is usually in close reach of water

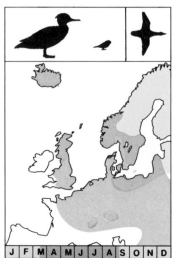

Largest of the sawbills, the beautiful Goosander has shown a welcome extension of range. It started to breed in Scotland in about 1871 and by the 1940s had spread to northern England.

During summer, it frequents large lakes and rivers, preferably in wooded country, though trees are absent from its Icelandic breeding grounds. Some of the waters it frequents may at this time of year be at quite high altitudes—up to 1,600 feet in Britain and 4,000 feet in central Europe. Winter habitats are normally large inland waters—many reservoirs providing ideal conditions. Goosander feed almost exclusively on fish, and their spread in Britain has not met with universal enthusiasm: anglers and water bailiffs fear damage to stocks of young trout and salmon, and the bird has been persecuted.

Like most sawbills, the species is usually a hole nester. Hollow trees provide nest sites in most places, the cavity being up to 30 feet from the ground. In Iceland, rock crevices or even exposed situations must suffice. The female often spends long periods off the nest fishing—a general feature of sawbill breeding biology. The eggs are kept warm by being buried in the nest's thick lining of down and wood chips. Still young, Goosander chicks often climb on to their mother's back while she is swimming, though five seems about the maximum that can be accommodated at once. Fledging takes about five weeks.

Red-breasted Merganser

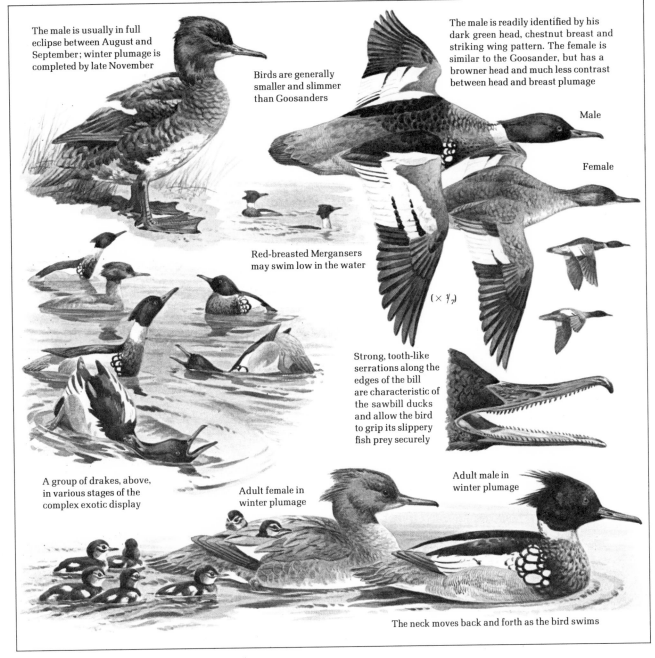

The male is usually in full eclipse between August and September; winter plumage is completed by late November

Birds are generally smaller and slimmer than Goosanders

The male is readily identified by his dark green head, chestnut breast and striking wing pattern. The female is similar to the Goosander, but has a browner head and much less contrast between head and breast plumage

Male

Female

Red-breasted Mergansers may swim low in the water

(× 1/7)

Strong, tooth-like serrations along the edges of the bill are characteristic of the sawbill ducks and allow the bird to grip its slippery fish prey securely

A group of drakes, above, in various stages of the complex exotic display

Adult female in winter plumage

Adult male in winter plumage

The neck moves back and forth as the bird swims

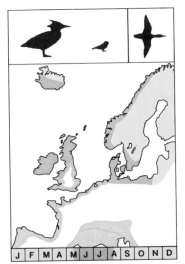

J F M A M J J A S O N D

Speeding along an estuary, neck and bill stretched out stiffly in a straight line with the body, Red-breasted Mergansers are easily distinguished from other maritime ducks.

Unlike the Goosander and Smew, this sawbill rarely occurs inland during the winter, and even during the summer it shows a fondness for sea lochs and fjords as breeding habitats, though large fresh-water lakes also suffice. Like the Goosander, it has recently extended its breeding range to include Britain. Both colonizations seem to have followed large influxes in hard winters, and although the Red-breasted Merganser's spread started 20 years later, it is now the commoner species. Fishing methods include not only div-

ing but also a habit of swimming about with only the head submerged. Young birds appear to fish in shallower water than adults.

Like those of all other sawbill ducks, Red-breasted Merganser courtship displays may be witnessed in the winter quarters. Groups of males cluster round a female, first adopting a hunched posture with the crest raised; then the head and neck are suddenly stretched stiffly forwards and upwards; then the crest is rapidly lowered. Finally, the bird bows, bringing its head down to the surface of the water.

Red-breasted Mergansers do not nest in tree holes, but the sites selected among rocks or vegetation are always very sheltered.

211

Shoveler

Shovelers dabbling in surface waters

When feeding, the bird paddles rapidly about with head held low as it sieves animal and plant matter through the fine comb-like plates edging the bill. The technique is called "dabbling"

Duck

In flight, the female Shoveler looks rather like the Mallard but with a single central white wing-bar; the Mallard has a double bar. The distinctive shape of the Shoveler's bill is a clear identification feature

The drake's dark head, white breast and chestnut belly are distinctive in flight

Drake

At birth, the duckling's bill is quite regular in shape, gradually acquiring the spatulate adult bill form during its first six weeks

From below, the wings appear to be set far back, an effect created by the very long bill

(× ¹/₇)

Drake

Duck

Duck

Male and female in winter plumage, with chick. When swimming, much of the drake's chestnut underside plumage is obscured

Drake

Eclipse plumage, above, is retained for longer than in most surface-feeders

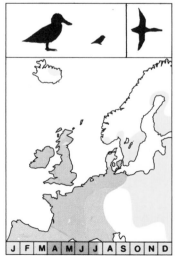

Huge bills and blue forewings on both sexes make the Shoveler the easiest dabbling duck to identify. As might be expected, the unusual bill shape denotes specialized feeding methods, and close examination shows how it operates. Delicate projections, somewhat like the teeth of a very fine comb, fringe the mandible edges, forming an efficient sieve. Basically a refinement of structures found in all ducks' bills, this device enables the Shoveler to live as a filter feeder. With the bill immersed, the bird swims about using the tongue to pump water in and out of the bill. As water is forced over the meshes of the "sieve", tiny food particles are trapped in sufficient quantity to provide worthwhile nourishment. Large groups of Shovelers often feed close together, and it is believed that this agitates the water, bringing more food into the surface layers. Such a feeding method is used to best advantage on shallow, well-vegetated inland waters, though Shovelers also visit estuaries in small numbers.

Specialized as they are, the Shoveler's feeding habits are clearly practical, for it is a numerous and widely distributed species. Breeding habits resemble those of most dabbling ducks, though the nests are often surprisingly exposed. Eight to 12 eggs are laid, and incubation takes 23 to 25 days. The drake sometimes helps the female tend the young, which fledge in six to six and a half weeks.

Shelduck

Flight is slower than that of the typical ducks, but wing beats faster than in geese

The chestnut band across the shoulders, and the distinctive pattern on the back, identify the Shelduck even at distance

On long-distance flights to their moulting areas, Shelduck fly in wedge formation or in oblique lines

Shelduck are sometimes seen resting on the open sea, but the species is generally restricted to the inter-tidal zone in Europe. Occasionally found on inland waters

Normally two, but sometimes more, adults take charge of several broods of young, forming a pack

(×¹⁄₈)

Drake

Juvenile

Duck

Adult males have a distinctive red knob at the base of the bill; in the female the bill is plain. Juveniles have no breastband. First winter and first summer birds have greenish heads and generally subdued colouring

The female nests in a disused rabbit burrow, lining a chamber, seven or eight feet from the entrance, with down. She leaves the nest twice daily to feed

| J | F | M | A | M | J | J | A | S | O | N | D |

Shelduck belong to a group of birds whose place in the animal kingdom is roughly between typical geese and typical ducks, and they are in many ways very different from other European wildfowl. Molluscs are their staple diet, and most important of those is the tiny snail *Hydrobia*: as many as 3,000 of these little animals have been found in a Shelduck's stomach. This mudflat organism is also an important food for many waders, but unlike those birds, Shelduck can obtain them by up-ending in shallow water, as well as by foraging on the mud. Since many *Hydrobia* retreat into the mud at low tide and only emerge when the sea covers them again, Shelduck are able to exploit them under considerably more advan-

tageous conditions than most waders.

Shelduck make their nests in burrows –commonly those of rabbits. Although the female incubates alone–hissing at intruders, like many hole-nesting birds –the male is never far away. Often both parents leave their young well before the end of the six-and-a-half to eight-week fledging period. Young Shelduck abandoned in this way join up into groups in the care of a few adults; meanwhile, their parents have migrated to one of the species' large communal moulting areas, such as the Knechtsand on the German Bight, or Bridgwater Bay on Britain's Severn estuary–places where until recently they have been endangered by air force bombing practice.

Eider

Below, the adult male is easily identified by his pied plumage and characteristic head shape. Right, flight is steady and very direct—often only a few feet above the waves

Juveniles, above, resemble females; young Eider mature very slowly

($\times\frac{1}{7}$)

Eider dive powerfully, using wings as well as feet for propulsion

Soft down is plucked from the female's breast and used to line the nest. Larger feathers are often intermingled

The Eider is a thoroughly marine species, frequently seen diving in quite heavy surf to take food from the rocky bottom. They are rarely seen inland except when migrating

Female Eider rarely leave their nests unattended, particularly when on exposed sites

Above, the wedge of feathers extending along the bill from the cheek is typical of the Eider. Left, adult drake

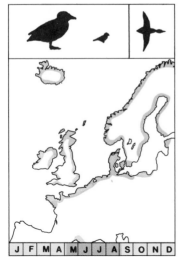

J F M A M J J A S O N D

Eider-down has long been used as a heat insulating material, and still has some economic importance. Though not greatly different from the down used by other ducks to line their nests, the Eider's is plentiful and easily collected. On Eider farms in Iceland and other parts of Scandinavia, several thousand pairs are induced to nest in semi-domestication by efficient protection and provision of artificial nest sites—one of the more praiseworthy forms of human exploitation of wildlife. Despite heavy mortality caused by oil spillage on the high seas, Eider are increasing, and a count in 1973 revealed nearly 600,000 in the Baltic alone.

These birds feed in shallow waters, rocky or muddy, and are much more in-clined to forage by up-ending than most diving ducks. A close study of their feeding behaviour on a Scottish estuary disclosed another feeding technique: the feet are used to excavate a crater in barely submerged mud and this is then explored with the bill. When they do dive, they swim with the wings half open. Mussels are the principal food, those taken ranging between two and 24 millimetres long; they may be crushed, but are usually eaten whole; crabs and starfish are also eaten.

Natural nest sites include turf, rocks and even ruined buildings. On hatching, Eider ducklings are led straight to the sea, where broods intermingle during the long fledging period of up to ten and a half weeks.

Common Scoter–Velvet Scoter

The male Scoter's wings are noticeably narrower than those of the female

The glossy jet-black plumage and attractive bill of the male, and the brown cap and pale cheeks of the female, are clear distinguishing features of the Common Scoter

Female Common Scoter

Male's bill varies yellow to deep orange

When riding on the water, Scoter often stretch upwards to flap their wings; if striking white wing-patches are exposed, the bird is a Velvet Scoter

$(\times \frac{1}{7})$

Flight, above, is very fast and direct—often in long lines and wedges—parallel to, and about half a mile from, the shore

A raft of Scoter in swell, below, has a characteristic snaking motion as parts of the group alternately vanish and reappear

Female Velvet Scoter

Male Velvet Scoter

Family group of Common Scoter; male and female swimming, with immature bird standing

White wing-patches show very clearly at distance. Young males have two head-patches, often indistinct

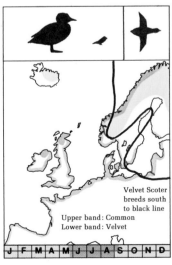

Velvet Scoter breeds south to black line

Upper band: Common
Lower band: Velvet

J F M A M J J A S O N D

The pathetic, oil-drenched specimens washed ashore after gales provide for most Europeans the closest glimpse they ever have of Scoter. The birds usually fly well offshore in long lines half hidden by waves, a habit which makes them vulnerable to the nets of bird-catchers on their Baltic migration route.

To see scoter at their best, it is necessary to take a boat trip to their feeding grounds—shallow areas of sea where mollusc-rich sand-banks come close to the surface. Here the Common Scoter may be found in dense rafts of hundreds or even thousands; the Velvet Scoter is less common, and rarely seen in groups of over 100, generally feeding in more scattered parties. While swimming underwater both species often open their wings, perhaps to assist steerage—a habit shared by Long-tailed Duck and Eider.

Lakes among northern forests are a typical summer habitat for both species, but the Common Scoter also inhabits treeless areas and tundra, while the Velvet Scoter shows a preference for more mountainous inland regions. Both species place their nests on the ground, sheltered under vegetation; Velvet Scoter sometimes nest at the foot of a tree. Clutch sizes for both species are in the range of six to ten eggs, and incubation takes about four weeks. Common Scoter require six to seven weeks to fledge; chicks of the Velvet Scoter are independent after four or five weeks.

Barnacle Goose

Generally, flocks do not mix with other species, though individual birds and small parties may do so

Typical open pattern of Barnacle Geese in flight

Adult

The Barnacle Goose is a frequent winter visitor to Great Britain and may be seen at varying times between mid-September and mid-May in most years

$(\times \frac{1}{9})$

The Barnacle Goose is identified at long range by its combination of black, white and grey. The pale cream face contrasts with the very dark crown and breast. Tail chevron is very prominent

Birds settle on the sea only in calm conditions; less inclined than Brent Geese to rest on water

When grazing, Barnacle Geese are less wary than most other species. Feeding is frequently interrupted by noisy quarrels between members of the group

The bill is very short and stubby, particularly in comparison with the grey geese. Barnacle Geese are generally rare outside their normal winter range

Juveniles have a dusky face and brownish upper plumage in their first year

Reclamation of coastal mudflats is not always disastrous for waders and wildfowl. Extensive reclamation carried out in Holland, for example, has denied the shore-living Brent Goose valuable feeding ground, while providing its relative the Barnacle Goose with a huge new acreage of pasture.

Barnacle Geese eat short rich turf on coastal meadows and certain types of salt-marsh. Recent research has shown that seeds also form a large part of their diet—a rather unusual feature among geese. They are taken in greatest quantity from rushes, probably by stripping fruit clusters directly from their spiky stems. Feeding takes place in daylight, the geese moving to and from their roosts on tidal flats at dusk and dawn. When there is a full moon, feeding may continue at night.

The quaint old myth that these geese hatch from barnacles is misleading in every sense—their nesting habits are entirely those to be expected of their family. Irish and Hebridean Barnacle Geese breed in Greenland; those from Solway in Spitsbergen, while birds wintering in Holland and on the Baltic island of Gotland breed in northern Russia. Nesting commences on snow-free areas before the Arctic thaw is completed. Sites chosen are either on rock outcrops or small islands—places giving protection from such predators as Arctic foxes. In common with other geese, the male guards his brooding mate and both parents tend the young.

216

Canada Goose

The chevron marking is proportionally farther from the end of the tail than in other related species

Largest of all the geese, the Canada Goose is easily identified from below by its black neck and white face-patch and by the pale belly and dark underwing

$(\times \frac{1}{10})$

After driving an intruder from the nest territory, a pair of Canada Geese indulge in a triumph display with sinuous movements of the neck

Originally introduced to Britain as ornamental birds, Canada Geese quickly spread in the wild to a variety of fresh-water habitats

Nests are built on the ground, near water, sometimes in colonies but more often in small groups

The take-off clearly displays the brown back, black tail and striking white chevron

Adult male and female; the sexes exhibit no obvious differences in form or coloration

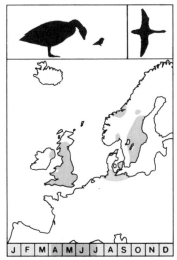

To bird-watchers in North America, this is the most familiar wild goose, and is a common sight on migration in spring or autumn throughout the continent. Although Canada Geese introduced from that continent have established themselves in parts of Europe, they have never quite emulated the success of their transatlantic forebears. In North America the Canada Goose is a highly variable species, with several races differing greatly in size and depth of colour. Those introduced into Europe belong to the large, pale Atlantic coast race; birds of other races, probably genuinely wild vagrants from North America, have occasionally appeared in Ireland and Scotland amongst flocks of Barnacle or White-fronted Geese. A survey in 1953 found some 1,500 pairs in Britain, and numbers have increased since then; the Swedish population is about 2,300 pairs, and there have recently been nesting occurrences in Norway and Denmark. In winter, Swedish birds visit coastal areas of the southern Baltic and northern North Sea, and some move inland as far as Switzerland.

Meadow and pasture near water are the typical habitat in Europe, and for breeding purposes the Canada Goose resorts to lakes, gravel pits and parkland. The nest of grass and reeds lined with down is usually close to water, sheltered by rough vegetation or bushes, and is often on an island. Five or six eggs are usually laid, and the young fledge after six and a half weeks.

217

White-fronted Goose

The adult White-fronted Goose in flight appears paler than the Bean Goose

Viewed from beneath, right, birds may be either heavily or lightly barred; juveniles lack underside barring and the white frontal blaze

$(\times\,^1/_{10})$

Adult   Adult   Juvenile

The White-front lacks the contrast between pale forewing and darker hind-wing typical of Greylag

Slimmer winged and more agile in flight than most grey geese, White-fronts can take spectacular evasive action on sighting guns

Family parties commonly graze together on open fields and pasture. If netted for ringing, birds are released in family groups, never singly

The Greenland race of White-front is readily identified by its orange bill

The Russian race, familiar in winter in western Europe, has a rose-red bill

Juveniles and birds in their first win-ter have very pale grey-yellow bills

Adult White-fronted Geese have a prominent white frontal blaze and well-marked underparts

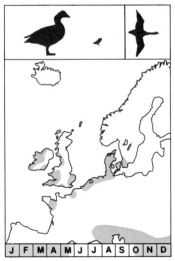

J F M A M J J A S O N D

Wild geese in flight can hardly fail to have romantic appeal. Many much smaller birds undertake longer migra-tions, but their journeys for the most part pass unnoticed. Geese always cause a sensation as a skein beats past in a long line, or in a V formation, strung out across the sky. The chorus of a flock in flight is a stirring sound, and amongst geese the White-front is perhaps the most musical of all—its call having a yodelling quality.

Two races occur in Europe: most numerous is the typical race, wintering in central and northern Europe and in England—these birds come from breed-ing grounds in Russia. A darker, orange-billed race breeding in Green-land winters in Scotland, Ireland and

Wales. Recent years have seen a pro-gressive shift of wintering flocks from central Europe to the Netherlands, where numbers now sometimes exceed 70,000—about half the total European winter population.

Wet pastureland, such as water-meadows, is the favourite habitat and grass is the main diet, although the Greenland race shows a liking for boggy areas, where it consumes the un-derground parts of white beak-sedge.

White-fronts breed in tundra on islands in rivers or raised areas in bogs. There is a tendency to nest colo-nially, but each gander defends a small territory around the nest. As with most geese, families stay together until the following season.

Brent Goose

Adult Brent Goose, foreground, in flight with immature bird

$(\times 1/9)$

Family groups are maintained, whether in single-race flocks or in mixed flocks

Adult, dark-bellied race

Adult, pale-bellied race

Brent often feed as the tide is turning, up-ending to reach submerged water-weeds

Brent fly in loose flocks, often low over the water, occasionally rising to 300 feet altitude

Brent are diurnal feeders, grazing on eel-grass on mudflats. Though small, and superficially like ducks, they are immediately identified as geese by the white chevrons

The Brent Goose is completely adapted to marine life and often rests on the sea

Juvenile birds are more heavily barred than adults and lack the prominent neck patch of the mature Brent

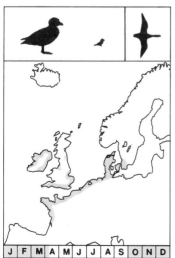

J F M A M J J A S O N D

Broad mudflats in bays and estuaries are the exclusive winter habitat of the Brent Goose—only in times of food shortage does it cross the sea wall to feed on fields like grey geese. At other times it sustains itself almost entirely on either eel-grass or *Enteromorpha* seaweed—plants which carpet the mud down to mid-tide level. A large form of eel-grass growing even lower on the shore was once an important food source, but during the 1930s a mysterious disease almost wiped it out on both sides of the North Atlantic. Robbed suddenly of this supply, Brent Goose populations dwindled alarmingly. The Brent had for long been a traditional quarry of the punt-gunner, but by the 1950s it was clear that the species could not survive continued hunting. Protective measures were introduced by several countries, since when its numbers have gradually increased; now estuary reclamation schemes pose a new threat to the future of the species.

Brent Geese nest in the high Arctic. The pale-bellied race from Canada, Greenland and Spitzbergen winters on the eastern seaboard of the USA, in Ireland and at a few localities on North Sea coasts. The dark-bellied race, more numerous in European wintering areas, breeds in the Soviet Arctic. Nests are sited on tundra, often on small islands. The clutch of three to five eggs hatches after four weeks' incubation by the female, but adverse weather causes periodic breeding failures.

Pink-footed–Bean Geese

Like other grey geese, Pink-foot fly in massed batallions or long skeins

The bill of the Bean Goose, right, is very variable; black with either orange or yellow patches individual to each bird

Bean Goose

The Pink-foot's bill is pink and black in adults; pink or ochre in immature birds

Pink-footed Goose

On the breeding grounds Pink-foot nest on cliffs and rocky outcrops to avoid the Arctic fox; occasionally birds will nest on open tundra

$(\times \frac{1}{6})$

Though normally daylight feeders, most geese will feed through the night in periods of bright, full, moonlight

Pink-footed Goose and Bean Goose; grey geese have no outward sexual differences

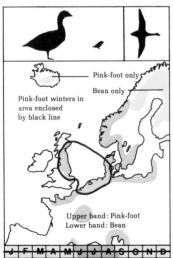

Pink-foot only

Bean only

Pink-foot winters in area enclosed by black line

Upper band: Pink-foot
Lower band: Bean

J F M A M J J A S O N D

Bean Geese and Pink-footed Geese are closely related, but their habits differ. Bean Geese frequently feed on pasture and in some areas roost inland. They are the most silent of the grey geese. Pink-foot feed largely on stubble, potato fields and other arable land. They roost on coastal mudflats, moving between shore and fields at dawn and dusk. Such movements, called flighting, become irregular during full moon, when feeding may continue at night. Flighting Pink-foot are highly vociferous, producing a thrilling cacophony in which the high-pitched voices of males can be distinguished from those of females, which are an octave lower.

Bean Geese have a much wider distribution than Pink-foot, but their num-bers have declined, perhaps due to changes in farming methods. However, they have accepted a predominantly arable habitat in many areas, and must have done so for a long time in England, where their name reputedly derives from a habit of feeding on wasted seeds from the bean harvest. Pink-foot are threatened by a proposed hydro-electric scheme which would flood their most important Icelandic breeding area.

Nesting Pink-foot choose sites on cliff ledges and rock outcrops, and breed in colonies. Bean Geese nest scattered on open tundra by lakes, swamps or rivers. With clutches of four to six eggs and an incubation period of about four weeks, basic breeding biology is similar in both species.

Greylag Goose

The rump and back are paler on the Greylag than on most other grey geese

(×1/6)

Fore-wing is palest of all geese

Plump, low-bodied domestic geese, often retaining plumage characteristics more typical of wild birds

Eastern race: colour of bill ranges from flesh to rose pink; belly is often spotted

Immediately before taking to the air, Greylag perform a series of characteristic "pre-flight" movements, jerking the head from side to side with increasing rapidity until they take flight

When coming in to land, Greylag often perform striking aerobatic movements known as "whiffling". The birds plunge downwards in a side-slipping dive, rolling and tilting in a totally abandoned manner

Head and bill are heavy and the Greylag's build is more robust than that of most of the grey geese

Though principally grassland grazers, Greylag occasionally feed on water-weed by up-ending

The furrowing along the neck, seen in all the grey geese, is caused by rows of elongated convex feathers

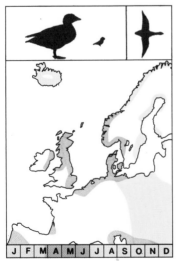

J F M A M J J A S O N D

Greylag Geese are the ancestors of all domesticated geese except the Chinese Goose, which descends from the Swan Goose of Asia. In their calls and general appearance, wild Greylags still bear an unmistakable resemblance to the farmyard bird. They are a widely distributed species which breeds farther south than any of the various grey geese occurring in Europe. Introducing it deliberately to new areas has increased its numbers and widened its range.

Behaviour patterns have been more intensively studied in the Greylag than in any other species of wildfowl. Like all geese, it has a complex social organization, maintained by an elaborate system of signals and postures. Pairs normally stay together for life, and family parties are maintained throughout the winter—factors which underlie the remarkable cohesiveness of goose flocks. A fascinating phenomenon revealed through such observations is that of imprinting—a process occurring in all wildfowl and many other birds, but first discovered, and extensively studied, in the Greylag.

Newly hatched goslings follow, and become strongly attached to, the first animal they see after birth. Normally this is their mother, but in experimental conditions it could be a duck, a bantam, even a human being. Whatever it is, the birds will subsequently transfer all their social behaviour to that animal, rather than to other Greylags.

221

Whooper Swan–Bewick's Swan

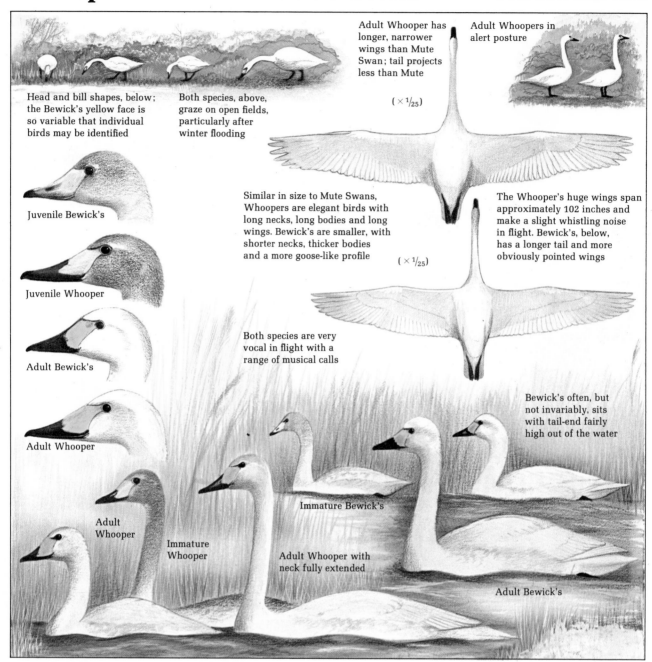

Head and bill shapes, below; the Bewick's yellow face is so variable that individual birds may be identified

Both species, above, graze on open fields, particularly after winter flooding

Adult Whooper has longer, narrower wings than Mute Swan; tail projects less than Mute

(× 1/25)

Adult Whoopers in alert posture

Juvenile Bewick's

Juvenile Whooper

Adult Bewick's

Adult Whooper

Similar in size to Mute Swans, Whoopers are elegant birds with long necks, long bodies and long wings. Bewick's are smaller, with shorter necks, thicker bodies and a more goose-like profile

(× 1/25)

The Whooper's huge wings span approximately 102 inches and make a slight whistling noise in flight. Bewick's, below, has a longer tail and more obviously pointed wings

Both species are very vocal in flight with a range of musical calls

Bewick's often, but not invariably, sits with tail-end fairly high out of the water

Adult Whooper

Immature Whooper

Immature Bewick's

Adult Whooper with neck fully extended

Adult Bewick's

Bewick's Swan winters inside area marked by black line

| J | F | M | A | M | J | J | A | S | O | N | D |

Whooper Swans and Bewick's Swans are above all wild birds, their ancestry untainted by any history of domestication like that of the Mute. Stirring calls, like bugles, seem almost to proclaim their freedom, though their wing beats are virtually silent. Audible at a great distance, these sounds are delivered through a specially elongated windpipe.

Only the Whooper Swan breeds in western Europe—in Lapland, Iceland and sporadically in Scotland. Its wintering areas are coasts, lakes and reservoirs mainly in southern Scandinavia and Britain, though a few travel as far as the Mediterranean. Bewick's Swan has a very northerly breeding range, confined to the high Arctic zone of the USSR, but is more widely distributed than the Whooper in winter. More partial to inland waters, it visits Holland and Germany in large numbers, and since the cold winter of 1955-6 has greatly increased its population wintering in England.

A sizeable population of Bewick's Swans winters at the Wildfowl Trust in Gloucestershire. Here, advantage has been taken of the great individual variation in bill pattern to chart family history in detail and it has been found, for example, that broods raised in successive years tend to associate in family flocks of up to 15 birds.

Whooper and Bewick's Swans make large nests similar to that of the Mute Swan, but with a more downy lining.

Mute Swan

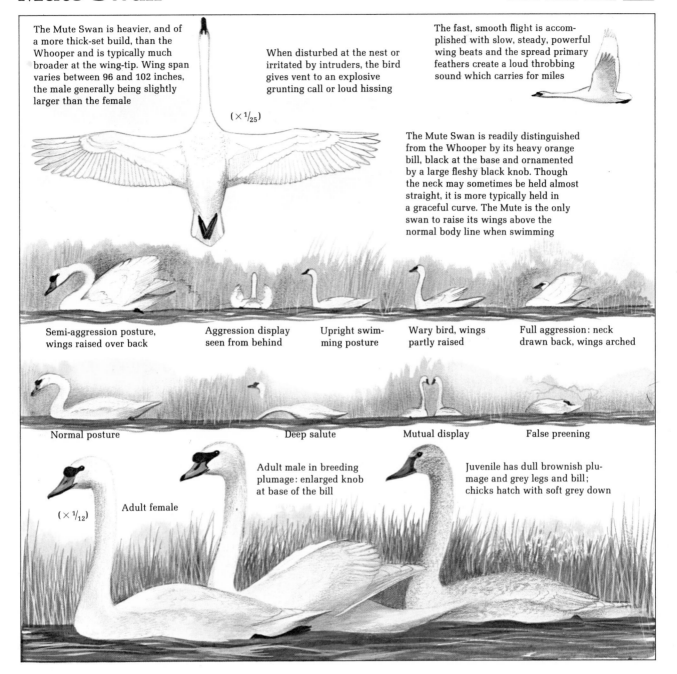

The Mute Swan is heavier, and of a more thick-set build, than the Whooper and is typically much broader at the wing-tip. Wing span varies between 96 and 102 inches, the male generally being slightly larger than the female

($\times \frac{1}{25}$)

When disturbed at the nest or irritated by intruders, the bird gives vent to an explosive grunting call or loud hissing

The fast, smooth flight is accomplished with slow, steady, powerful wing beats and the spread primary feathers create a loud throbbing sound which carries for miles

The Mute Swan is readily distinguished from the Whooper by its heavy orange bill, black at the base and ornamented by a large fleshy black knob. Though the neck may sometimes be held almost straight, it is more typically held in a graceful curve. The Mute is the only swan to raise its wings above the normal body line when swimming

Semi-aggression posture, wings raised over back

Aggression display seen from behind

Upright swimming posture

Wary bird, wings partly raised

Full aggression: neck drawn back, wings arched

Normal posture

Deep salute

Mutual display

False preening

Adult male in breeding plumage: enlarged knob at base of the bill

Juvenile has dull brownish plumage and grey legs and bill; chicks hatch with soft grey down

($\times \frac{1}{12}$) Adult female

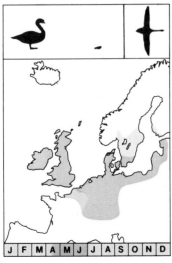

Compared with other swans, the Mute is indeed a poor vocalist, its repertoire consisting of mere grunts and hisses. On the wing, however, it compensates for the deficiency with loud, throbbing wing beats—an exhilarating sound whose rhythm is said to have inspired Wagner when composing the *Ride of the Valkyrie*.

This species is the most common swan of Europe, and in most parts of the Continent it is the only one which breeds. Its present distribution is partly the result of domestication at various times in the past. The ancient ceremony of swan-upping is still performed every year on the Thames: young swans are rounded up and the bills given distinctive marks.

Various water plants and a few small animals constitute the Mute Swan's diet. Large flocks congregate on certain estuaries, and sometimes make serious inroads into the limited stocks of eel-grass. To breed, they resort to inland lakes and rivers, siting the huge and conspicuous nest close to water. Unlike the nests of ducks and geese, these are built by both sexes and the lining contains little down. The male's threat display deters most humans, though the damage inflicted by actual attacks has been exaggerated. Incubation of the three to eight eggs lasts 35 days, and is mainly the female's task, though the male takes over while she is feeding—mainly at night. The cygnets fledge in 13 weeks.

J F M A M J J A S O N D

Herring Gull

Typical underwing pattern of adult

Frequently seen following coastal ships, particularly fishing boats

Juvenile

Birds of all ages are commonly seen together in flight

Adult in winter has streaked head markings

Head projects farther forward than that of the Common Gull

The Herring Gull is much heavier in build than the Common Gull and has a different wing-tip pattern

(× ⅟₇)

Second winter plumage

Immature plumage as seen in flight

Immature Herring Gull

Herring Gull, below, in the characteristic posture adopted while uttering the loud and raucous display call

Sub-adult Herring Gulls often appear extremely ragged and untidy when moulting. In some adult birds, the black tips fade to brown and the white "mirrors" on the wing-tips wear off. The adult's bill is yellow; the legs always a pale flesh-pink. Herring Gulls of the eastern Baltic and Mediterranean have yellow legs

Adult in summer has white head

The only grey-backed gull that nests on roofs in seaside towns

(× ⅟₅)

The Herring Gull is large, robust, raucous and aggressive, distinguished from the Common Gull by its size, structure and shade of grey

J F M A M J J A S O N D

This is the seagull of everyone's imagination. It scavenges rubbish tips and harbours, follows boats for jettisoned titbits and even includes buildings and chimney-pots among its possible nest sites. A dangerous menace on aircraft runways, it has an alarming list of damage and fatalities to its name. It is abundant and on the increase. None the less, Herring Gulls are beautiful and fascinating, and studies of their social organizations have contributed enormously to the understanding of animal behaviour.

They normally nest colonially, traditional breeding areas including coastal promontories, cliffs and dunes. Buildings, lake shores and china-clay pits are more recent colonizations. The nest is a thick pile of grass, seaweed and jetsam amassed by both parents. Two or three eggs are laid at two- or three-day intervals, and sporadic incubation begins before the clutch is complete. In common with all gulls, both male and female brood the eggs for 28 to 33 days. The young leave the nest after a few days, but stay within their parents' territory during their six-week fledging period. The few which stray outside are likely to be eaten by neighbouring adults. Again in common with all gulls, food is brought by both parents, and includes a great variety of material obtained by scavenging. Herring Gulls regularly break open such hard-shelled prey as crabs or molluscs by dropping them from a height.

Common Gull

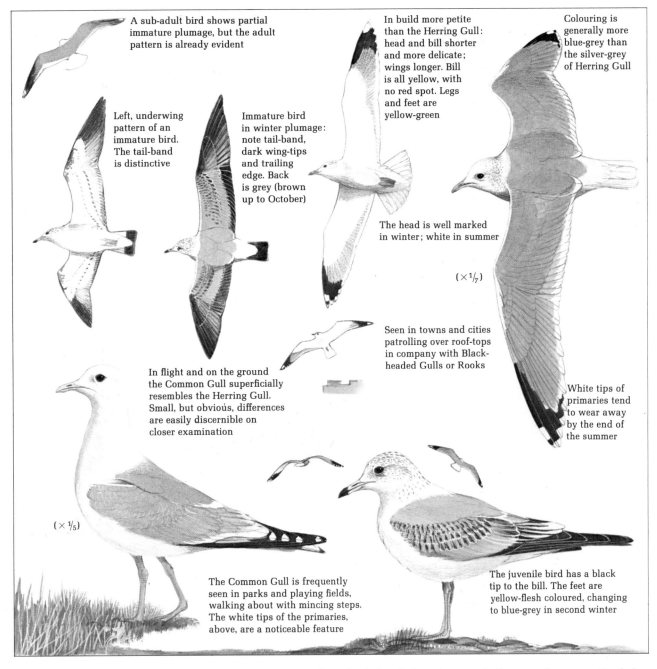

A sub-adult bird shows partial immature plumage, but the adult pattern is already evident

In build more petite than the Herring Gull: head and bill shorter and more delicate; wings longer. Bill is all yellow, with no red spot. Legs and feet are yellow-green

Colouring is generally more blue-grey than the silver-grey of Herring Gull

Left, underwing pattern of an immature bird. The tail-band is distinctive

Immature bird in winter plumage: note tail-band, dark wing-tips and trailing edge. Back is grey (brown up to October)

The head is well marked in winter; white in summer

$(\times \frac{1}{7})$

Seen in towns and cities patrolling over roof-tops in company with Black-headed Gulls or Rooks

In flight and on the ground the Common Gull superficially resembles the Herring Gull. Small, but obvious, differences are easily discernible on closer examination

White tips of primaries tend to wear away by the end of the summer

$(\times \frac{1}{5})$

The Common Gull is frequently seen in parks and playing fields, walking about with mincing steps. The white tips of the primaries, above, are a noticeable feature

The juvenile bird has a black tip to the bill. The feet are yellow-flesh coloured, changing to blue-grey in second winter

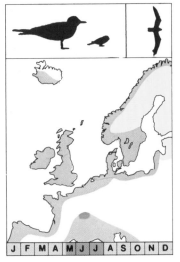

Similar in size to the Black-headed Gull, similar in appearance to the Herring Gull but not quite as abundant as either, the Common Gull is often overlooked—yet it is a widespread species. Its breeding range includes not only northern Eurasia but also parts of Alaska and Canada. It is a gull of sheltered waters, and although strongly migratory, it rarely ventures far out to sea for feeding purposes. Coastal mudflats and agricultural land provide it with much of its food, and in suburban areas it shows particular fondness for playing fields. For roosting, both tidal waters and inland sites such as reservoirs may be used. Feeding methods include not only the usual scavenging techniques of other gulls but also piracy, similar to that practised by skuas, of other gulls carrying food; the Black-headed Gull is often a victim of such pirate attacks.

Common Gulls' nests vary from scrapes with a minimal lining to bulky structures of grass and seaweed. Usually these are on rocks or among vegetation, often near the water's edge, but occasionally they are placed in trees—and in one instance even on an old Rook's nest. They may be solitary or colonial, and are sometimes associated with other gulls and terns. Two or three eggs are laid, and both sexes incubate them for 22 to 25 days. Both parents also feed the chicks, which, like those of all other gulls, are able to walk from an early age.

225

Great Black-backed Gull

Deceptively small, adults weigh four and a half pounds and have a wing span of 65 inches. Though often appearing slow and ponderous, the bird is fast and agile in pursuit of wounded birds or when chasing other gulls to force them to disgorge food

In flight, the wings appear broader than those of other gulls. The head projects well forward and the huge bill gives the bird a rapacious look. Wing beats are slow and regular, interspersed with long glides

Usually flies in small parties; some individuals flapping while others are in gliding flight

Adult, above, showing extent of dark underwing patch

Fourth-year plumage

Third-year plumage

Second-year plumage

Immature birds are extensively mottled, but pre-adult plumage changes are complex

(×¹⁄₇)

(×¹⁄₅)

The extent and intensity of black in the plumage is not a reliable distinguishing feature. Though very dark on the upper surfaces, the Great Black-backed Gull is not as black as the northern races of the Lesser Black-backed Gull

Details of the wing-tip plumage pattern vary between individuals

A huge, heavy-headed gull; males have heavier bills than females. Head has a distinctively long profile compared with the rounder heads of the smaller gulls

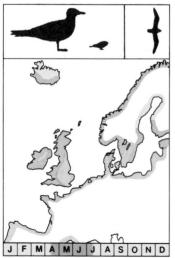

J F M A M J J A S O N D

Most of the larger gulls feed in part by the capture of living prey, but this huge and formidable species is the most serious predator of them all. Regular victims include other seabirds and their young as well as rabbits and rodents. Large animals are picked clean, finishing up with the skin turned inside out. Relatively small victims, such as gull chicks, may be swallowed whole, the operation being aided by the bird's ability to increase the distance between the halves of its lower jaw—a capacity shown by many other birds, but especially well developed in gulls.

Great Black-backs are regular predators only during the breeding season. At other times they live by scavenging on carrion, offal and refuse, especially that discarded by fishing boats. Increased fishing activity may be the reason for their multiplication during recent decades. This trend is disturbing to those concerned with the protection of seabird colonies. Campaigns to reduce the numbers of Great Black-backed Gulls have had some success, for example at Skokholm, off the south coast of Wales, where predation of Manx Shearwaters has been significantly reduced.

Often a solitary nester, the Great Black-back amasses a large pile of seaweed, grass and other litter in which to lay the clutch of two to three eggs. Incubation, by both parents, lasts 26 to 28 days, and the young fledge in seven or eight weeks.

Lesser Black-backed Gull

An adult of the British race in winter plumage. The Scandinavian race, seen in UK on passage, in winter, is much darker with an almost black back

Colour pattern is almost identical to the Great Black-back but the mantle is paler. Bill and legs are yellow, fading to pinkish or greyish tone in the winter. Despite many small differences, the bird may be difficult to distinguish from larger species when viewed at a distance

Individuals and small parties commonly seen inland during October-March

Flies with slow, measured beats; often glides and tilts

Second summer

Second winter

Immature bird

Immature: darker than Herring Gull

Individual birds vary greatly in plumage, and accurate identification may rest with the projection of the wing-tips when the wings are folded

(×⅐)

British race; adult in summer plumage has a pure white head

Scandinavian race: very dark back

The underwing pattern shows very clearly as the bird takes off

(×⅕)

Compared with the Herring Gull, the head is more delicate, body and wings longer and more slender. When at rest, the long wings project backwards well beyond the tail

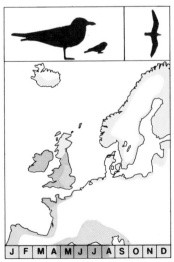

J F M A M J J A S O N D

Lesser Black-backed and Herring Gulls are very closely related. When the Herring Gull's distribution is traced westwards around the Arctic, it is found to merge, by a series of increasingly dark races, with that of the Lesser Black-backed Gull. The two can thus be regarded as the extremes of a single variable species, maintaining their separate identities in an area of overlap. In Europe, they behave as separate species, sometimes nesting side by side, but each breeding only with its own kind. Even so, the barrier separating them is a fragile one; hybrids occasionally occur, and can be artificially induced by the simple expedient of exchanging eggs between Lesser Black-backed and Herring Gull nests. Change-lings thus produced assume the identity of the foster species and in adult life will mate with the "wrong" species to produce hybrid offspring.

Not surprisingly, the two species are virtually identical in many of their habits. Lesser Black-backs do not feed on rubbish tips as often as Herring Gulls, but with them they add to the bird-strike menace at airports. For such a migratory bird, unexpectedly large winter roosts of Herring Gulls occur on several reservoirs in Britain. Black-backed Gulls' breeding sites are as varied as Herring Gulls', but where both occur together on rocky coasts, Lesser Black-backs prefer flat ground, while Herring Gulls predominate on cliff ledges.

227

Black-headed Gull

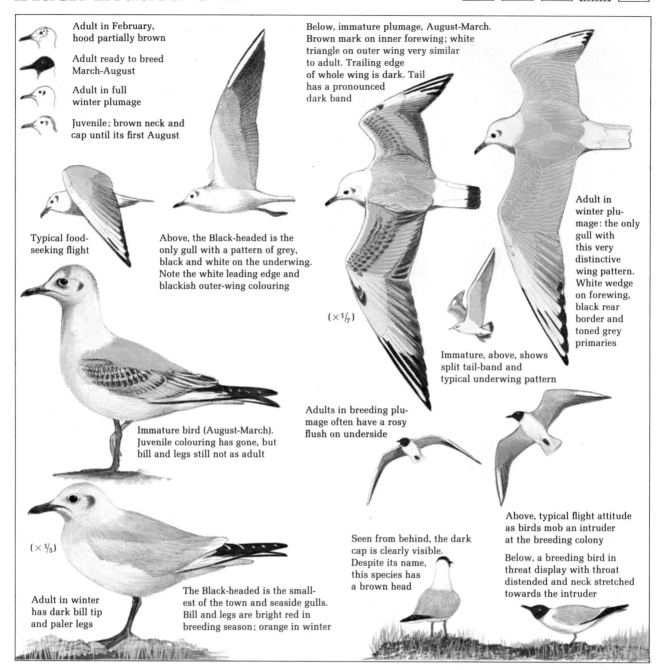

Adult in February, hood partially brown

Adult ready to breed March-August

Adult in full winter plumage

Juvenile; brown neck and cap until its first August

Typical food-seeking flight

Above, the Black-headed is the only gull with a pattern of grey, black and white on the underwing. Note the white leading edge and blackish outer-wing colouring

Below, immature plumage, August-March. Brown mark on inner forewing; white triangle on outer wing very similar to adult. Trailing edge of whole wing is dark. Tail has a pronounced dark band

Adult in winter plumage: the only gull with this very distinctive wing pattern. White wedge on forewing, black rear border and toned grey primaries

Immature, above, shows split tail-band and typical underwing pattern

Adults in breeding plumage often have a rosy flush on underside

Immature bird (August-March). Juvenile colouring has gone, but bill and legs still not as adult

(× 1/7)

(× 1/5)

Adult in winter has dark bill tip and paler legs

The Black-headed is the smallest of the town and seaside gulls. Bill and legs are bright red in breeding season; orange in winter

Seen from behind, the dark cap is clearly visible. Despite its name, this species has a brown head

Above, typical flight attitude as birds mob an intruder at the breeding colony

Below, a breeding bird in threat display with throat distended and neck stretched towards the intruder

J F M A M J J A S O N D

Many North American birds occur as vagrants in western Europe. Far fewer European birds stray against the prevailing winds west across the Atlantic, but the Black-headed Gull does so regularly. It seems likely that with the Little Gull, another wanderer from Europe, it will eventually breed there. This would seem to be the logical outcome of the Black-headed Gull's spectacular increase and range expansion in Europe during the past century. Even since 1900 it has increased a hundredfold in Sweden and Finland, and a survey of England and Wales in 1958 showed 27 per cent increase in 20 years.

Success of this kind is usually a result of a bird's rapid adaptation to the changes wrought by twentieth-century Man. This certainly seems true of the Black-headed Gull. Long known as a follower of the plough, it now benefits from playing fields, rubbish dumps, park lakes and even suburban gardens, gleaning rubbish and foraging for soil invertebrates. Once a rare bird in London, it is estimated that 192,000 roosted there during December 1968.

Breeding sites include marshes, saltings, sewage farms and gravel pits. Nests are closely grouped in colonies, sometimes of several thousand pairs. On marshy sites, some nests are built as floating structures amongst vegetation. Three eggs are usual, and incubation lasts 23 to 24 days. The young fledge at five to six weeks.

Glaucous Gull–Iceland Gull

Glaucous, above, is slow and ponderous in flight

Adult Iceland Gull in winter

Adult Glaucous, winter

The Iceland Gull, right, and Glaucous Gull, far right, are drawn to same scale; the Glaucous is as large as the Great Black-backed Gull, the Iceland similar in size to the Herring Gull. The Iceland Gull has shorter tail, more delicate head and narrower, more pointed, wings than the Glaucous Gull

Adults of both species have same basic wing patterning

Adult Glaucous

Second-summer Glaucous Gull

Small Glaucous

Comparison of bill sizes: the bill of the Iceland Gull is both lighter and shorter than that of the bigger Herring Gull

Herring Gull

Iceland Gull

(×⅐)

Large Glaucous

Immature Glaucous Gull

Immature Glaucous, above, and adult Iceland, below, drawn to same scale

Third-winter Iceland Gull has pale plumage and black-banded yellow bill

(×⅙)

First-winter Iceland Gull has a more delicate bill than the Glaucous, more rounded head and longer wings

Adult Iceland Gull

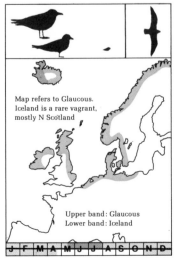

Map refers to Glaucous. Iceland is a rare vagrant, mostly N Scotland

Upper band: Glaucous
Lower band: Iceland

J F M A M J J A S O N D

Relationships among some North Atlantic gulls have puzzled researchers. The Iceland Gull, for example, looks like a smaller edition of the Glaucous Gull, but its behaviour and habits resemble those of the Herring Gull, to which it is probably closely allied.

Glaucous Gulls are in many respects paler versions of the Great Black-backed Gull, which they approach closely in size. They show the combination of scavenging and predatory habits characteristic of typical gulls, the former practice being particularly a feature of Arctic seabirds. The Little Auk is perhaps its most frequent victim, often snapped up from one of the rafts of densely packed birds which stud the surface of the sea around a colony.

Captured on the water in this way, it would be difficult for the Glaucous Gull to dismember a Little Auk, and usually it is swallowed whole. Arctic Tern chicks are also a common prey, though Glaucous Gulls find it difficult to penetrate far into a colony due to determined mobbing by parents. Alternatively, sea invertebrates and rubbish gleaned around human settlements may make up the diet.

Despite their name, Iceland Gulls breed only in Greenland and Arctic Canada. They winter in small numbers in the Baltic and around Britain. Although they indulge, like their larger relative, in predation and scavenging, fish, sometimes obtained by diving, form a major part of their diet.

229

Great Skua–Pomarine Skua

Pomarine Skua: wing beats are slow, steady and powerful

Marauding skua tumbles a Gannet by grabbing its tail. Often, the victim will disgorge its food

Great Skuas on passage, above, may fly steadily at about 100 feet or fly low over the waves

Immature Pomarine, dark phase plumage

Pomarine, immature dark phase

Pomarine adult, pale phase

Adult Great Skua

The adult Pomarine Skua is readily identified by its long tail feathers. Even the stubs of broken feathers show clearly

Great Skuas frequently harass other seabirds

The Pomarine Skua is a heavy, powerful bird, intermediate between the Arctic and Great Skuas. Plumage is very variable–from very pale to very dark phases. Pomarine is more solidly built and has broader wings than the Arctic Skua; the species always has prominent wing-flashes like those of the Great Skua

The distinct white wing-flashes are similar on both upper and lower surfaces

$(\times \frac{1}{7})$

$(\times \frac{1}{7})$

Great Skua in full aggression display

Swooping to attack an intruder at the nest

Great Skua, above, has no prominent tail feathers

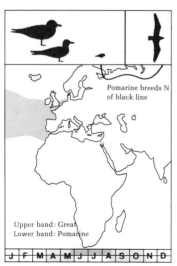

Pomarine breeds N of black line

Upper band: Great
Lower band: Pomarine

J F M A M J J A S O N D

Skuas have perfected a feeding strategy which biologists term kleptoparasitism, but which the layman might prefer to call piracy. The technique consists simply of harrying other seabirds in the air to make them release food. Birds as large as Gannets may be pursued in this way.

The Great Skua not only uses this feeding method but is also a redoubtable predator, taking the eggs, young and adults of many species. It is recorded as having killed such formidable adversaries as the Grey Heron and Great Black-backed Gull. Many attacks are made in flight, sometimes resulting in injury to the aggressor itself, who may then fall victim to other Great Skuas ready to seize any opportunity of feeding, even it if involves cannibalism. The Puffin is a frequent victim, often captured as it emerges from the entrance of its burrow.

Open woodland is the breeding habitat, and nest sites vary from solitary to social. Territories are defended with great violence; even humans are subjected to low-level frontal attacks, the bird striking the head with trailing feet. The nest is a meagrely lined scrape, and the clutch usually contains two eggs. Both sexes incubate, the off-duty bird often maintaining a look-out from some eminence. Incubation lasts 28 to 30 days, and the young fledge in six to seven weeks. Great Skuas winter mainly in the North Atlantic but one Scottish-ringed bird was recovered in Guyana.

Arctic Skua–Long-tailed Skua

Immature Long-tailed Skua, left, is slimmer than the Arctic; has longer, narrower wings and longer tail, the central feathers of which are rounded (compare with Arctic). The body is typically much less robust than that of the Arctic

These brown, falcon-like, predatory seabirds have a swift, flapping flight interspersed with glides, often low over the waves. Plumage very variable—pale through to dark phases. Heavier build than Long-tailed

Arctic immature (dark phase)

Immature Arctic from beneath

(×⅐)

Below, juvenile Long-tailed Skua showing pale belly, well-marked underwing and barred under-tail coverts. Wing-flash is very prominent. Tail feathers grow in four-inch annual increments so that in the second year the bird resembles adult Arctic

Immature, August-March

(×⅐)

Flight is graceful and leisurely, with ephemeral floating quality. Where identification is in doubt in UK the bird is usually an adult Arctic Skua

Left, adult Arctic pale phase from beneath. Right, the same bird viewed from above. Adults have long projecting tail feathers

Arctic Skuas hunting, above, illustrating a variety of plumage phases. When a victim is sighted, wing action increases in speed with the wings almost meeting beneath the body. The change in pace is visible at long range

Adult Long-tailed (pale phase)

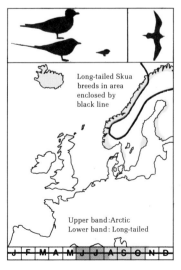

Long-tailed Skua breeds in area enclosed by black line

Upper band: Arctic
Lower band: Long-tailed

J F M A M J J A S O N D

Two distinct colour phases exist within Arctic Skua populations, one with pale underparts, the other with dark. Proportions of the two vary geographically; in southern Norway and the Baltic most birds are dark, but the number of light-coloured birds increases with northerly latitude, and in northern Norway reach 90 per cent of the population. Light-coloured birds are numerous at Scottish colonies, especially in the Outer Hebrides. Arctic Skuas are more frequently piratical than Great Skuas, choosing terns and Kittiwakes as their main victims, although on tundra they feed largely on small rodents and birds.

Like Great Skuas they usually nest in loose colonies on open ground, and make determined attacks on all intruders. Off-duty or non-breeding birds frequently indulge in spectacular aerial chases over the breeding grounds. Birds usually breed for the first time at four years of age. The two eggs hatch in 26 days, and the young fledge after four to five weeks.

Long-tailed Skuas are the smallest and most graceful of their family, and are virtually always of the pale phase. They are Arctic or sub-Arctic breeders, whose nesting activity is closely related to the population cycles of lemmings, which form their main prey. Because they move straight out into the Atlantic rather than hugging the coasts, Long-tailed Skuas are much less often seen on migration than Arctic Skuas.

231

Adult in winter

Immature bird, left, is exceptionally well marked; size, however, distinguishes it from Little Gulls

Above, Kittiwake has typically pure-white underwing . . .

. . . and long, slender outer wing with a noticeably straight leading edge

(× 1/7)

Broad tail-band and striking wing pattern make this a handsome bird, but colour fades to pale brown by the end of the first summer. In flight, the Kittiwake resembles the Common Gull, but its wing beats are generally shallower and more rapid

Among the most social of all cliff-nesting birds, Kittiwakes may crowd the face of a vertical cliff—placing their nests on the narrowest of ledges, sometimes so precarious that the bird must press awkwardly against the rock to avoid being blown off

Right, food is either picked deftly from the surface in flight or in a series of shallow dives made after alighting

(× 1/5)

Though rare, young adults and immature birds are sometimes seen inland in October and November. The species has recently started nesting on building ledges in coastal towns and dock areas

The Kittiwake is instantly identified by its yellow bill, black legs and dark eyes. It is the only common gull with very short, completely black legs

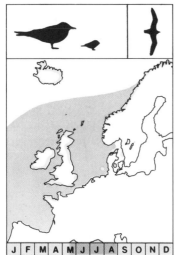

J F M A M J J A S O N D

Adaptations for oceanic feeding and cliff-ledge nesting make the Kittiwake a very distinctive gull. Spending little time on land, its legs are relatively short and lack the hind toe. Fish are its food in the breeding season and surface invertebrates during wintertime oceanic wanderings.

In common with several species of gull, and with the Fulmar, Kittiwakes have increased enormously during the twentieth century. It is astonishing that this increase went unnoticed until 1959, when a careful census in Britain was compared with past records. The results indicated an increase of about 50 per cent every ten years, and a census in 1969 showed the growth rate still being maintained. On British coasts

about half a million pairs now breed, and the increase also has been noted all round the North Sea. Such a population explosion was probably overlooked because, until recently, growth was mainly confined to existing colonies, with few new ones being established. While other gulls have increased by capitalizing on the side effects of industrial society, the Kittiwake has benefited from the cessation of human exploitation: eggs were plundered and adults shot on a large scale during the nineteenth century.

Kittiwake nests are built on a foundation of green seaweeds, cemented to a cliff ledge with guano—or to the window ledges of waterside buildings in British and Norwegian towns.

Little Gull

An adult in winter plumage, right: grey and white above with dark head-patches. Distinguished by small size, tern-like flight and, in full adults, complete absence of black on the upper wing surface

Below, immatures and right, a sub-adult (black spots)

An immature bird in flight, left, is generally identified by the relationship of wing pattern to size, but care must be taken to avoid confusion with the immature Kittiwake, which has similar patterning but is larger and more typically a gull in behaviour

On inland and coastal waters, feeding birds beat back and forth over the surface, dipping sharply into the water to pick up food. Some birds hover

An adult in flight shows marked contrast between upper- and underwing

(× ¹/₇)

Very characteristic of the Little Gull is the habit, on landing, of pausing with the wings held high over the back

Size alone identifies this graceful, delicate gull. At rest, the adult, left, shows its rosy breast and deep grey-black underwing with a white border. The juvenile has an all-white underwing

(×¹/₅)

Immature birds, left, perch on posts and breakwaters along the shoreline. Note the small, delicate head and the typical gentle expression. The bird should be compared with Kittiwake

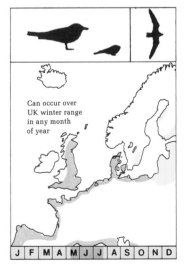

Can occur over UK winter range in any month of year

J F M A M J J A S O N D

Curiously patchy distribution and baffling migratory patterns characterize this the smallest of the gulls.

Most of its breeding range lies in the USSR, split into three distinct regions. In Europe, it breeds at only a very few scattered outposts no farther west than Holland. The winter range is mainly around the Black Sea and Mediterranean, but some occur on the North Sea and Atlantic coasts of Europe. Here, occurrences are inexplicably irregular, flocks of some hundreds inhabiting certain Scottish localities in autumn, but only isolated individuals appearing in England. Strangest of all, the Little Gull is a regular vagrant to the eastern seaboard of North America, and now breeds there in small numbers.

Both in habits and flight action, the Little Gull much resembles marsh terns, such as the Black Tern, in whose company it often nests. Breeding habitats are marshes and swampy grasslands with plenty of open water rich in the insect life on which it feeds. Outside the breeding season, sustenance is small fish and crustaceans. Most colonies contain less than 50 pairs, though larger ones occur where the species is more widely distributed. Nests, usually quite large structures of grass, are sited amongst rushes or similar emergent water plants. Two or three eggs form a normal clutch, but up to seven have been recorded. Young birds leave the colony with their parents in family parties which later disperse.

233

Common Tern

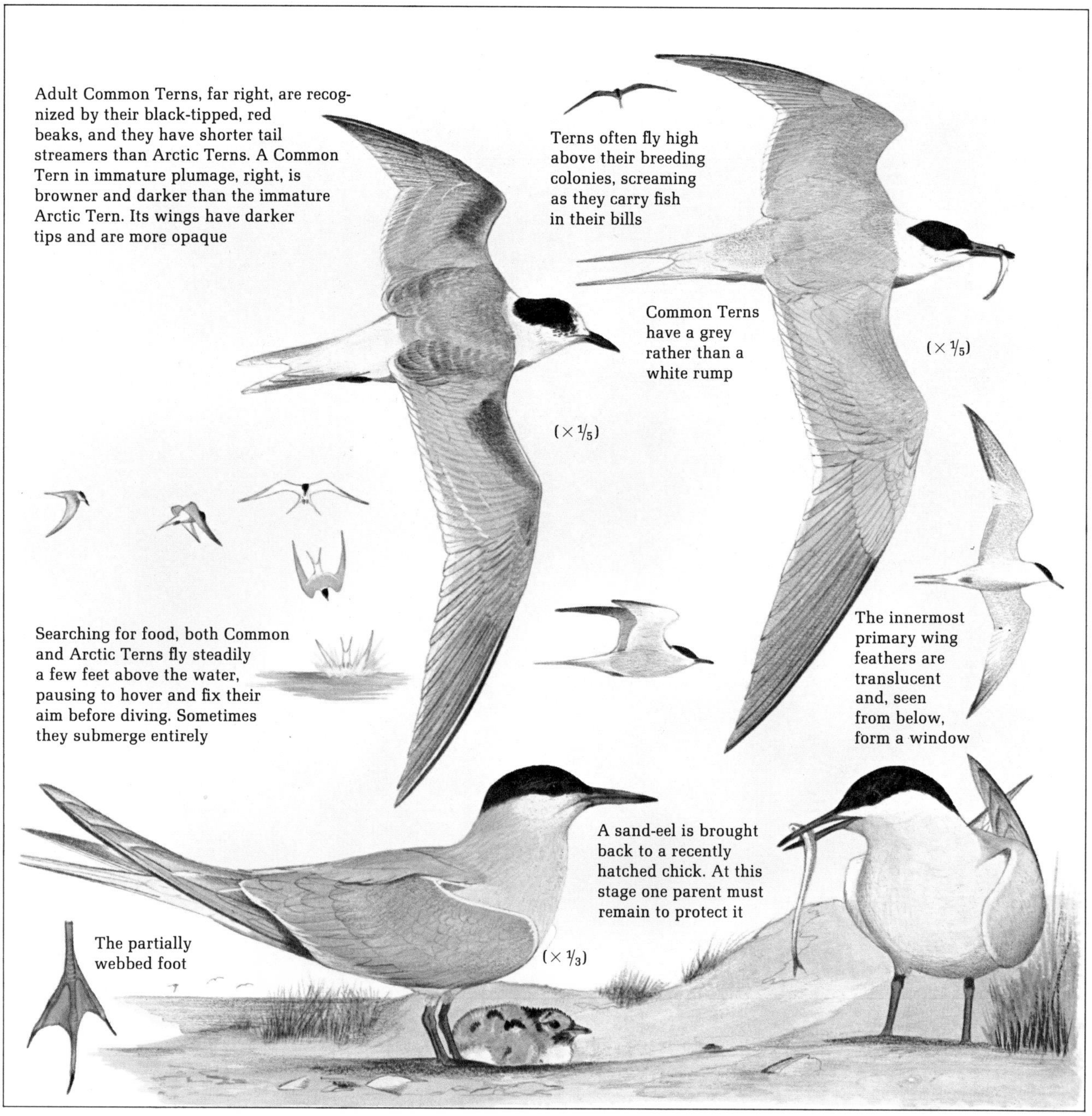

Adult Common Terns, far right, are recognized by their black-tipped, red beaks, and they have shorter tail streamers than Arctic Terns. A Common Tern in immature plumage, right, is browner and darker than the immature Arctic Tern. Its wings have darker tips and are more opaque
Terns often fly high above their breeding colonies, screaming as they carry fish in their bills
Common Terns have a grey rather than a white rump
(× 1/5)
(× 1/5)
Searching for food, both Common and Arctic Terns fly steadily a few feet above the water, pausing to hover and fix their aim before diving. Sometimes they submerge entirely
The innermost primary wing feathers are translucent and, seen from below, form a window
A sand-eel is brought back to a recently hatched chick. At this stage one parent must remain to protect it
The partially webbed foot
(× 1/3)

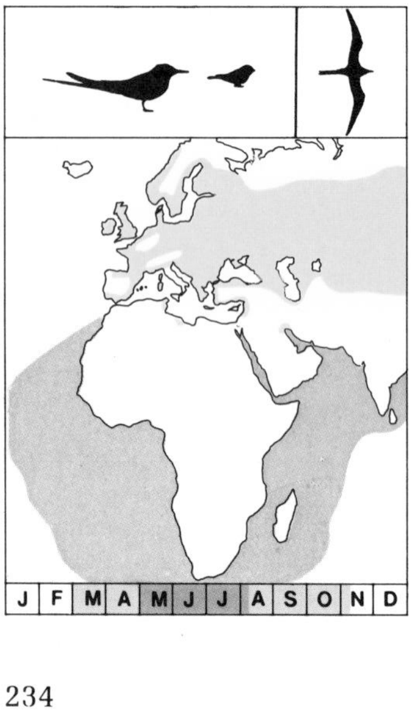

J F M A M J J A S O N D

Common and Arctic Terns share many features: see facing page. The Common Tern's breeding range starts at the southern limit of the Arctic Tern's – some mixed colonies occur, but the zone of overlap is small. Not only does the Common Tern breed on Mediterranean as well as North Sea shores, it also ranges inland, with colonies on many wetland areas far from the sea – even at 14,000 feet in Tibet.

Colonies, especially inland, are often small – occasional pairs nesting even on artificial sites on inland waters. Mobbing (i.e. nest defence) is less vicious than by the Arctic Tern.

Common Terns feed in fresh water or close inshore (the Arctic fishes well out to sea) and thus take more insects and crustaceans; whitebait is a favoured fish. Its insect-catching techniques over water resemble the Black Tern's and craneflies are taken over land.

During courtship, a male flies around with a fish in its beak, which is presented to a prospective partner. In both species, young are kept in the nest for the first few days with one parent in attendance. Thereafter they leave the nest and hide in nearby vegetation, allowing both partners to fish for them. In dense colonies, robbing of fish is common; pairs which have lost their own young are prime culprits. Sometimes up to 12 birds will harry a single parent, when it will be lucky to get one in ten fish to each chick.

Arctic Tern

Pure red beak and long tail streamers typify the adult Arctic Tern in summer. Underparts are often all grey, dark in contrast to the pure white of the Common Tern

Adult Common Tern, summer

Adult Arctic Tern, summer

Juvenile Common Tern

Juvenile Arctic Tern

In winter, Arctic and Common Terns both have white foreheads and the crown is flecked with white. In winter, an Arctic Tern's beak is wholly black, in summer red. The Common Tern has a largely black beak in winter, and in summer it is red with a black tip. Arctic Terns have black legs in winter, Common Terns red. Immature Arctic Terns have all-black beaks, immature Common Terns blackish beaks with a red base

Adult Arctic Tern, winter

Juvenile Arctic Tern

(× ⅕)

Adult Arctic Terns have much paler wings than juveniles

(× ⅓)

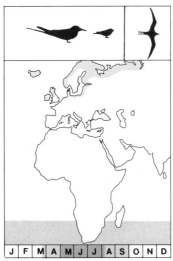

An Arctic Tern's leg, right, is noticeably shorter than a Common Tern's, left

Note how the tail streamers extend well beyond the length of the tail

To enter an Arctic Tern colony is unnerving; birds regularly strike an observer's head, and may even draw blood. Colonies, sometimes thousands strong, are often tenanted by other nesting birds, such as Eiders, which gain security from the Tern's efficient mobbing of gulls and foxes. The clamour of the birds is interrupted at intervals by brief, eerie spells of silence, while the terns sweep out to sea in a massed flock – a phenomenon known as a "dread". Colonies are sited on rocky islets, beaches, or short turf, always close to the sea. Arctic Terns take up to five years to establish themselves in the breeding colony; thereafter, one or two chicks may be raised from the clutch of two or three eggs.

It has been calculated that the Arctic Tern enjoys a greater amount of daylight than any other animal. Breeding around the shores of the Arctic Ocean and northern Atlantic and Pacific it migrates to spend our winter in the Antarctic summer, remaining in the region of maximum day length all the year round. Birds ringed in Britain have been recovered in Australia. On average, Arctic Terns cover some 20,000 miles a year on migration alone; the oldest-known bird reached 27 years, so a lifetime's mileage may exceed a return trip to the moon.

The rapid moult necessitated by such long migrations occurs in the Antarctic, where food-rich waters replenish energy for the return flight.

J F M A M J J A S O N D

Little Tern

Its small size, yellow legs and black-tipped yellow beak all reliably identify the Little Tern in the field. At a distance the hurried flight separates it from its larger relatives

Winter

Summer

In winter, the black crown recedes and becomes flecked with grey. In summer, adult Little Terns are the only European Sea Terns retaining a white forehead

When Little and Common Terns are together, the Little Tern can be distinguished by its dumpy body and tail with a shallow notch and short streamers. The Little Tern also has a distinctive flight pattern: it hovers on rapidly flicking wings with head held low before taking the plunge

Above: a black eye-stripe running from crown to beak develops in summer

Below, the Little Tern's typical hurried flight on rapidly beating wings

(× ⅓)

Above: a face-on view of the head pattern. Centre: a female settles on her eggs. Right: the male brings a sand-eel to a chick at the very exposed nest

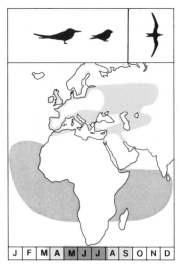

J F M A M J J A S O N D

Smallest of the European sea terns, the Little Tern has the widest breeding range, nesting in every continent. In Britain it is widespread but almost exclusively coastal, breeding in small scattered colonies on sandy beaches or shingle spits. Elsewhere, sand bars on inland waters are also regularly used.

The American population of Little Terns suffered badly last century from slaughter for the millinery trade. A new danger now threatens in many parts of the world, for its nesting grounds are the same open beaches beloved of holidaymakers. The two or three eggs in their scrape are so well camouflaged that humans crush them underfoot or cause desertion by disturbance: less bold in defence of their nests than Common or Arctic Terns, their protesting calls go unnoticed. Though still a regular sight on our coasts, the British population is dangerously low at less than 2,000 pairs.

Little Terns feed close inshore, often in tidal creeks and pools, hovering more and flying with quicker wing beats than other terns. Rarely nesting more than a few yards from the tideline, mortality from wind-blown sand and foam is added to the damage caused by disturbance. The diet includes small crustaceans and worms, sand eels and whitebait.

On migration, Little Terns join local populations of their own species, and this makes their precise movements difficult to determine.

Sandwich Tern—Gull-billed Tern

An adult Sandwich Tern in winter plumage. It is larger than the Common Tern, with longer, thinner wings, more prominent head and bill and a shorter tail

(×⅕)

Gull-billed Tern

Sandwich Tern

Sandwich and Gull-billed Terns are thin, lanky, rather angular birds: easily distinguished from Common and Arctic Terns either in flight or on the ground

Below, Gull-billed Terns. They resemble Sandwich Terns in shape except for their shorter, stouter, all-black beaks. They also have shorter tails, which, with the back, are grey as opposed to white

Dark wing-tips are caused by feather wear

Gull-billed Tern, winter

Gull-billed Tern, summer

Adult Gull-billed Tern

Sandwich Tern in display

Below, adult Sandwich Terns. The shaggy breeding cap begins to whiten early in the season. Young birds do not have the yellow tip to the bill

Below, the Sandwich Tern chick has distinctive spiky down on its upperparts

(×⅓)

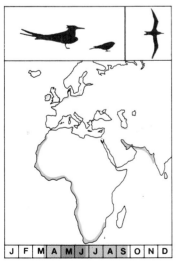

J F M A M J J A S O N D

The densely packed coastal colonies of this large and handsome tern are exciting to visit – a hubbub of grating calls. Observers should however approach with care, since birds can be frightened right away especially when reconnoitring early in the season.

First-comers select a site for the colony, within which are "sub-colonies" whose members show close synchronization of breeding times – an adaptation conferring high breeding success. Less aggressive than Common or Arctic Terns, Sandwich Terns often nest close to them, or to Black-headed Gulls, benefiting from their neighbours' zeal in mobbing intruders.

In early spring, aerial displays are frequent, small groups flying to great heights before planing down, calling. One or two eggs are laid in May and incubated for three to four weeks. Staple food for chicks and adults is fish, especially sand-eels and sprats.

Sandwich Terns dive deeper and from greater heights than smaller species. Their feeding range may be wide: a tag from a young salmon appeared at a Scottish colony just 48 hours after the fish was marked 42 miles away. They are highly mobile birds, extensive interchange taking place between different European countries.

Gull-billed Terns resemble Sandwich Terns in size and general appearance, but have a heavy, all-black bill. They are inland birds, feeding mainly on insects.

237

Black Tern

Adult Black Tern, summer

Adult Black Tern— paler than a juvenile

Adult Black Tern in summer—grey underwing

Adult, from below

Adult, from above

White-winged Black Terns— shorter, squarer tail, broader wings, red feet, shorter bill

Forked tail, black head and almost uniform grey wings are all conspicuous

(×⅕)

A juvenile Black Tern's tail is less deeply forked than the adult's. It has darker plumage, a white collar and the distinctive black cap

(×⅕)

Juvenile White-winged Terns have paler wings than juvenile Black Terns. They also have a white rump and a dark back

Below, a juvenile Black Tern showing the dark shoulder patch which separates it from all other Terns

Both species have similar quick wing beats and drop repeatedly to pick insects from the water

(×½)

In spring and autumn Black Terns move in-land to large lakes and reservoirs

Raft nests are built in fresh-water marshes

Widely distributed throughout the world, Black Terns breed on flooded marshland, where they have the benefit of a mosaic of open water and vegetation. Here, aquatic insects abound, which the birds pick from the surface in flight. Unlike Sea Terns, Black Terns are unwilling to plunge and rarely take fish, though unwary tadpoles and frogs may fall victim.

Black Terns patrol suitable waters in groups, calling frequently. During courtship, display flights occur: one resembles the fish flight of Sea Terns without the fish; another starts with several birds circling high and calling, finally breaking off in small groups, which glide down on set wings. Their nests are floating piles of weed or rushes, but some are built in sedge clumps. Both sexes incubate the two or three eggs, and displays occur at the nest, notably the "stooping" male posture, bill pointing downwards, wings and tail stretched up in line with it. Hatching after three weeks, chicks stay in the nest for over a week before moving into the surrounding vegetation, where they are fed by their parents for four or more weeks, even when able to fly. Eurasian Black Terns breed east to the River Yenisey, in the USSR, but winter entirely in tropical Africa, mainly north of the equator.

Black Terns ceased to breed regularly in Britain in 1885, but have nested again several times since the Second World War.

J F M A M J J A S O N D

Manx Shearwater

Small parties of Manx Shearwaters knife across the waves on stiffly held wings, one moment flicking over to show the black back, the next to show the white belly. They use every available current of air to continue gliding and only on very calm days or on take-off are the wings used for any length of time in flapping flight. Balearic Shearwaters, the southern European race, have dull brown underparts

$(\times\frac{1}{9})$

Shearwaters gather to feed in rafts on the water surface well out to sea, or, in the evening, close inshore off rocky coasts. The major food source is small shoaling fish. Much feeding is done in flight, the bird hovering briefly, then making a shallow dive. Flocks on the sea will carefully watch where gulls are going to feed, then make for the same area themselves

These birds have the "tube nose" of the petrel family

$(\times\frac{1}{3})$

Manx Shearwaters are especially clumsy on land after dark, and have to scramble up rocks to gain height for take-off

Manx Shearwaters have a distinctive musty smell. The young have such large fat reserves that in some areas they are killed and eaten as "mutton birds"

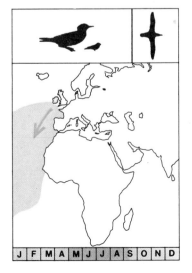

An ocean wanderer on a global scale, yet easily accessible at its breeding colonies, the Manx Shearwater is one of the most intensively studied seabirds. It nests in burrows on inshore islands, visiting and courtship taking place at night to the accompaniment of unearthly screams and cackles. Manx Shearwaters eat small fish taken from the sea surface, and may feed at great distances from the colony. Their homing ability is spectacular: Shearwaters transported to Boston, USA, from Skokholm, off the south coast of Wales, were back at the colony in $12\frac{1}{2}$ days. Adults leave the colony to feed for some ten days before egg laying in early May, and thereafter the parents alternate continuous incubation spells of a week

or more. The single white egg hatches after seven or eight weeks. Both parents feed the chick by regurgitation.

The colony is quietest and visits slacken during full moon. Feeding intervals up to three days are common. The fledgling is deserted at two months, and a week or so later makes its way to the sea. Manx Shearwaters breed first at five or six years, and may live for a further 20 or more.

The introduction of Brown Rats to breeding islands has reduced or extinguished many colonies. Britain (at least 175,000 pairs) is the stronghold in western Europe, but other races nest in the Mediterranean and Pacific. North Atlantic birds normally winter off Rio de Janiero.

Fulmar

Fulmars have extraordinary powers of flight, which recall the even more accomplished Albatross. The stronger the wind, the more impressive they are. Masters of the up-current, they can wheel and turn with precision close to the cliff face. Feet are usually tucked into the feathers to assist streamlining, but may be used near the nest to assist manoeuvring. They have a distinctive underwing pattern, and lack the black wing-tips of gulls

Normal flight is similar to the Manx Shearwater, sweeping low across the waves on stiff wings, but Fulmars flap more frequently. In side view, below, the dumpy body shows clearly. The Blue Fulmar, a darker grey bird, is seen in northerly waters

(× ⅑)

(× ⅓)

The complex beak structure includes the double tubular "nostril", whose function is still debated. It may assist speed assessment

On land, Fulmars are clumsy, shuffling on their tarsi rather than standing. The nestlings are unusually well equipped for self-defence, directing a foul smelling jet of stomach oil at the intruder

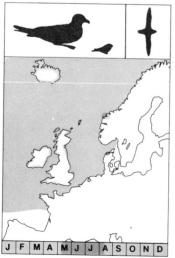

J F M A M J J A S O N D

With its ghost-grey plumage and mastery of flight, an aura of romance surrounds this outstandingly successful seabird. Until 1878 its only known British colony was on remote St Kilda. Then a few pairs were found in the Shetlands, and it has since spread right round Britain, where recent surveys put the number of occupied nest sites at 305,000. The expansion started while many island communities still harvested Fulmars for flesh, oil and feathers.

The Fulmar's success has probably been based on human activities – first whaling, and later commercial fishing, both producing much waste offal, on which Fulmars feed. Its expansion seems surprising since only a single egg is laid each year, and breeding does not start until the age of seven or eight. This is offset by a life-span of 25 years.

Fulmars return to the breeding cliffs in November or December from extensive wanderings in the North Atlantic, but do not nest until May. Pairs leave the colony for a fortnight's "honeymoon" prior to laying in order to build up food reserves. Courtship involves gaping and an incredible cackling chorus. Chicks are fed on regurgitated food and stomach oil. The distinctive musty smell, common to petrels, lingers even on stuffed birds 100 years old. After seven weeks on the ledge, the chick weighs more than an adult and is ready to leave. The parents cease feeding it a few days before its departure.

Razorbill

In flight, an adult with summer plumage shows a dark head. The Guillemot has a very similar profile

Juvenile

The main function of the handsome black and white horny beak of the adult is probably as a court-ship embellishment. In winter, it is replaced by a smaller sheath on the same skullbone foundation

Under way, Razorbills fly fast and straight, but while manoeuvring must extend their feet to steer or to brake

Adult, winter

On the cliff, a pair indulge in mutual preening, a gentle neck-nibbling rou-tine forming part of the courtship display. A chick, below, will be taken to sea half grown

Adult, summer

Downwind, Razorbills fly very fast indeed

(×⅓)

Razorbills are difficult to distinguish from Guillemots in winter as they fly past low over the waves a few hundred yards from the shore: at this time the different shapes of the beaks are less marked

Wings held stiffly, feet spread to slow it down, a Razorbill descends to the sea from the cliff. Several attempts at landing may be made on windy days

The bird is aptly enough named. Its beak is both sharp and heavy, and the vertical white bar sets the Razorbill apart from the Guillemot. Minute furry feathers form the white stripe running from eye to beak

Razorbills dive from the surface, using wings and feet under water

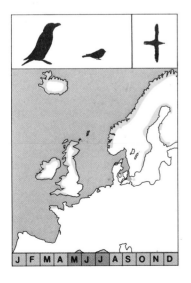

With its deep, compressed bill, this bird resembles a smaller version of its extinct, flightless relative, the Great Auk. It nests in small caves in cliffs, or among boulders and scree, usually on uninhabited islands. Ledge nests are rare. Though similarly coloured, the single egg is more rounded than the Guillemot's. Although their nests are less vulnerable, Razorbills, like Guille-mots, take their 18-day-old half-grown young to sea at dusk. The chick is fed with a beakful of small fish – Guille-mots give longer, single fish. Sand eels, sprats, crustaceans and molluscs figure in the diet.

Razorbills return to their breeding areas from January onwards. Prior to nesting, displays occur on the sea near the colony. Line ahead formation swim-ming and mass diving are seen, and pairs circle round one another on the water. After moving onshore, "billing" and head shaking – bill open to show the yellow interior – are frequent, and birds often leave the cliffs with a slow-motion "butterfly flight". They are noisy, and have a deep-throated call which is similar to that of the Guillemot.

In pre-Roman times, Razorbills were eaten by maritime tribesmen. Today, they are threatened by oil pollution and by fishermen who feel that Razorbills and other auks are competing for the commercial harvest of the seas. Never-theless, their numbers appear to have decreased less than those of the Guillemots and Puffins.

Guillemot—Black Guillemot

In summer, Guillemots show a dark head and neck while flying. Black Guillemots, below left, are unmistakable in summer plumage. In winter, Guillemots can be difficult to tell from Razorbills as they fly past low over the waves usually a few hundred yards from the shore: at this time the different shapes of the beaks are less marked

"Bridled" head marking

"Bridled" marking, winter

The "bridled" marking, above, running back from the eye, is found in most colonies, though more frequently in the north. In winter, the throat and cheeks show more white

$(\times \frac{1}{3})$

Juvenile Black Guillemot. An adult in winter plumage is similar but has red feet

Adult Black Guillemot

Adult Black Guillemots

Juvenile Black Guillemot, winter

In winter, a complete reversal of plumage colouring takes place in the Black Guillemots, upperparts become grey, underparts white

Guillemots in winter plumage flying at speed, low over sea

Birds gather in loose rafts inshore and make shallow hunting dives from the surface. Below left, adult Guillemot, summer

Adult Guillemot, winter

Guillemots are distinguished from Razorbills by their larger size and slender, dagger-shaped beak. The chocolate colour also sets them apart, except in northernmost Europe, where the Guillemot is black. The egg, superbly adapted to cliff life, rolls around its centre of gravity when disturbed, rather than over the ledge

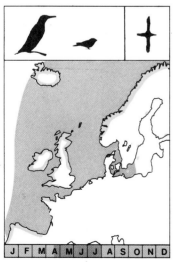

Guillemots nest in dense colonies on tops of sea stacks and cliff ledges. Seen close to, their heads seem to be continually bowing and their displays sometimes resemble the Razorbill's. A cacophony of trumpeting calls continually rises from the colony. They panic easily, and many chicks are lost in the scramble following disturbance. Eggs are more secure: their conical shape means they spin on one spot rather than roll over the ledge, and they are made additionally safe by their coating of guano. They even become more stable as incubation proceeds, the centre of gravity shifting towards the narrow end. Nevertheless, marauding gulls account for any untended egg or chick, and mortality is high. Chicks are fed on single large fish, given head first. So hazardous is life on the cliff that chicks depart half grown, using spread feet and whirring wings to slow their descent. They leave at dusk (to avoid predators), parents in attendance, then move out to sea to feed.

Black Guillemots are smaller and much less numerous, breeding singly or in groups, scattered round rocky coasts. Displays include water dances and underwater chases in which the vermilion foot may be important. Cavities among boulders or cliffs are usual nest sites and they are the only European auks to lay two eggs. Greater site safety is reflected in the longer stay of the chick, over twice as long as that of the Guillemot.

Gannet

A long neck and tail, with a narrow, cigar-shaped body

Adults

A dagger-shaped beak and forward-facing eyes giving binocular vision make the gannet a deadly underwater hunter

Adult

Adult

(× 1/15)

Right, the gannet's eyes viewed from beneath: they are placed to give downward as well as forward vision. The skull is specially strengthened to withstand impact and the body is protected by a layer of fat and a cushion of elastic air sacs

The differing plumages are best seen in flight. Juveniles start life dark grey, the area of white on the wings increasing over the first few years until the clean black and white, yellow-headed plumage of the adult is attained

Juvenile

Sub-adult

Head of juvenile

The gannet's long wings, with a span of six feet, are well suited to gliding, which reduces the amount of energy consumed in flight

Sighting a fish

Immature

Adult

(× 1/8)

Diving gannets often drop vertically from 100 feet or more, and normally hold the wings right back before entry. If a fish-shoal is near the surface, dives are made at an oblique angle from only a few feet

Juveniles show a pale belly

The hind toe is joined to the front three by a web on the inside of the leg

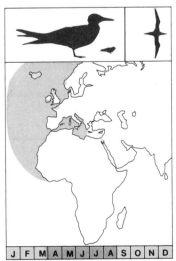

J F M A M J J A S O N D

The Gannet is a species on the increase. Considering it only lays one egg a year and takes up to five years to reach breeding age, its success is astonishing. One possible reason is the increased availability of fish offal from trawlers, another that the taking of young birds for human food has almost ceased.

The nest is a conical mound of seaweed and flotsam, cemented with guano. Both parents incubate, covering the egg with the feet because a brood patch is lacking. The chicks are in the nest for some 15 weeks, fed on regurgitated fish. When ready to leave they weigh more than adults, the reserve tiding them over the first week or two of independence. This extra weight made them desirable food for human

communities on isolated islands, and in some places they are still harvested. By contrast, their tropical cousins, the boobies, leave the nest after 12 weeks, but remain with their parents, being taught to fish for several months.

Colonies, usually on isolated offshore rocks, are often large: Boreray, off the Outer Hebrides, has over 70,000 pairs. When the young are well grown, a colony of this size will consume well over 100 tons of fish daily, including herring, mackerel and whiting.

Gannets migrate farthest in their first year, reaching West African waters. Sub-adults move less far south, wintering in the Mediterranean and Biscay. Adults disperse through home waters outside the breeding season.

243

Cormorant

Cormorants may breed in trees, and as a result kill them with their droppings

In flight, Cormorants look awkward and distinctly prehistoric. They can soar to great heights, often doing so inland

Immature bird revealing white underparts

Adult in flight

During the breeding season adults have a white patch on the face and on the flanks

(× ⅙)

The southern race of Cormorant sports white plumes on the head during the breeding season

Head of immature bird

Colonies are usually sited on much flatter ground than those of the Shag

Juvenile

Immature

On hot days, a nestling Cormorant, below right, is commonly seen with its throat distended, panting in order to reduce body heat

The pose so familiar in heraldry is in fact the bird drying its wings

The Shag, below, has a much more slender beak than the Cormorant and carries it at less of an angle

When on the water, Cormorants point their beaks upwards in a distinctive manner

Big fish are brought to the surface before being swallowed

Birds often fly low over the water

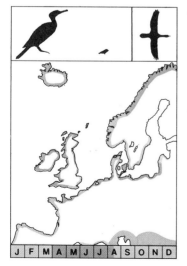

A bird of world-wide distribution, the Cormorant is common in coastal waters and on some inland lakes and reservoirs. Most colonies are on low, rocky islets, but inland, trees are often used, which soon die as a result of the guano deposits. Its nest is a heap of seaweed or branches lined with finer material, and the three or four chalky blue eggs are incubated for about a month, hatching to reveal naked and reptilian-looking youngsters. Two months elapse before they can fly.

Cormorants are skilled fishers, diving for 20 to 30 seconds to fish near the bottom at up to five fathoms depth, keeping wings closed under water. On coasts they are particularly fond of flatfish, and are estimated to catch up to two pounds of fish per day. As a result, they can come into conflict with fishermen, and bounties are sometimes paid on them. In open sea, the Cormorants' effect on fish stocks is probably small, but may be more significant in enclosed waters – though in some lakes they benefit salmon stocks by concentrating on fish which eat young salmon. In China, Cormorants have been trained to fish for Man for at least 1,000 years, and the Stuart Kings of England also employed them. The birds are kept on a long lead with a leather collar, which prevents fish being swallowed.

Cormorants do not undertake clearly marked migrations, but disperse up to several hundred miles after breeding. Populations appear fairly stable.

Shag

A Shag's tail, far left, has 12 feathers, the Cormorant's, left, 14

Immature Cormorant

Head of immature Cormorant. It has a larger area of bare skin than the immature Shag, and a deeper, heavier beak

Juvenile and immature Shags, left and right, always have much darker underparts than Cormorants, and unlike that species are never white below. A young Shag, below right, shows some pale feather-edges on the upper wing and body

Immature Shag

Right, the "landing gape", a conciliatory display used after landing

"Aware" posture when approaching female, nest or young

An adult in breeding season. The yellow gape patch is lost in winter. General colouring is a rich, oily green

(× ⅙)

Shags share the Cormorant's wing-drying attitude, but the wings are usually held straighter

Only the male performs the gape-dart, left, and throw-back, right

The juvenile's head shape contrasts with the Cormorant's

These birds have an extraordinary "jump-dive"

Shags mostly fly low

Both Shags and Cormorants land with an awkward flop

Adult Shags in winter show small, pale chin patches

Tails of Shag and Cormorant "float" flat

Sometimes only the head appears

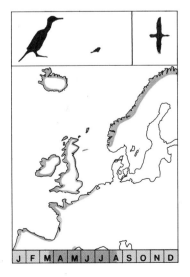

J F M A M J J A S O N D

Smaller and slimmer than Cormorants, adult Shags are dark all over except for the yellow face patch. A metallic sheen on the feathers has given rise to the name "Green Cormorant". Like Cormorants, Shags are usually silent except at breeding or roosting sites, where growling calls are uttered.

Shags are more maritime than Cormorants, restricted largely to rocky coasts. Birds found inland are usually storm-blown victims of autumn gales – with a curious propensity for landing in busy streets and other unlikely places.

The nest is an exceedingly smelly pile of rotting seaweed, low on a cliff or cave ledge, or in a cavity under boulders. Protection from spray (which can fatally chill young) or from waves is of paramount importance. Competition for sites may be intense and inexperienced young birds often have their nests washed away. Nesting commonly starts in late February, but sometimes much earlier: laying has been recorded on November 20. The clutch usually contains three eggs. Generally, breeding is timed to hatch the young during the period of maximum abundance of food.

Shags disperse from breeding sites in the same way as Cormorants, but usually move less far. Populations have increased in many areas, though local catastrophes can occur as in 1968, when poisoning by an abnormal growth of dinoflagellate algae (a "red tide") killed large numbers of Shags on the north-eastern coast of England.

Puffin

Adult Puffins cannot be mistaken for other auks, except in flight at a considerable distance

Fast-beating wings carry these heavy birds at a good speed. Downwind, they can move very fast indeed

Such a neatly arranged row of sand eels is made possible by a specially hinged beak. The loose fold of orange lip permits upper and lower halves of the bill to close parallel. The eels are gripped firmly along the whole length of the bill, rather than just in a narrow angle at the innermost end

Only one feature of the adult Puffin changes in the breeding season – the beak. Its modified, parrot-like shape and vivid colouring give the bird a comical appearance. The Puffin is a smaller bird than a Razorbill or Guillemot

Adult in winter, showing its differently shaped beak. The change takes place at sea

$(\times \frac{1}{3})$

Adults by their burrows

A juvenile has its own shape of beak, and its face is much greyer than an adult's. Easily confused with a young Razorbill

Swimming attitude of an adult. Below, before returning to the breeding cliffs, adults form rafts on the sea

Puffins are at home in rough sea conditions, diving with ease and bouncing undeterred off waves that hinder their flight path in take-off

The beak is in fact quite a slender structure

Puffins are probably the best known of all seabirds, and their comical appearance is familiar to many who have never seen one in the flesh. Yet despite the affection in which it is held, the Puffin's numbers have been decreasing.

Puffins nest colonially in burrows lined with dry grass on soft ground at the top of rocky islands. The birds arrive in early spring, numbers building up just offshore for some days before flying on to the land *en masse*. Courtship involves much clashing of the brightly coloured bills, and furious fights occasionally take place. A single white egg is laid, and both parents incubate in turn through the six weeks it takes to hatch. The chick is fed on sand eels, whiting and sprats brought in beakfuls of up to 11 at a time. Like many seabird young, it fasts for about a week, using up fat reserves after the parents leave it at six weeks old. Young Puffins need a good drop to enable them to make their first flight, and during the (sometimes long) walk to a take-off point they are very vulnerable to predators. Although the journey is usually made in the dim visibility of dusk, Great Black-backed Gulls and Great Skuas still take their toll.

But predation alone does not explain the Puffin's decline, and pollution by chemical wastes and oil are also likely causes. The question requires much more research, which is made difficult by the fact that puffins winter far out to sea. When they die, they sink.

Biology
of the
Bird

Anatomy of a Bird

Of all forms of animal locomotion flight is perhaps the most demanding, imposing severe restrictions on size and body form. For this reason, birds show greater uniformity of structure than, say, mammals or reptiles, and even the largest birds are still dwarfed by giants among land and water animals.

Lightness is crucial, and although some bulky structures, such as the massive flight muscles, are indispensable, they must be concentrated as close as possible to the bird's centre of gravity. Nearly all muscles are situated on, or very close to, the body, and limb movements are effected by means of long tendons passing through slings and "pulley" arrangements at the main joints. Even the head, the most massive extremity, has been perfectly tailored to reduce weight; the bill is finely honeycombed with air spaces and teeth were eliminated very early in the evolution of birds.

Feathers confer on birds an important advantage lacking in the other flying animals: their hind legs remain entirely free. By contrast, bats (and the extinct pterosaurs) have their hind-limbs integrated into their membranous wings—rendering them almost helpless on the ground. Nevertheless, even converting the fore-limbs alone into wings has drawbacks: these limbs are useless for manipulating food or other material. To compensate, birds have long flexible necks and extremely mobile and versatile jaw mechanisms quite capable of the most delicate manipulations. Lacking teeth, birds need some other means of grinding their food, particularly so in those species feeding on hard seeds. The grinding function is performed by the muscular gizzard, a specialized part of the stomach, and in many species the action is aided by grit swallowed by the bird.

Senses of sight and hearing are acute, but few birds appear to have any highly developed sense of smell. The eyes are huge, almost meeting at the centre of the skull, and are capable of resolving very fine detail over most of the field of view. Sensitivity to movement is also well developed—a vital factor in the bird's ability to navigate. Similarly, the bird's ears can detect very rapid changes in sound. Spectrographic analysis of bird songs reveals that many of the song patterns are far too rapid for the human ear to detect—yet these are full of significance to the birds themselves.

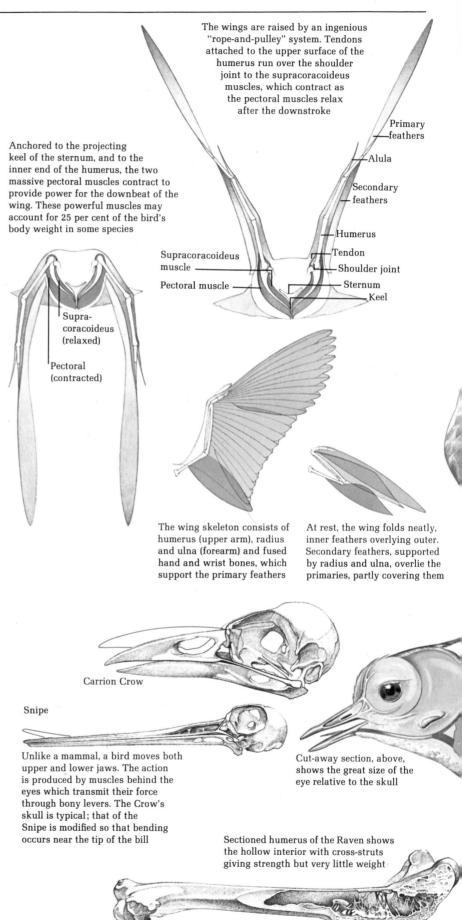

The wings are raised by an ingenious "rope-and-pulley" system. Tendons attached to the upper surface of the humerus run over the shoulder joint to the supracoracoideus muscles, which contract as the pectoral muscles relax after the downstroke

Primary feathers
Alula
Secondary feathers
Humerus
Tendon
Supracoracoideus muscle
Shoulder joint
Pectoral muscle
Sternum
Keel

Anchored to the projecting keel of the sternum, and to the inner end of the humerus, the two massive pectoral muscles contract to provide power for the downbeat of the wing. These powerful muscles may account for 25 per cent of the bird's body weight in some species

Supra-coracoideus (relaxed)
Pectoral (contracted)

The wing skeleton consists of humerus (upper arm), radius and ulna (forearm) and fused hand and wrist bones, which support the primary feathers

At rest, the wing folds neatly, inner feathers overlying outer. Secondary feathers, supported by radius and ulna, overlie the primaries, partly covering them

Carrion Crow

Snipe

Unlike a mammal, a bird moves both upper and lower jaws. The action is produced by muscles behind the eyes which transmit their force through bony levers. The Crow's skull is typical; that of the Snipe is modified so that bending occurs near the tip of the bill

Cut-away section, above, shows the great size of the eye relative to the skull

Sectioned humerus of the Raven shows the hollow interior with cross-struts giving strength but very little weight

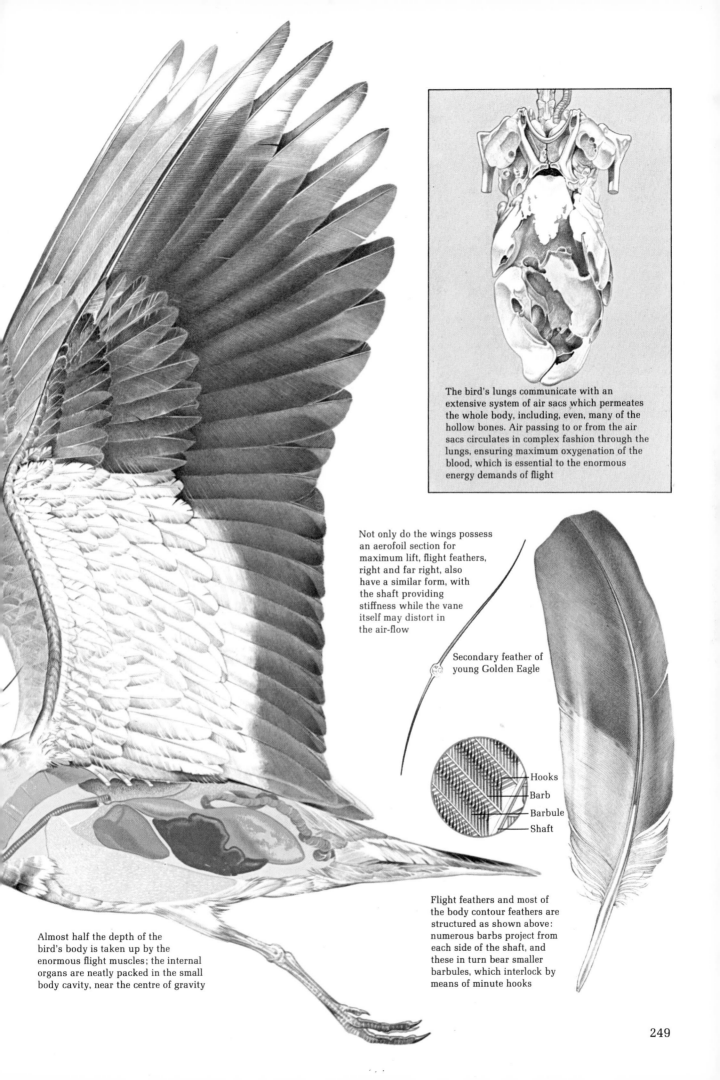

The bird's lungs communicate with an extensive system of air sacs which permeates the whole body, including, even, many of the hollow bones. Air passing to or from the air sacs circulates in complex fashion through the lungs, ensuring maximum oxygenation of the blood, which is essential to the enormous energy demands of flight

Not only do the wings possess an aerofoil section for maximum lift, flight feathers, right and far right, also have a similar form, with the shaft providing stiffness while the vane itself may distort in the air-flow

Secondary feather of young Golden Eagle

Hooks
Barb
Barbule
Shaft

Flight feathers and most of the body contour feathers are structured as shown above: numerous barbs project from each side of the shaft, and these in turn bear smaller barbules, which interlock by means of minute hooks

Almost half the depth of the bird's body is taken up by the enormous flight muscles; the internal organs are neatly packed in the small body cavity, near the centre of gravity

249

Techniques of Flight

Every bird observed on the wing will be seen to show a preference for one of four main techniques of flight—gliding, soaring, flapping or hovering—though many species will utilize combinations of these basic techniques according to their physical environment and feeding method.

Gliding—the simplest technique—requires minimal expenditure of energy; the bird is kept aloft simply by the pressure difference above and below the wing caused by the air-flow over the aerofoil. However, friction inevitably reduces the bird's air speed and without further action it would simply stall. Speed is maintained by using the pull of gravity; the bird glides in a descending path, rising at intervals either by changing to flapping flight or by utilizing a rising current of air.

Soaring birds rely entirely on upward-moving air currents, usually the thermal updraughts caused by differential heating of land surfaces. By subtle movements of the body and wings the bird exploits the currents to fly horizontally or to climb and may remain on the wing for hours without any great expenditure of its energy resources. Birds commonly soar in rising spirals – remaining within the roughly cylindrical column of the thermal, but breaking away at the top to glide down to a lower point on the next thermal.

Flapping flight requires a very high output of energy, quite beyond many large soaring birds such as the storks and eagles, and the former—because they have no opportunity to feed *en route*—must conserve energy and ride the air currents throughout their annual migrations. Flapping flight has two variations; one used for take-off and rapid climbing, the other for normal horizontal flight. In simple forward flight, the bird uses its wing like an oar—powerful downstrokes generating sufficient thrust and lift to keep the bird airborne. The upstroke in this form of flight is passive. Take-off and rapid climbing require greater lift and upward force is generated on both upstroke and downstroke.

Hovering is a highly specialized form of flight, finding its highest development in the humming-birds. Among European birds the Kestrel is the most adept, though others, such as terns, hover briefly before diving for food. Most hovering birds fly into the wind so that their air speed and the wind speed cancel out, allowing the bird to remain in one spot: humming-birds, however, can hover in still air and even fly backwards or sideways for a limited length of time.

  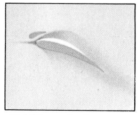 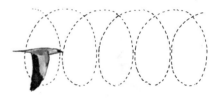

Normal smooth air-flow   Air-flow broken   Stability regained

In order to function efficiently, the wings must have the aerofoil section illustrated above. The pressure difference created by the air-flow over and beneath the wing provides the lifting force necessary to keep the bird airborne. To fly slowly, the bird must increase the "angle of attack", that is, incline the wing more steeply into the air-flow, but too great an angle of attack will allow the air-stream to break free from the aerofoil surface as turbulence: the pressure difference is lost and the bird stalls. At slow speed, the alula (the tiny "bastard wing" on the leading edge of the main wing) is extended to form a slot which smooths the air-flow over the wing surface and maintains the bird's stability.

In forward flight, the bird's wing describes a roughly circular path relative to the body, sweeping forward and down on the power-stroke; back and up on the return. However, viewed in forward flight this action is seen as a rowing motion—difficult to discern in many tiny, fast-flying species but quite clear in slower-moving birds like Rooks and geese

The techniques of flight

Many soaring birds make use of the upward currents of air caused by physical obstacles such as woods, buildings and cliff faces. Thermals are more localized updraughts of warm air which form over land wherever the surface is subject to differential heating. Rising air commonly occurs over ploughed land and over towns; cool air descends over "cold" (heat absorbing) areas, notably over woodland and areas of water. Migrant birds make full use of thermals during their annual journeys and such species generally avoid long sea crossings.

Gliding and soaring flight saves vital energy for seabirds which habitually roam over vast areas of ocean. Flying over waves, the bird gains speed in the faster-moving air 50 to 100 feet above the surface, then glides down through progressively slower-moving air, eventually turning into the wind to soar upwards again. Soaring Gannets, far right, accumulate in groups in the standing waves which form down-wind of a physical obstruction

Deflected air-flow

Thermal air-flow

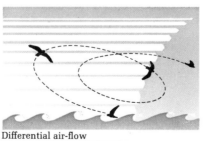

Differential air-flow

Standing wave air-flow

Main power-stroke

Summit of
take-off stroke

Bottom of
main power-stroke

Tail as
rudder

Start of take-off stroke

Mid-power-stroke

Alighting

Take-off, left, requires extra thrust. Unexpectedly, this is produced by a backward-flicking upstroke, primaries flattened. Lift exists only if air flows over the wings. **Wing-flapping,** to maintain that airflow, is a more subtle motion than it appears. As wings beat downwards for the main power-stroke, immediately above, the primary feathers do not merely flail. By virtue of being stiffened at their leading edges, they twist. Air

is swept not only down but back. Simultaneously, the wings move forwards in relation to the body, producing extra lift. More forward thrust is given at the bottom of the power-stroke, top right, when the wings "row" backwards. On the upstroke, centre right, the primaries twist again, into a near-vertical position, making least resistance to the air. **Turning,** top right, involves pronounced swivelling of the tail like a rudder

Landing is a feat of co-ordination. Eyes are fixed on the perch. The body rears to a near-vertical attitude, increasing the wings' angle of attack to the point where a stall is induced. Descent to a perch requires a massive reduction in lift, achieved in part by raising the tail for maximum air spillage. Whatever the approach, speed is checked by spreading wings and tail to act as brakes, and by beating the wings against the direction of movement. Finally, the legs reach for the perch. Any tendency to stall before the last moment is checked by spreading the alula

Landing may be a perfectly co-ordinated action, but the impact is substantial. To withstand it, a bird has modifications of the pelvis and hind limbs. The former is relatively very large and fused with the backbone to form a strong and rigid structure. This provides a large area of attachment for the massive leg muscles, which to assist balance are situated high on the limb, near the centre of gravity

A sure and automatic grip on its perch is vital if a bird is to sit there for hours on end, if necessary asleep. The toes are flexed by a tendon that passes round the intertarsal or "ankle" joint. The weight of the bird on its legs makes the intertarsal bend; if it bends, the tendon stretches, if the tendon stretches, the toes have no option but to grip

251

The Unspoken Language

The patterns of behaviour adopted by birds are just as closely tailored to their varying life styles as are their physical adaptations and their plumage colours. Thus, for example, birds which feed on items found only by diligent searching—such as tiny insects among vegetation—usually forage most efficiently alone. Such species usually also nest alone and maintain a sizeable territory around the nest site in which to search for food. Most passerines fall into this category and such familiar aspects of behaviour as the songs and display flights of the male birds all function to maintain this territorial claim against competing neighbours and to advertise the male's presence to potential mates in the area.

Birds using abundant and easily exploited food supplies, such as seeds and flying insects, often feed in flocks and many also nest colonially. Among colonial nesters, territory is reduced to a tiny area around the nest, and the main features of behaviour are the elaborate patterns of social signals necessary to prevent friction within the colony.

The study of behaviour—ethology—has shown that many activities involve a stereotyped performance known as a "fixed action pattern", triggered by a specific stimulus.

Basic maintenance activities, a vital element in any bird's behavioural repertoire, are generally seen when the bird is at rest but not sleeping. Care of the plumage, by preening and by bathing, is particularly important as, in addition to flight, the feathers provide the bird's only insulation.
Most birds have an oil gland situated at the base of the tail, and during preening its secretion is spread on to the feathers to maintain their suppleness and resistance to wear, and to waterproof the plumage. Preening is often accompanied by ruffling actions, which re-align the feathers, and by "comfort" movements such as leg and wing stretching

Social organization in gregarious species is maintained by a complex and often subtle "language" of actions and postures. Stability and cohesion within a flock is assured by a strict hierarchy, or "pecking order", in which every bird knows its place. The order results from numerous encounters between individuals, but the clashes seldom involve fighting; the exchange is invariably by signal—threat by one bird, submission by the other. Members of a pair signify recognition and acceptance by greeting ceremonies which block any spontaneous aggressive responses

Among birds with identical male and female plumage colouring, the sexes are differentiated by their behaviour patterns. Such species show particularly clearly how signals and responses can function as a visual language. In the Herring Gull, for example, the intrusion of any individual into a male's territory will immediately provoke a threat posture from the resident. If the intruder is a male he will respond aggressively and a brief fight may ensue—invariably ending in victory for the holder of the territory, and the withdrawal of the intruding bird

Blackbird sunbathing: wings outspread, tail fanned, feathers well separated

Blackbird bathing: feathers are cleaned and cleared of parasites by water bathing or dusting

Pheasant, right, roosts alone in a tree, often silhouetted against the evening sky

Birds spend a great deal of time preening their feathers, oiling them and drawing each in turn through the bill to repair "breaks" in the mesh of barbules

Dunlin, above, roost communally, often closely grouped and facing into the prevailing wind

Red spot stimulates young Herring Gull to beg even from a crude bill model

The V formation of the crane flock has aerodynamic, energy-saving advantages

The bright red interior of the Kittiwake's mouth features in greeting displays

Communal feeding increases flock security—a sentinel bird is always alert to any approaching danger

The upright posture of the gull at left indicates hostility towards an intruder

The intruder, in this case a male, reacted to the "resident's" threat with aggression; his bluff called, he retreats

The majority of birds form monogamous relationships in which both parents share in the feeding and protection of the young. This behavioural trait is particularly important in species whose young are nidicolous–those born blind, unfeathered and unable to fend for themselves. Polygamous and promiscuous relationships, in which the female alone must tend the eggs and young, are less common.

Although monogamous birds do perform courtship displays, some of which are quite striking, the most bizarre and elaborate rituals occur in the promiscuous species. Extreme forms of display carry an increased risk from predators as the performing bird is very conspicuous and also preoccupied with its activity. The dangers may be minimized if the display is performed communally at a "lek", as in the case of the Ruff and

Black Grouse, so that at least one bird is almost certain to see any approaching threat and give the alarm.

A phenomenon common to many patterns of behaviour is the incorporation of activities more appropriate to some quite different function: thus, courtship may include begging and ritual feeding, as in the Herring Gull, or the offering of nest material–an important part of the Great Crested Grebe's display.

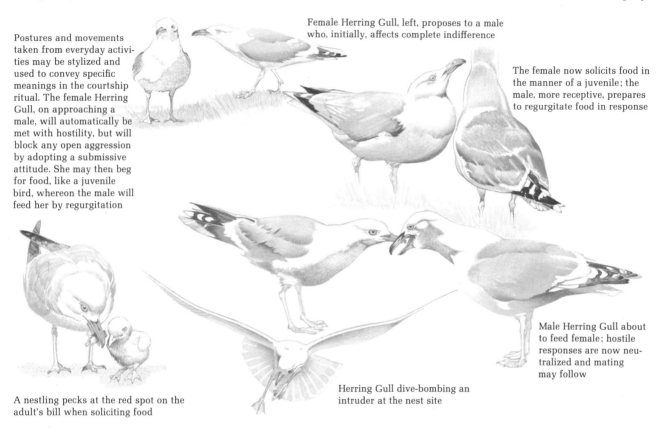

Postures and movements taken from everyday activities may be stylized and used to convey specific meanings in the courtship ritual. The female Herring Gull, on approaching a male, will automatically be met with hostility, but will block any open aggression by adopting a submissive attitude. She may then beg for food, like a juvenile bird, whereon the male will feed her by regurgitation

Female Herring Gull, left, proposes to a male who, initially, affects complete indifference

The female now solicits food in the manner of a juvenile; the male, more receptive, prepares to regurgitate food in response

Male Herring Gull about to feed female; hostile responses are now neutralized and mating may follow

A nestling pecks at the red spot on the adult's bill when soliciting food

Herring Gull dive-bombing an intruder at the nest site

Development within the egg
The number of eggs comprising the clutch, and the size, shape, colour and weight of the eggs, varies enormously from one species to another as does the period of time taken for the development and subsequent incubation of the egg. However, the processes taking place within the egg are essentially the same in all birds and are here illustrated by the domesticated hen, which, like other game-birds, wildfowl, waders, cranes, grebes and divers, is a nidifugous species. Most other species have nidicolous young. Gulls and terns produce well-developed young, but these remain on, or near, the nest for some time after birth

Day 1: the spherical yolk floats in the fluid albumin (white) with the blastodisc, an early stage of the embryo, uppermost

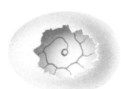

Day 3: the tiny embryonic heart, with the main blood vessels already formed, is beating before the chick is recognizable

Day 9: now clearly visible, the chick is receiving oxygen through pores in the shell, and nutrients from the yolk via the network of blood vessels

Day 15: eyes, bill and feet are prominent features of the chick as it develops rapidly at the expense of the life-giving nutrient yolk mass

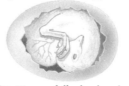

Day 21: now fully developed, the chick breaks out of the shell with the aid of the sharp "egg-tooth" on the tip of the diminutive bill

Nidifugous young are down-covered and mobile; nidicolous young are born blind and helpless

Bird-watching in Europe

Many of the wild areas of Europe are fast disappearing—whittled away by the relentless encroachment of twentieth-century civilization. Natural forest is cut down to be replaced by less interesting plantations of commercial softwoods, while wetlands, with their characteristic and fascinating birdlife, are drained to create land for development.

To ensure the survival of at least some of the more important wilderness areas, conservation organizations have been set up in most European countries, many of which own or manage nature reserves. Some are run by the State, like the Nature Conservancy in Britain, while others are voluntary, depending for their funds on the subscriptions of their members. The Royal Society for the Protection of Birds (RSPB) is a British organization concerned primarily with areas of ornithological value; similar organizations exist in most of the countries of Europe and their addresses are given in the list below.

Large and important reserves often have a resident staff of trained guides and wardens, and a clearly marked network of footpaths—often with hides positioned at particularly favourable observation points. Tours of the area, led by an expert guide, are commonly available and many of the major reserves run training courses in bird-ringing. Smaller reserves may only have a part-time warden—if any—and in these areas above all the bird-watcher should remember his responsibilities: these remaining wild areas are precious not only to the wildlife they support but to future generations of Europeans.

CONSERVATION IN EUROPE

AUSTRIA
Österreichische Gesellschaft für Vogel Kunde,
Naturhistorisches Museum,
A-1014 Vienna 1.

BELGIUM
Institut Royal des Sciences Naturelles de Belgique,
Rue Vautier 31,
Bruxelles 4.

DENMARK
Dansk Ornithologisk Forening,
Faelledvej 9 Mezz,
Dk 2200, Copenhagen N.

EIRE
Irish Society for the Protection of Birds,
Dept. of Lands,
24 Upper Merrien Street,
Dublin 2.

FINLAND
Societas pro Fauna et Flora Fennica,
Zoological Museum of the University,
Novra Järnvagsgaten 13,
Helsinki 10.

FRANCE
Ligue pour la Protection des Oiseaux,
57 Rue Cuvier,
BP505,
75005 Paris.

GERMANY (Federal Republic)
Deutscher Bund für Vogelschutz,
705 Waiblingen,
Lange Strasse 34.

GREAT BRITAIN
British Trust for Ornithology,
Beech Grove,
Tring,
Herts. HP23 5NR.

Royal Society for the Protection of Birds,
The Lodge,
Sandy,
Beds. SG19 2DL.

Scottish Ornithologists Club,
21 Regent Terrace,
Edinburgh, EH7 5BT.

ITALY
La Lega Italiana per la Protezione degli Uccelli,
Lungano Guicciardina 9,
50125 Firenze.

LUXEMBOURG
Ligue Luxembourgeoise pour L'Etude et la Protection des Oiseaux,
32 Rue de la Forêt, Luxembourg.

THE NETHERLANDS
Nederlandse Vereniging Tot Berscherming Van Vogels,
Driebergseweg 16B,
Zeist 2740.

NORWAY
Zoologisk Museum,
Sarsgatan 1,
Oslo 5.

PORTUGAL
Sociedada Portuguesa de Ornitologia,
Seccâo de Zoologica,
Faeuldade Ciencas,
Oporto.

SPAIN
Sociedad Española de Ornitologica,
Castellana 80,
Madrid.

SWEDEN
Svenska Naturskyddsföreningen,
Kungsholms Strand 125,
112 34 Stockholm.

Sveriges Ornitologiska Förening,
Runebergsgatan 8,
114 29 Stockholm.

SWITZERLAND
Schweizerische Vogelwarte,
6204 Sempach, Lucerne.

AREAS OF SPECIAL INTEREST

Denmark
1 Skagen
2 Rold Skov
3 North Sjaelland
4 Copenhagen
5 West Sjaelland
6 Lolland-Falster-Mon
7 Langeland
8 South Jutland
9 Blaavandshuk
10 Ringkøbing Fjord
11 Limfjorden

Great Britain
1 Shetland–Fair Isle
2 Speyside
3 Foulsheugh
4 Firth of Forth
5 Farne Islands
6 The Wash
7 Minsmere
8 Thames–Medway
9 London Reservoirs
10 Portland–Weymouth
11 Slimbridge
12 Skokholm–Skomer
13 Dee Estuary
14 The Hebrides

Ireland
1 Malin Head
2 Lough Neagh
3 Strangford Lough
4 Dublin–North Bull Island
5 Wexford Slobs
6 Cape Clear Island
7 Kerry Islands
8 Lough Akeagh
9 Lough Erne

The Netherlands
1 Zwartemeer
2 Oostelijk Flevoland
3 De Hoge Veluwe
4 Naarder Meer
5 Lake Nieuwkoop
6 Rhine Delta
7 Alkmaarder Meer
8 Zwanenwater
9 Texel

Belgium
1 Kalmthout Heath
2 Campine
3 Genk
4 Hautes- Fagnes National Park
5 Harchies
6 Blankaart
7 Yser Estuary
8 Zwin

France
1 Sologne	10 Port du Gavarnie
2 Brenne	11 Les Landes
3 Dombes	12 Ile d'Olonne
4 Lac du Bourget	13 Baie de Bourgneuf
5 Vanoise National Park	14 Lac de Grand Lieu
6 Camargue	15 Golfe du Morbihan
7 Languedoc	16 Sept-Iles
8 Gorges du Tarn	17 St. Malo
9 St. Flour	18 Baie de Veys

Spain
1 Montana de Covadonga	8 Ronda
2 Pyrénées	9 Southern Andaluci
3 Andorra	10 Coto de Dña Ana
4 La Escala	11 Huelva
5 Ebro Delta	12 Badajoz
6 Majorca	13 Sierra Guadarrama
7 Sierra Nevada	

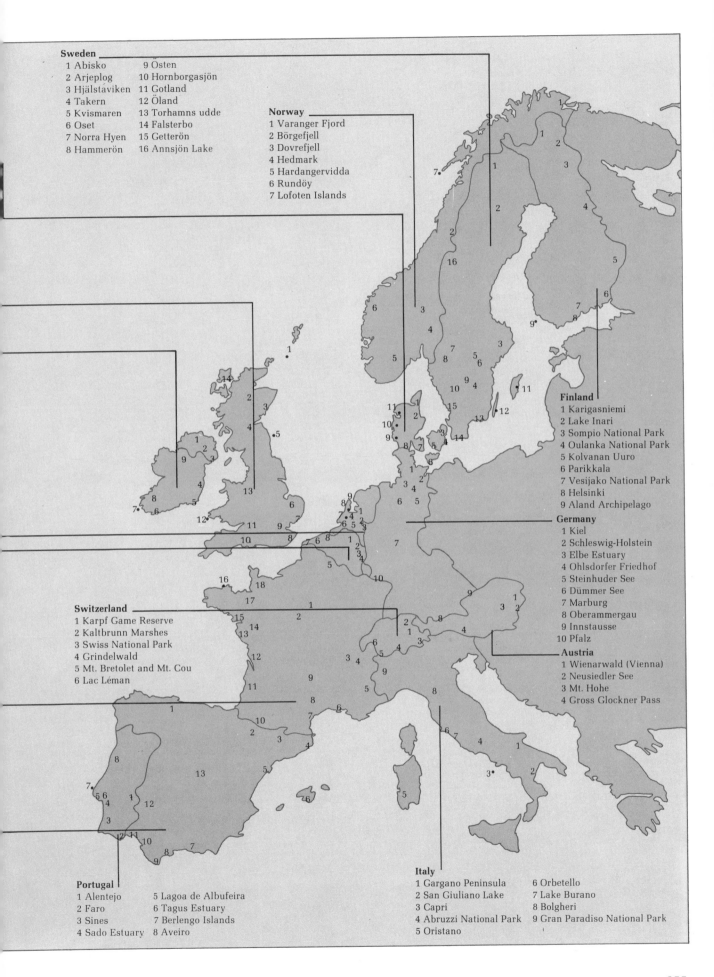

Sweden
1 Abisko 9 Östen
2 Arjeplog 10 Hornborgasjön
3 Hjälstaviken 11 Gotland
4 Takern 12 Öland
5 Kvismaren 13 Torhamns udde
6 Oset 14 Falsterbo
7 Norra Hyen 15 Getterön
8 Hammerön 16 Annsjön Lake

Norway
1 Varanger Fjord
2 Börgefjell
3 Dovrefjell
4 Hedmark
5 Hardangervidda
6 Rundöy
7 Lofoten Islands

Finland
1 Karigasniemi
2 Lake Inari
3 Sompio National Park
4 Oulanka National Park
5 Kolvanan Uuro
6 Parikkala
7 Vesijako National Park
8 Helsinki
9 Aland Archipelago

Germany
1 Kiel
2 Schleswig-Holstein
3 Elbe Estuary
4 Ohlsdorfer Friedhof
5 Steinhuder See
6 Dümmer See
7 Marburg
8 Oberammergau
9 Innstausse
10 Pfalz

Austria
1 Wienarwald (Vienna)
2 Neusiedler See
3 Mt. Hohe
4 Gross Glockner Pass

Switzerland
1 Karpf Game Reserve
2 Kaltbrunn Marshes
3 Swiss National Park
4 Grindelwald
5 Mt. Bretolet and Mt. Cou
6 Lac Léman

Portugal
1 Alentejo 5 Lagoa de Albufeira
2 Faro 6 Tagus Estuary
3 Sines 7 Berlengo Islands
4 Sado Estuary 8 Aveiro

Italy
1 Gargano Peninsula 6 Orbetello
2 San Giuliano Lake 7 Lake Burano
3 Capri 8 Bolgheri
4 Abruzzi National Park 9 Gran Paradiso National Park
5 Oristano

Checklist of Scientific Names and Common Names

Avocet	*Recurvirostra avosetta*	Brent, dark-bellied	*Branta b. bernicla*
		Brent, pale-bellied	*Branta b. hrota*
Bee-eater	*Merops apiaster*	Canada	*Branta canadensis*
Bittern	*Botaurus stellaris*	Greylag	*Anser anser*
Little	*Ixobrychus minutus*	Pink-footed	*Anser fabalis brachyrhynchus*
Blackbird	*Turdus merula*	White-fronted	*Anser albifrons*
Blackcap	*Sylvia atricapilla*	White-fronted, Greenland race	*Anser a. flavirostris*
Bluethroat, Red-spotted	*Luscinia s. svecica*	Goshawk	*Accipiter gentilis*
White-spotted	*Luscinia s. cyanecula*	Grebe, Black-necked	*Podiceps nigricollis*
Brambling	*Fringilla montifringilla*	Great Crested	*Podiceps cristatus*
Bullfinch	*Pyrrhula pyrrhula*	Little	*Tachybaptus ruficollis*
Bunting, Cirl	*Emberiza cirlus*	Red-necked	*Podiceps griseigena*
Corn	*Emberiza calandra*	Slavonian	*Podiceps auritus*
Ortolan	*Emberiza hortulana*	Greenfinch	*Carduelis chloris*
Reed	*Emberiza schoeniclus*	Greenshank	*Tringa nebularia*
Rock	*Emberiza cia*	Grouse, Black	*Lyrurus tetrix*
Snow	*Plectrophenax nivalis*	Red	*Lagopus l. scoticus*
Buzzard	*Buteo buteo*	Willow	*Lagopus l. lagopus*
Honey	*Pernis apivorus*	Guillemot	*Uria aalge*
Rough-legged	*Buteo lagopus*	Black	*Cepphus grylle*
		Gull, Black-headed	*Larus ridibundus*
Capercaillie	*Tetrao urogallus*	Common	*Larus canus*
Chaffinch	*Fringilla coelebs*	Glaucous	*Larus hyperboreus*
Chiffchaff, southern race	*Phylloscopus c. collybita*	Great Black-backed	*Larus marinus*
Chiffchaff, northern race	*Phylloscopus c. abietinus*	Herring	*Larus a. argentatus*
Chough	*Pyrrhocorax pyrrhocorax*	Herring, Scandinavian race	*Larus a. omissus*
Alpine	*Pyrrhocorax graculus*	Iceland	*Larus glaucoides*
Coot	*Fulica atra*	Lesser Black-backed	*Larus f. graellsii*
Cormorant	*Phalacrocorax carbo*	Lesser Black-backed,	
Cormorant, southern race	*Phalacrocorax c. sinensis*	Scandinavian race	*Larus f. fuscus*
Corncrake	*Crex crex*	Little	*Larus minutus*
Crane	*Grus grus*		
Crossbill	*Loxia curvirostra*	Harrier, Hen	*Circus cyaneus*
Crow, Carrion	*Corvus c. corone*	Marsh	*Circus aeruginosus*
Hooded	*Corvus c. cornix*	Montagu's	*Circus pygargus*
Cuckoo	*Cuculus canorus*	Hawfinch	*Coccothraustes coccothraustes*
Curlew	*Numenius arquata*	Heron, Grey	*Ardea cinerea*
		Night	*Nycticorax nycticorax*
Dabchick	*Tachybaptus ruficollis*	Purple	*Ardea purpurea*
Dipper, Black-bellied	*Cinclus c. cinclus*	Squacco	*Ardeola ralloides*
Dipper, British race	*Cinclus c. gularis*	Hobby	*Falco subbuteo*
Diver, Black-throated	*Gavia arctica*	Hoopoe	*Upupa epops*
Great Northern	*Gavia immer*		
Red-throated	*Gavia stellata*	Jackdaw	*Corvus monedula*
Dotterel	*Eudromias morinellus*	Jay	*Garrulus glandarius*
Dove, Collared	*Streptopelia decaocto*		
Rock	*Columba livia*	Kestrel	*Falco tinnunculus*
Stock	*Columba oenas*	Kingfisher	*Alcedo atthis*
Turtle	*Streptopelia turtur*	Kite, Black	*Milvus migrans*
Duck, Ferruginous	*Aythya nyroca*	Red	*Milvus milvus*
Long-tailed	*Clangula hyemalis*	Kittiwake	*Rissa tridactyla*
Tufted	*Aythya fuligula*	Knot	*Calidris canutus*
Dunlin, northern race	*Calidris a. alpina*		
Dunlin, southern race	*Calidris a. schinzii*	Lammergeier	*Gypaetus barbatus*
Dunnock	*Prunella modularis*	Lapwing	*Vanellus vanellus*
		Lark, Crested	*Galerida cristata*
Eagle, Booted	*Hieraletus pennatus*	Linnet	*Acanthis cannabina*
Golden	*Aquila chrysaetos*		
Short-toed	*Circaetus gallicus*	Magpie	*Pica pica*
Imperial	*Aquila heliaca adalberti*	Mallard	*Anas platyrhynchos*
Egret, Cattle	*Bubulcus ibis*	Martin, Crag	*Hirundo rupestris*
Little	*Egretta garzetta*	House	*Delichon urbica*
Eider	*Somateria mollissima*	Sand	*Riparia riparia*
		Merganser, Red-breasted	*Mergus serrator*
Falcon, Eleonora's	*Falco eleonorae*	Merlin	*Falco columbarius*
Fieldfare	*Turdus pilaris*	Moorhen	*Gallinula chloropus*
Finch, Snow	*Montifringilla nivalis*		
Firecrest	*Regulus ignicapillus*	Nightingale	*Luscinia megarhynchos*
Flamingo	*Phoenicopterus ruber*	Nightjar	*Caprimulgus europaeus*
Flycatcher, Collared	*Ficedula albicollis*	Nutcracker	*Nucifraga caryocatactes*
Pied	*Ficedula hypoleuca*	Nuthatch	*Sitta europaea*
Spotted	*Muscicapa striata*		
Fulmar	*Fulmarus glacialis*	Oriole, Golden	*Oriolus oriolus*
		Ortolan	*Emberiza hortulana*
Gadwall	*Anas strepera*	Osprey	*Pandion haliaetus*
Gannet	*Sula bassana*	Ouzel, Ring	*Turdus t. torquatus*
Garganey	*Anas querquedula*	Ring, Alpine	*Turdus t. alpestris*
Godwit, Bar-tailed	*Limosa lapponica*	Owl, Barn	*Tyto a. guttata*
Black-tailed	*Limosa limosa*	Barn, continental race	*Tyto a. alba*
Goldcrest	*Regulus regulus*	Little	*Athene noctua*
Goldeneye	*Bucephala clangula*	Long-eared	*Asio otus*
Goldfinch	*Carduelis carduelis*	Scops	*Otus scops*
Goosander	*Mergus merganser*	Short-eared	*Asio flammeus*
Goose, Barnacle	*Branta leucopsis*	Tawny	*Strix aluco*
Bean	*Anser f. fabalis*	Oystercatcher	*Haematopus ostralegus*
Bean, eastern race	*Anser f. rossicus*		

Partridge	*Perdix perdix*
Red-legged	*Alectoris rufa*
Peregrine	*Falco peregrinus*
Phalarope, Grey	*Phalaropus fulicarius*
Red-necked	*Phalaropus lobatus*
Pheasant	*Phasianus colchicus*
Pigeon, Feral	*Columba livia*
Wood	*Columba palumbus*
Pintail	*Anas acuta*
Pipit, Meadow	*Anthus pratensis*
Rock	*Anthus s. petrosus*
Rock, Scandinavian race	*Anthus s. littoralis*
Tawny	*Anthus campestris*
Tree	*Anthus trivialis*
Water	*Anthus s. spinoletta*
Plover, Golden	*Pluvialis a. apricaria*
Golden, northern race	*Pluvialis a. altifrons*
Grey	*Pluvialis squatarola*
Kentish	*Charadrius alexandrinus*
Little Ringed	*Charadrius dubius*
Ringed	*Charadrius hiaticula*
Pochard	*Aythya ferina*
Red-crested	*Netta rufina*
Pratincole, Red-winged	*Glareola p. pratincola*
Ptarmigan	*Lagopus mutus*
Puffin	*Fratercula arctica*
Quail	*Coturnix coturnix*
Rail, Water	*Rallus aquaticus*
Raven	*Corvus corax*
Razorbill	*Alca torda*
Redpoll, Arctic	*Acanthis f. hornemanni*
Redpoll, Mealy	*Acanthus f. flammea*
British/central European race	*Acanthus f. cabaret*
Redshank	*Tringa totanus*
Redstart	*Phoenicurus phoenicurus*
Black	*Phoenicurus ochruros*
Redwing	*Turdus iliacus*
Robin	*Erithacus rubecula*
Roller	*Coracias garrulus*
Rook	*Corvus frugilegus*
Ruff	*Philomachus pugnax*
Sanderling	*Calidris alba*
Sandpiper, Common	*Tringa hypoleucos*
Curlew	*Calidris ferruginea*
Green	*Tringa ochropus*
Purple	*Calidris maritima*
Wood	*Tringa glareola*
Scaup	*Aythya marila*
Scoter	*Melanitta nigra*
Velvet	*Melanitta fusca*
Serin	*Serinus serinus*
Shag	*Phalacrocorax aristotelis*
Shearwater, Manx	*Puffinus puffinus*
Shelduck	*Tadorna tadorna*
Shoveler	*Anas clypeata*
Shrike, Great Grey	*Lanius excubitor*
Lesser Grey	*Lanius minor*
Red-backed	*Lanius collurio*
Woodchat	*Lanius senator*
Siskin	*Carduelis spinus*
Skua, Arctic	*Stercorarius parasiticus*
Great	*Stercorarius skua*
Long-tailed	*Stercorarius longicaudus*
Pomarine	*Stercorarius pomarinus*
Skylark	*Alauda arvensis*
Smew	*Mergus albellus*
Snipe	*Gallinago gallinago*
Jack	*Lymnocryptes minimus*
Sparrow, Hedge	*Prunella modularis*
House	*Passer domesticus*
Tree	*Passer montanus*
Sparrowhawk	*Accipiter nisus*
Spoonbill	*Platalea leucorodia*
Starling	*Sturnus vulgaris*
Stilt, Black-winged	*Himantopus himantopus*
Stint, Little	*Calidris minuta*
Temminck's	*Calidris temminckii*
Stonechat	*Saxicola torquata*
Stork, White	*Ciconia ciconia*
Swallow	*Hirundo rustica*
Red-rumped	*Hirundo daurica*

Swan, Bewick's	*Cygnus bewickii*
Mute	*Cygnus olor*
Whooper	*Cygnus cygnus*
Swift	*Apus apus*
Alpine	*Apus melba*
Teal	*Anas crecca*
Tern, Arctic	*Sterna paradisaea*
Black	*Chlidonias niger*
Common	*Sterna hirundo*
Gull-billed	*Gelochelidon nilotica*
Little	*Sterna albifrons*
Sandwich	*Sterna sandvicensis*
Thrush, Blue Rock	*Monticola solitarius*
Mistle	*Turdus viscivorus*
Rock	*Monticola saxatilis*
Song	*Turdus philomelos*
Tit, Bearded	*Panurus biarmicus*
Blue	*Parus caeruleus*
Coal, British race	*Parus a. britannicus*
Coal, continental race	*Parus a. ater*
Coal, Irish race	*Parus a. hibernicus*
Crested	*Parus cristatus*
Great	*Parus major*
Long-tailed, British race	*Aegithalos c. rosaceous*
northern race	*Aegithelos c. caudatus*
Marsh	*Parus palustris*
Willow, British race	*Parus m. montanus*
Willow, northern race	*Parus m. borealis*
Treecreeper	*Certhia familiaris*
Turnstone	*Arenaria interpres*
Twite	*Acanthis flavirostris*
Vulture, Black	*Aegypius monachus*
Egyptian	*Neophron percnopterus*
Griffon	*Gyps fulvus*
Wagtail, Blue-headed	*Motacilla f. flava*
Grey	*Motacilla cinerea*
Pied	*Motacilla alba yarrelli*
White	*Motacilla a. alba*
Yellow, British race	*Motacilla flava flavissima*
Yellow, Scandinavian race	*Motacilla f. thunbergi*
Yellow, Spanish race	*Motacilla f. Iberiae*
Warbler, Barred	*Sylvia nisoria*
Bonelli's	*Phylloscopus bonelli*
Cetti's	*Cettia cetti*
Dartford	*Sylvia undata*
Fan-tailed	*Cisticola juncidis*
Garden	*Sylvia borin*
Grasshopper	*Locustella naevia*
Great Reed	*Acrocephalus arundinaceus*
Icterine	*Hippolais icterina*
Marsh	*Acrocephalus palustris*
Melodious	*Hippolais polyglotta*
Reed	*Acrocephalus scirpaceus*
Sardinian	*Sylvia melanocephala*
Savi's	*Locustella luscinioides*
Sedge	*Acrocephalus schoenobaenus*
Subalpine	*Sylvia cantillans*
Willow, northern race	*Phylloscopus t. acredula*
Willow, southern race	*Phylloscopus t. trochilus*
Wood	*Phylloscopus sibilatrix*
Waxwing	*Bombycilla garrulus*
Wheatear	*Oenanthe o. oenanthe*
Wheatear, Greenland race	*Oenanthe o. leucorrhoa*
Black	*Oenanthe leucura*
Black-eared	*Oenanthe hispanica*
Whimbrel	*Numenius phaeopus*
Whinchat	*Saxicola rubetra*
Whitethroat	*Sylvia communis*
Lesser	*Sylvia curruca*
Wigeon	*Anas penelope*
Woodchat	*Lanius senator*
Woodcock	*Scolopax rusticola*
Woodlark	*Lullula arborea*
Woodpecker, Black	*Dryocopus martius*
Great Spotted	*Dendrocopos major*
Green	*Picus viridis*
Grey-headed	*Picus canus*
Lesser Spotted	*Dendrocopos minor*
Wren	*Troglodytes troglodytes*
Wryneck	*Jynx torquilla*
Yellowhammer	*Emberiza citrinella*

Glossary

Adult: difficult to define; size is misleading. Essentially a bird with definitive mature plumage.
Albinism: abnormal (white) colouring caused by absence of pigmentation.
Alula: the small "bastard" wing on the leading edge of the wing used to control stall tendency at very low speed.
Ankle: the intertarsal joint. May be mistakenly assumed to be the "knee" joint.
Axillaries: feathers in the "armpit" of the bird.

Brood: the young from a single clutch of eggs; hence **brooding**, the adult's action in sitting on the young to keep them warm.

Carpal joint: the small bones of the "wrist" joint—the forward-pointing joint of the folded wing.
Chevron: V-shaped marking.
Chick: colloquial term for a young bird between hatching and first flight.
Cock: general term for the male bird. More specific terms used for some species, eg cob (swan); drake (duck); gander (goose).
Commensal: sharing similar environment and food.
Contour feather: any feather forming part of the outer surface of the bird's plumage.
Coverts: the contour feathers that overlap the main wing or tail feathers.
Cryptic: colouring or patterning of the plumage which breaks up the outline of the bird and hence conceals or camouflages it.
Cursorial: adapted to running; a ground-dwelling species.

Diurnal: living and feeding mainly by day.
Decurved: bent downwards.

Eclipse: dull plumage assumed notably by male ducks for a period after the breeding season.
Exotic: term describing a species not normally found in the area under consideration.

False preening: a behavioural quirk, roughly similar in human terms to scratching the head.
Family: taxonomic term; a grouping of genera.

Feral: literally meaning wild. In ornithology, used to denote a once-domesticated species that has reverted to the wild state.
Fledging: the process by which a young bird acquires its first covering of feathers; hence **fledgling**—a young bird recently fledged.

Gape: produced by a bird opening its beak.
Genus: taxonomic grouping of birds having a common ancestor.
Guano: dung or excrement.

Hen: general term for the female bird. More specific terms are used for some species, eg greyhen (female Black Grouse), reeve (female Ruff).
High Arctic: the true Arctic, where the ground is permanently frozen and there are no trees.

Immature: after a young bird leaves the nest in juvenile plumage, which can last varying lengths of time, there follows a complete or partial moult into immature plumage. This persists until the attainment of full adult plumage.

Lek: communal display ground used by some species (see page 168, the Ruff).

Metabolism: the chemical changes which take place constantly in the cells and tissues of the body.
Moult: the periodic loss and replacement of plumage. The term also used to denote the time of year when birds are in the process of moulting.

Nuptial: pertaining to the breeding season, e.g. "nuptial finery" used to describe the male bird's breeding plumage.

Passerine: a member of the huge order *Passeriformes*, which includes more than half the known bird species. Often referred to as the perching birds since the order is characterized by foot structure adapted for efficient gripping.
Pelagic: species which spend the greater part of their time at sea, far from land.

Phase: also **morph**. Denotes a particular form of the species where a colour variation exists, eg dark phase, grey phase.
Polygamy: the formation of a sexual bond between one male and more than one female.
Primaries: those main flight feathers attached to the "hand" bones and forming the outer section of the wing.

Recurved: bent upwards.
Resident: non-migratory; some resident species do undertake localized movements or longer, seasonal journeys within Europe.
Ringing: the marking of individual birds, by the application of an identifiable ring on the leg, to facilitate the recording of population movements. A variation is the clip, applied to the wing, and commonly used to mark ducks.
Roosting: the bird is said to be roosting when either actually sleeping or resting for more than a brief nap.
Rufous: reddish-brown.

Scapulars: feathers above shoulder.
Secondaries: feathers attached to the "forearm" and forming the inner section of the wing.
Sedentary: resident, but scarcely moving from the immediate vicinity of the birthplace.
Sub-adult: young bird, with a mixture of immature and adult plumage; the last stage before full adult plumage.
Subarctic: superficially Arctic regions (not necessarily within the Arctic circle) where the ground is not permanently frozen and which can support small trees.

Taiga: coniferous forest land, lying south of tundra.
Tarsal bones: those bones comprising the "ankle".
Taxonomy: the science of classification.
Tundra: vast, treeless regions which make up most of N Russia, with arctic climate and vegetation.

Vagrant: a definition of scarcity applied to birds which leave their normal range to make infrequent visits to the area in question.
Vermiculation: irregular, wavy marking, reminiscent of tracks made by worms.
Vinaceous: wine coloured.

Index

Index

Sources of Reference
A wide range of books and periodicals were consulted in the preparation of *The Birdlife of Britain*, and the publishers and authors are particularly indebted to the following:
  A Field Guide to Birds' Nests, B. Campbell and I. J. Ferguson-Lees, Constable 1972; *A Field Guide to the Nests, Eggs and Nestlings of British and European Birds*, Colin Harrison, Collins 1975; *A Guide to Bird-watching in Europe*, I. J. Ferguson-Lees, Bodley Head 1975; *A New Dictionary of Birds*, Landsborough Thomson, Nelson 1964; *Atlas of European Birds*, Nelson 1960; *Birds of the World* (vols. one to ten), John Gooders (ed.), IPCS 1969-71; *Book of British Birds*, AA/Reader's Digest 1969; *Field Guide to the Birds of Britain and Europe*, Heinzel, Fitter and Parslow; *Finches*, Ian Newton, Collins New Naturalist 1972; *Handbook of Water-fowl Behaviour*, P. A. Johnsgard, Constable 1965; *The Handbook of British Birds* (five vols.), Witherby, Jourdain, Ticehurst, Tucker, Witherby 1943-4 (revised edition); *The Herring Gull's World*, Niko Tinbergen, Collins 1953; *The Life of Birds*, Joel Carl Welty, Constable 1964 and *The World Atlas of Birds*, Mitchell Beazley 1974.